Horace Hayman Wilson, Fitzedward Hall

Hindu mythology and tradition

Horace Hayman Wilson, Fitzedward Hall

Hindu mythology and tradition

ISBN/EAN: 9783742806697

Manufactured in Europe, USA, Canada, Australia, Japa

Cover: Foto ©Thomas Meinert / pixelio.de

Manufactured and distributed by brebook publishing software
(www.brebook.com)

Horace Hayman Wilson, Fitzedward Hall

Hindu mythology and tradition

Horace Hayman Wilson, Fitzedward Hall

Hindu mythology and tradition

A SYSTEM

OF

HINDU MYTHOLOGY AND TRADITION.

TRANSLATED

FROM THE ORIGINAL SANSKRIT,

AND

ILLUSTRATED BY NOTES

DERIVED CHIEFLY FROM OTHER PURÁŃAS.

BY THE LATE

H. H. WILSON, M.A., F.R.S.,

BODEN PROFESSOR OF SANSKRIT IN THE UNIVERSITY OF OXFORD,
ETC., ETC.

EDITED BY

FITZEDWARD HALL.

LONDON:

TRÜBNER & CO., 60, PATERNOSTER ROW.

1870.

VISHŃU PURÁŃA.

BOOK V. (continued).

CHAPTER XVII.

Akrúra's meditations on Krishńa: his arrival at Gokula: his delight at seeing Krishńa and his brother.

AKRÚRA, having set off in his quick travelling-car, proceeded to visit Krishńa at the pastures * of Nanda; and, as he went along, he congratulated himself on his superior good fortune, in having an opportunity of beholding a descended portion of the deity.† "Now," thought he, "has my life borne fruit; my night is followed by the dawn of day: since I shall see the countenance of Vishńu, whose eyes are like the expanded leaf of the lotos.‡ I shall behold that lotos-eyed aspect§ of Vishńu, which, when seen only in imagination, takes away the sins of men. I shall, to-day, behold that glory of glories,‖, the mouth of Vishńu,¶ whence proceeded

---

* Gokula.   † Namely, Chakrín, in the original.
‡ Here follows, in the Sanskrit, a stanza left untranslated:

अथ मे सफले नेत्रे अथ मे सफला गिर: ।
यद्मे परस्परालापो हृदा विष्णुं भविष्यति ॥

Srí·thara gives this stanza; but Ratnagarbha does not appear, from my MSS. of his commentary, to recognize it.
§ Literally, "the lotos-eye."

‖ आत्म आत्माम् । Variant, preferred by the commentator Ratnagarbha: आत्म देवानां, "light of the gods".
¶ The original has Bhagavat.

V.   1

the Vedas and all their dependent sciences.* I shall
see the sovereign of the world, by whom the world is
sustained;† who is worshipped as the best of males,‡
as the male of sacrifice§ in sacrificial rites. I shall see
Keśava, who is without beginning or end; by worshipping whom with a hundred sacrifices, Indra obtained the sovereignty over the gods. That Hari,
whose nature is unknown to Brahmá, Indra, Rudra,
the Aświns, the Vasus, Ádityas, and Maruts, will (this
day,) touch my body. The soul of all, the knower of
all, he who is all, and is present in all, he who is per-
manent, undecaying, all-pervading, will converse with
me. He, the unborn, who has preserved the world in
the various forms of a fish, a tortoise, a boar, a horse,[1]

---

[1] The commentator‖ explains this to mean Hayagríva,—or
Vishńu with the neck and head of a horse,—who, it is said, in the
Second Book¶ of the Bhágavata, appeared at the end of a great

---

* To render vedánga.
† Akhiládhára.
‡ Purushottama. See Vol. I., p. 16, note ‡.
§ Yajna-purusha. See Vol. I., p. 163, note *.
‖ The words of the commentators are, in common, simply अश्व: ।
हयग्रीव: । But I show, presently, that they must be wrong
¶ The passage referred to is Chapter VII., 11, where Brahmá is the
speaker. The original and Burnouf's translation are subjoined:

सर्वे ममास भगवान्हयश्रीर्षाथो
साद्यात्म यत्पुरुषस्तपनीयवर्णः ।
छन्दोमयो मखमयोऽखिलदेवतात्मा
वाचो बभवुरमृतीः श्वसतोऽस्व मस्त: ॥

"Dans mon sacrifice, Bhagavat lui-même fut Hayaçircha, le mâle du
sacrifice, dont la couleur est celle de l'or, dont les Vêdas et les sacrifices sont la substance, et les divinités l'âme; quand il respira, de ses
narines sortirent de ravissantes paroles."
Professor Wilson's view of the meaning of the stanza just quoted is
more than usually imaginative.

a lion,* will, this day, speak to me. Now, the lord of
the earth, who assumes shapes at will, has taken upon
him the condition of humanity, to accomplish some
object cherished in his heart. That Ananta, who holds

---

sacrifice performed by Brahmá, and breathed from his nostrils
the texts of the Vedas. The fourth Avatára is always, elsewhere, said to be the Vámana, or dwarf.†

In the *Bhágavata-puráńa*, VIII., XXIV., 7, 8, it is said, that, as
Brahmá slumbered, the Vedas slipped out of his mouth, and Hayagríva
came, and furtively carried them off. Hari, or Vishńu, it is subsequently
stated, at last slew Hayagriva.

According to Vol. II., p. 125, Vishńu is worshipped, in Bhadráśwa, as
Hayaśiras,—the Hayaśirsha of the verses cited above, and of the *Bhágavata-puráńa*, V., XVIII., 1. For Aśwaśiras, as an epithet of Náráyańa, or Vishńu, see the *Mahábhárata*, *Sánti-parvan*, śl. 13100, &c.

With this divinity Professor Wilson has confounded the demon Hayagríva, for whom see Vol. II., p. 70, note §, and p. 210, note 1. Aśwagríva, mentioned in the *Mahábhárata*, *Ádi-parvan*, śl 2533, is, presumably,
identical with the latter, who has a fellow in Aśwaśiras,—*ibid.*, śl. 2531
and 2646.

The passage in Vol. I., Preface, p. LXXXVI., where "Vishńu, as Hayagríva" is spoken of, I have not yet been able to verify. In the mean-
time, it may pretty safely be surmised that there is a mistake.

Hayaśirsha, Hayaśiras, and Aśwaśiras are, being interpreted, 'Horse-
headed'; Hayagríva and Aśwagríva, 'Horse-necked.'

In the *Sabdakalpadruma*, the first definition of Hayagríva makes him
an epiphany of Vishńu, for the sake of recovering the Vedas, which had
been carried off by Madhu and Kaitabha. The passage there quoted—
Mahábhárata, *Sánti-parvan*, śl. 13497—13503,—does not, however, mention Hayagríva at all, but Aśwaśiras.

My friend Mr. C. P. Brown informs me, that, in the Madras Presidency,
Hayagríva is a not uncommon name for a Brábman to bear. The fact
is noteworthy. Hayagrivahan, "Slayer of Hayagríva," is an epithetical
designation of Hayaśirsha, *i. e.*, Vishńu.

* *Sinha*: which here denotes *nŕi-sinha*, the commentators say. See
Vol IV., p. 277, text and note ‡.

† See Vol. III., p. 18, text and note 1.

1*

the earth upon his crest, and who has descended upon
earth for its protection, will (this day,) call me by my
name. Glory to that being, whose deceptive adoption
of father, son, friend, brother, mother, and relative
the world is unable to penetrate! Glory to him, who
is one with true knowledge, who is inscrutable,* and
through whom, seated in his heart, the Yogin crosses
the wide expanse of worldly ignorance and illusion!
I bow to him, who, by the performers of holy rites,
is called the male of sacrifice (Yajnapurusha); by
pious worshippers† is termed Vásudeva; and, by the
cultivators of philosophy,‡ Vishńu. May he in whom
cause, and effect, and the world itself is comprehended be propitious to me, through his truth; for
always do I put my trust in that unborn, eternal Hari,
by meditation on whom man becomes the repository
of all good things."§

His mind thus animated by devout faith, and meditating in this manner, Akrúra (proceeded on his road,
and) arrived at Gokula a little before sunset, at the
time of the milking of the cows.‖ And there he saw
Kŕishńa, amongst the cattle, dark as the leaf of the

* *Ameya.*
† *Sátwata.*
‡ *Vedánta.*

§ यथा तव जगन्नाभि धातर्ये तत्प्रतिष्ठितम् ।
 सद्रसत्तेन सत्त्वेन मय्यसौ यातु सौम्यताम् ॥
 कृते सकलकल्याणभाजनं यच आयते ।
 पुरुषत्तमं नित्यं व्रजामि शरणं हरिम् ॥

‖ The original here has "at the milking-place of the cows", आदोहने
नवाम् । Śridhara's and Ratnagarbha's comment: आदोहने । दोहनस्थाने ।

full-blown lotos; his eyes of the same colour,* and
his breast decorated with the Śrívatsa† mark; long-
armed, and broad-chested; having a high nose,‡ and
a lovely countenance brightened with mirthful smiles;
treading firmly on the ground, with feet whose nails
were tinted red; clad in yellow garments, and adorned
with a garland of forest-flowers; § having a fresh-
gathered creeper in his hand, ‖ and a chaplet of white
lotos-flowers on his head. ¶ Akrúra** also beheld,
there, Balabhadra, white as a swan, a jasmine, or the
moon, and dressed in blue raiment; having large and
powerful arms, †† and a countenance as radiant as a
lotos in bloom,—like another Kailása-mountain, crested
with a wreath of clouds.

When Akrúra saw these two youths, his countenance expanded with delight, ‡‡ and the down of his
body stood erect (with pleasure). For this he thought
to be supreme happiness and glory; this, the double
manifestation of the divine Vásudeva. §§ This was the
twofold gratification of his sight, to behold the creator

---

* मखष्टपद्मपत्राक्षम् ।
† See Vol. IV., p. 268.
‡ प्रजम्बबाहुमासीनं तुङ्गोरःस्थलसुन्दरम् ।
§ वन्यपुष्पविभूषितम् ।
‖ सार्द्रनीललताहस्तम् । Variant, accepted by the commentator Ratnagarbha: सेन्द्रनीलाचसार्भं तम् ।
¶ सिताम्भोजावतंसकम् ।
** *Yadu-nandana*, "descendant of Yadu," in the or-ginal.
†† Add "and shoulders".
‡‡ विकसद्गुरुसरोरुहः ।
§§ एतत्परं धाम तदेतत्परं पदम् ।
      भगवद्वासुदेवांशो द्विधा योऽत्रावस्थितः ॥

of the universe: now he hoped that his bodily form
would yield fruit. -- as it would bring him in contact
with the person of Kṛishṇa,*—and that the wearer of
infinite forms would place his hand on his back; the
touch of whose finger alone is sufficient to dispel sin,
and to secure imperishable felicity; that hand which
launches the fierce irresistible discus, blazing with all
the flames of fire, lightning, and the sun, and, slaugh-
tering the demon-host, washes the collyrium from
the eyes of their brides; that hand into which Bali
poured water, and thence obtained ineffable enjoyments below the earth,† and immortality, and dominion over the gods for a whole Manwantara, without
peril from a foe. "Alas! He will despise me for my
connexion with Kaṁsa,—an associate with evil, though
not contaminated by it. How vain is his birth, who
is shunned by the virtuous!‡ And yet, what is there,

* साफल्यमद्यणोर्युगमेतदञ
दृष्टे अगद्वातरि यातमुच्चैः ।
अथक्रमेतन्न्नगवत्प्रसादा-
द्न्तेऽऽऽक्रसङ्गे फलवन्म स्यात् ॥

† The original implies that Bali, who had dwelt below the earth, obtained, &c.:

* * * * * बलिर्मंगोच्चा-
नवाप भोगान्वसुधातलस्थः ।

For Bali,—a Daitya, son of Virochana.—successively sovereign of Pátála and an Indra, see Vol. II., p. 69, and p. 210, note 1; Vol. III.,
p. 18, note 1, and p. 23.
    The translation, towards the end of the present chapter, is very free,
generally.

‡ अयेष मां कंसपरिग्रहेण
दोषासदोभूतमदोषदुष्टम् ।
कर्ता न मोगोवहतं धिगस्तु
तज्जन्म तत्साधु बहिष्कृतो यः ॥

in this world, unknown to him who resides in the
hearts of all men, who is ever existent, exempt from
imperfection, the aggregate of the quality of purity,
and identical with true knowledge?* With a heart
wholly devoted to him, then, I will approach the lord
of all lords, the descended portion of Purushottama,
of Vishńu, who is without beginning, middle, or end."

Some of my MSS. have, instead of न मौनोपहृतं, अवमानोपहृतम् ।
This variant is noted by the commentator Ratnagarbha, and appears in
the text of Śrídhara.

* ज्ञानात्मकस्खामलसत्वराशे-
रपेतदोषस्य सदा स्फुटस्य ।
किं वा जगत्यत्र समस्तपुंसा-
मज्ञातमस्याप्ति हृदि खितस्य ॥

CHAPTER XVIII.

Grief of the Gopís, on the departure of Kríshńa and Balaráma with Akrúra: their leaving Gokula. Akrúra bathes in the Yamuná; beholds the divine forms of the two youths, and praises Vishńu.

THUS meditating, the Yádava approached Govinda, (and addressed him,) and said "I am Akrúra," and bowed his head down to the feet of Hari.* But Kríshńa laid upon him his hand, which was marked with the flag, the thunderbolt, and the lotos, and drew him (towards him), and affectionately embraced him. Then Ráma† and Keśava entered into conversation with him, and, having heard from him all that had occurred, were much pleased, and led him to their habitation: there they resumed their discourse, and gave him food to eat, and treated him with proper hospitality.‡ Akrúra told them how (their father) Ánakadundubhi,§ the princess Devakí, and (even his own father,) Ugrasena had been insulted by the iniquitous demon,‖ Karúsa: he also related to them the purpose for which he had been despatched. When he had told them all these things, the destroyer of Keśin¶ said to him: "I

---

* चरणौ नमाम शिरसा हरि: ।

† The original has Bala.

‡ सह ताभां तदाकूर: हतसंवादनादिक: ।
  भुक्तभोज्यो यथान्यायमाघषे ततक्ष्यो: ॥

§ See Vol. IV., p. 101, text and note 1.

‖ Dánava.

¶ Keśi-súdana. Compare the cognate epithet of Kríshńa, Madhusúdana, "slayer of Madhu."

was aware of all that you have told me, lord of liberal gifts.* Ráma and I will go, to-morrow, to Mathurá, along with you. The elders of the cowherds shall accompany us, bearing ample offeriugs.† Rest here tonight, and dismiss all anxiety.‡ Within three nights I will slay Kaṁsa and his adherents."

Having given orders, accordingly, to the cowherds, Akrúra, with Keśava and Ráma, § retired to rest, and slept soundly in the dwelling of Nanda. The next morning was bright; and the youths prepared to depart for Mathurá, with Akrúra. The Gopís, seeing them about to set forth, were much afflicted; they wept bitterly; their bracelets were loose upon their arms; and they thus communed together:‖ "If Govinda depart for Mathurá, how will he return to Gokula? His ears will there be regaled with the melodious and polished conversation of the women of the city. Accustomed to the language of the graceful females of Mathurá, he will never again endure the rustic expressions of the Gopís. Hari, the pride of the station,¶ is carried off; and a fatal blow is inflicted upon us by inexorable destiny. Expressive smiles, soft language, graceful airs, elegant gait, and significant

---

* Here follows a stanza left untranslated:

आरभ्ये च महाभाग यदुद्वीपपियं मतम् ।
विचिन्नं नाब्धितत्ते विद्धि कंसं इतं मया ॥

These verses are recognized, in their texts and comments, by both the scholiasts. Furthermore, they are found translated at length in Professor Wilson's Hindu-made English version.

† Upáyana.

‡ निग्रेयं नीयतां वीर न चिन्तां कर्तुमर्हसि ।

§ Balabhadra, in the Sanskrit.

‖ The translation is, hereabouts, free and expanded.

¶ Goshṭha.

glances belong to the women of the city.* Hari is of rustic breeding; and, captivated by their fascinations, what likelihood is there of his returning to the society of any one amongst us?† Keśava, who has mounted the car, to go to Mathurá, has been deceived by the cruel, (vile), and desperate Akrúra. Does not the unfeeling traitor know the affection that we all here feel for our Hari, the joy of our eyes, that he is taking him away? Unkind that he is, Govinda is departing from us, along with Ráma. Haste! Let us stop him. Why talk of telling our seniors that we cannot bear his loss? What can they do for us, when we are consumed by the fires of separation? The Gopas, with Nanda at their head, are, themselves, preparing to depart. No one makes any attempt to detain Govinda. Bright is the morning that succeeds to this night, for the women of Mathurá; for the bees of their eyes will feed upon the lotos-face of Achyuta. Happy are they who may go hence without impediment, and behold, enraptured, Kŕishńa on his journey. A great festival will give pleasure, to-day, to the eyes of the inhabitants of Mathurá, when they see the person of Govinda.‡ What a blissful vision will be seen by the happy women (of the city), whose brilliant eyes shall regard, unchecked,

* भावगर्भस्थितं वाक्यं विलासललिता गतिः ।
नागरीणामधैवैतत्कटाचेचितमेव च ॥

† याम्यो हरिरयं तासां विलासनिगडैर्युतः ।
भवतीनां पुनः पार्श्वं कया युक्त्या समेष्यति ॥

‡ धन्यास्ति पचि ये क्रष्णमितो याच्यजिनवारिताः ।
उद्वहिष्यन्ति पश्यन्तः खदेहं पुलकाचितम् ॥
मधुरानगरोपीरनयनां महोत्सवः ।
गोविन्दावयवैर्दृष्टिरतीवाच भविष्यति ॥

the countenance of Krishńa!* Alas! The eyes of the
Gopís have been deprived of sight by the relentless
Brahmá,† after he had shown them this great treasure.
In proportion as the affection of Hari for us decays,
so do our limbs wither, and the bracelets slip from
our arms.‡ And now the cruel Akrúra urges on the
horses. All conspire to treat unhappy females with
unkindness. Alas! alas! We see, now, only the dust
of his chariot-wheels. And now he is far away: for
even that dust is no longer to be seen." Thus lamented
by the women,§ Keśava and Ráma quitted the dis-
trict of Vraja.¹ Travelling in a car drawn by fleet
horses, they arrived, at noon, at the banks of the Yamuná, when Akrúra requested them to halt a little,
whilst he performed the usual daily ceremonial in the

---

¹ In the Bhágavata, Hari Vaṁśa, &c., several adventures of
Krishńa, during his residence at Vraja, are recorded, of which our
text makes no mention. Of these, the two most popular are
Krishńa's taking away the clothes of the Gopís whilst bathing,
and his liberating the Gopas from the mouth of Aghásura, ‖—dis-
guised as a vast serpent,—into which they had entered, thinking
it a cavern in a mountain. The omission of these two legends,
or of any of the rest, is not much to be regretted.

---

* The original has Adhokshaja, for the signification of which word see
Vol. I., p. 28, note †
† Vidbátrí, in the Sanskrit. Vide infra, p. 15, note ¶.
‡ अनुरागेण शिथिलमस्मासु व्रजता हरे: ।
   शिथिल्यमुपयान्त्यायु करेषु वलयान्यपि ॥
§ र्खेवमतिष्ठार्देन गोपीजनमिरोषित: ।
‖ That is to say, Agha the Asura. He was Kaṁsa's generalissimo;
and it seems that little more than this fact is known of him. See the
Bhágavata-puráńa, X., Prior Section, Chapter XII.

river.[1*] Accordingly, the intelligent Akrúra bathed, and rinsed his mouth; and then, entering the stream, he stood meditating upon the supreme being.† But he beheld (mentally,[2]) Balabhadra, having a thousand hooded heads, a garland of jasmine-flowers, and large red eyes,‡ attended by Vásuki,§ Rambha,‖ and other mighty serpents,¶ praised by the Gandharvas, decorated with wild flowers, wearing dark-coloured garments, crowned with a chaplet** of lotoses, ornamented with brilliant ear-rings, inebriate, and standing at the bottom of the river, in the water.[3] On his lap he also

---

[1] The noonday prayer, or Sandhyá.

[2] By his Dhyána, or force of meditation, in which it is attempted to bring before the mind's eye some definite form of the object of adoration. In this case, Akrúra is compelled to see a form he did not anticipate. The Hari Vaṁśa,†† very clumsily, sets him to meditate upon the serpent Śesha, which spoils the story; intended, as that is, to exhibit the identity of Balaráma and Kŕishńa with the Supreme.

[3] Balaráma was, thus, visible in his real character of Śesha,‡‡—the chief of serpents, the couch of Vishńu, and supporter of the world.

---

* अथाह कृष्णमकूरो भवश्रां तावदाखताम् ।
   यावत्करोमि कालिन्त्यामाह्रिकार्यमथासि ॥

The Yamuná is here called Kálindi.

† To translate Brahma.

‡ वसिद्रपत्रपपत्रोणिषयम् ।

§ See Vol. II., p. 74.

‖ See Vol II., p. 287, note *. The conjecture which I there ventured thus turns out to be correct.

¶ Pavanáśin.

** Avatamsaka.

†† Chapter XCIII.

‡‡ See Vol. II., pp. 74 and 85, and p. 211, note 1; also, Vol. IIL, pp. 30, 31.

beheld, at his ease,* Krishńa, of the complexion of a
cloud,¹ with full and coppery eyes, having an elegant
form, and four hands, armed with the discus and other
weapons, wearing yellow clothes, decorated with many-
coloured flowers, and appearing like a cloud embellished with streams of lightning and the bow of Indra.†
His breast was marked with the celestial sign;‡ his
arms were radiant with bracelets; a diadem shone on
his brow;§ and he wore a white lotos for his crest.‖
He was attended by Sanandana¶ and other holy sages,
who, fixing their eyes upon the tips of their noses,
were absorbed in profound meditation.**

When Akrúra beheld Balaráma†† and Krishńa in this
situation, he was much amazed, and wondered how
they could so quickly have got there from the chariot.
He wished to ask them this; but Janárdana deprived
him of the faculty of speech, at the moment. Ascending, then, from the water, he repaired to the car; and
there he found them both, (quietly) seated, in the same
human persons as before. Plunging, again, into the
water, there he again beheld them, hymned, as before,

---

¹ Or, rather, he beheld Ghanaśyáma,—an appellation of Krishńa,
who is so called from being as black (śyáma) as a cloud (ghana).

---

* Aklishťa.
† Śakra, in the original.
‡ To render śrivatsa. Vide supra, p. 5.
§ श्रीवत्सवषषं चारुकेयूरमुकुटोज्वलम् ।
‖ Avataṁsaka.
¶ See Vol. II., p. 226; and p. 227, note 1.
** सनन्दनाधीर्मुनिभि: सिद्धयोगैरकल्मषै: ।
विचिन्तमानं तचक्षीर्नासायन्वलोचनै: ॥
†† The Sanskrit has Bala.

by the Gandharvas, saints,* sages,† and serpents. Apprehending, therefore, their real character, he thus eulogized the eternal deity, who consists of true knowledge:‡

"Salutation to thee, who art uniform and manifold, all-pervading, supreme spirit, of inconceivable glory, and who art simple existence!§ Salutation to thee, O inscrutable, who art truth, and the essence of oblations!‖ Salutation to thee. O lord, whose nature is unknown, who art beyond primeval matter, who existest in five forms,¶ as one with the elements, with the faculties.** with matter, with the living soul, with supreme spirit!†† Show favour (to me), O soul of the universe, essence of all things, perishable or eternal, whether addressed by the designation of Brahmá, Vishṇu, Śiva, or the like. I adore thee, O god,‡‡ whose nature is indescribable, whose purposes are inscrutable, whose name, even, is unknown;§§ for the at-

---

* *Muni.*
† *Siddha.*
‡ तुष्टाव सर्वविद्यानमयमच्युतमीश्वरम् ।
§ शक्रूर उवाच ।
सन्धारूपिणेऽचिन्त्यमहिम्ने परमात्मने ।
व्यापिने नैकरूपैकरूपाय नमो नमः ॥
‖ *Havis.*
¶ See Vol. I., p. 2, note 1, where this passage is referred to and enlarged on.
** *Indriya.*
†† *Átman* and *paramátman.* The first is the same as *jivátman.* See Vol. IV., p. 253, note *.
‡‡ *Parameśvara.*
§§ अनाख्येयाभिधान ि *Abhidhána* here takes the place of the more ordinary *náman*, the term rendered "appellation", just below. See Vol. IV., p. 346, supplement to p. 267, note *.

tributes of appellation or kind* are not applicable to
to thee, who art THAT.[1] the supreme Brahma, eternal,
unchangeable, uncreated.† But, as the accomplishment of our objects cannot be attained except through
some specific form,‡ thou art termed. by us, Krishna,
Achyuta, Ananta, or Vishnu.§ Thou, unborn (divinity),
art all the objects of these impersonations; thou art
the gods, and all other beings; thou art the whole
world; thou art all. Soul of the universe, thou art
exempt from change; and there is nothing except thee
in all this existence. Thou art Brahmá, Pasupati, Ar-
yaman,‖ Dhátri, and Vidhátri;¶ thou art Indra,** air,
fire, the regent of the waters,†† the god of wealth,‡‡ and
judge of the dead;§§ and thou, although but one, pre-
sidest over the world, with various energies addressed
to various purposes. Thou, identical with the solar
ray, createst the universe; all elementary substance is

---

[1] Tad, 'that'; all that is, or that can be conceived.

---

* It should seem, from a collation of passages, that *játi*, the expression here used, is synonymous with *rúpa.* Do *náman* and *játi* signify
'genus' and 'species'? See Vol. II., p. 328, text and note ‡; and p. 337,
supplementary note to p. 59, l. 8.

† *Aja.*

‡ कल्पमामृते ।

§ ततः ब्रह्माच्युतानन्तविष्णुसंज्ञाभिरीड्यसे ।

‖ Corrected from "Áryaman".

¶ Dhátri and Vidhátri are said to be Brahmá as protector and creator.
See Colebrooke's *Miscellaneous Essays*, Vol. I., p. 191. In lieu of Dhátri,
some MSS. yield Vishnu.

** To represent *tridasapati*, 'lord of the gods.'

†† *Toyesa*: Varuna, to-wit.

‡‡ *Dhana-pati*; namely, Kubera.

§§ The original yields Antaka, who is one with Yama. See Vol. II.,
p. 216, note 1.

composed of thy qualities; and thy supreme form is
denoted by the imperishable term SAT (existence).
To him who is one with true knowledge; who is, and
is not, perceptible, * I bow. Glory be to him, the lord
Vásudeva, to Sankarshańa, to Pradyumna, and to Aniruddha!"[1]

---

[1] Akrúra's piety is, here, prophetic: the son and grandson of
Kŕishńa (see Vol. IV., p. 112,) are not yet born. But this is the
Vaishńava style of addressing Kŕishńa, or Vishńu, as identical
with four Vyúhas,—'arrangements' or 'dispositions',—Kŕishńa,
Balaráma, Pradyumna, and Aniruddha.† See the Asiatic Re-
searches, Vol. XVI., p. 35.‡ In this, as in several other places,
the Vishńu Puráńa differs from some of the other narratives of
Kŕishńa, by the length and character of the prayers addressed to
Vishńu. The Hari Vaṁśa, for instance, here has no prayer or
panegyric at all; the Bhágavata inserts one.

---

* *Sat* and *asat*, 'real' and 'unreal'.

† Ratnagarbha, one of the commentators on the *Vishńu-puráńa*, refers,
to a similar purport, to the *Mahábhárata*. The passage intended is,
apparently, in the *Śánti-parvan*,—*śl.* 12888, *et seq.*

‡ Or Professor Wilson's collected Works, Vol. I., p. 45.

CHAPTER XIX.

Akrúra conveys Krishńa and Ráma near to Mathurá, and leaves
them: they enter the town. Insolence of Kaṁsa's washerman:
Krishńa kills him. Civility of a flower-seller: Krishńa gives
him his benediction.

THUS, the Yádava (Akrúra), standing in the river,
praised Krishńa, and worshipped him with imaginary*
incense and flowers. Disregarding (all) other objects,
he fixed his (whole) mind upon the deity; and, having
continued, for a long time, in spiritual contemplation,†
he (at last,) desisted from his abstraction, conceiving
he had effected the purposes of soul.‡ Coming up from
the water of the Yamuná, he went to the car; and
there he beheld Ráma and Krishńa, seated as before.
As his looks denoted surprise, Krishńa said to him:
"Surely, Akrúra, you have seen some marvel in the
stream of the Yamuná; for your eyes are staring, as
if with astonishment." Akrúra replied: "The marvel
that I have seen in the stream of the Yamuna I behold
before me, even here, in a bodily shape: for he whom
I have encountered in the water, Krishńa, is, also,
your wondrous self, of whose illustrious person the
whole world is the miraculous development.§ But

---

* *Mano-maya.*
† *Brahma-bhúta.*
‡ जतङ्कत्वमिवात्मानं मन्वमानो महामतिः ।
This is in the same stanza with what immediately follows, and should
have been connected with it, in the translation.
§ अमदेतन्महाबर्षं रूपं यस्ख महात्मनः ।
तेजांबर्यंवरेखांहं भवता कृष्ण संगतः ॥

enough of this. Let us proceed to Mathurá. I am
afraid Kaṁsa will be angry at our delay: such is the
wretched consequence of eating the bread of another."*
Thus speaking, he urged on the quick† horses; and
they arrived, after sunset, at Mathurá. When they
came in sight of the city, Akrúra said to Kŕishńa and
Ráma: "You must now journey on foot, whilst I proceed alone in the car.‡ And you must not go to the
house of Vasudeva; for the elder has been banished,
by Kaṁsa, on your account."

Akrúra, having thus spoken, left them, and entered
the city; whilst Ráma and Kŕishńa continued to walk
along the royal road. Regarded, with pleasure, by
men and women, they went along sportively, looking
like two young elephants. As they roamed about,
they saw a washerman§ colouring clothes; and, with
smiling countenances, they went and threw down
some of his fine linen.‖ The washerman was the
servant of Kaṁsa, made insolent by his master's favour;¶ and he provoked the two lads with loud and

---

* तत्किमेतेन मधुरां व्रजामो मधुसूदन ।
  विभेमि कंसादिग्जन्म परपिष्टोपजीविनाम् ॥

† *Váta-raṁhas.*

‡ पद्यां यातं महावीर्यौ रचेनैको विश्रामयहम् ।

§ *Rajaka.* From the context the word seems to denote a dyer.

‖ अयाचेतां तुच्छपाणि वासांसि रविरागनी ।

The lads did not "throw down some of his fine linen", but asked
him for it.

रविरागि तौ is the reading preferred by the commentator Ratnagarbha; रविरागनी, that accepted by Śridhara: and neither of them
mentions that of the other.

¶ कंसस्य रजकः सोऽय प्रसादाऽद्धविकाय: ।

Instead of प्रसादा॰, some MSS. have प्रमादा॰.

scurrilous abuse, until Krishna struck him down, with his head to the ground, and killed him. Then, taking the clothes, they went their way, clad in yellow and blue raiment, until they came to a flower-seller's shop. The flower-seller looked at them with astonishment, and wondered who they could be, or whence they could have come. Seeing two youths so lovely, dressed in yellow and blue garments, he imagined them to be divinities descended upon earth. Being addressed by them with mouths budding like lotoses, and asked for some flowers, he placed his hands upon the ground, and touched it with his head, saying: "My lords have shown me great kindness, in coming to my house,*— fortunate that I am. I will pay them homage." Having thus spoken, the flower-seller, with a smiling aspect, gave them whatever choice flowers they selected, to conciliate their favour. Repeatedly prostrating† himself before them, he presented them with flowers, beautiful, fragrant, and fresh.‡ Krishna, then, being much pleased with him, gave him this blessing: "Fortune, good friend, who depends upon me, shall never forsake you. Never shall you suffer loss of vigour or loss of wealth. As long as time shall last, your descendants shall not fail.§ Having long tasted various de-

---

* प्रसादपरमौ नाथौ मम गेहमुपागतौ ।

† प्रणम्य, which implies nothing more than a respectful inclination of the head and uplifting of the hands.

‡ Amala.

§ यावद्दिनानि तावच्च न नशिष्यति संतति: ।

This lection, Ratnagarbha's, is the one followed by the Translator. Śrídhara's and that of nearly all my best MSS. begins the verse with the words यावत्त्वत्राम ।

lights (on earth), you shall, finally, obtain, by calling me to recollection, a heavenly region, the consequence of my favour. Your heart shall ever be intent on righteousness; and fulness of days shall be the portion of your posterity. Your descendants shall not be subject to natural infirmities, as long as the sun shall endure."* Having thus spoken, Kŕishńa and Ráma,† worshipped by the flower-seller, went forth from his dwelling.[1]

---

[1] These incidents are told, with some unimportant differences, in the other accounts of Kŕishńa's youth.

---

* गोपसर्गादिकं दोषं युष्मत्संततिसंभवः ।
    संप्राप्स्यति महाभाग यावत्सूर्यो धरिष्यति ॥

† Baladeva, in the original.

CHAPTER XX.

Krishńa and Balaráma meet Kubjá; she is made straight by the former: they proceed to the palace. Krishńa breaks a bow intended for a trial of arms. Kamsa's orders to his servants. Public games. Krishńa and his brother enter the arena: the former wrestles with Chánúra, the latter, with Mushíika, the king's wrestlers, who are, both, killed. Krishńa attacks and slays Kaṁsa: he and Balaráma do homage to Vasudeva and Devakí: the former praises Krishńa.

AS they proceeded along the high road, they saw coming (towards them) a young girl, who was crooked, carrying a pot of unguent. Krishńa addressed her sportively, and said: "For whom are you carrying that unguent? Tell me, lovely maiden;* tell me truly." Spoken to as it were through affection, Kubjá,† well disposed towards Hari, replied to him also mirthfully, being smitten by his appearance: "Know you not, beloved, that I am the servant of Kaṁsa, and appointed, crooked as I am, to prepare his perfumes?‡ Unguent ground by any other he does not approve of: hence I am enriched through his liberal rewards." Then said Krishńa: "Fair-faced damsel, give us of this unguent,—

---

* *Indivara-lochaná.*

† No proper name, here and near the top of the next page, but "the deformed girl". The word *kubjá* is rendered "crooked", above.

‡ कान्त कस्मात् आनासि कंसेनाभिनियोजिताम् ।
नैकवक्रेति विख्यातामनुलेपनकर्मणि ॥

The name of the damsel, we are thus told, was Naikavakrá. In the *Bhágavata-puráńa*, X., Prior Section, XLII., 3, her name appears as Trivakrá. She was so called, the commentator Śrídhara remarks, because triply deformed,—namely, in the neck, in the chest, and in the waist.

fragrant, and fit for kings,—as much as we may rub
upon our bodies." "Take it," answered Kubjá. And
she gave them as much of the unguent as was sufficient for their persons. And they rubbed it on various parts of their faces and bodies,[1] till they[*] looked
like two clouds, one white and one black, decorated
by the many-tinted bow of Indra. Then Krishńa,[†]
skilled in the curative art, took hold of her, under the
chin, with the thumb and two fingers, and lifted up
her head, whilst, with his feet, he pressed down her
feet; and, in this way, he made her straight. When
she was thus relieved from her deformity, she was a
most beautiful woman;[‡] and, filled with gratitude and
affection, she took Govinda by the garment, and invited
him to her house. Promising to come at some other
time, Krishńa[§] smilingly dismissed her, and then

---

[1] They had their bodies smeared in the style called Bha-
ktichchheda (भक्तिच्छेदानुलिप्ताङ्गौ); that is, with the separating
or distinguishing (chheda) marks of Vaishńava devotion (bhakti),—
certain streaks on the forehead, nose, cheeks, breast, and arms,
which denote a follower of Vishńu. See the Asiatic Researches,
Vol. XVI., p. 33.[||]

---

[*] The original here gives them the epithet *purusharshabha*.
[†] Śauri, in the Sanskrit. See the original in the next annotation.
[‡] ततस्तां चिबुके शौरिरङ्गापनविधानवित् ।
उत्वच्च तोलयामास ह्यङ्गुलेनायपाणिना ॥
चकर्ष पद्भ्यां च तथा चरुलं केग्रवोऽनयत् ।
तत: सा च्रुतां मात्रा शोचितामभवद्वरा ॥
For some of the additions to the literal sense of the original, the
Translator has drawn on Śrídhara.
[§] The Sanskrit has Hari.
[||] Or Professor Wilson's collected Works, Vol. I., p. 41.

laughed aloud, on beholding the countenance of Baladeva.[1]*

Dressed in blue and yellow garments, and anointed
with fragrant unguents,† Keśava and Ráma proceeded
to the hall of arms, which was hung round with garlands.: Inquiring of the warders which bow he was
to try, and being directed to it, he took it, and bent
it.§ But, drawing it with violence, he snapped it in
two;[2] and all Mathurá resounded with the noise which
its fracture occasioned. Abused by the warders for
breaking the bow, Kŕishńa and Ráma retorted, and de-
fied them, and left the hall.||

When Kamsa knew that Akrúra had returned, and
heard that the bow had been broken, he thus said to
Cháńúra and Mushtika, (his boxers): "Two youths,
cowherd boys, have arrived. You must kill them both,
in a trial of strength,¶ in my presence; for they prac-

---

[1] The story is similarly told in the Bhágavata, &c.

[2] The bending or breaking of a bow is a favourite incident
in Hindu heroic poetry; borrowed, no doubt, from the Rámáyańa, where, however, it has an object: here it is quite gratuitous.

---

* Ráma, in the original.

† भक्तिच्छेदानुलिप्माङ्गौ । See note 1 in the preceding page.

: According to the original, in all my MSS., &c., the youths, not the
hall, were thus adorned.

§ चायीगं च धनूरतं ताभां पृष्टेव रविभिः ।
  आख्यातं सहसा क्रष्णो गृहीलापूरयन्बभु: ॥

Instead of चायोगं च, the lection of Śrídhara, Ratnagarbha has
चायोगवं, and says that we here have the name of the bow, Áyogava.
The commentators mention and explain other readings; and my MSS.
supply still more.

॥ रविवैबं निहलीभी निक्नालौ कार्मुकालयात् ।

¶ Malla-yuddha. See note ¶ in p. 39, infra.

tise against my life. I shall be well pleased if you kill
them in the match, and will give you whatever you
wish; not else. These two foes of mine must be killed
by you, fairly or unfairly. The kingdom shall be ours
in common, when they have perished." Having given
them these orders, he sent, next, for his elephant-
driver, and desired him to station his (great) elephant,
Kuvalayápída,—who was as vast as a cloud charged
with rain,—near the gate of the arena, and drive him
upon the two boys, when they should attempt to
enter.* When Kaṁsa had issued these commands, and
ascertained that the platforms were all ready (for the
spectators), he awaited the rising of the sun, unconscious of impending death.†

In the morning, the citizens assembled on the platforms set apart for them; and the princes, with the
ministers and courtiers,‡ occupied the royal seats.
Near the centre of the circle, judges of the games§
were stationed by Kaṁsa, whilst he himself sat apart,
close by, upon a lofty throne. Separate platforms
were erected for the ladies of the palace,‖ for the

---

* प्रोवाचोदैस्त्वया मह्रसमाजद्वारि कुञ्जरः ।
  स्थाप्यः कुवलयापीडस्तेन तौ गोपदारकौ ॥

Instead of मह्र॰, there occurs, as a common variant, the lection accepted
by Śridhara, मेऽस्य । This, mistaken for मेघ॰, with the supposition that
त्वया was misread तोय॰, is the only ground that I have discovered for
the Translator's clause "who was as vast as a cloud charged with rain."

† The original has आसन्नमर॒ण:, which only implies that his death
was near, not that he knew it to be so.

‡ These two words are to represent ámátya. Bhṛitya, 'dependants',
is a variant.

§ मह्रमात्रिकवर्गः । Variant: मह्रपार्श्विकवर्गः ।

‖ Antaḥpura.

courtesans,* and for the wives of the citizens.¹ Nanda
and the cowherds had places appropriated to them, at

---

¹ The Bhágavata enters into even fewer particulars than our
text, of the place set apart for the games. The Hari Vamsa
gives a much more detailed description, which is, in some respects, curious. The want of any technical glossary, and the general manner in which technical terms are explained in the ordinary dictionaries, render it difficult to understand exactly what
is intended; and any translation of the passages must be defective. The French version,† however, probably represents a
much more splendid and theatrical scene than the text authorizes,
and may, therefore, admit of correction. The general plan is
nothing more than an enclosed space, surrounded by temporary
structures of timber or bamboos, open or enclosed, and decorated
with hangings and garlands. It may be doubted if the details
described by the compiler of the Hari Vamsa were very familiar
even to him; for his description is not always very consistent or
precise. Of two commentators, one evidently knows nothing of
what he attempts to explain; but, with the assistance of the
other, the passages may be thus, though not always confidently,
rendered:

"The king, Kamsa, meditating on these things, went forth,
from his palace, to the place which had been prepared for the
sight of the ceremonial ('), to inspect the scaffolds (²) which had
been constructed. He found the place close set with the several
platforms (³) of the different public bodies (⁴), strongly put together,
and decorated with roofed pavilions of various sizes, supported
by columns, and divided into commodious chambers.(⁵) The edifice was extensive,‡ well arranged, secured by strong rafters, (⁶)
spacious and lofty, and commodious and secure. Stairs led to
the different galleries. (⁷)§ Chairs of state (⁸) were placed in

---

* Vára-mukhyá.
† M. Langlois's translation, Vol. I., pp. 354, 355, and pp. 362—364.
‡ Swáyata. Variant: swáyuta.
§ The translation of the last two sentences educes much more from
the original than even the commentaries warrant.

the end of which sat Akrúra and Vasudeva. Amongst
the wives of the citizens appeared Devakí, mourning

---

various parts of it. The avenues that conducted to it were nar-
row ([9]). It was covered with temporary stages and sheds, ([10])
and was capable of sustaining the weight of a multitude.

"Having seen the place of the festival thus adorned, Karńsa
gave orders, and said: 'To-morrow let the platforms, and terraces, and pavilions ([11]) be decorated with pictures, and garlands,
and flags, and images; ([12]) and let them be scented with fragrant
odours, and covered over with awnings. ([13]) Let there be ample
heaps of dry pounded cow-dung ([14]) provided on the ground, *
and suitable refreshment-chambers be covered over, and decorated
with bells and ornamented arches. ([15]) Let large water-jars be
securely fixed in order, capable of holding a copious supply, and
provided with golden drinking-cups. Let apartments be prepared ([16]), and various kinds of beverage, in appropriate vessels,
be ready. Let judges of the games be invited, and corporations,
with their chiefs. Let orders be issued to the wrestlers, and
notice be given to the spectators; and let platforms, for their ac-
commodation, be fitted up in the place of assembly.'" ([17])†

---

    * *Aksha-váta* is the reading of my oldest MS., instead of the ordinary
ranga-váta.

    † *Harivaṁśa, ll.* 4527 — 4537:

एवं राजा विचिन्त्यास निष्क्रम्य खगृहोत्तमात् ।
प्रेक्षागारं अगामाशु मझानामवलोककः ॥
स दृष्ट्वा सर्वनियुक्तं प्रेक्षागारं नृपोत्तमः ।
श्रेणीनां दृढसंयुक्तिमेघवाटिनिरन्तरम् ॥
सोत्तमागारयुक्ताभिर्वडभीभिर्विभूषितम् ।
कुटीभिश्च प्रवृद्धाभिरिकक्षक्षीय भूषितम् ॥
सर्वतः सारनिर्व्यूहं खायतं सुप्रतिष्ठितम् ।
उद्यासिष्टसुखिष्टमद्वारोहणमुत्तमम् ॥
नृपासनपरिचिन्नं संचारपथसंकुलम् ।
छन्नं तद्वेदिकाभिश्च मानवौघभरक्षमम् ॥
स दृष्ट्वा भूषितं रङ्गमाज्ञापयत बुद्धिमान् ।
श्वः सचिवाः समाज्ञाय सपताकाखध्वेव च ॥

for her son,* whose lovely face she longed to behold,
even in the hour of his destruction. When the musical

When the meeting takes place, the site of the games is thus
described: "Upon the following day, the amphitheatre([18]) was
filled by the citizens, anxious to behold the games. The place
of assembly ([19]) was supported by octagonal painted pillars,([20])
fitted up with terraces, and doors, and bolts, with windows, circular or crescent; shaped, and accommodated with seats with
cushions;([21]) and it shone like the ocean, whilst large clouds
hang upon it, with spacious, substantial pavilions,([22]) fitted up
for the sight of the combat; open to the front,([23]) but screened
with beautiful and fine curtains,([24]) crowned with festoons of
flowers, and glistening with radiance, like autumnal clouds. The
pavilions † of the different companies and corporations, vast as
mountains, were decorated with banners, bearing upon them the
implements and emblems of the several crafts.([25]) The chambers
of the inhabitants of the inner apartments shone near at hand,
bright with gold, and painting, and net-work of gems: they were
richly decorated with precious stones, were enclosed below with
costly hangings,([26]) and ornamented above with spires and banners, and looked like mountains spreading their wings in the sky;

सुवासिता वपुष्मन्त उपनीतोत्तरच्छद: ।
क्रियन्तां मञ्चवाटाश्च वङ्गभी वीजयन्तया ॥
चचवटि करीषश्च कर्य्यन्तां राग्र्योऽबयाः ।
घष्टाक्षोरक्षशीभाश्च बलयन्तानुरूपतः ॥
क्राष्यन्तां सुनिलतानाश्च पागसुधा यथाक्रमम् ।
उद्भारसहाः सर्वे सकाष्णघटोत्तराः ॥
बलयचोपवर्य्यन्तां कषायाचीव कुभ्रन्ना: ।
मास्निकाश्च निमस्क्यन्तां श्रेखश्च सपुरोगमाः ॥
आग्रा च देया मन्ननां प्रेषकार्ना तथैव च ।
समाजे मञ्चवाटाश्च कर्य्यन्तां सुपकल्पिताः ॥

* पुत्रगृद्धिनी, which means that Devaki loved her son.

† *Mancha*; previously rendered "scaffolds"; "pavilions" being used to
represent *vadabhi* or *valabhi*.

instruments sounded, Cháńúra sprang forth, and the
people cried "Alas!" and Mushtika slapped his arms

while the rays of light reflected from the valuable jewels were
blended with the waving of white chowries and the musical
tinkling of female ornaments. The separate pavilions of the
courtesans were graced by lovely women, attired in the most
splendid dresses, (²⁷) and emulated the radiance of the cars of the
gods. In the place of assembly there were excellent seats,
couches made of gold, and hangings of various colours, inter-
mixed with bunches of flowers; and there were golden vases of
water, and handsome places for refreshment, filled with fruits of
various kinds, and cooling juices, and sherbets fit for drinking. (²⁸) And there were many other stages and platforms, *
constructed of strong timber; and hangings, by hundreds and
thousands, were displayed; and, upon the tops of the houses,
chambers (²⁹) fitted up with delicate jalousies, through which the
women might behold the sports, appeared like swans flying
through the air.

"In front stood the pavilion of Kaṁsa, surpassing all the rest
in splendour, looking like Mount Meru, in radiance; its sides, its
columns, being covered with burnished gold; fastened with
coloured cords, and every way worthy the presence of a king."†

---

* These two substantives.are to render *mancha*. See note † in the
preceding page.

† *Harivánśa, śl.* 4642—4656:

तस्मिन्नहनि निर्वृत्ते द्वितीये समुपस्थिते ।
आपूर्यत महारङ्गः पौरैर्यूथदिदृक्षुभिः ॥
सविचाष्टासिचरणः सार्गलद्वारवेदिकः ।
सगवाक्षार्धचन्द्रश्च सतल्पोत्तमभूषितः ॥
प्राग्विश्वारनिमुंक्तैर्माल्यदामावतंसितैः ।
चलन्तैर्विराजद्भिः शारदैरिव तोयदैः ॥
मञ्चागारैः सुनिर्मुक्तैर्युद्धाय सुविभूषितैः ।
समाअवाटः शुशुभे समेघौघ इवाम्बवः ॥
स्वकर्मद्रव्ययुक्ताभिः पताकाभिरिरंकृतम् ।
श्रेणीनां च गणानां च मञ्चा भान्त्यचलोपमाः ॥

in defiance. Covered with must* and blood from the
elephant, whom, when goaded upon them by his

In justification of the rendering of the above, an explanation
of the technical terms, taken either from dictionaries or from the
commentators, † may be subjoined. (¹) Kaṁsa went to the Prekshágára (प्रेक्षागार), literally, 'house of seeing;' but it is evident, from its interior being visible to spectators on the tops of
the houses,—as subsequently mentioned,—that it was not a

अन्तःपुरजतानां च प्रेषागाराखनेकशः ।
रेजुः काष्ठर्जिचचाणि रत्नज्वालाकुलानि च ॥
तानि रत्नौघक्कप्राणि ससानुप्रगृहाणि च ।
रेजुर्जवनिकाचेपैः सपत्ता इव ते नगाः ॥
तथ चामरहासेय भूषणानां च गिरिज्जितैः ।
मणीनां च वराहीणां विचिचयेद्दर्चिषः ॥
नखिकागां पृथक्भूम्खाः गुर्भैराखरणाम्बरैः ।
श्रोभिता वारमुख्याभिर्विमानमतिमोंजसः ॥
तवाखनानि मुख्यानि पर्यंद्क्राव हिरद्मयाः ।
प्रकोर्ष्टाथ क्रुषाचिषाः सपुष्पखवकानुमाः ।
बीवर्षाः पानकुम्भाच पानभूम्यच श्रोभिताः ।
फलावदंगपूर्णांच चाङ्र्यैः पानयोजिताः ॥
चन्बे च मद्या बहवः काष्ठसंचयबन्धनाः ।
रेजुः सखरखास्तव यतघोऽव सहस्रशः ॥
उत्तरागारिकाद्याच्ये सूच्माजाला्वलोकिनः ।
खीणां प्रेषागृहा भान्ति राजहंसा इवाम्बरे ॥
प्राच्युखखासनियुक्तो मेषगुक्कसमप्रभः ।
इकपचनिभक्तखिचनियोगघोभितः ॥
प्रेषागारः स कंसख प्रचकाशेऽधिकं श्रिया ।
घोभितो माख्यदामैव निवासक्तलघयः ॥

---

* This word, a popularized form of the Persian *mast*, مست, is here
used to translate *mada*, the ichor which exudes from the temples of a
rutting elephant. *Mast* is an adjective, signifying 'proud', 'in rut'.

† Nílakaṉṭha and Arjuna Miśra. To the scantlings of scholia, adduced
in the following pages, that are taken from the former, I have annexed
his name. The remaining elucidations which Professor Wilson indicates
to be commentatorial are derived from the latter.

driver, they had slain, and armed with his tusks. Balabhadra and Janárdana confidently* entered the arena,

---

theatre, or covered edifice.   If a building at all, it was merely
a sort of stockade.   One commentator † calls it "a place made
for seeing the sacrifice": धनुर्महमेषणार्थं कृतं खानम् । (²) Manchá-
nám avalokakaḥ (मञ्चानामवलोकक:).   The Mancha is commonly
understood to signify a raised platform, with a floor and a roof,
ascended by a ladder: see Dictionary.   (³) Mancha-váta (मञ्चवाट).
Váta is either 'site' or 'inclosure,' and is used, here, without
much affecting the sense of Mancha.   The compound is explained,
by the commentators, ‡ 'prepared places' (रचितभूमय:), or 'the
sites of the platforms' (मञ्चभूमय:).   (⁴) The Śreñis (श्रेणीनां), as-
sociations of artificers practising the same art.   One of the commentaries understands the term to be here used to denote, not
their station, but their labours: "The structure was the work of
the artificers" (प्रयतं श्रेणीनाम्).   (⁵) Several words occur, here,
of technical import.   The passage is:

सोत्समागारयुक्ताभिर्वलभीभिर्विभूषितम् । §
कुटीभिश्व प्रवृद्धाभिरेकस्तभीश्व भूषितम् ॥

Valabhi is said, by the commentator, to mean a structure with a
pent roof, supported by six columns; Kuṭi, a circular one, having
seven roofs (something, perhaps, like a Chinese pagoda,) and
four columns.   The Eka-stambha is a chamber, supported by
one column: वलभीभिरभवतो नमत्यबृद्धाभिरह्रीभि: षट्भाभि: ।
कुटीभिश्व प्रवृद्धाभि: कोचक: समस्तद्दिक्षेचतुसभि:॥ (⁶) Sáranirvyúha

---

* गर्वलीलाविलोकिती ।
† Nilakaṇṭha.
‡ The ensuing definitions I find in Arjuna Miśra only.
§ Some MSS. begin this line with उत्तरागार° .
‖ What is meant, here, as the first sentence is from Nilakaṇṭha, who
therein explains, first, वलभीभि:, and then ह्रीभि:, which he reads
instead of कुटीभि:. The rest of the Sanskrit, giving a definition of
the latter term, is, perhaps, altered from the same commentator.

like two lions amidst (a herd of) deer. Exclamations
of pity arose from all the spectators, along with ex-

(सारनिर्व्यूहं).* It is difficult to understand the necessity of rafters
in an inclosure in which the platforms and stages seem to have
been erected independently of any floor or wall; but the com-
mentary† explains Nirvyúha, "strong brackets, projecting from
a house:" सारनिर्व्यूहं वृहं नामद्वारा गृहानिर्गतदारूरूपाणि यच ।
(⁷) Aślishta-suślishta-manchárobaṇam. The first epithet is explained, 'not contracted' (असंकुचितम्);‡ the second, 'well constructed' (साधुरचितम्); and, for the 'ascending' (Árohaṇa),
we have सोपानपङ्क्तिर्यच 'where was a line of steps' or 'ladders'.
There is another reading of the text, however, which may be
rendered: "Having steps well secured in their ascent above"
(उद्कमवबसुश्लिष्टं§ मन्त्रारोहणम्). (⁸)'Seats for kings' (नृपास-
नानि‖). (⁹) Such is the literal purport of Sanchára-patha-sankula
(संचारपथसंकुल); implying, possibly, the formation of passages
by fences on either side. (¹⁰) This is doubtful. The phrase is
(छन्नं तद्वेदिकाभि:) Chhannaṁ tad-vedikábhiḣ. Chhanna means,
literally, 'covered,' and can scarcely be used in the sense of
'overspread' or 'filled with.' Vediká means an elevated floor or
terrace, with which a hall or edifice cannot well be 'covered',
and, therefore, requires the sense here given to Chhanna. The
commentators are silent. (¹¹) The Manchavátás and Valabhis, as
above. The other term is Vithi, 'a shop,' 'a stall,' 'a terrace,'
'a road.' (¹²) Let them be Vapushmantah (वपुष्मन्त:), "having
painted or sculptured figures" (चित्रपुतयादियुक्ता:).¶ The other

---

* I have altered, here and below, "niryyúha", and the same form in
Sanskrit. सारनिर्युहं is a variant.

† Nilakántha's.

‡ Nilakántha's explanation of अश्लिष्ट ।

§ उद्कमवबमश्लिष्टं—the reading of Arjuna Miśra,—and उद्याश्लिष्ट-
सुश्लिष्टं are further variants that I find.

‖ See the original, at the foot of p. 26, supra.

¶ Nilakántha.

pressions of astonishment. "This, then," said the
people, "is Křishńa. This is Balabhadra. This is he

commentary renders it merely 'pleasant' or 'agreeable' (सुहृद्वीया:).
(¹³) 'Covered above with cloths' (उपनीतोत्तरच्छद:). The use of
the awning or Shamiyána is very common in India. (¹⁴) For the
wrestlers to rub over their bodies, to absorb the perspiration
(मज्जानं खेदापमार्जनार्थम्). (¹⁵) This is, all, rather questionable.
The passage is, most usually:

घण्टास्तोरबयोभाय बलयस्यानुरूपत: ।

Vali, or Bali, in one sense, means 'the edge of a thatch,'. and
may be put for some sort of temporary structure,—a kind of re-
tiring or refreshment-room for the boxers and wrestlers. In some
copies, it is read पटास्तरयोभा:, "beautiful with cloths spread,"
on which the performers may sit, when disengaged; perhaps, a
sort of carpet on the ground. (¹⁶) The expression is, again, Vali
(बलयखोपकल्थ्यताम्). Another sense of the word is "offering
of viands, or of the remains of a sacrifice, to all beings;" * but
that cannot be its purport here: nor is it ever used in the sense
of viands in general. The verb Kalp or Klip also usually implies
'making'. (¹⁷) Manchaváta;† 'in the Samája' or 'assembly'.
(¹⁸) Mahárunga (महारङ्ग), "the great place of the performance."
Ranga is 'acting' or 'representation'; also, the place or site of
it. (¹⁹) All the copies consulted, except one, offer an irregularity
of construction, which, although defended by the commentators,
is a license scarcely allowable. The epithets of the first verse
are, all, in the plural number; they then occur in the singular,
to agree with the only substantive in the description, Samájaváta.
According to the commentaries, the plural term Mancháh (मञ्चा:)
understood is the substantive to the epithets of the first stanza;
and Samájaváta (the singular), to those of the other verses.
This awkwardness is, however, avoided by the reading of an old
and very good copy, which puts it, all, in the singular;‡ as:

---

* See Vol. III., p. 118, and p. 220, note 1.
† To render "platforms". My oldest MS. has मञ्चयोभा: ।
‡ So do the Calcutta edition of the *Harivaṁśa*, my oldest MS., and,
so far as I know them, MSS. generally.

by whom the fierce night-walker Pútaná was slain;[*]
by whom the waggon was overturned, and the two

सविभाष्टाक्षिचरक्ष: खार्गेष्ठद्वारवेदिक: ।
समवाषार्धचक्रच सतलोत्तमभूषित: ॥

([20]) The expression is Charaṅa; literally, 'foot;' explained, by
the commentator.[†] Stambha, 'post' or 'pillar'. ([21]) The reading
of most of the copies is Sayanottama (शयनोत्तम), which may be
taken as the sense of Talottama, 'couches or benches with cushions.' ([22]) Manchágáraih (मञ्चागारैं:). 'temporary houses.' ([23]) Or,
'fronting to the east' (प्राच्मुखि:); ([24]) Nirmuktaih (निर्मुक्तैं:); explained, by the commentator,[§] to mean 'fine threads', 'net-work',
or 'gauze', through which persons, females especially, may see,
without being seen. ([25]) स्वकर्मेद्र्व्ययुक्ताभि: पताकाभि: । ([26]) "With
ridges and projections" (सस्सानुप्रगृहाणि). The commentator[||]
explains this: "with flags on the top of them" (उपरिदेषे सप-
ताकानि). ([27]) This appears to be intended for an epithet of the
women; although Ástaraṅa is not usually applied to dress:
आस्तरखाम्बरि: शोभिता वारमुखाभि: ।[¶]
([28]) फलावदंशपूर्वाच चाङ्गेर्य: पानयोजिता: ।
Phala, of course, is 'fruit'. Avadaṁsa is explained, in lexicons,
"what is eaten to excite thirst:" one comment[**] gives it, "what
may be sucked," as tamarinds and the like. Chángeri is explained "fluids for drinking, made with sorrel or acid fruits";
that is, sherbets. ([29]) उत्तमागारिका: or उत्तरागारिका: is an
epithet of the Prekshágára,[††] or look-out house of the women
(स्त्रीषां प्रेषागृहा:), situated on the tops of their houses, according

[*] See Vol. IV, p. 276.
[†] ?
[‡] Nílakaṅṭha.
[§] Idem.
[||] Idem.
[¶] Parts of two lines. See the original, in p. 29, supra.
[**] Nílakaṅṭha's.
[††] The original exhibits the plural, as does the translation which Pro-
fessor Wilson here annotates.
V.   3

Arjuna-trees felled.* This is the boy who trampled and danced on the serpent Káliya;† who upheld the mountain Govardhana for seven nights;‡ who killed, as if in play, the iniquitous Arishta,§ Dhenuka,|| and Kesin.¶ This, whom we see, is Achyuta.** This is he who has been foretold by the wise, skilled in the sense of the Puráńas, as Gopála, who shall exalt the depressed Yádava race. This is a portion of the all-existing,†† all-generating Vishńu, descended upon earth,

---

to the commentators;‡‡ गृहोपरि गृहं यत्तदुत्तमागारं तत्रभवाः * * * प्रेशागृहाः; an arrangement very compatible with the form of Indian houses, which have flat roofs, commonly enclosed by a trellis-work or jalousie of masonry.§§ It is observable, that, in the Vishńu Puráńa, and in the Mahábhárata, on various public occasions, the women take their places on the platforms, or in the pavilions, without curtains or screens.

---

* See Vol. IV., pp. 279 and 281.

† *Ibid.,* p. 291.

‡ *Ibid.,* pp. 315, 316.

§ *Ibid.,* pp. 333, 334.

|| *Ibid,* pp. 297, 298.

¶ *Ibid.,* p. 340.

** Here the original, according to all my MSS., &c., has the following stanza, unrendered by the Translator, as in his Hindu-made version:

श्वयं चास्र महाबाङर्बलभद्रोऽयमोऽयतः ।
प्रयाति लीलया योषिन्मनोनयनमन्द्दनः ॥

Both the commentators recognize these verses; and Ratnagarbha expounds them.

†† *Sarva-bhúta.* Ratnagarbha explains it by *sarvátman.*

‡‡ The words quoted are Nílakańtha's. Arjuna Miśra has something different.

§§ Professor Wilson's translation of the two passages quoted in pp. 25, 26, and pp. 27, 28, *supra,* and his notes on the same, have suggested numerous remarks which I have withheld; the subject of this episodical matter not being one with which the *Vishńu-puráńa* is very intimately connected.

who, will, assuredly, lighten her load." Thus did the
citizens describe Ráma and Kŕishńa, as soon as they
appeared; whilst the breast of Devakí glowed with
maternal affection;* and Vasudeva, forgetting his infirmities, felt himself young (again), on beholding the
countenances of his sons as a season of rejoicing. The
women of the palace, and the wives of the citizens,
wide opened their eyes, and gazed intently upon
Kŕishńa.† "Look, friends," said they to their companions; "look at the face of Kŕishńa. His eyes are
reddened by his conflict with the elephant; and the
drops of perspiration stand upon his cheeks, outvying
a full-blown lotos in autumn, studded with glittering
dew.‡ Avail yourself, now, of the faculty of vision.
Observe his breast, – the seat of splendour, marked
with the mystic sign,§ — and his arms, menacing destruction to his foes. Do you not notice Balabhadra,
dressed in a blue garment,—his countenance as fair as
the jasmine, as the moon, as the fibres of the lotos-
stem? See how he gently smiles at the gestures of
Mushṭika and Cháńúra, as they spring up. And now
behold Hari advance to encounter Cháńúra. What!
Are there no elders, judges of the field?‖ How can
the delicate form of Hari,—only yet in the dawn of

* उरस्ताप देवक्याः स्नेह्न्नुतपयोधरम् ।
Here we have an expression of the idea, that, when a woman is deeply
moved in her maternal feelings, she experiences a secretion of milk.

† द्रष्टुं न विरराम तम् ।
‡ This sentence is somewhat interpolated, and otherwise freely rendered.
Avaśyáya, as appears from the context, here means, as the commentators
interpret it, 'hoar-frost,' rather than "dew".
§ To render *śrívatsa*. See Vol. IV., p. 268.
‖ *Yukta-kárin*.

3*

adolescence,—be regarded as a match for the vast and adamantine bulk of the great demon?* Two youths, of light and elegant persons, are in the arena, to oppose athletic fiends, headed by the cruel Chánúra.† This is a great sin: in the judges of the games, for the umpires to suffer a contest between boys and strong men."

As thus the women of the city conversed (with one another), Hari, having tightened his girdle, danced in the ring, shaking the ground (on which he trod). Balabhadra, also, danced, slapping his arms in defiance. Where the ground was firm, the invincible Krishńa contended, foot to foot, with Chánúra. The practised demon Mushtika was opposed by Balabhadra. Mutually entwining, and pushing, and pulling, and beating each other with fists, arms, and elbows, pressing each other with their knees, interlacing their arms, kicking with their feet, pressing with their whole weight upon one another,[1] fought Hari and Chánúra. Desperate

---

[1] The terms here used are technical, and refer to the established modes of wrestling amongst Hindu athletæ.§ 1. Saṁnipáta (संनिपात) is described "mutual laying hold of."‖ 2. Avudhúta (अवधूत), "letting go of the adversary." 3. Kshepaṅa (वेपण) "pulling to and casting back." 4. Mushti-nipáta (मुष्टि-

---

* क्व वज्रकठिनाभोगिशरीरोऽयं महासुरः ।
† इमौ सुललितौ रङ्गे वर्त्तेते नवयौवनौ ।
    दैतेयमल्लाद्याशूरप्रमुखास्त्वलितिदारुणाः ॥
‡ Vyatikrama.
§ The following definitions are taken from the two commentaries.
‖ परस्परं संश्लेषः । Śrídhara. 'Mutual onset', परस्परं संघर्षः । Ratnagarbha.

was the struggle, though without weapons, and one
for life and death, to the great gratification of the

निपात),* "striking with fists." 5. Kíla-nipátana (कीलनिपातन).
"striking with the elbow." 6. Vajra-nipátana (वज्रनिपातन).
"striking with the fore-arm."† 7. Jánu-nirgháta (आनुनिर्घात),‡
"pressing or striking with the knees." 8. Báhu-vighaṭṭana (बाहु-
विघट्टन),§ "interlacing the arms." 9. Pádoddhúta (पादोद्धूत),
"kicking." 10. Prasṛishṭá ¶ (प्रसृष्टा), "intertwining of the whole
body." In some copies,** another term occurs, Aśma-nirgháta
(अश्मनिर्घात), "striking with stones," or "striking blows as
hard as with stones;" for stones could scarcely be used in a

---

* The original has no such term, but मुष्टिभि:, "with the fists."

† _Aratni-dwaya._ _Aratni_ never, I believe, signifies "fore-arm"; and
the definition of the fifth technicality shows that it cannot bear the import of 'elbow', its more ordinary signification, when it does not denom-
inate a measure. Again, as it does not here mean 'fist',—one of its
senses,—it seems likely that it must denote the ulnar side of the hand.
So, indeed, the term is explained by Arjuna Miśra, where he comments
on the _Mahábhárata, Vana-parvan, śl._ 15781. His words are: अरत्निना ।
करतलपार्श्वेन ।

‡ The Sanskrit has आनुभि:, simply. See note **, below.

§ I find a different reading. See note **, below. The Translator's definition, which is conjectural, is little likely to be correct.

। पन्यामुत्षेपणम् । परस्परं पादक्षेतोत्षूलनम् । Ratnagarbha.

¶ Variant: _prasṛishṭa._

** The subjoined verse is rejected, without remark, by Ratnagarbha,
and is absent from my two old copies of the mere text, but occurs,
though uncommented, in Śrídhara's text, and in several of my MSS.:

आनुभिश्वाश्मनिर्घातैस्तथा बाह्नविघट्टिति: ।

Some excellent copies give, instead of अश्मनिर्घाति:, अश्ममभि-
घाति: ।

Professor Wilson, when he accepted, in his translation, the seventh
and eighth technicalities, should have accepted _aśma-nirgháta_, also,
which cannot be divorced from the other two, since it stands, in the
original, between them.

spectators.* In proportion as the contest continued, so Chánúra was gradually losing something of his original vigour,† and the wreath upon his head trembled from his fury and distress;[1] whilst the world-comprehending‡ Krishńa wrestled with him as if but in sport. Beholding Chánúra losing, and Krishńa gaining, strength, Kamsa, furious with rage, commanded the music to cease. As soon as the drums and trumpets were silenced, a numerous band of heavenly instruments was heard in the sky;§ and the gods invisibly exclaimed: "Victory to Govinda! Keśava, kill the demon Chánúra!" Madhusúdana, having, for a long time, dallied with his adversary, at last lifted him up,

---

contest specified as "one without weapons"‖ (अशस्त्रं • • युद्धम्).¶

[1] Krishńa contended with Chánúra, "who, through distress and anger, shook the flowers of his crest:"

खेदाच्चालयता कोपान्निजमौलिकेसरम् ।

The two last terms are explained: "the flower of the wreath on his head:" स्वशीर्षापीड़भूतं पुष्पम् ।**

---

* अशस्त्रमतिघोरं तत्त्वयोर्युद्धं सुदारुणम् ।
  बलप्राणविनिष्पाद्यं समाजोत्सवसन्निधौ ॥

† प्राणहानिमवापाग्र्यां तावत्तावज्झवाह्णवम् ।

‡ Jagan-maya.

§ मृदङ्गादिषु तूर्येषु प्रतिषिद्धेषु तत्क्षणात् ।
  खे संगतान्यवाद्यन्तदेवतूर्याण्यनेकशः ॥

‖ As to the use of stones in the combat, which is designated as aśastra, we must suppose,—if the verse quoted above has not been foisted into the text,—that the term śastra, embodied in this epithet, is employed technically, so as to comprehend those rude and ready missiles.

¶ See note *, above.

** Ratnagarbha.

and whirled him round, with the intention of putting
an end to him. Having whirled Chánúra round a
hundred times, until his breath was expended in the
air, Kríshńa[*] dashed him on the ground, with such
violence as to smash his body into a hundred fragments, and strew the earth with a hundred pools of
gory mire.[†] Whilst this took place, the mighty Baladeva was engaged, in the same manner, with the demon
bruiser,[‡] Mushtika. Striking him on the head with his
fists, and on the breast with his knees, he stretched
him on the ground, and pummelled him there, till he
was dead. Again, Kríshńa encountered the royal
bruiser[§] Tosalaka,[‖] and felled him to the earth with
a blow of his left hand. When the other athletæ[¶]

---

[*] Called, in the original, not by his name, but by the epithet *ami-trajit*.

[†] भूमावास्फोटितत्तेन वाबूरः यतधा त्रवम् ।
रत्नखावमहापङ्कं चकार यतधा भुवम् ॥

[‡] *Malla*.

[§] *Malla-rája*, "prince of *mallas*". For *malla*, see note ¶, below.

[‖] Corrected from "Tomalaka". Professor Wilson's MS. may have
shown a broken श. Most copies yield Tośalaka, the reading, apparently,
accepted by Ratnagarbha, and that of the *Bhágavata-puráńa*, which has,
likewise, the short form, Tośala. In very good MSS. of the *Harivaṁśa* I find Toshala and Toshalaka. Professor Wilson's Bengal translation
has Salaka.

[¶] *Malla*; which Professor Wilson renders, indifferently, by "athlete",
"boxer", and "bruiser". The last two terms are inadequate, while the
first is inadequative, as being much too wide for the occasion. 'Pancratiast', in an accommodated acceptation, may answer to represent *malla*;
for the pancratiast fought nude, whereas it appears that his Hindu ana-
logue contended clothed.

The fighting of Hari, Chánúra, and Baladeva clearly evinces, that the
malla-yuddha corresponded to the classical παγκράτιον or παμμάχιον,—
not, indeed, the regular agonism, so much as the lawless description
that was practised at Sparta,—the characteristic of which was a combination of boxing and wrestling.

saw Chánúra, Mushtika, and Tosalaka killed, they fled
(from the field); and Krishṅa and Sankarshaṅa danced,
victorious,* on the arena, dragging along with them,
by force, the cowherds of their own age. Kaṁsa, his
eyes reddening with wrath, called aloud to the surrounding people: "Drive those two cowboys out of
the assembly: seize the villain Nanda; and secure him
with chains of iron: put Vasudeva to death with tortures intolerable to his years: and lay hands upon†
the cattle, and whatever else belongs to those cowherds
who are the associates of Krishṅa."

Upon hearing these orders, the destroyer of Madhu
laughed at Kaṁsa, and, springing up to the place

Nilakaṅṭha, commenting on the *Mahábhárata*, *Vana-parvan*, *śl.* 15779,
quotes from some *Niti-śástra*, as follows:

वामपाणिकचोत्पीडा भूमौ निष्पेषणं बलात् ।
मूर्ध्नि पादप्रहरणं आगुनोदरमर्दनम् ॥
मालूराकारया मुष्ट्या कपोले दृढताडनम् ।
कफोणिपातोऽप्यसकृत्सर्वतक्षलताडनम् ।
तालेन युद्धे श्रामणं मारणं कृतमष्टधा ॥
चतुर्भिः षक्तियं हन्यात्पञ्चभिः षक्तियाधमम् ।
षड्भिर्वैश्यं सप्तभिस्तु षूद्रं संकरमष्टभिः ॥

It appears, from this, that the Hindu pancratium recognized eight
modes of procedure: tearing out the hair, felling to the ground, kicking
on the head, punching the belly with the knee, pommelling the cheeks
with clenched fists, elbowing, slapping, and whirling round. Four of
these modes of annoyance, counted from the first, are reckoned legitimate
as against an ordinary Kshattriya; five, as against a reprobate or titular
Kshattriya; six, as against a Vaiśya; seven, as against a Śúdra; and
all eight, as against an adversary of mixed extraction.

Our modern fancy have nothing to learn, on the score of humanity,
from their Aryan predecessors of the ring, any more than from the
roughs of Sparta, among whom even biting and scratching were not accounted foul play.

* *Harshita*, 'delighted.'

† Insert 'the towns', *pur.*

where he was seated, laid hold of him by the hair of
his head, and struck his tiara* to the ground. Then,
casting him down upon the earth, Govinda threw himself upon him. Crushed by the weight of the upholder
of the universe, the son of Ugrasena (Kamsa), the king,
gave up the ghost. Krishna† then dragged the dead
body, by the hair of the head, into the centre of the
arena; and a deep furrow was made by the vast and
heavy carcass of Kamsa, when it was dragged along
the ground by Krishna, as if a torrent of water had
run through it.[1] Seeing Kamsa thus treated, his brother
Sunáman‡ came (to his succour): but he was encountered, and easily killed, by Balabhadra. Then
arose a general cry of grief from the surrounding

---

[1] Et latus mediam sulcus diducit arenam. §

The yielding sand being furrowed into a ditch, or a water-
course, by the dead bodies being dragged over it.

The text is:

गौरवेणातिमहता परिखा तेन कृष्यता ।
कता कंसस्य देहेन वेगेनैव महाअसः ॥

* *Kirita.*
† Madhusúdana, in the original.
‡ Corrected from "Sumálin". This mistake is easily accounted for.
In Professor Wilson's favourite MS., which is carelessly transcribed, and
has few of the copyist's inadvertencies corrected, we read:

सुमालिनामा बलभद्रेण लीलयैव निपातितः ।

Professor Wilson's Hindu-made version has Sumáli.

By striking out the syllables -माlि°, the verse is restored to its
proper form. But the Translator, in due adherence to his copy, should
have given the name as Sumálináman.

For Sunáman, see Vol. IV., p. 98.

§ This looks as if intended for Juvenal., Sat. I., 157:

Et latum media sulcum diducit arena.

‖ Literally: "By the trailing body of Kamsa, with *its* prodigious weight,
a channel *was* made, as by the velocity of a great stream."

circle, as they beheld the king of Mathurá* (thus)
slain, (and treated) with (such) contumely, by Kṛishṇa.
Kṛishṇa, accompanied by Balabhadra, embraced the
feet of Vasudeva and of Devakí: but Vasudeva raised
him up;† and, he and Devakí recalling to recollection
what he had said to them at his birth, they bowed to
Janárdana; and the former thus addressed him: "Have
compassion upon mortals, O god, benefactor, ‡ and lord
of deities. It is by thy favour to us two, that thou hast
become the (present) upholder (of the world). That,
for the punishment of the rebellious,§ thou hast descended (upon earth,) in my house, having been propitiated (by my prayers), sanctifies our race. Thou
art the heart‖ of all creatures; thou abidest in all creatures; and all that has been, or will be, emanates from
thee, O universal spirit.¶ Thou, Achyuta, who com-
prehendest all the gods, art eternally worshipped with
sacrifices: thou art sacrifice itself, and the offerer of
sacrifices. The affection that inspires my heart, and
the heart of Devakí, towards thee, as if thou wast our
child, is, indeed, but error and a great delusion.**
How shall the tongue of a mortal such as I am call
the creator of all things, who is without beginning or

---

* See Vol. IV., p. 338.
† The original makes both the father and mother show him this honour:

उत्थाप्य वसुदेवस्तं देवकी च अनार्हणम् ।

‡ *Varada.*
§ *Durvṛitta.*
‖ *Anta.*

¶ प्रवर्त्तंते समस्तांस्त्वत्तो भूतभविष्यती ।
** सापह्नवं मम मनो यदेतत्त्वयि जायते ।
देवकीबालजमीति तद्वन्मविडम्बना ॥

end, son? Is it consistent that the lord of the world, from whom the world proceeds, should be born of me, except through illusion?* How should he, in whom all fixed and moveable things are contained, be conceived in the womb, and born of a mortal being?† Have compassion, therefore, indeed, O supreme lord, and, in thy descended portions, protect the universe. Thou art no son of mine. This whole world, from Brahmá to a tree,‡ thou art. Wherefore dost thou, who art one with the Supreme, beguile us? Blinded by delusion, I thought thee my son; and for thee, who art beyond all fear, I dreaded the anger of Kaṁsa; and, therefore, did I take thee, in my terror, to Gokula, where thou hast grown up. But I no longer claim thee as mine own.§ Thou, Vishńu,—the sovereign lord of all,‖ whose actions Rudra, the Maruts, the Aświns, Indra,¶ and the gods cannot equal, although they behold them; thou, who hast come amongst us, for the benefit of the world,—art recognized; and delusion is no more."

* जगदेतज्जगन्नाथ संभूतमखिलं यतः ।
कया युत्या विना मायां सोऽजन्तः संभविष्यति ॥
† स कोष्ठोत्सङ्कशयनो मनुष्याख्यायते कथम् ।
‡ आब्रह्मपादपमयं जगदेतत् । See Vol. III., p. 202, note ‖.
§ This sentence is not rendered very literally.
‖ This phrase is to represent ila.
¶ The original has Śatakratu. See Vol. I., p. 150.

CHAPTER XXI

Krishna encourages his parents; places Ugrasena on the throne;
becomes the pupil of Sándipani, whose son he recovers from
the sea: he kills the marine demon Panchajana, and makes a
horn of his shell.

HAVING permitted to Devakí and Vasudeva (an
interval of) true knowledge, through the contemplation
of his actions, Hari again spread the delusions of his
power* over (them and) the tribe of Yadu. He said
to them: "Mother; venerable father; you have, both,
been long observed, by Sankarshaṅa and myself, with
sorrow, and in fear of Kaṁsa. He whose time passes
not in respect to his father and mother is a vile being,
who descends, in vain, from virtuous parents.† The
lives of those produce good fruit who reverence their
parents, their spiritual guides, the Brahmans, and the
gods. Pardon, therefore, father, the impropriety of
which we may have been culpable, in resenting, without
your orders, — to which we acknowledge that we are
subject, — the oppression we suffered from the power
and violence of Kaṁsa.": Thus speaking, they offered
homage to the elders of the Yadu tribe, in order, and,
then, in a suitable manner, paid their respects to the
citizens. The wives of Kaṁsa, and those of his father, §

* मायां॰ * वैष्णवीम् ।

† कुर्वतां याति यः कालो मातापिचोरपूजनम् ।
तत्खण्डमायुषो व्यर्थं साधूनामुपजायते ॥

: This sentence is much expanded in translation.

§ मातरश्च, "and his — *Kaṁsa's* — mothers," *i. e.*, it seems, his
mother and his mother-in-law.

then surrounded the body of the king, lying on the
ground, and bewailed his fate, in deep affliction. Hari,
in various ways, expressed his regret (for what had
chanced), and endeavoured to console them, his own
eyes being suffused with tears. The foe of Madhu then
liberated Ugrasena from confinement, and placed him
on the throne, which the death of his son had left
vacant.[*] The chief of the Yádavas,[†] being crowned,
performed the funeral rites of Kaṁsa, and of the rest
of the slain. When the ceremony was over, and Ugrasena had resumed his royal seat, Kṛishṇa (addressed
him,) and said: "Sovereign lord, command, boldly,
what else is to be done.[§] The curse of Yayáti has
pronounced our race unworthy of dominion;[1] but, with
me for your servant, you may issue your orders to the
gods. How should kings disobey them?"[||]

Thus having spoken, the human[¶] Keśava summoned,
mentally, the deity of the wind,—who came upon the
instant,—and said to him: "Go, Váyu, to Indra, and
desire him[**] to lay aside his pomp,[††] and resign to

---

[1] The curse pronounced on the elder sons of Yayáti, on their
refusing to take upon them their father's infirmities. See Vol. IV.,
p. 43.

* अभविष्वत्तथैवेनं निजराज्ये हतात्मजम् ।

† Yadu-siṁha.

‡ Hari, in the original.

§ उवाचाज्ञापय विभो यत्कार्यमविषङ्कितः ।

|| मयि भूत्वे स्थिते देवानाज्ञापयतु किं नृपैः ।

¶ कार्यमानुषः ।

** Vásava, in the original.

†† 'Pride', rather,—garva; namely, says Ratnagarbha, at the recollection of Kṛishṇa's having lifted up Mount Govardhana.

Ugrasena his (splendid) hall, Sudharman.* Tell him
that Kŕishńa commands him to send the royal hall,
the unrivalled gem of princely courts, for the assemblage of the race of Yadu."† Accordingly, Váyu⁝
went, and delivered the message to the husband of
Śachí,§ who∥ (immediately) gave up to him the hall
Sudharman; and Váyu conveyed it to the Yádavas,
the chiefs of whom, thenceforth, possessed this celestial court, emblazoned with jewels, and defended by
the arm of Govinda.¶ The two excellent Yadu youths,
versed in all knowledge, and possessed of all wisdom,**
then submitted to instruction, as the disciples of
teachers. Accordingly, they repaired to Sándípani —
who, though born in Kásí,†† resided at Avantí,‡‡ — to
study (the science of) arms, and, becoming his pupils,
were obedient and attentive to their master; exhibiting

---

* Or the name may be read Sudharmá. Both forms are authorized.

† हृष्णो ब्रवीति राजाईमेतद्रत्नमनुत्तमम् ।
सुधर्माख्या सभा युत्तमखां यदुभिरासितुम् ॥

‡ The Sanskrit has Pavana.

§ In the original, Śachípati, an epithetical designation of Indra. See
Vol. II., p. 72, note 2.

∥ Here the original calls Indra by his appellation Purandara.

¶ वायुनोपहृतां दिव्यां सभां ते यदुपुङ्गवाः ।
बुभुजुः सर्वरत्नाढ्यां गोविन्दभुजसंश्रयात् ॥
The ordinary reading, and that accepted by Ratnagarbha, ends the
second line with -संश्रयाः ।

** Sarva-jnána-maya.

†† Káśya, "of the Káśi tribe." See my Benares, &c., p. 9, note 1;
also, Vol. IV., p. 345, supplement to p. 159, note ††. But the Translator has the support of both the commentators. Káśya is the word
used in the corresponding passage of the Bhágavata-puráńa, viz., X.,
Prior Section, XLV., 31; but Śrídhara offers no explanation of it.

‡‡ The city so called. The Sanskrit has Avantipura. See Vol. III.,
p. 246. I have corrected "Avanti".

an example, to all men, of the observance of instituted rules.* In the course of sixty-four days,† they had gone through the elements of military science, with the treatises on the use of arms, and directions for the mystic incantations, which secure the aid of supernatural weapons.[1]‡ Sándípani, astonished at such proficiency, and knowing that it exceeded human faculties, imagined that the Sun and Moon had become his scholars. When they had acquired all that he could teach, they said to him: "Now say what present shall be given to you, as the preceptor's fee."§ The prudent Sándípani, perceiving that they were endowed with more than mortal powers, requested them to give him his dead son, (drowned) in the sea of Prabhása.[2]

---

[1] They read through the Dhanur-veda,‖ which treats of military matters; with the Rahasya, 'the mystical part,'¶ and the Sangraha, 'collection' or 'compendium',—said to be, here, the Astra-prayoga,** 'the employment of weapons.'

[2] Prabhása is a place of pilgrimage in the west of India, on the coast of Gujerat, near the temple of Somanátha, and town of Puttun Somnath. It is also known by the name of Somatírtha; Soma, or the Moon, having been here cured of the con-

---

* "An example of the observance of instituted rules" is to translate áchára. See Vol. III., p. 107, note ‡.

† Ahorátra, 'nyctbemera.' The term, apparently, is chosen with a view to imply diligent studentship.

‡ These three expansions are to represent the expressions specified in note 1 in this page.

§ Guru-dakshiná.

‖ See Vol. III., p. 67.

¶ The mantras and Upanishads, the commentators allege.

** Śrídhara and Ratnagarbha.

Taking up their arms, they marched against the Ocean. But the all-comprehending Sea said to them: "I have not killed the son of Sándípani.* A demon† named Panchajana,‡ (who lives) in the form of a conch-shell, seized the boy. He is still under my waters.§ On hearing this, Kŕishńa plunged into the sea; and, having slain the vile Panchajana, he took the conch-shell, — which was formed of his bones, (and bore it as his horn),—the sound of which fills the demon-hosts with dismay, animates the vigour of the gods, and annihilates unrighteousness.‖ The heroes also recovered the boy from the pains of death, and restored him, in his former person, to his father. Ráma and Janárdana

---

sumption brought upon him by the imprecation of Daksha, his father-in-law. Mahábhárata, Śalya Parvan; Vol. III., p. 249.

* गृहीताखी ततखौ तु सार्धपाचो महोदधिः ।
उवाच न मया पुचो इतः सान्दीपनेरिति ॥

Various MSS. have, instead of सार्धपाच:, सार्धहृख:, पाचपाच:, जमेगातं:, and भचेगातं: । It is impossible to say what reading the Translator accorded the preference to.

† Daitya.

‡ For his origin, see Vol. II., p. 69, note ‖.

§ The Sea here addresses Kŕishńa as asura-súdana, "slayer of demons."

‖ Professor Wilson has here omitted to translate a stanza, of some little importance, if only by way of connecting what precedes with what follows. It is recognized by both the commentators, and runs thus:

तं पाञ्चजन्यमापूर्य गत्वा यमपुरीं हरिः ।
बलदेवच बलवान्जित्वा वैवस्तं यमम् ॥

We learn, from this, that Hari blew Pánchajanya,—the name of his newly acquired shell,—and proceeded to the city of Yama; and that Baladeva conquered Yama, son of Vivaswat.

For the origin of Yama, see Vol. III., p. 20; for the situation of Yama's city, Vol. II., p. 239.

then returned to Mathurá, which was well presided over * by Ugrasena, and abounded in a happy population, both of men and women.[1]

---

[1] The incidents of the two last chapters are related in the Bhágavata and Hari Vaṁśa,—often in the words of the text, but with many embellishments and additions, especially in the latter. The Brahma Vaivarta, on the other hand, makes still shorter work of these occurrences than our text.

* *Pálita.*

CHAPTER XXII.

Jarásandba besieges Mathurá; is defeated, but repeatedly renews the attack.

PARÁŚARA.—The mighty Kaṁsa had married the two daughters of Jarásandha,* one named Asti, the other, Prápti.† Jarásandha was king of Magadha,‡ and a very powerful prince;[1] who, when he heard that Krishṅa§ had killed his son-in-law, was much incensed, and, collecting a large force, marched against Mathurá, determined to put the Yádavas and Krishṅa to the sword.‖ Accordingly, he invested the city with three and twenty numerous divisions of his forces.[2] Ráma and Janárdana sallied from the town, with a slender, but resolute, force, and fought bravely with the armies

---

[1] See Vol. IV., pp. 150, 151.

[2] With twenty-three Akshauhiṅis, each consisting of 109,350 ¶ infantry, 65,610 horse, 21,870 chariots, and as many elephants. ** The Hari Vaṁśa †† enumerates, as the allies, or tributaries, of Jarásandha, a number of princes from various parts of India. But this is a gratuitous embellishment.

---

* See Vol. IV., pp. 150 and 173; also, note in p. 344.

† Corrected from "Asti" and "Prápti".

‡ Corrected, here and everywhere, from "Magadha". See Vol. IV., p. 151, note ‡.

§ Hari, in the original.

‖ This sentence is rendered with great looseness.

¶ Corrected from "109,300".

** So say the commentators on the Amara-kośa, II., VIII., II., 49. For a venerable statement of the component parts of an akshauhiṅi, see the Mahábhárata, Ádi-parvan, śl. 292—296.

†† Śl. 5013—5022.

of Magadha.* The two youthful leaders prudently resolved to have recourse to their ancient weapons; and, accordingly, the bow of Hari, with two quivers filled with exhaustless† arrows, and the mace: called Kaumodaki,§ and the ploughshare‖ of Balabhadra, as well as the club ¶ Saunanda, descended, at a wish, from heaven. Armed with these weapons, they (speedily) discomfited the king of Magadha and his hosts, and reentered the city, (in triumph).

Although the wicked (king of Magadha,) Jarásandha was defeated, yet Kríshńa knew, that, whilst he escaped alive, he was not subdued; and, in fact, he soon returned, with a (mighty) force, and was again forced, by Ráma and Kríshńa, to fly. Eighteen times[1] did the haughty prince of Magadha** renew his attack

---

[1] The Bhágavata†† and Hari Vaṁśa‡‡ say 'seventeen times.' The latter indulges in a prolix description of the first encounter, nothing of which occurs in the Bhágavata, any more than in our text.

* निक्रम्यास्वपरीवारावुभौ रामजनार्दनौ ।
   युयुधाते समं तत्र बलिनौ बलिशलिनः ॥

† *Akshaya,* 'indestructible.'

‡ *Gadá.*

§ A present from Varuńa, according to the *Mahábhárata, Ádi-parvan, śl.* 8200. It takes its name from Kumodaka, an epithetical appellation of Kríshńa.

‖ *Hala,* which means, ordinarily, 'plough.' For its synonym, *sira,* synecdochically used in the same way as in the text, see Vol. III., p. 332, note ¶.

¶ *Musala;* a weapon shaped like a pestle, it should seem.

** To render मागधो राजा ।

†† X., Latter Section, I., 44.

‡‡ *Śl.* 5126.

4*

upon the Yádavas, headed by Ḱrishńa, and was as often defeated and put to the rout, by them, with very inferior numbers. That the Yádavas were not overpowered by their foes was owing to the present might of the portion of the discus-armed Vishńu.* It was the pastime† of the lord of the universe, in his capacity of man, to launch various‡ weapons against his enemies: (for) what effort of power to annihilate his foes could be necessary to him whose fiat creates and destroys the world? But, as subjecting himself to human customs, he formed alliances with the brave, and engaged in hostilities with the base.§ He had recourse to the four devices of policy,—or, negotiation, presents, sowing dissension, and chastisement,‖—and, sometimes, even betook himself to flight. Thus, imitating the conduct of human beings, the lord of the world pursued, at will, his sports.¶

---

* यद्बलं याद्वानां तैरजितं यद्नेकशः ।
तन्तु संनिधिमाहात्म्यं विष्णोरंशस्य चक्रिणः ॥

† *Lilá.* See Vol. IV., p. 325, note §.

‡ *Aneka-rúpa.*

§ तथापि यो मनुष्याणां धर्मतमनुवर्तते ।
कुर्वन्बलवता संधिं हीनैर्युद्धं करोत्यसौ ॥

Ratnagarbha reads the first verse as follows:

तथा चे चे मनुष्याणां धर्माख्तद्नुवर्तनम् ।

Other variants, of little importance, might be added from my MSS. unaccompanied by commentary.

‖ *Sáman, upapradána, bheda,* and *dańda-páta.* See, further, the *Amara-kośa,* II., VIII., I., 20.

¶ मनुष्यदेहिनां चेष्टामिवेवमनुवर्ततः ।
लीला जगत्पतेयस्य चरूतः संप्रवर्तते ॥

CHAPTER XXIII.

Birth of Kálayavana: he advances against Mathurá. Krishńa builds Dwáraká, and sends thither the Yádava tribe: he leads Kálayavana into the cave of Muchukunda: the latter awakes, consumes the Yavana king, and praises Krishńa.

PARÁSARA.—Syála* having called Garga,† the Brahman, whilst at the cow-pens, impotent, in an assembly of the Yádavas,‡ they all laughed; at which he was highly offended, and repaired to the shores§ of the western sea,‖ where he engaged in arduous penance, to obtain a son, who should be a terror to the tribe of Yadu.¶ Propitiating Mahádeva, and living upon iron-sand** for twelve years, the deity†† (at last) was pleased with him, and gave him the (desired) boon. The king of the Yavanas, who was childless,

---

* On the credit of both the commentators, we here have no proper name, but the word for brother-in-law, *syála*. According to Ratnagarbha, Śiśiráyaṇa is thus alluded to, and proleptically; for Garga was still to marry his sister, Gaurí.

† Corrected from "Gárgya", with the suffrage of several MSS. Probably the Garga is meant who—as we read in the *Bhágavata-purdña*, X., Prior Section, Chapter XLV.,—served as instructor to Krishńa and Balaráma. See Vol. IV., p. 273. But Gárgya seems to be the reading of the *Harivaṁśa*, śl. 1957—1959.

Two Gargas, then, are named in the present Chapter. See p. 58, *infra*.

‡ यदूनां संनिधौ ।

§ There is no word for this in the Sanskrit.

‖ Instead of *dakshiṇábdhi*, the reading of Śrídhara, most MSS. have *dakshiṇápatha*, 'the south', the lection preferred by Ratnagarbha.

¶ सुतमिच्छंस्तपस्तेपे यदुचक्रभयावहम् ।

** *Ayaś-chúrṇa*; 'iron-filings', more likely.

†† Hara, in the original.

became the friend of Garga;* and the latter begot a
son, by his wife, who was as (black as) a bee, and was,
thence, called Kálayavana.[1] The Yávana king, having
placed his son, whose breast was as hard as the point
of the thunderbolt, upon the throne, retired to the
woods. Inflated with conceit of his prowess, Kálayavana demanded of Nárada who were the most mighty
heroes on earth. To which the sage answered "The
Yádavas." Accordingly, Kálayavana assembled many
myriads of Mlechchhas and barbarians,[2]† and, with a

___

[1] This legend of the origin of Kálayavana is given, also, by
the Hari Vaṁśa.‡ The Bhágavata, like our text, comes, at
once, to the siege of Mathurá by this chief; but the Hari Vaṁśa
suspends the story, for more than thirty chapters, to narrate an
origin of the Yádavas, and sundry adventures of Kṛishńa and
Ráma to the south-west. Most of these have no other authority,
and are, no doubt, inventions of the Dakhní compiler; and the
others are misplaced.

[2] So the Bhágavata describes him, § as leading a host of
Mlechchhas (or barbarians) against Kṛishńa; but, in the Mahábhárata,—Sabhá Parvan, Vol. 1., p. 330,—where Kṛishńa describes
the power of Jarásandha, he admits that he and the Yádavas fled
from Mathurá to the west, through fear of that king; but no
account is given of any siege of Mathurá by Kálayavana. The
only indication of such a person is the mention,‖ that Bhagadatta,

___

* स भाजयामास च तं यवनेग्रो ग्रगाह्मजः ।

The original, it will be observed, does not here name Garga, which I
have corrected from "Gárgya".

† म्लेच्छकोटीसहस्राणां सहस्रैर्बहुभिर्वृतः ।

‡ Chapter CXV.

§ It calls him Yavana the Asura.

‖ Śl. 578, 579:

मुदं च नरकं चैव याति यो यवनाधिपः ।
अपर्यन्तबलो राजा प्रतीच्यां वरुणो यथा ॥

vast armament of elephants, cavalry, and foot, advanced, impatiently, against Mathurá and the Yádavas;

---

the Yavana king, who rules over Muru[*] and Naraka, in the west and south, is one of his most attached feudatories. This king is, in various other places, called king of Prágjyotisha; as he is in a subsequent passage of the same book,—Sabhá Parvan, p. 374;[†] and this name is always applied to the the west of Assam.[‡] His subjects are, however, still Yavanas and Mlechchhas; and he presents horses, caps set with jewels, and swords with ivory hilts, —articles scarcely to be found in Assam, which cannot well be the seat of his sovereignty. It seems most likely, therefore, that the story may have originated in some knowledge of the power and position of the Greek-Bactrian princes, or their Scythian successors; although, in the latter compilations, it has been mixed up with allusions to the first Mohammedan aggressions. See Asiatic Researches, Vol. VI., p. 506, and Vol. XV., p. 100.

भगद्त्तो महाराज वृद्धस्य पितुः सखा ।
स वाचा प्रणतस्तस्य कर्मणा च विग्रेषतः ॥

Here, Bhagadatta—with the epithet *aparyanta-bala*, 'of boundless might',—is said to be paramount over Muru and Naraka, in like manner as Varuṇa rules the west. The direction of Bhagadatta's kingdom is not assigned.

M. Fauche's translation of this passage, while correcting Professor Wilson's view of its meaning, as to some points, turns an epithet into a king, and gives him what belongs to Bhagadatta:

"De lui relève encore le roi Aparyantabala, souverain des Yavanas, qui règne sur le Mourou et le Naraka, comme Varouṇa sur la plage occidentale;

"Et Bhagadatta, le vieil ami de ton père, *Bhagadatta*, qui se courbe plus que toute autre, puissant roi, devant sa parole et son geste."

For the position of Varuṇa's city, see Vol. II., p. 239.

[*] It has more than once been conjectured that we should read Maru, in this place. But Muru and Naraka, I take it, are, here, not names of countries,—as is generally supposed,—but two demons, so called, at last slain by Kṛishṇa. See Chapter XXIX. of this Book.

[†] *Śl.* 1836.

[‡] *I. e.*, to the ancient Kámarúpa; for which see Vol. II., p. 132, and p. 133, note 1.

wearying, every day, the animal that carried him, but
insensible of fatigue, himself.

When Krishna knew of his approach, he reflected,
that, if the Yádavas encountered the Yavana, they
would be so much weakened by the conflict, that they
would then be overcome by the king of Magadha;*
that their force was much reduced by the war with
Magadha,† whilst that of Kálayavana was unbroken;
and that the enemy might be, therefore, victorious.‡
Thus, the Yádavas were exposed to a double danger. §
He resolved, therefore, to construct a citadel, for the
Yadu tribe, that should not be easily taken,—one that
even women might defend, and in which, therefore,
the heroes of the house of Vrishni‖ should be secure;
one in which the male combatants of the Yádavas
should dread no peril, though he, himself, should be
drunk, or careless, asleep, or abroad. Thus reflecting,
Krishna¶ solicited a space of twelve furlongs from the
ocean; and there he built the city of Dwáraká,[1] defended by high ramparts,** and beautified with gardens

---

[1] According to the Mahábhárata, he only enlarged and fortified
the ancient city of Kusasthalí, founded by Raivata. Sabhá
Parvan.†† See, also, Vol. III., p. 253, of this work.

---

* कृष्णोऽपि चिन्तयामास रचितं यादवं बलम् ।
  यवनेन रणे गम्यं मागधस्य भविष्यति ।
† Literally, "by the king of the Magadhas," मागधेन ।
‡ A free translation; and so is much of what follows.
§ There is no Sanskrit for this sentence. It is taken from the com-
mentaries.
‖ Vrishni-pungava. For Vrishni, see Vol. IV., p. 58.
¶ The original has Govinda.   ** Mahá-vapra.
†† Śl. 614. M. Fauche, in his translation, converts Raivata into a
mountain.

and reservoirs of water, crowded with houses and buildings,[*] and splendid as the capital of Indra, Amarávatí.[†] Thither Janárdana conducted the inhabitants of Mathurá, and then awaited, at that city, the approach of Kálayavana.[‡]

When the hostile army encamped round Mathurá, Krishńa,[§] unarmed, went forth, and beheld the Yavana king. Kálayavana, the strong-armed, recognizing Vásudeva, pursued him,—him whom the thoughts of perfect ascetics[||] cannot overtake. Thus pursued, Krishńa entered a large cavern, where Muchukunda, the king of men, was asleep. The rash[¶] Yavana, entering (the cave), and beholding a man lying asleep there, concluded it must be Krishńa, and kicked him; at which Muchukunda awoke, and, casting on him an angry glance, the Yavana was instantly consumed, and reduced to ashes.[**] For, in a battle between the gods and demons, Muchukunda had, formerly, contributed to the defeat of the latter; and, being overcome with sleep, he solicited of the gods, as a boon, that he should enjoy a long repose. "Sleep long, and soundly,"[††] said the gods; "and whoever disturbs you shall be instantly burnt to ashes by fire emanating from your body."[1]

---

[1] The name of Muchukunda, as one of the sons of Mándhátri,[‡‡]

[*] *Prákára*; 'strong buildings', Ratnagarbha says.
[†] See Vol. II., p. 240, text and notes.
[‡] आसन्ने कालयवने मथुरां च स्वयं ययौ ।
[§] The Sanskrit has Govinda.   [||] *Mahá-yogin.*   [¶] *Sudurmati.*
[**] दृष्टमात्रस्तु तेगासौ अज्वाल यवनोऽधिना ।
तत्क्रोधजेन भैवेय भक्षीभूतश्च तत्क्षणात् ॥
[††] These words are interpolated by the Translator.
[‡‡] Corrected from "Mańdhátri".

Having burnt up the iniquitous Yavana, and beholding the foe of Madhu, Muchukunda asked him who he
was. "I am born," he replied, "in the Lunar race, in
the tribe of Yadu, and am the son of Vasudeva."
Muchukunda, recollecting the prophecy of old Garga,
fell down before the lord of all, Hari, saying:" Thou
art known, supreme lord, to be a portion of Vishńu;*
for it was said, of old, by Garga,† that, at the end of
the twenty-eighth Dwápara age, Hari would be born
in the family of Yadu. Thou art he, without doubt,—
the benefactor of mankind; for thy glory I am unable
to endure. Thy words are of deeper tone than the
muttering of the rain-cloud; and earth sinks down
beneath the pressure of thy feet. As, in the battle between the gods and demons, the Asuras were unable
to sustain my lustre, so even am I incapable of bearing
thy radiance.‡ Thou alone art the refuge of every

occurs in Vol. III., p. 268; but no further notice is taken of him.
The Bhágavata§ specifies his being the son of that king, and
relates the same story of his long sleep as the text. The same
occurs in the Hari Vamśa.‖ The general character of the legends
in this chapter is that of reference to something familiar, rather
than its narration. In the Hari Vamśa the opposite extreme is
observable; and there the legends are as prolix as here they are
concise. The Bhágavata follows a middle course; but it seems
unlikely, that, in either of the three, we have the original fables.

* प्राह ज्ञातो भवान्विष्णोरंशस्त्वं परमेश्वरः ।
Instead of विष्णोरंशः, some MSS. have विष्णुः पूर्वः ।
† Probably, the Garga mentioned in Vol. II., p. 213.
‡ देवासुरे महायुद्धे दैत्यसैन्ये महाभटाः ।
   न शेकुर्मम तत्तेजस्त्वत्तेजो न सहाम्यहम् ॥
§ X., Latter Section, II.
‖ Chapter CXV.

living being who has lighted on the world. Do thou, who art the alleviator of all distress, show favour upon me, and remove from me all that is evil.* Thou art the oceans, the mountains, the rivers, the forests; thou art earth, sky, air, water, and fire: thou art mind, intelligence, the unevolved principle,† the vital airs, the lord of life; the soul;‡ all that is beyond the soul; the all-pervading; exempt from the vicissitudes of birth; devoid of (sensible properties,) sound and the like; undecaying, illimitable, imperishable, subject neither to increase nor diminution:§ thou art that which is Brahma,—without beginning or end. From thee the immortals, the progenitors, the Yakshas, Gandharvas,|| and Kinnaras, the Siddhas, the nymphs of heaven,¶ men, animals,** birds, reptiles,†† deer,‡‡ and all the vegetable world, proceed; and all that has been, or will be, or is now, moveable or fixed. All that is amorphous, or has form; all that is gross, subtile, moveable, or stable,§§ thou art, O creator of the world; and beside thee there is not anything. O lord, I have been whirl-

---

* संमसीइ प्रपन्नार्तिहरतो हर ममाशुभम् ।

† *Avyákṛita.*

‡ *Puṁs.*

§ *Nása.*

|| Corrected from "Gandharbhas".

¶ *Apsaras.*

** *Paśu,* which often means 'sacrificial animals'. Compare the title Paśupati; also, the terms *paśubandha* and *nirúdhapaśubandha,* Vol. III., p. 40, note §, and p. 113, note †.

†† *Sarisṛipa;* rather "reptiles" than "insects", as it is rendered in Vol. II., p. 92.

‡‡ 'Wild beasts', rather; *mṛiga.*

§§ Ratnagarbha has, instead of सूक्ष्मं चरं स्थिरं, सूक्ष्मतरं तथा: and this reading gets rids of two tautologies; for "moveable or fixed" occurs just before.

ed round, in the circle of worldly existence, for ever;
and have suffered the three classes of affliction;* and
there is no rest† whatever. I have mistaken pains for
pleasures, like sultry vapours: for a pool of water;
and their enjoyment has yielded me nothing but sorrow. § The earth, dominion, ‖ forces, treasures, friends,¶
children, wife, dependants, all the objects of sense,**
have I possessed, imagining them to be sources of
happiness; but I found, that, in their changeable nature, †† O lord, they were nothing but vexation. The
gods themselves, though (high) in heaven, were in
need of my alliance. Where, then, is everlasting repose?
Who, without adoring thee,—who art the origin of all
worlds,—shall attain, O supreme deity, that rest which
endures for ever? Beguiled by thy delusions, and

---

* These are alluded to in the opening stanza of the *Sánkhya-káriká*:

दुःखत्रयाभिघाताज्जिज्ञासा तदपघातके हेतौ ।
दृष्टे सापार्था चेन्नैकान्तात्यन्तोऽभावात् ॥

"Because of the disquietude *which results* from threefold pain, *there
arises* a desire to know the means of doing away therewith *effectually*.
If *it be objected, that,* visible *means to this end being available,* such desire is unprofitable, I demur; for that *these means do* not, entirely and
for ever, *operate exemption from disquietude*."

The three sorts of pain, the *ádhyátmika*, *ádhibhautika*, and *ádhidaivika*,
are, in the words of Colebrooke, "evil proceeding from self," "from external beings," and "from divine causes". See his *Miscellaneous Essays*,
Vol. I., p. 238.

† *Nirvŕiti.*
‡ *Mŕiga-tŕishńá,* the mirage.
§ तथा मात्र गृहीतानि तानि तापाय चाभवन् ।
‖ *Ráshtra.*
¶ Insert 'adherents', *paksha.*
** शब्दाद्या विषयाः ।
†† परिणामे, 'in the end,' 'at last,' 'after all.'

ignorant of thy nature,* men, after suffering the various penalties of birth, death, and infirmity, behold the countenance of the king of ghosts,† and suffer, in hell, dreadful tortures,—the reward of their own deeds. Addicted to sensual objects, through thy delusions I revolve in the whirpool of selfishness and pride; and, hence, I come to thee, as my final refuge, who art the lord deserving of all homage, than whom there is no other asylum;‡ my mind afflicted with repentance for my trust in the world, and desiring the fulness of felicity, emancipation from all existence."§

---

* असद्रूपविद्रव ।

† *Preta-rája*, an epithet of Yama.

‡ परमपदं यतो न किंचित् ।

§ निर्वाणे परिखतधाबि खाभिलाष: ।

This means: "longing for emancipation,—of uncreated glory." So says Ratnagarbha, who also allows the epithet of 'emancipation' to signify "resort of perfect *yogins*". Śrīdhara gives the second interpretation only.

The 'emancipation' of the Hindus is not release "from all existence", but from consciousness of pleasure and pain. The distinction is, at all events, good, as a piece of idealism.

CHAPTER XXIV.

Muchukunda goes to perform penance. Krishńa takes the army and treasures of Kálayavana, and repairs, with them, to Dwáraká. Balaráma visits Vraja: inquiries of its inhabitants after Krishńa.

THUS praised by the wise Muchukunda, the sovereign of all things, the eternal lord, Hari, said to him: "Go to whatever celestial regions you wish, lord of men, possessed of might irresistible, honoured * by my favour. When you have fully enjoyed all heavenly pleasures, you shall be born in a distinguished family, retaining the recollection of your former births; and you shall, finally, obtain emancipation."† Having heard this promise, and prostrated himself before Achyuta, the lord of the world, Muchukunda went forth from the cave, and, beholding men of diminutive stature, now first knew that the Kali age had arrived. The king, therefore, departed to Gandhamádana,: the shrine § of Naranáráyańa,‖ to perform penance.

Krishńa, having, by this stratagem, destroyed his

---

* *Upabŕinhita.*

† भुक्ता भोगान्महादिव्यान्अविष्वसि महाकुले ।
जातिस्मरो मन्मसादान्ततो मोषमवाप्स्यसि ॥

: Probably, the mountain spoken of in Vol. II., p. 115.

§ *Sthána.* A shrine of Naranáráyańa is referred to in Chapter XXXVII. of this Book.

‖ A name of Krishńa, for which see the *Mahábhárata, Sánti-parvan,* śl. 12658; also, the *Bhágavata-puráńa,* V., XIX., 9.

"In various parts of the *Mahábhárata,* Krishńa and Arjuna are singularly represented as having formerly existed in the persons of two Rishis, Náráyańa and Nara, who always lived and acted together." *Original Sanskrit Texts,* Part IV., p. 192.

The Devarshis Nara and Náráyańa are mentioned in Vol. I., p. 111, note 1, and in Vol. III., p. 68, note 1. Also see Vol. IV., p. 246, note 1.

enemy, returned to Mathurá, and took captive his army, rich in horses, elephants, and cars, which he conducted to Dwáraká,* and delivered to Ugrasena; and the Yadu race was relieved from all fear of invasion.† Baladeva, when hostilities had entirely ceased, being desirous of seeing his kinsmen, went to Nanda's cow-pens,‡ and there again conversed with the herdsmen and their females, with affection and respect. By some, the elders, he was embraced; others, the juniors, he embraced; and with those of his own age, male or female, he talked and laughed.§ The cowherds made many kind speeches to Haláyudha;|| but some of the Gopís spoke to him with the affectation of anger,¶ or with feelings of jealousy, as they inquired after the loves of Krishńa with the women of Mathurá. "Is all well with the fickle and inconstant Krishńa?" said they. "Does the volatile swain, the friend of an instant, amuse the women of the city by laughing at our rustic efforts (to please him)? Does he ever think of us, singing in chorus to his songs? Will he not come here once again, to see his mother? But why talk of these things? It is a different tale to tell, for him without us, and for us without him. Father,

---

* The original has Dwáravatí, of which "Dwáraká" is a synonym.
† Parábhibhava.
‡ Nanda-gokula.
§ केचापि संपरिष्वक्तः कांचित परिष्वजे ।
  हासं चक्रे समं कैश्चिन्मैनीपीजनैस्तथा ॥
The Translator's specifications of "elders", &c., are taken from the commentators.
|| "Ploughshare-weaponed," literally; a name of Baladeva or Balabhadra. *Vide supra*, p. 51, text and note ||.
¶ Prema-kupita. Compare the terms in Vol. IV., p. 323, notes § and **.

mother, brother, husband, kin,—what have we not
abandoned for his sake? But he is a monument of
ingratitude.* Yet tell us, does not Kŕishńa talk of
coming here? Falsehood is never, O Kŕishńa, to be
uttered by thee. Verily, this is Dámodara,† this is
Govinda, who has given up his heart to the damsels
of the city,—who has, no longer, any regard for us,
but looks upon us with disdain.": So saying, the
Gopís, whose minds were fixed on Kŕishńa, § addressed
Ráma, in his place, calling him Dámodara and Govinda, ‖ and laughed, and were merry; ¶ and Ráma
consoled them by communicating to them agreeable,
modest, affectionate, and gentle messages from Kŕishńa.
With the cowherds he talked mirthfully, as he had
been wont to do, and rambled, along with them, over
the lands of Vraja.[1]

---

[1] This visit of Balaráma to Vraja is placed, by the Hari
Vaṁśa, anterior to the fall of Mathurá; by the Bhágavata, long
subsequent to the establishment of the Yadus at Dwáraká.

* अज्ञातसद्भ्वज: ।

† See Vol. IV., p 281.

: दामोदरोऽसौ गोविन्दः पुरस्त्रीसक्तमानसः ।
अपेतप्रीतिरस्मासु दुर्द्यः प्रतिभाति नः ॥

"Of this Dámodara, or Govinda, whose heart is attached to the
women of the city, the love has departed, as towards us; and, therefore,
he is hard to be seen. And yet he delights us."

Ratnagarbha has दामोदरासौ; i. e., he puts 'Dámodara' in the vocative. By reading, also, अप्रेतप्रीति:,—in which, likewise, he is peculiar,—
he gives the sentence a very different meaning; but his explanation of
this expression by गतप्रीति: can scarcely be accepted.

§ Hari, in the original.

‖ The Sanskrit has Kŕishńa.

¶ आमन्त्रितः स कृष्णेति पुनर्दामोदरेति च ।
अहुः सुस्वरं गोप्यो हरिणा हतचेतसः ॥

CHAPTER XXV.

Balaráma finds wine in the hollow of a tree; becomes inebriated; commands the Yamuná to come to him, and, on her refusal, drags her out of her course: Lakshmí gives him ornaments and a dress: he returns to Dwáraká, and marries Revatí.

WHILST the mighty * Śesha, [1] † the upholder of the globe, was thus engaged in wandering amidst the forests, with the herdsmen, in the disguise of a mortal, —having rendered great services to earth, and still considering what more was to be achieved,—Varuńa, ‡ in order to provide for his recreation, said to (his wife,) Váruńí § (the goddess of wine): "Thou, Madirá, ‖ art ever acceptable to the powerful Ananta. ¶ Go, therefore, auspicious and kind goddess, ** and promote his enjoyments." Obeying these commands, Váruńí went and established herself in the hollow of a Kadamba-tree, in the woods of Vŕindávana. Baladeva, roaming about, (came there, and,) smelling the pleasant fragrance of liquor, †† resumed his ancient passion for strong drink. The holder of the ploughshare, ‡‡ observ-

---

[1] The great serpent, of whom Balaráma is an incarnation.

* Mahátman.
† See Vol. II., pp. 74, 85, and 211, note 1.
‡ See Vol. II., p. 85.
§ See Vol. I., p. 146, note 1; and Vol. II., p. 212.
‖ Different, of course, from the Madirá named in Vol. IV., p. 109.
¶ The same as Śesha. See Vol. II., p. 211.
** गच्छ मुदे शुभे | Ratnagarbha reads, instead of मुदे, मुदा |
†† Madirá.
‡‡ Lángalin, in the original; the same, in effect, as Haláyudha. Vide supra, p. 63, note ‖.

ing the vinous drops distilling from the Kadamba-tree, was much delighted, (and gathered) and quaffed them,[1] along with the herdsmen and the Gopís; whilst those who were skilful with voice and lute celebrated him in their songs.* Being inebriated (with the wine), and the drops of perspiration standing like pearls upon his limbs, he called out, not knowing what he said:"† Come hither, Yamuná river. I want to bathe." The river, disregarding the words of a drunken man, came not (at his bidding). On which, Ráma,‡ in a rage,

---

[1] There is no vinous exudation from the Kadamba-tree (Nau-clea Kadamba); but its flowers are said to yield a spirit, by distillation; —whence Kádambarí§ is one of the synonyms of wine, or spirituous liquor. The grammarians, however, also derive the word from some legend; stating it to be so called, because it was produced from the hollow of a Kadamba-tree on the Go-manta‖ mountain: नोमन्तपर्वते कदम्बकोटरात्खाता। The Hari Vaṁśa,¶ which alone makes the Gomanta mountain the scene of an exploit of Kṛishṇa and Ráma, makes no mention of this origin of wine; and the Bhágavata** merely says, that Váruńí took up her abode in the hollow of a tree.†† There must be some other authority, therefore, for this story.

---

* उपगीयमानो ललितं गीतवाब्यविशारदैः।
This verse, it is observable, has an excessive syllable at the end of its first half.

† Vihwala.

‡ The Sanskrit has Lángalin. See the preceding page, note ‡‡.

§ Personified, Kádambarí is said to be daughter of Chitraratha and Madirá. For Chitraratha, see Vol. II., p. 86, note 1.

‖ Corrected, here and below,—and in the Sanskrit,—from "Gomantha". For the mountain in question, see Vol. II., p. 141, note 2, ad finem. The Harivaṁśa places it near the Sahya mountains.

¶ Chapter XCVII.

** X., Latter Section, XVI., 19.

†† Compare the Harivaṁśa, Chapter XCVIII.

took up his ploughshare,* which he plunged into her
bank, and dragged her to him, calling out:† "Will you
not come, you jade?‡ Will you not come? Now go
where you please, (if you can)." Thus saying, he compelled the dark river to quit its ordinary course, and
follow him whithersoever he wandered through the
wood.§ Assuming a mortal figure,, the Yamuná, with
distracted looks, approached Balabhadra,¶ and entreated him** to pardon her, and let her go. But he
replied: "1 will drag you with my ploughshare, in a
thousand directions, since you contemn my prowess
and strength."†† At last, however, appeased by her
reiterated prayers, he let her go, after she had watered
all the country.[1]‡‡ When he had bathed, the goddess

---

[1] The Bhágavata and Hari Vaṁśa §§ repeat this story; the
latter, very imperfectly. The former adds, that the Yamuná is

---

* *Hala.* Vide *supra*, p. 51, note ‖.
† गृहीला तां तटे तेन चक्म॑ मद्विह्ह्रू: ।
‡ *Pápa.*
§ सा ह्ह्रा सहसा तेन मार्गं संत्यज्य जिश्रगा ।
यचाचे बलभद्रोऽसी श्रावयामास तद्वनम् ॥
Śrídhara, like one of my MSS. unaccompanied by commentary, has, not
ह्ह्रा, but ह्ण्ण्रा, the reading followed by the Translator.

‖ भरीरिवी ।
¶ Ráma, in the original.
** The Sanskrit here exhibits Musaláyudha, "Bludgeon-armed", a name
of Baladeva. Vide *supra*, p. 51, note ¶.
†† सोऽप्रवीद्वजानाचि मम ग्रौर्यबले यदि ।
सोऽहं लां ह्लपातेन विनेष्वामि सहस्रधा ॥
‡‡ ह्लुह्लयातिवंचासान्तया नद्या प्रसादित: ।
भूभागे श्राविते तक्सिन्नुमोच यमुनां बल: ॥
§§ Chapter CIII.

5*

of beauty,* Lakshmí, came, and gave him a beautiful
lotos to place in one ear, and an ear-ring for the other;†
a fresh necklace of lotos-flowers, sent by Varuńa; and
garments of a dark blue colour, as costly as the wealth
of the ocean:‡ and, thus decorated with a lotos in one
ear, a ring in the other,§ dressed in blue garments,
and wearing a garland, Balaráma appeared united with
loveliness. Thus decorated, Ráma sported two months
in Vraja, and then returned to Dwáraká, where he
married Revatí, the daughter of King Raivata,‖ by
whom he had (two sons,) Niśaṭha¶ and Ulmuka.[1]

still to be seen following the course along which she was dragged
by Balaráma. The legend, probably, alludes to the construction
of canals from the Jumna, for the purposes of irrigation; and the
works of the Mohammedans in this way—which are well known,
—were, no doubt, preceded by similar canals, dug by order of
Hindu princes.
[1] See Vol. IV., p. 109.

* The Sanskrit has only Kánti for "the goddess of beauty." It is a
name of Lakshmí, who is mentioned, in the original, several stanzas
further on.
† अवतंसोत्पलं चारु गृहीलिकं च कुण्डलम् ।
Professor Wilson has rendered the explanation of the commentators.
‡ This expression is to render samudrárha.
§ कृतावतंसः स तदा चारुकुण्डलभूषितः ।
‖ See Vol. III., pp. 249—254.
¶ Corrected from "Nishaṭha".

CHAPTER XXVI.

Kríshńa carries off Rukmińí: the princes who come to rescue her repulsed by Balaráma. Rukmin overthrown, but, spared by Kríshńa, founds Bhojakańa. Pradyumna born of Rukmińí.

BHÍSHMAKA* was king of Vidarbha,† residing at Kuńdina.¹: He had a son named Rukmin, and a beautiful daughter termed Rukmińí. Kríshńa fell in love with the latter,§ and solicited her in marriage; but her brother, who hated Kríshńa, would not assent to the espousals. At the suggestion of Jarásandha, and with the concurrence of his son, the powerful (sovereign) Bhíshmaka affianced Rukmińí to Śiśupála.¶ In order to (celebrate) the nuptials, Jarásandha and other princes, the friends of Śiśupála,** assembled

---

¹ Vidarbha is the country of Berar; and the name remains in the present city of Beder. The capital, however, Kuńdinapura, is, commonly, identified with a place called Kundapoor, about forty miles north-east of Amarávatí (in Berar).

---

* The elongated form of Bhishma, as this king is called in the *Mahábhárata*.

† Literally, "in the country of the Vidarbhas": विदर्भविषये ।

‡ See Vol. II., p. 158, note 3.

§ And she, we are told, with him:

रुकिस्वीं चकमे कृष्ण: सा च तं चारुहासिनी ।

Cháruhásini is an epithet, not a second name, of Rukmińí. For Cháruhásini, another of Kríshńa's numerous wives, see Vol. IV., p. 112; also, *infra*, p. 81, note §, and p. 83, note §.

∥ Called Chakrin, in the Sanskrit.

¶ The beginning of this Chapter is translated in *Original Sanskrit Texts*, Part IV., p. 179, note 161.

** See Vol. IV., pp. 104 and 106.

in the capital of Vidarbha;* and Kŕishńa, attended by Balabhadra and many other Yádavas, also went to Kuńdina,† to witness the wedding. When there, Hari contrived, on the eve of the nuptials, to carry off the princess;[1] leaving Ráma and his kinsmen to sustain the weight of his enemies.‡ Pauńdraka,§ the illustrious Dantavakra,|| Vidúratha,¶ Śiśupála, Jarásandha, Sálwa,** and other kings, indignant (at the insult), exerted themselves to kill Kŕishńa, but were repelled by Balaráma and the Yádavas.†† Rukmin, vowing that he would never enter Kuńdina again, until he had slain Keśava in fight, pursued and overtook him.‡‡ (In the combat that ensued), Kŕishńa destroyed, with his discus,§§ as if in sport, the host (of Rukmin),—with all

---

[1] When she had gone forth from the city to worship Ambiká: Bhágavata. Indráńí, the wife of Indra: Hari Vaṁśa.|||| Our text tells the circumstance more concisely than the others.

---

* भीष्मकस्य पुरीं अगमुः ।
† Corrected, throughout this Chapter, from "Kundina".
‡ विपक्षभारमासज्य रामादीश्वव बन्धुषु ।
§ See Chapter XXXIV. of this Book.
|| See Vol. IV., p. 103.
¶ Vide ibid., p. 153.
** Exchanged for "Salya", which I nowhere find, and which is, probably, corrupted from Sálya, a reading peculiar to Professor Wilson's favourite MS. Sálwa was king of the Saubhas, according to the Harivaṁśa, śl. 6143.
†† रामावीर्यंदुपुङ्क्तैः ।
‡‡ हनुं कृष्णमभिद्रुतः ।
§§ The "discus", chakra, is not here mentioned; but Kŕishńa is designated as Chakrin. The original of the passage where the discus was supposed to be spoken of is as follows:
निर्जितः पातितखोर्व्यां खीलयैव स चक्रिणा
I find no reading but this.
|||| Śl. 6612.

its horse, and elephants, and foot, and chariots,—and overthrew him, and hurled him on the ground, and would have put him to death, but was withheld by the entreaties of Rukminí.* "He is my only brother," she exclaimed, "and must not be slain by thee. Restrain your wrath, O divine lord; and give me my brother, in charity." Thus addressed by her, Krishńa, whom no acts affect,† spared Rukmin;[1] and he (in pursuance of his vow,) founded the city Bhojakata,[2]: and (ever afterwards) dwelt therein.§ After the defeat of Rukmin, Krishńa married Rukminí,¶ in due form; having, first, made her his own by the Rákshasa ritual.[3]** She bore him the gallant Pradyumna, a

---

[1] After depriving him of his eyebrows and hair. In the Bhágavata, Balaráma also interferes in favour of Rukmin, and reproves Krishńa for disfiguring him.

[2] Of course, this was somewhere in the neighbourhood of Kuńdina, or Vidarbha, and is, usually, supposed to be situated on the Narmadá.

[3] That is, by violence. Thus Manu: "The seizure of a maiden, by force, from her house, while she weeps, and calls for

---

* हलुं ज्ञतमतिः ज्रष्टो एकिलं चुज्रुर्मेदम् ।
  मवम्य धाचितो म्रह्म्वकिमला मग्वान्ह्रिः ॥

† *Aklishla-karman.* See Vol. IV., p. 282, note †.

: See Vol. II., p. 158, note 3.

§ Ratnagarbha, with whom agree several of my MSS. unaccompanied by commentary, omits a passage of three stanzas, beginning with the verses cited in note *, above, and ending at the point indicated. Quite possibly, too, this passage has been unwarrantably introduced into the text as recognized by Śrídhara. He does not gloss any part of it.

‖ Madhusúdana, in the original.

¶ She was one of Krishńa's chief wives. See Vol. IV., p. 112.

** See Vol. III., p. 105.

portion of the deity of love.* The demon Śambara†
carried him off; but he slew the demon.‡

---

assistance, after her kinsmen and friends have been slain in
battle, or wounded, and their houses broken open, is the mar-
riage styled *Rákshasa.*" § III., 33.|| According to the Bhága-
vata, Rukmińí sends to invite Krishńa to carry her off, and instructs him how to proceed.

---

* "The deity of love" is to render Madana, a name of Káma or Ananga.
† See Vol. II., p. 70.

‡ अहार म्वरो यं वै यो अघान च ग्म्वरम् ।

§ This is from the translation of Sir William Jones.

|| हृत्वा छित्त्वा च भित्त्वा च क्रोशन्तीं रुदतीं गृहात् ।
प्रसह्य कन्याहरणं राक्षसो विधिरुच्यते ॥

CHAPTER XXVII.

Pradyumna stolen by Śambara; thrown into the sea, and swallowed by a fish; found by Máyádevi: he kills Śambara, marries Máyádevi, and returns, with her, to Dwáraká. Joy of Rukmiṅi and Kṛishṅa.

MAITREYA.—How, Muni, happened it that the hero Pradyumna was carried away by Śambara? And in what manner was the mighty Śambara killed by Pradyumna?

PARÁŚARA.—When Pradyumna was but six days old, he was stolen, from the lying-in chamber, by Śambara, terrible as death;* for the demon foreknew that Pradyumna, if he lived, would be his destroyer.† Taking away the boy, Śambara cast him into the ocean, swarming with monsters,:—into a whirlpool of roaring waves, the haunt of the huge creatures of the deep.§ A large fish swallowed the child; but he died not, and was born anew, from its belly:[1] for that fish,

---

[1] The Bhágavata tells the story in the same manner; but the Hari Vaṁśa omits the part of the fish.

---

* Here, as below, the original has *kálaśambara*, *i. e.*, according to Ratnagarbha, "black Śambara", or "Śambara, equal to death." Śrídhara gives only the latter interpretation.

† षडे८ह्नि आतमाषं तु प्रसुवं सूतिकागृहात् ।
  मसेष हृत्वेति मुने हतवान्कालशम्बरः ॥

: *Gráhogra.*

§ कल्लोलजनितावर्ते सुघोरे मकरालये ।
  पतितं तत्र पैवेको मत्स्यो जग्राह बालकम् ।
  न ममार च तत्रापि अठरेण न जीर्यते ॥

with others, was caught by the fishermen, and delivered, by them, to the great Asura Sambara. His
wife Máyádeví, the mistress of his household, superin-
tended the operations of the cooks, and saw, when the
fish was cut open, a beautiful child, looking like a
new shoot of the blighted tree of love. Whilst won-
dering who this should be, and how he could have got
into the belly of the fish, Nárada came, to satisfy her
curiosity, and said to the graceful dame: "This is the
son of him by whom the whole world is created and
destroyed, * —the son of Vishńu, who was stolen, by
Sambara, from the lying-in chamber, and tossed (by
him,) into the sea, where he was swallowed by the
fish. He is now in thy power. Do thou, beautiful
woman, tenderly † rear this jewel of mankind." Thus
counselled by Nárada, Máyádeví took charge of the
boy, and carefully reared him, from childhood, being
fascinated by the beauty of his person. Her affection
became still more impassioned, when he was decorated
with the bloom of adolescence. The gracefully-moving‡
Máyávatí,§ then, fixing her heart and eyes upon the
high-minded Pradyumna, gave him, whom she re-
garded as herself, all her magic (and illusive) powers.||

So reads Srídhara. Ratnagarbha ends the second verse with अढरा-
गच्छीपितः; several MSS. unaccompanied by commentary, with अढरैषन-
ळदीपितः ।

* समस्तयमतः सृतिसंहारकारिषः ।   † विकब्धा ।

‡ *Gajá-gámini*; literally, "having the gait of an elephant."

§ Another name of Máyádeví. Some MSS. yield, here and elsewhere,
Máyárati.

|| मायावती दृदौ चासी मायाः सर्वा महात्मने ।
प्रद्युम्नायालम्भूताय तस्यदुग्धदचेत्रसा ॥

Observing these marks of passionate affection, the
son of Kŕishńa* said to the lotos-eyed (Máyádeví):
"Why do you indulge in feelings so unbecoming the
character of a mother?" To which she replied: "Thou
art not a son of mine; thou art the son of Vishńu,
whom Kála Śambara† carried away, and threw into
the sea. Thou wast swallowed by a fish, but wast
rescued, by me, from its belly.‡ Thy fond mother, O
beloved, is still weeping for thee." When the valiant §
Pradyumna heard this, he was filled with wrath, and
defied Śambara to battle. In the conflict that ensued,
the son of Mádhava‖ slew the whole host of Śambara.
Seven times he foiled the delusions of the enchanter,
and, making himself master of the eighth, turned it
against Śambara,¶ and killed him. By the same faculty he ascended into the air,** and proceeded to his
father's house, where he alighted, along with Máyávatí, in the inner apartments. When the women beheld Pradyumna, they thought it was Kŕishńa himself.
Rukmińí, her eyes dimmed with tears, spoke tenderly
to him, and said: "Happy is she who has a son like
this, in the bloom of youth. Such would be the age

This is the reading of Ratnagarbha. Śridhara begins the second verse
with the words प्रयुन्नायातिरागाम्बा ।
* Kŕishńí, in the original.
† See note • in p. 73, *supra.*
‡ चित्र: समुद्रे मत्स्स्य संमाप्तो अठराज्जथा ।
§ *Mahá-bala.*
‖ Mádhavi, in the Sanskrit.
¶ Here the original again has *kála-śambara.*
** In the original there is only the word उत्पत्स, to denote this pro-
cedure. Neither of the commentators remarks on the passage. See
Vol. III., p. 311, note ‖.

of my son Pradyumna, if he was alive. Who is the
fortunate mother adorned by thee? And yet, from
thy appearance, and from the affection I feel for thee,
thou art, assuredly, the son of Hari."

At this moment, Kṛishṇa, accompanied by Nárada,
arrived; and the latter said to the delighted Rukmiṇí:*
"This is thine own son, who has come hither, after
killing Śambara, by whom, when an infant, he was
stolen from the lying-in chamber. This is the virtuous
Máyávatí, his wife, and not the wife of Śambara. Hear
the reason. When Manmatha (the deity of love,) had
perished,[1] the goddess of beauty,† desirous to secure
his revival, assumed a delusive form, and, by her
charms, fascinated the demon Śambara, and exhibited
herself to him in various illusory enjoyments.‡ This

---

[1] When he was reduced to ashes by a fiery glance from
Śiva, in resentment of his inflaming him with passion for Umá.
This legend is a favourite with the Śaiva Puráṇas, and is told
in the Linga and Káliká; also, in the Padma Puráṇa, and Káśi
Khaṇḍa of the Skanda Puráṇa. They do not say much about
his resuscitation, however; Śiva, in pity of Ratí's grief, restoring
him only to a bodiless existence, as Ananga, whose place is to
be in the hearts of men. The Linga adds, that, when Vishṇu,
in consequence of the curse of Bhṛigu, shall be born as the son
of Vasudeva, Káma shall be born as one of his sons.

* ब्रत:पुरचरीं देवीं रकिणी प्राह हर्षयन् ।
I find no variants of this passage.

† This expression is to render rúpiṅí, "the beautiful one,"—an epithet,
here, of Rati.

‡ Śridhara has ब्रवाचायुपभोगेषु । Ratnagarbha, while mentioning this
lection, prefers विहारायुपभोगेषु; and some MSS. of the mere text exhibit विवाहायुपभोगेषु । The Translator seems to have taken the first

thy son is the descended Káma; and this is (the goddess) Rati, his wife.[1] There is no occasion for any
uncertainty: this is thy daughter-in-law." Then Rukminí was glad, and Keśava, also. The whole city
resounded with exclamations of joy;* and all the
people of Dwáraká† were surprised at Rukminí's recovering a son who had so long been lost.‡

---

[1] The daughter of Daksha, but not enumerated amongst those
formerly specified (Vol. I., p. 109). She was born from his perspiration, according to the Káliká Puráńa.

---

of these readings; in which, apparently, he thought he saw वायव*,
in the sense of something 'airy' or 'unreal'. The whole expression
signifies "sexual congress and other enjoyments".

* नगरी च समस्ता वा वायु साध्वित्तभावत ।

† The original has Dwáravati.

‡ The rendering of this Chapter deviates rather more widely than usual
from literality.

CHAPTER XXVIII.

Wives of Kŕishńa. Pradyumna has Aniruddha: nuptials of the latter. Balaráma, beat at dice, becomes incensed, and slays Rukmin and others.

RUKMIŃÍ bare to Kŕishńa these other sons: Chárudeshńa, Sudeshńa, Chárudeha,* Susheńa, Chárugupta, Bhadracháru, Cháruvinda,† Sucháru, and the very mighty Cháru;‡ also, one daughter, Chárumatí. Kŕishńa had seven other beautiful wives:§ Ká-

---

* *Mahábala*, in one MS., follows Chárudeha. It would be difficult to prove that it is not a proper name.

† Instead of Susheńa and Cháruvinda, the *Bhágavata-puráńa* has Vicháru and Cháruchandra.

‡ A single copy has Chandra.

Several other sons of Rukmińí, elsewhere recognized as such, are here unnoticed. See Vol. IV., p. 112, note **.

§ The original is as follows:

अन्याश्च भार्याः कृष्णस्य बभूवुः सप्त शोभनाः ।

It is signified, by this verse, that seven beautiful wives are about to be named; but it is not expressly said that the specification is restricted to seven wives, or to beautiful ones only. The commentators, however, endeavour to reduce the catalogue to a septenary. Śrídhara's identification, in order to this reduction, is spoken of, by the Translator, in his note in p. 81, *infra*, but is not accepted by him. Further particulars Śrídhara does not enter into; and the Translator, who does not even allude to Ratnagarbha's roll of the ladies, assumes that we are to find, here, precisely the same seven—and no more,—that are enumerated at the beginning of Chapter XXXII. of this Book. But, as will appear from my annotations that follow, it is more or less possible that several wives are designated over and above the heptad with which the commentators content themselves. My Ajmere MS. ends the verse quoted above with बभूवुस्तनुमध्योभगाः; thus premising 'very beautiful' wives, —not simply 'beautiful',—and omitting all definition of their number.

Ratnagarbha asserts that the seven are: Mitravindá, Satyá, Jámbavatí, Rohińí, Suśílá, Satyabhámá, and Lakshmańá; and the words connected with these names are, he pronounces, epithets. Unlike Śrídhara, he

líndí,* Mitravindá,† the virtuous: Nágnajití,§ the
queen‖ Jámbavatí;¶ Rohiní,** of beautiful form;†† the

takes Jámbavatí to be a different person from Rohiní; and he considers
Kálindí to be a synonym of Mitravindá.
      In Vol. IV., p. 112, we read that Kríshúa's principal wives "were
Rukminí, Satyabhámá, Jámbavatí, Chárnhásini, and four others." If we
knew who these four others were, it could be ascertained how far the
principal wives tallied with the beautiful ones, and whether the group
under discussion contains additions to those two categories.
      * For her origin, see Vol. IV., p. 286, note *. Her offspring, as
named in the *Bhágavata-purána*, were Sruta, Kavi, Vrisha, Vira, Su-
bábu, Bhadra, Sánti, Darśa, Púrnamása, and Somaka.
      † Corrected from "Mitravrindá", which I find nowhere but in a care-
lessly executed copy of Sridhara's text and commentary, to which Professor Wilson was very partial, and which he too often used without
controlling it.
      Mitravindá's children, the *Bhágavata-purána*, alleges, were ten: Vríka,
Harsha, Anila, Grídhra, Vardhana, Annáda, Mahása, Pávana, Vahni, and
Kshudhi.
      ‡ The original is सत्या नार्जविती तथा । According to Sridhara,
in his commentary on the *Bhágavata-purána*, the lady here intended is
Satyá, patronymically called Nágnajiti. For the Translator's "the virtuous Nágnajití", we should, therefore, read 'Satyá, daughter of Nagnajit.'
M. Langlois makes the same mistake, in his translation of the *Hari-
vaṁśa*, Vol. I., p. 500. See further, note § in the preceding page, and
note ‡‡ in p. 82, *infra*.
      § Mother, the *Bhágavata-purána* alleges, of Vira, Chandra, Aśwasena,
Chitragu, Vegavat, Vrisha, Áma, Sanku, Vasu, and Kunti.
      ‖ देवी जाम्बवती चापि । It is barely possible that we should read
'Devi,' not "the queen". Compare the *Harivaṁśa*, śl. 9179.
      For Jámbavatí, see Vol. IV., p. 79.
      ¶ The *Bhágavata-purána* represents her as mother of Sámba, Sumitra,
Purujit, Satajit, Sahasrajit, Vijaya, Chitraketu, Vasumat, Dravida, and
Krata.
      ** An elder Rohiní was one of Kríshúa's numerous step-mothers. See
Vol. IV., pp. 109 and 260.
      Kríshúa's wife Rohiní had, on the authority of the *Bhágavata-purána*,
the following sons: Váma, Áyus, Satyaka, Díptimat, Támratapta, and
others unnamed.
      †† जामरूपिणी । Possibly, this is a proper name, Kámarúpiní; but,
probably, it is an epithet. See the *Harivaṁśa*, śl. 6701.

amiable and excellent daughter of the king of Madra,*

---

* *Madrarája.* Leaving out of question the interpretation "king of
Madra", our choice lies, according to circumstances, between "king of
the Madras" and "King Madra." In the purest Sanskrit, only the former
of these two significations is admissible. There are many cases, in later
literature, similar to *Madrarája*, thus considered; such as *Káśirája*, *Vatsa-
rája*, *Bhojarája*, *Bhojapati*, &c. &c. Instances in which there is not the
option spoken of above, but in which, at variance with classical canons, sub-
stantival members of a compound stand in apposition, are *Varadarája*,
Bhojadeva, *Kámadeva*, *Mádhavadeva*, *Nandiśa*, *Venkateśa*, *Bháilleśa*, *Ka-
pileśwara*, *Rámeśwara*, *Gorakshanátha*, *Seshanága*, *Aghásura*, &c. &c.
Mádrí's father might, as has been said, be *Madrarája* in the sense of
"King Madra"; only no such ruler has been discovered among Krishńa's
contemporaries. Conclusively, Lakshmańá—as the lady who bears the
patronym of Mádri is distinctively called,—is said, in the *Bhágavata-
puráńa*, to have been daughter of *Madrádhipati*, which it would be very
unsafe to translate otherwise than by "king of the Madras".

In Sanskrit, names of countries and kingdoms are denoted, very frequently, by compounds ending with a word for country or kingdom,—
deśa, *vishaya*, *rájya*, *ráshtra*. Examples of such names standing independently are rare, and seem to be confined to feminines. Most generally,
a plural is employed; and this plural imports a people. Thus, where we
should be disposed to say "he lives in Málava", an ancient Hindu would
have said "he lives in the country of the Málavas", वसति मालवदेशे,
or, in accordance with the somewhat more prevalent idiom, "he lives
among the Málavas", वसति मालवेषु.

The preponderant usage here referred to may, perhaps, be accounted
for in this wise. The earliest Hindus were grouped in tribes, not in
nations; and these tribes were distinguished by lineage, not by place of
abode. The titles which they bore were eponymous; and it should seem
that they were long in acquiring fixed habitations. Hence, it may be
surmised,—and not for the reason that led Louis Philippe to style himself "king of the French",—it is that we read of, for instance, "the
king of the Panchálas"; somewhat as, from a sense of vagueness, the
Yavanas, Húnas, Chínas, Turushkas, and Śakas were never localized,
further than by the indeterminate forms *Yavana-deśa*, "country of the
Yavanas," and the like. In later times, as history informs us, kingdoms of more or less definite bounds were established, and lasted for
long periods. But the old idiom had become so firmly rooted as, in
spite of the altered state of things, to hold its ground; and the option
of mentioning a region or state (by its simple name), instead of its
people, was seldom accepted. The sole exceptions seem to be afforded

(Mádrí);* Satyabhámá,† the daughter of Sattrájita;‡ and Lakshmaná, of lovely smiles.¹§ Besides these,

---

¹ The number specified, however, both in this place and in Chapter XXXII., is nine, instead of eight. The commentator ‖ endeavours to explain the difference, by identifying Rohiní with Jámbavatí. But, in the notices of Kríshńa's posterity, both in

by the names of cities which were, of themselves, kingdoms; and most Hindu cities bore appellations of the feminine gender. The Kurukshetra, Mashńára, Sáchiguńa, and Avachatnuka of the *Aitareya-bráhmaṇa* I take to be cities with masculine names,—like Kanyakubja, &c.,—not countries. If this view be not fallacious, we can, therefore, only plead convenience, when we speak of Abhira, Ánarta, Chedi, Kerala, Kośala, Kuru, Madra, Magadha, Málava, Śúrasena, &c. &c., after the manner of the latest and most corrupt Sanskrit, and of the living vernaculars of India. Similarly, we find, in Latin, only *Sabinorum ager* or *Sabinus ager*, and *in Sabinis versari, in Sabinos proficisci*; but, in the present day, we have *la Sabina*. The Greeks, it is true, devised the name Σαβίνη; and, in the same way, they invented the names Abiria, Cirrhadia, Gandaritis, *etc.*, though the ancient Hindus recognized no countries denominated Abhira, Kiráta, Gandhára, &c.

* I have parenthesized this name, as being added by the Translator. The original has **सुशीला श्रीसमझूना** I The latter word is, palpably, an epithet of the former, and suggested thereby. The *Harivamśa, śl.* 6700, places this point beyond all doubt. We must read, therefore, "Suśílá," and eliminate "amiable and excellent". *Vide supra*, p. 78, note §. Suśílá appears, in p. 107, *infra*, under her patronym Mádri.

To Mádri the *Bhágavata-puráṇa* assigns progeny bearing the names of Praghosha, Gátravat, Siṁha, Bala, Prabala, Úrdhwaga, Mahásakti, Saha, Oja, and Parájita.

† According to the *Bhágavata-puráṇa*, she had ten children: Bhánu, Subhánu, Swarbhánu, Prabhánu, Bhánumat, Chandrabhánu, Bríhadbhánu, Atibhánu, Śríbhánu, and Pratibhánu.

‡ Corrected from "Śatrujit". The original has Sáttrájiti, patronymic of Sattrájita, for whom and his daughter Satyabhámá, see Vol.IV., pp. 79, 80.

§ **चारुहासिनी** I Here we have, possibly, another name of Lakshmaná, rather than an epithet. For Chárubásiní, see Vol. IV., p. 112, note ‖. Also see note § in p. 83, *infra*. My Ajmere MS. gives **प्रियदर्शना**; and Priyadarśaná, too, is a lady's name, as in my *Vásavadattá*, p. 236.

‖ Śrídhara is intended. *Vide supra*, p. 78, note §.

V.   G

he* had sixteen thousand other wives.[1]†

---

this work and in the Bhágavata, she is distinct from Jámbavatí. She seems, however, to be an addition to the more usually specified eight, of whose several marriages the Bhágavata gives the best account. In addition to the three first, — respecting whom particulars are found in all,—Kálindí, or the Yamuná,‡ is the daughter of the Sun, whom Kŕishńa meets on one of his visits to Indraprastha, § and who claims him as the reward of her penance. His next wife, Mitravindá, is the daughter of his maternal aunt, Rájádhidevi (Vol. IV., pp. 101 and 103), and sister of Vinda and Anuvinda, kings of Avanti: ‖ she chooses him at her Swayaṁvara. The Hari Vaṁśa ¶ calls her Sudattá,** daughter of Śibi; and she is, subsequently, termed Śaibyá by our text.†† Nágnajití, or Satyá,‡‡ the next wife, was the daughter of Nagnajit, king of Kauśala, §§ and was the prize of Kŕishńa's overcoming seven fierce bulls, whom no other hero had encountered with success. Bhadrá,‖‖ princess of Kekaya, ¶¶—also Kŕishńa's cousin, the daughter of Śrutakirtti (Vol. IV., pp. 101 and 103), — was his next; and his eighth wife was Mádrí, *** the daughter of the

---

* Chakrin, in the original.

† In all, Kŕishńa's wives amounted to sixteen thousand and one hundred, as we read in Vol. IV., p. 112. But *vide infra*, p. 105, note §§.

‡ See Vol. III., p. 20.

§ A city on the Jumna, near the present Delhi. It belonged to the Páńdavas.   ‖ See Vol. IV., supplementary note on p. 10:.

¶ *Śl.* 9179 and 9187. In *śl.* 6703 of the same work, this or another daughter of Śibi seems to be called Tanwi.

** Corrected from "Saudattá". See note ‖ in the page following.

†† In p. 107, *infra*.

‡‡ Transformed, in the text, into "the virtuous". See note ‡ in p. 79, *supra*.

§§ The *Bhágavata-puráńa* describes Nagnajit as *Kauśalya*, which Śrídhara interprets by *Ayodhyá-pati*, "King of Ayodhyá"; and this city was the capital of Kosala.

‖‖ Her children, we read in the *Bhágavata-puráńa*, were Sangrámajit, Bŕihatsena, Śúra, Praharańa, Arijit, Jaya, and Subhadra.

¶¶ See Vol. IV., p. 103, text and note §. The *Bhágavata-puráńa* simply gives Bhadrá the epithet Kaikeyí.   *** See note * in the last page.

The heroic Pradyumna was chosen, for her lord, at
her public choice of a husband, by the daughter of
Rukmin;* and he had, by her, the powerful and gallant prince Aniruddha, who was fierce in fight,† an
ocean of prowess, and the tamer of his foes. Keśava
demanded, in marriage, for him, the granddaughter of

king of Madra,‡—named, according to the Bhágavata, Lakshmaná, § and, to the Hari Vaṁśa, Subhimá;‖ distinguishing, as
does our text, clearly, Lakshmaná from Mádrí, and, like it,
having no satisfactory equivalent for Bhadrá. The Hari Vaṁśa
does not name Rohiní, but specifies other names, as Bṛihati,¶ &c.
In the life of Kṛishńa—taken from the Bhágavata, through a Persian translation,—published by Maurice, there is a curious instance
of the barbarous distortion of Sanskrit names by the joint labours of the English and Persian translators. The wives of
Kṛishńa are written: Rokemenee (Rukmiṇí), Setubhavani (Satyabhámá), Jamoometee (Jámbavatí), Kalenderee (Kálindí), Lech-
meena (Lakshmaná), Soeta (Satyá), Bhedravatee (Bhadrá), Mi-
babenda (Mitravindá).

¹ These, according to the Mahábhárata, Ádi Parvan, were
Apsarasas, or nymphs. In the Dána Dharma, they become
Kṛishńa's wives through a boon given him by Umá.

* Kakudmati was her name. See Vol. IV., p. 112, text and note ††.
The Bhágavata-puráńa calls her Rukmavatí, also. For Rukmin, vide
supra, p. 67.
† रघे कुब: ।
‡ Vide supra, p. 80, note *.
§ Corrected from "Lakshaná". Vide supra, p. 80, note *. In the
Harivaṁśa, śl. 6702 and 9179, Lakshmaná takes the place of Mádrí, and
is followed, according to the Calcutta and Bombay editions, by जाम्-
बिखनी, for which see Vol. IV., p. 112, note ‖. Is it a third synonym?
Vide supra, p. 81, note §.
‖ Corrected from "Saubhimá". See the Harivaṁśa, śl. 9180.
Professor Wilson's "Saudattá" and "Saubhímá" were taken, I suspect,
from the "Soudattá" and "Soubhímá" of M. Langlois; his ou, a trans-
lettering of ड, u, being supposed to represent औ, au.
¶ Daughter of Śibi. Harivaṁśa, śl. 9192.
6*

Rukmin; and, although the latter was inimical to
Křishńa,[*] he betrothed the maiden[†] (who was his
son's daughter,) to the son of his own daughter (her
cousin Aniruddha). Upon the occasion of the nuptials,
Ráma and other Yádavas attended Křishńa[‡] to Bhojakata, the city of Rukmin. After the wedding[§] had
been solemnized, several of the kings, headed by him
of Kalinga,[||] said to Rukmin: "This wielder of the
ploughshare[¶] is ignorant of the dice, which may be
converted into his misfortune. Why may we not contend with him, and beat him. in play?"[**] The potent
Rukmin replied to them, and said "So let it be." And
he engaged Balaráma[††] at a game of dice, in the
palace. Balaráma[‡‡] soon lost to Rukmin a thousand
Nishkas.[1] He then staked and lost another thousand,

---

[1] The Nishka is a weight of gold, but, according to different
authorities, of very different amount. The commentator[§§] here
terms it a weight of four Suvarńas, each about 175 grains Troy.

* Sauri, in the original.
† Subhadrá. See Vol. IV., p. 112.
‡ The Sanskrit has Hari.
§ Of Prádyumni,—according to the original,—that is to say, Aniruddha.
|| कलिङ्गराजप्रमुखाः:, "the king of Kalinga, and others."
¶ Halin, i. e., Balaráma. Vide supra, p. 63, note ". and p. 65, note ::.
** अनभज्ञो हली द्यूते तथाख वसनं महत् ।
न अयामो वसं कआद्यूतेनेन महाद्युते ॥
Ratnagarbha has अनभिज्ञ: instead of अनभज्ञ: ।
†† Ráma, in the original.
‡‡ The Sanskrit has Bala.
§§ Śrídhara. Ratnagarbha is silent.
, || In reckoning money by tale, the nishka, according to the first chapter
of the Lilávatí, is equivalent to sixteen drammas. See Colebrooke's Al-
gebra, &c., p. 1.

and then pledged ten thousand, which Rukmin, who
was well skilled in gambling, also won. At this, the
king of Kalinga laughed aloud;* and the weak and
exulting Rukmin grinned, and said:† Baladeva is
losing; for he knows nothing of the game; although,
blinded by a vain passion for play, he thinks he understands the dice.": Haláyudha, galled by the broad
laughter of the Kalinga prince,§ and the contemptuous
speech of Rukmin, was (exceedingly) angry, and, overcome with passion, increased his stake to ten millions
of Nishkas. Rukmin accepted the challenge, and,
therefore, threw the dice. Baladeva won, and cried
aloud "The stake is mine." But Rukmin called out,
as loudly, that he was the winner. "Tell no lies,
Bala," said he. "The stake is yours; that is true: but
I did not agree to it. Although this be won by you,
yet still I am the winner."¶ A deep voice was then
heard in the sky, –inflaming still more the anger of
the high-spirited Baladeva,–saying: "Bala has rightly
won the whole sum, and Rukmin speaks falsely.
Although he did not accept the pledge in words, he
did so by his acts,** (having cast the dice)." Bala-

---

* *Swanavat.*

† दन्तान्विदर्श्यबुडो रुक्मी चाह महोद्धतः ।

: मुधैवाचावलेपान्धो यः खं मेनेऽचकोविदम् ।

So read most MSS., and Srídhara. Ratnagarbha has:

मुधैवाचावलेपान्धो योऽवमेनेऽचकोविदान् ।

§ रुह्य कलिङ्गराजानं प्रकाशद्वस्ननगनम् ।

चलीकोमीर्लं बल : "Have done with lies, Bala."

¶ एवं खया चेद्विजितं मया न विजितं बवम् ।

** The expression in the original looks proverbial:

अनुत्कापि वचः किंचित्कृतं भवति कलेबा ।

ráma,* thus excited, his eyes red with rage, started
up, and struck Rukmin with the board on which the
game was played,† and killed him.[1] Taking hold of
the trembling king of Kalinga, he knocked out the
teeth which he had shown when he laughed.‡ Laying
hold of a golden column, he dragged it from its place,
and used it as a weapon to kill those princes who had
taken part with his adversaries.§ Upon which, the
whole circle, crying out with terror, took to flight, and
escaped from the wrath of Baladeva.‖ When Kŕishńa¶
heard that Rukmin had been killed by his brother, he
made no remark, being afraid of Rukmińí (on the one
hand,) and of Bala (on the other); but, taking with
him the (newly) wedded Aniruddha, and the Yádava
tribe, he** returned to Dwáraká.

---

[1] The Bhágavata and Hari Vaṁśa—which, both, tell this story,—
agree in the death of Rukmin; but, in the Mahábhárata, he appears, in the war, on the side of the Páńḍavas. The occurrence
is a not very favourable picture of courtly manners; but scenes
of violence have never been infrequent at the courts of Rajpoot
princes.

---

* The Sanskrit has Bala.
† Ashṭápada.
‡ See the original words quoted in note § in the preceding page.
§ आक्षिप्य च महात्स्कं आतस्पमयं बलः ।
अघान चे ऽन्ये तत्यशा भूभुतः कुपितो बलात् ॥
‖ ततो हाहाक्षतं सर्वं पलायनपरं द्विज ।
तद्राजमक्षलं सर्वं बभूव कुपिते बले ॥
¶ Madhusúdana, in the original.
** Keśava, according to the reading accepted by Śrídhara. The other,
Ratnagarbha's lection, represents Bala as leading off Keśava and the rest.

CHAPTER XXIX.

Indra comes to Dwáraká, and reports to Krishńa the tyranny of
Naraka. Krishńa goes to his city, and puts him to death.
Earth gives the ear-rings of Aditi to Krishńa, and praises him.
He liberates the princesses made captive by Naraka, sends them
to Dwáraká, and goes to Swarga, with Satyabhámá.

ŚAKRA,* the lord of the three worlds, came
mounted on his fierce† (elephant,) Airávata, to (visit)
Sauri (Krishńa,) at Dwáraká.‡ Having entered the
city, and been welcomed by Hari, he related (to the
hero) the deeds of the demon§ Naraka.‖ "By thee,
Madhusúdana, lord of the gods," said Indra, "in a
mortal condition, all sufferings have been soothed.
Arishťa, Dhenuka, Chánúra, Mushťika,¶ Keśin, who
sought to injure helpless man,** have, all, been slain
by thee. Kaḿsa, Kuvalayápíḍa, the child-destroying
Pútaná, have been killed by thee; and so have other
oppressors of the world. By thy valour and wisdom

---

* Or Indra. For him and his mother, see Vol. II., p. 27. Śakra and
Hari were, both, sons of Aditi. See Vol. I., p. 151; and Vol. III., p. 18,
text and notes 1 and †.

† *Matta.*

‡ Dwáravatí, in the original.

§ Daitya. See the next note.

‖ The less famous Naraka was son of Viprachitti, son of Kaśyapa and
Danu, and, hence, was a Dánava, according to our Puráńa. See Vol. II.,
pp. 70—72. The Naraka of the text was not a Dánava; nor can he be
called a Daitya, except by a very loose use of the term. As appears
from note 1 in the next page, his father was Vishńu; and our text expresses that his mother was Bhúmi.

¶ Ratnagarbha's text does not mention the two pancratiasts Chánúra
and Mushťika.

** *Tapaswi-jana.*

the three worlds have been preserved;* and the gods,
obtaining their share of the sacrifices offered by the
devout, enjoy satisfaction. But now hear the occasion
on which I have come to thee, and which thou art
able to remedy.† The son of the earth,¹: called Naraka, who rules over the city of Prágjyotisha,²§ in-
flicts a great injury upon all creatures. Carrying off
the maidens of gods, saints,‖ demons, and kings, he
shuts them up in his own palace.¶ He has taken away
the umbrella of Varuńa,** impermeable to water, the
jewel-mountain crest of Mandara,†† and the celestial
nectar-dropping ear-rings of my mother:: Aditi;§§ and

---

¹ By Vishńu, as the Varáha Avatára;‖‖ but found and adopted
by Janaka. Káliká Puráńa.

² In the centre of the country of Kámarúpa,¶¶ inhabited by
Kirátas; the site of the shrines of Deví, as Dikkaravásiní and
Kámákhyá.*** Káliká Puráńa.

---

* चुभद्गोर्दुष्छबतुत्रिपरिचाते अगत्तये ।
† सोऽहं स्राम्रतमायातो यत्रिमित्तं जगार्दन ।
तक्तूला तत्रतीकारमचलं कर्तुमर्हसि ॥

: *Bhauma.*

§ The original does not make him ruler over that city, but simply
says that it was the scene of his cruelties.

For Prágjyotisha, *vide supra*, p. 55, note :.

‖ *Siddha.*

¶ *Mandira.*

** Called Prachetas, in the Sanskrit.

†† See Vol. II., p. 115.

:: See note * in the preceding page.

§§ Corrected, here and everywhere below, from "Aditi".

‖‖ See Vol. I., p. 61, note 2, *ad finem.*

¶¶ *Vide supra*, p. 54, note 2.

*** In Assam, according to Professor Wilson, in his collected Works,
Vol. III., p. 77. Also see Vol. I., Preface, p. XC. of the present work,
where correct "Kámákhyá".

he now demands my elephant, Airávata.* I have,
thus, explained to you, Govinda, the tyranny of the
Asura. You can best determine how it is to be prevented."†

Having heard this account, the divine Hari: (gently)
smiled, and, rising from his throne,§ took Indra | by
the hand. Then, wishing for the eater of the serpents,
Garuḍa immediately appeared; upon whom his master,
having first seated Satyabhámá upon his back, ascended, and flew to Prágjyotisha. Indra¶ mounted
his elephant, and, in the sight of the inhabitants of
Dwáraká, went to the abode of the gods.

The environs of Prágjyotisha were defended by
nooses, constructed by the demon Muru,** the edges of
which were as sharp as razors;†† but Hari, throwing
his discus Sudarsana:: (amongst them), cut them to
pieces. Then Muru started up; but Kesava slew him,

---

* अमृतस्रावविधी दिव्ये मक्षातुः इष्व कुण्डले ।
अहार सोऽसुरोऽदित्वा वाञ्छद्विरावतें गजम् ॥

So reads Śrídhara. Ratnagarbha has, for the first verse:

अमृतस्रावविधी दिव्ये मणिगिर्मितकुण्डले ।

Some MSS., further, deviate from Śrídhara's reading only by नाक्षा ते,
instead of मक्षातुः; from which it appears that the ear-rings were called
Divya.

† यद्य प्रतिपत्तव्यं तत्त्वयं प्रविमृश्यताम् ।
: "Son of Devaki," after the Sanskrit.
§ Varásana.
| In the original, Vásava.
¶ Śakra, in the Sanskrit.
** Vide supra, p. 54, notes 2 and ||, and p. 55, note *.
†† प्रारज्योतिषपुरख्यासीतसमन्ताच्छतयोजनम्
आधिता मौरवैः पाशैः पुरार्तिभूर्द्विजोत्तम ॥
:: We have before had mention of it. See Vol. II., p. 52.

and burnt his* seven thousand sons, like moths,†
with the flame of the edge of his discus. Having slain
Muru, Hayagríva,‡ and Panchajana, § the wise Hari
rapidly reached the city of Prágjyotisha. There a
(fierce) conflict took place with the troops of Naraka,
in which Govinda destroyed thousands of demons;
and, when Naraka came into the field, showering upon
the deity all sorts of weapons, the wielder of the discus
and annihilator of the demon-tribe cut him in two with
his celestial missile.¶ Naraka being slain, Earth,**
bearing the two ear-rings of Aditi, approached the lord
of the world,†† and said: "When, O lord, I was upheld
by thee in the form of a boar, thy contact then engendered this my son. He whom thou gavest me has
now been killed by thee. Take (therefore,) these two
ear-rings, and cherish his progeny. Thou, lord, whose
aspect is (ever) gracious,‡‡ hast come to this sphere,
in a portion of thyself, to lighten my burthen. Thou
art the eternal§§ creator, preserver,‖‖ and destroyer

---

* मुरोय, or else मुरोषु, in the original. The variant of some
copies, मुरस्य, substitutes Mura for Muru. These persons—whose names
are often confounded in MSS.,—were, both, slain by Kŕishńa. The latter
is said, by Sridhara, to have been a Rákshasa.

† Salabha.

‡ Vide supra, p. 2, note ¶.

§ Vide supra, p. 48.

‖ Samupádravat, "assaulted."

¶ ग्रस्ताखवर्षं मुञ्चन्तं भौमं तं नरकं बली ।
   चिप्ता चक्रं द्विधा चक्रे चक्री दैतेयचक्रहा ॥

** Bhúmi.

†† Jagannátha.

‡‡ प्रसादसुमुखः ।

§§ Avyaya. See Vol. I., p. 17, note *.

‖‖ Vikartṛi; 'transformer,' literally: "by means of rain and the like,"
say the commentators.

of the universe; the origin of all worlds; and one with
the universe.* What praise can be worthily offered to
thee?† Thou art the pervader, and that which is pervaded; the act, the agent, and the effect; the universal
spirit of all beings. What praise can be worthily offered to thee?: Thou art the abstract soul, the sentient and the living soul of all beings, the imperishable.
But, since it is not possible to praise thee worthily,
then why should the hopeless attempt proceed?§
Have compassion, O universal soul, and forgive the
sins which Naraka has committed. Verily, it is for the
sanctification of thy son, that he has been killed by
thee."‖ The lord, who is the substance of all creatures,¶ having replied to the Earth** "Even so," proceeded to redeem the (various) gems from the dwelling of Naraka. In the apartments of the women††
he found sixteen thousand and one hundred damsels.[1]

---

[1] These were captive princesses, according to the Bhágavata;

---

* Of this passage there are several different readings, of little consequence.

† क्षूयते ऽ क्षुत किं तव ।

: Here the translation is not literal.

§ परमात्मा त्वमात्मा च भूतात्मा पाम्यचो भवान् ।
यदा तदा स्तुतिर्नाखि किमर्षा ते प्रवर्तते ॥

Ratnagarbha says: नास्तित्वमेवाह । किमर्षा । किमास्रया ।
For the expressions *paramátman, átman,* and *bhútátman,* here employed,
vide supra, p. 14, note ††.

‖ बदोषाय त्वत्सुत: स निपातित: । So reads Sridhara; and his explanation has been followed by the Translator. Ratnagarbha speaks of
this lection, but prefers to end the verse with तत्सूति: परिपाक्वतां; in
accepting which he connects बदोषाय with त्म्यतां, which precedes it.

¶ *Bhúta-bhávana,* "creator of beings."
** Dharañí.
†† *Kanyá-pura.*

He also beheld (in the palace,) six thousand large *
elephants,† each having four tusks; twenty-one lakhs ‡
of horses of Kámboja§ and other excellent breeds. ||
These¶ Govinda despatched to Dwáraká, in charge of
the servants of Naraka. The umbrella of Varuṇa, the
jewel-mountain, which he also recovered, he placed
upon Garuda; ** and, mounting him, himself, and
taking Satyabhámá with him, he set off to the heaven
of the gods, to restore the ear-rings of Aditi.[1]

Apsarasas, or celestial nymphs, according to the Kálika Puráṇa;
and these, upon their rescue by Kṛishṇa, became his wives.††

[1] The legend of Naraka is related, in more detail, in the Bhágavata and Hari Vaṁśa, but is still more fully narrated in the
Kálika Upapuráṇa. It may be considered as one of the various
intimations that occur in the Puráṇas, of hostilities between the
worshippers of Vishṇu and Śiva; Naraka being, in an especial
degree, favoured by the latter.

* Ugra.

† According to the reading of some MSS., there were as many horses,—
common ones, it is to be supposed, since a particular kind is specified
just below.

‡ Niyuta; a term variously defined by different authorities. See notes
on the beginning of Chapter III. of Book VI.

§ काम्बोजानाम् । For the Kámbojas, see Vol. III., p. 291, note 1.

|| I find nothing, in the original, answering to the words "and other
excellent breeds".

¶ That is to say, agreeably to the original, the girls, the elephants,
and the horses.

** दृष्ट्वे वारणं कच्चं तथैव मणिपर्वतम् ।
आरोपयामास हरिर्गरुडे पन्नगाग्रणे ॥

I find no variants of this stanza, save as to its closing word, which
Ratnagarbha reads पतगेश्वरे ।

†† According to the text of our Puráṇa, also, Kṛishṇa married them.
Vide infra, p. 105.

CHAPTER XXX.

Kŕishńa restores her ear-rings to Aditi, and is praised by her:
he visits the gardens of Indra, and, at the desire of Satyabhámá,
carries off the Párijáta-tree. Śachi excites Indra to its rescue.
Conflict between the gods and Kŕishńa, who defeats them.
Satyabhámá derides them. They praise Kŕishńa.

GARUDA, laden with the umbrella of Varuńa, and
the jewel-mountain, and bearing Hŕishíkeśa* (on his
back, to the court of Indra), went (lightly), as if in
sport, along. When they arrived at the portals of
Swarga, Hari blew his shell; on which the gods advanced to meet him, bearing respectful offerings.†
Having received the homage of the divinities, Kŕishńa
went to the palace of the mother of the gods, whose
turrets‡ resembled white clouds; and, on beholding
Aditi, paid his respects to her, along with Śakra; and,
presenting to her her own ear-rings, informed her of
the destruction of (the demon) Naraka. The mother
of the world, well pleased, then fixed her whole
thoughts upon Hari, the creator, and thus pronounced
his praise: "Glory to thee, O god with the lotos-eyes,
who removest all fear from those that worship thee.
Thou art the eternal, universal, and living soul; the
origin of all beings;§ the instigator of the mental fac-

---

* "And his wife:" सभायं च हृषीकेशम् । For Hŕishíkeśa, see Vol. I.,
p. 2, note 1.

† सार्घपाणा: ।

‡ Śikhara.

§ सनातनात्मसर्वात्मभूतात्मभूतभावन ।

ulty and faculties of sense;* one with the three qualities; beyond the three qualities; exempt from con-
traries; pure; existing in the hearts of all; void of
colour, extension, and every transient modification;†
unaffected by (the vicissitudes of) birth, or death,
sleep, or waking. Thou art evening,‡ night, and day;
earth, sky, air, water, and fire; mind, intellect, and individuality.§ Thou art the agent of creation, duration,
and dissolution; the master over the agent;—in thy
forms which are called Brahmá, Vishńu, and Śiva.
Thou art gods, Yakshas, Daityas, Rákshasas, Siddhas,
Pannagas, Kúshmáńdas, Piśáchas, Gandharvas, men,
animals,¶ deer,** elephants, reptiles,†† trees, shrubs,
creepers,‡‡ climbers,§§ and grasses;‖‖ all things large,
middling, small, immense, or minute: thou art all
bodies whatsoever, composed of aggregated atoms.¶¶
This thy illusion beguiles all who are ignorant of thy
true nature,—the fools who imagine soul to be in that

---

* प्रणेता मनसो बुद्धेरिन्द्रियाणाम् ।
† सितदीर्घादिगिःषेषकल्पनापरिवर्जित ।
‡ Sandhyá.
§ भूतादि: । Ratnagarbha explains it by ahamkára. For bhútádi, see
Vol. I., p. 33, note *.
‖ Corrected from "Punnagas". Pannaga is the same as sarpa, for
which see Vol. I., p. 63. The next term, "Kúshmáńdas," is rendered
"goblins" in Vol. IV., p. 277.
¶ Paśu; "sacrificial animals." Vide supra, p. 59, note **.
** Mṛiga, "wild beasts."
†† Sarisṛipa. See Vol. I., p. 84, note §; and Vol. II., p. 92, text and
note §.
‡‡ Latá.
§§ Valli.
‖‖ For similar enumerations, see Vol. I., p. 84; and Vol. II., p. 92.
¶¶ इहमेहा भवास्तर्वे ये केचिन्नुनाजनबधा: ।

which is not spirit.* The notions that "I am—this is mine", which influence mankind, are but the delusions of the mother of the world, originating in thy active agency.† Those men who, attentive to their duties, diligently worship thee, traverse all this illusion, and obtain spiritual freedom. Brahmá and all the gods, men, and animals,‡ are, alike, invested by the thick darkness of fascination, in the gulf of the illusions of Vishńu. That men who, having worshipped thee, should seek the gratification of their desires, and their own preservation,—this, O lord, is, also, thy delusion. It is the sport of thy fascinations that induces men to glorify thee, to obtain, thereby, the continuance of their race, or the annihilation of their enemies, instead of eternal liberation.§ It is the fault of the impure acts of the unrighteous (to proffer such idle requests to one able to confer much more important benefits), — like asking for a rag to cover one's nakedness‖ from the tree that bestows whatever is solicited.¶ Be propitious,

---

* माया तवेयमज्ञातपरमार्थातिमोहिनी ।
भगवत्यवाद्यविज्ञानं यया मूढोऽनुवर्षते ॥

At the end of the second verse, in lieu of अनुवर्षते, the reading of Śridhara, Ratnagarbha has अनुबध्यते. Another lection which I find is निबध्यते ।

† अहं ममेति भावोऽन यत्पुंसामभिजायते ।
संसारमातुर्मायायाह्नवेतन्नान्य चेष्टितम् ॥

‡ Paśu.

§ आराध्य त्वामभीप्सन्ते कामान्नात्मलभवत्पयम् ।
वदेते पुरुषा माया सैवेयं भगवंस्तव ॥
मया त्वं पुत्रकामिन्वा वैरिपक्षक्षयाय च ।
आराधितो न मोक्षाय मायाविलसितं हि तत् ॥

‖ Kaupina.

¶ Kalpadruma.

then, imperishable, author of all the error that deceives
the world; and dispel, O lord of all creatures, the conceit of knowledge, which proceeds from ignorance.*
Glory to thee, grasper of the discus, wielder of the bow,
brandisher of the mace, holder of the shell! For such
do I behold thee, in thy perceptible form. Nor do I
know that form of thine which is beyond perception.
Have compassion on me, supreme god." †

Vishńu, thus hymned by Aditi, smiled, and said to
the mother of the gods:: "Mother, goddess, do thou
show favour unto me, and grant me thy blessing." §
"So be it," replied Aditi, "even‖ as thou wilt; and,
(whilst thou dwellest) amongst mortals, the first of
men,¶ thou shalt be invincible by gods or demons."
Then Satyabhámá, accompanied by the queen of Indra,**
addressed Aditi respectfully, and solicited her benedic-
tions; and Aditi (in reply,) said to her: "Fair-browed
dame, thou shalt never suffer decay, nor loss of beauty.
Thou shalt be the asylum of all loveliness, dame of

---

* अज्ञानं ज्ञानसन्नावभूतं भूतेश नाशय ।
Ratnagarbha says: ज्ञानसन्नावभूतम् । ज्ञानवानहमिख्रभिमानात्म-
कम् । And Śrídhara comments to precisely the same effect.

† एतत्पश्यामि ते रूपं खुलचिह्नोपलचितम् ॥
न आनामि परं यत्ते प्रसीद परमेश्वर ॥

‡ *Surárańí.* Similarly, Kunti is called *Páńdavárańí,* in the *Mahábhárata.*
For *arańí,* see Vol. III., p. 330, note *.

§ वरदा भव ।

‖ Corrected from "ever",—a typographical error. The original is
यथेच्छा ते ।

¶ *Purusha-vyághra,* 'tiger of a man,' and in the vocative. See Vol. IV.,
p. 320, note ¶; also, *supra,* p. 22, note *.

** Śakráńí, in the original.

faultless shape."* With the assent of Aditi, Indra†
then respectfully saluted Janárdana in all due form,
and conducted him and Satyabhámá through Nandana
and other pleasant gardens of the gods; where Keśava,
the destroyer of Keśin,‡ saw the Párijáta-tree,§ the
favourite of Śachí, which was produced when the
ocean was churned for ambrosia: the bark was of gold;
and it was embellished with young sprouting leaves of
a copper colour, and fruit-stalks bearing numerous
clusters of fragrant fruit.‖ When Satyabhámá noticed
this tree, she said to her beloved lord, Govinda: "Why
should not this divine tree¶ be transported to Dwáraká? If what you say is true, and I am really dear to
you, then let this tree be taken away from hence, and
planted in the garden** of my dwelling. You have
often said to me: 'Neither Jámbavatí nor Rukminí is
so dear to me, Satyá, as you are.' If you have spoken
the truth, and not mere flattery,†† then let this Párijáta-
tree be the ornament of my mansion. I long to shine
amidst my fellow-queens, wearing the flowers of this
tree in the braids of my hair."‡‡

---

* मन्यवादाम ते सुधु अरा वैद्यमेव च ।
अविद्यावनयवारि सर्वकामा अविष्यसि ॥
† The Sanskrit has *deva-rája*.
‡ *Keśisúdana*. I have corrected "Keśi". See Vol. IV., p. 340.
§ See Vol. I., p. 144, and p. 146, note 1.
‖ This description of the Párijáta-tree is rendered very freely. The
original gives it one epithet not here translated,—*sugandháḍhya*, 'rich in
fragrance'. The text followed is that of Śrídhara, from which various
MSS. offer many unimportant deviations.
¶ Professor Wilson read देवपादप.; but, no doubt, we should read
देव पादप:. A variant is found: द्रष्ण पादप: ।
** *Nishkuṭa.* †† *Upachára.* ‡‡ *Keśa-paksha.*
V. 7

Thus solicited by Satyabhámá, Hari smiled upon her, and, taking the Párijáta-plant, put it upon Garuda.* The keepers of the garden (remonstrated and) said: "This Párijáta-tree belongs to Sachí, the queen of the sovereign of the gods. It is not proper, Govinda, for you to remove it. At the time when the ocean was churned for the beverage of immortality,† this tree was produced, for the purpose of providing Sachí with flowery ornaments. You cannot be suffered to depart with it.‡ It is through ignorance that this is sought for by any one; as it is the especial property of her on whose countenance the king of the gods delights to look. And who shall go away with impunity, who attempts to carry it off?§ Assuredly, the king of the gods will punish this audacity; for his hand launches the thunderbolt, and the immortals attend upon his steps.‖ Forbear, then, Kŕishńa; nor provoke the hostility of all the gods.¶ The wise will not commence actions that can be productive only of unpleasant consequences."** Satyabhámá, on hearing these words, was exceedingly offended, and said: "What right has

---

* Called, in the original, Garutmat.

† अमृतमन्थने ।

‡ न चेमी गृहीतेवं गमिष्यसि ।

§ देवराजो मुखप्रेची यस्यासक्ताः परिग्रहम् ।
मौढ्यात्मार्थयसे चेमी गृहीतेवं हि को व्रजेत् ॥.
Some MSS. read देव, instead of चेमी ।

‖ वज्रोत्कटकरं प्रक्रमणुवाकान्ति चामराः ।

¶ तद्बलं सकलैर्देवैर्वियहेण तवाच्युत ।

** विपाकवट्टु यत्कर्म तन्न प्रंचन्ति पण्डिताः ।
"The wise do not commend an act disagreeable in its consequences.'

Śachí, what has Indra,* to the Párijáta-tree? It was
produced at the churning of the ocean, as the common
property of all worlds. Wherefore, gods, should Indra†
alone possess it? In the same manner, guardians of
the grove, as nectar, as the moon, as (the goddess) Śrí
(herself), so the Párijáta-tree is the common property
of all the world; and, since Śachí, confiding in the
strength of her husband's arm, would keep it to herself, away with submission to her!‡ Satyá takes away
the tree. Go quickly; and let Paulomí§ be told what
I have said. Repeat to her this contemptuous message
from Satyabhámá: 'If you are the beloved wife of your
lord, if your husband is obedient to your authority, let
him prevent my husband from carrying off this tree.
I know your husband, Śakra; I know the sovereign of
the divinities; and I, who am a mortal,‖ take this Párijáta-tree away from you.'"

Accordingly, the warders (of the garden) went and
reported to Śachí the message (of Satyabhámá). Śachí
appealed to her husband, and excited the king of the
gods to resent this affront;¶ and Indra, accordingly,
attended by the army of the celestials, marched to attack Hari, in defence of the Párijáta-tree. The gods
were armed with clubs,** swords,†† maces, and darts;

---

* Śakra, in the Sanskrit.
† The original has Vásava.
‡ तत्क्षमतामर्ष चाक्षा ।
§ Patronymic of Puloman, father of Śachí. See Vol. II., p. 72, note 2.
For a less famous Paulomí, see Vol. I., p. 152, note 1, ad finem.
‖ Manushí, 'a woman.' Śachí, no less than Satyabhámá, was "a
mortal".
¶ शची कोत्साहयामास विद्याधिपतिं पतिम् ।
** Parigha.   †† Nistriṁśa.

and Indra* wielded the thunderbolt. As soon as Govinda saw the king of the gods† advancing against
him, on his elephant, attended by the immortals,‡ he
blew his shell, so that the sound filled all the regions,
and he showered, smilingly, myriads of arrows upon
his assailants.§ Beholding the air, in all directions,
overspread with his darts, the celestials (in return,)
hurled innumerable missiles; but every one of these
the destroyer of Madhu,‖ and lord of all worlds, cut,
playfully, into a thousand pieces (with his shafts). The
devourer of serpents (Garuḍa,) laid hold of the noose
of the sovereign of the waters,¶ and tore it to fragments with his beak, as if it had been a little snake.
The son of Devakí threw his mace at the club of Yama,
and cast it, broken, upon the ground. He cut in bits **
the litter†† of the lord of wealth,‡‡ with his discus; a
glance of his eye eclipsed the radiance of the sun;§§ he
severed Agni into a hundred parts, with his arrows,
and scattered the Vasus through the realms of space.
With his discus he cut off the points of the tridents‖‖
of the Rudras, and cast themselves upon the earth; and,

---

* Śakra, in the original.
† For "the king of the gods" the Sanskrit has Śakra.
‡ Literally, 'the gods,'—*deva*.
§ सुमोष च शरजातं सहस्रायुतसंमितम् ।
Professor Wilson's favourite MS. indefensibly ends this verse with
सहस्रायुतसंमितं; whence "smilingly". Read: "And he discharged a
volley of arrows, amounting to myriads of thousands."
‖ Madhusúdana.   ¶ Namely, Varuńa.
** *Tilaśas.* This word denotes that the pieces were no larger than
sesamum-seeds.
†† *Śibiká.*   ‡‡ Kubera, to wit.
§§ चकार गौरिरत्नं च रुद्ध्यूतं इतीव्यसम् ।
‖‖ *Śúla,* 'pikes.'

with the shafts shot from his bow, he dispersed the
Sádhyas, Viśwas,* Maruts, and Gandharvas, like
fleeces of cotton from the pods of the Simel† tree,
through the sky. Garuda,‡ also, diligently plied his
beak, and wings, and nails, and bit, and bruised, and
scratched the deities who opposed his lord.§
  Then the king of the gods and the foe of Madhu ‖
(encountered, and) overwhelmed each other with
countless shafts, like rain-drops falling from two heavy
clouds. Garuda, in the conflict, engaged with Airávata;
and Janárdana was opposed to all the deities. When
all the other weapons had been cut to pieces, Indra¶
stood armed with his thunderbolt, and Krishña, with
the discus Sudarśana.** Beholding them thus prepared
for fight, all the people of the three spheres exclaimed

---

* *Viśwe.* These deities are not mentioned severally, but always col-
lectively. See Vol. III., p. 189, note beginning near the foot.

† ग्राम्बितूखवत् । The original has, thus, *Śálmali.* See Vol. IV.,
p. 240, note ‖.   ‡ The Sanskrit has Garutmat.

§ बद्धाणपि वम्नेव पक्षाभां मखराङ्गुरैः ।
   अवयंवाडयद्देवान्हारयंत पचार वै ॥

Herein is exemplified the figure of speech which is called, in Sanskrit,
yathá-sankhyá. A similar, but more complete, instance of construction by
the correspondent order of terms is afforded in the following couplet:

    "Vir simplex, fortasse bonus, sed pastor ineptus,
    Vult, tentat, peragit, plurima, pauca, nihil."

Stanzas of like verbal collocation might be adduced, in any quantity,
from medieval compositions. In the Third Book of Sir Philip Sidney's
Arcadia is a sonnet contrived, throughout, like its beginning:

    "Vertue, beautie, and speech, did strike, wound, charme,
    My heart, eyes, eares, with wonder, love, delight."

‖ Madhusúdana.   ¶ Vásava, in the original.

** हिमेष्वेवमाबेषु यस्त्रेष्वस्त्रेषु च सरण ।
   अयाह गाखयो वज्र ङ्गव्यबर्क सुदर्शनम् ।

"Alas! alas!" Indra* launched his bolt; but in vain; for Hari caught and arrested it. He forbore, however, to hurl his discus, and only called out to Indra to stay.† Satyabhámá, seeing Indra disarmed, and his elephant disabled by Garuda, and the deity, himself, about to retreat, said to him: "King of the triple sphere, it ill becomes the husband of Sachí to run away. Ornamented with Párijáta-garlands, she will approach you. Of what use‡ is the sovereignty of heaven, embellished with the Párijáta-tree, no longer beholding Sachí meet you with affection, as of yore? Nay, Sakra: fly not! You must not suffer shame. Here, take the Párijáta-tree. Let the gods be no longer annoyed. Sachí, inflated with pride of her husband, has not welcomed me to her dwelling with respectful presents. As a woman, I am light of purpose, and am anxious for my husband's fame. Therefore have I instigated, Sakra, this contest with you. But I do not want the Párijáta-tree; nor do I wish to take that which is another's property. Sachí is proud of her beauty. What woman is not proud of her husband?" Thus spoken to (by Satyabhámá), the king of the gods turned back, and said to her: "Desist, wrathful dame, from afflicting your friend by further reproaches. § I am not ashamed of being vanquished by him who is the author of the creation, preservation,

---

* Mahendra, in the Sanskrit.
† Hereabouts the translation is free.
‡ The insertion, here, of the words "to you", justified by the original, would make this sentence intelligible. The Sanskrit is as follows:

बीकृयं देवराज्यं ते पारिजातखगुल्लजलम् ।
अपक्षतो यथापूर्वं प्रखयादामतां प्रचीम् ॥
§ माइ पैनामलं नखिड खखुः खेदातिनिखरैः ।

and destruction of the world'; who is the substance of
all things;* in whom, without beginning or middle,
the universe is comprised; and from whom, and by
whom, identical with all things, it proceeds, and will
cease to be.† What disgrace is it, O goddess, (to any
one,) to be discomfited by him who is the cause of
creation, continuance, and dissolution? His form is the
parent of all worlds, though infinitely subtile, and
known to those only by whom all that may be known
is known. Who is able to overcome the unborn, uncon-
stituted, eternal lord, who has willed to become a
mortal, for the good of the world?"[1]

---

[1] The Bhágavata: merely says: "Incited by his wife, Krishńa
took away the Párijáta-tree, having subdued the gods, and
planted it in the garden of Satyabhámá." The Hari Vaṁśa
makes a long story of it, and tells it with some variations,
especially in the commencement; Satyabhámá's desire for the
Párijáta-tree having been excited by Nárada's presenting a flower
from it to Krishńa's other spouse, Rukmiṇí.

---

* *Viśwa-rúpin.*

† अखिलमेतत् कस्मैतदृणादिमधे
   यमाधत्तश्च न विन्दति धर्मभूतात् ।

‡ X., Latter Section, IX., 39, 40:

   नोदितो भार्ययोत्याञ्च पारिजातं गच्छति ।
   भारोच सेह्यान्विबुधान्निर्जिल्योपानयत्पुरम् ॥
   स्थापितः सत्यभामाया गृहोद्यानोपयोभिनः ।
   अन्वनुर्धमराः सर्वांस्तन्म्बासवलं षड़ाः ॥

Krishṅa, with Indra's consent, takes the Párijáta-tree to Dwáráká; marries the princesses rescued from Naraka.

KEŚAVA, being thus eulogized by the king of the gods, smiled, and spake gravely to him (in reply). "Thou art Indra," said he, "the king of the celestials. We are (but) mortals, O lord of the world. Thou must pardon, therefore, the offence that I have committed. Let this Párijáta-tree be taken to its appropriate situation. I removed it in compliance with the words of Satyá. Receive back, also, this your thunderbolt, cast at me: for this is your proper weapon, *—the destroyer of your foes." Indra† answered, and said: "Thou beguilest us, O lord, in calling thyself a mortal. But we know thee to be the lord, although not endowed: with subtlety of discernment. Thou art that thou art, engaged in the (active) preservation § of the earth; thou extractest the thorns implanted in her bosom, destroyer of the demon-race.‖ Let this Párijáta-tree be transferred to Dwáráká;¶ and it shall remain upon earth as long as thou abidest in the world of mortals."** Hari, having assented to the proposal of Indra,†† returned to

---

* *Praharaṅa.*
† Śakra, in the original.
‡ That is to say, "although we are not endowed."
§ *Trḋṅa.*
‖ अनतः य्रखनिष्कर्षं करोच्वसुरसूदन ।
¶ The Sanskrit has Dwáravatí.
** मार्त्तलोके त्वया मुक्ते नार्थं संस्तास्यते भुवि ।
†† *Devendra*, in the Sanskrit.

earth, hymned by attendant sages,* saints,† and quir-
isters of heaven.

When Kŕishńa arrived over Dwáraká, he blew his
shell, and delighted all the inhabitants with the sound.
Then, alighting from Garuda, he proceeded, with Satyabhámá, to her garden,‡ and there planted the great
Párijáta-tree, the smell of which perfumed the earth
for three furlongs,§ and an approach to which enabled
every one to recollect (the events of) a prior existence;
so that, on beholding their faces in that tree, all the
Yádavas contemplated themselves in their (original)
celestial forms.‖ Then Kŕishńa took possession of the
wealth, elephants, horses, and women, which he had
recovered from Naraka, and which had been brought
(to Dwáraká) by the servants (of the demon); and, at
an auspicious season, he¶ espoused all the maidens
whom Naraka had carried off (from their friends):
at one and the same moment,** he†† received the
hands of all of them, according to the ritual, in separate
mansions.‡‡ Sixteen thousand and one hundred was
the number of the maidens.§§ And into so many dif-

---

* *Siddha.*
† *Ŕishi.*
‡ *Nishkuʈa.*
§ *Yojana.*

‖ तत्स्ते यादृवाः स्वैं देष्वम्भानमानुषाण् ।
दद्यु: पादपे तस्मिन्कुर्वन्तो मुखदर्शनम् ॥

¶ The Sanskrit here has Janárdana.
** *Kála.*
†† Govinda, in the original.
‡‡ Instead of पुत्रगेहेषु, there is a variant, पुत्रदेहेषु, importing "in
multiplied persons."
§§ Our Puráńa is at variance with itself as to the number of Kŕishńa's
wives. See Vol. IV., p. 112, with which compare pp. 81, 82, *supra.*

ferent forms did the foe of Madhu* multiply himself;
so that every one of the damsels thought that he had
wedded her, in his single person.† And the creator of
the world, Hari, the assumer of universal shape, abode
severally in the dwelling of each of these his wives.‡

---

* Madhusúdana.

† एकैकशेन ताः सर्वा मेनिरे मधुसूदनम् ।
मामेव पाणिग्टहृषं भगवान्कृतवानिति ॥

Śridhara, at least according to my single MS. of his commentary,
begins this stanza with एकैकरूपेन, at the expense of metrical correctness.

‡ निम्नासु च जगत्स्रष्टा तासां गेहेषु केशवः ।
उवास विप्र सर्वासां विश्वरूपधरो हरिः ॥

CHAPTER XXXII.

Children of Kríshńa. Ushá, the daughter of Báńa, sees Aniruddha in a dream, and becomes enamoured of him.

PARÁŚARA.—I have enumerated to you Pradyumna and the other sons of Rukminí. Satyabhámá bore Bhánu[*] and Bhaimarika.[†] The sons of Rohiní were Díptimat, Támrapaksha,[:] and others. The powerful Sámba[§] and other sons were born of Jámbavatí. Bhadravinda[||] and other valiant youths were the sons of Nágnajití. Śaibyá (or Mitravindá¶) had several sons, of whom Sangrámajit was the chief. Vríka and others were begotten (by Hari) on Mádrí.[**] Lakshmaná had Gátravat and others; and Śruta and others were the sons[††] of Kálindí[1],[::] Kríshńa[§§] had sons, also, by his

---

[1] The Bhágavata says, each of his eight queens had ten sons,

---

[*] Two MSS. have Bháru.

[†] Corrected from "Bhairika." In giving this mangled form of the name, Professor Wilson was misled by an error in his favourite MS. The scansion of the line shows that a syllable is missing. Messrs. Böhtlingk and Roth have helped to perpetuate "Bhairika".

[:] Corrected from "Támrapakshi", in which reading Professor Wilson was again led astray by an error in the MS. referred to in the last note. Messrs. Böhtlingk and Roth wrongly credit our Translator with "Támrapakshin". One of my MS. yields Támravarńa; another, "Díptimat and others". Also *vide supra*, p. 79, note ★★.

[§] Corrected from "Śamba". [||] My Ajmere MS. has Bhadramanda.

[¶] Supplied by the Translator, on the authority of the commentator Śrídhara. Ratnagarbha considers Śaibyá as one of Kríshńa's eight wives of the first order;·but he does not identify her, by name, with any one of those specified in note § to p. 78, *supra*.

[**] *Vide supra*, p. 81, note ★.

[††] There were three of them,—unnamed,—according to the reading of my Arrah MS. [::] *Vide supra*, p. 78, note §, and p. 81, note 1.

[§§] Chakrin, in the original.

other wives,—in all, one hundred and eighty thousand.
The eldest of the whole was Pradyumna, the son of
Rukmiņí: his son was Aniruddha, from whom Vajra *
was born: his mother was Úshá,†—the daughter of
Báņa, and granddaughter of Bali,:—whom Aniruddha
won in war.§ On that occasion, a fierce battle took
place between Hari and Śankara, in which the thousand
arms of Báņa were lopped away by the discus of the
former.‖

MAITREYA.—How happened it, (venerable) Brahman,
that a contest on account of Úshá arose between Śiva ¶
and Kŕishńa? And in what manner did Hari cut off
the thousand arms of Báņa?** This, illustrious sir,
thou art able to narrate.††

PARÁŚARA.—Úshá, the daughter of Báņa, having
seen Párvatí sporting with (her lord,) Śambhu, was
inspired with a wish for similar dalliance. The beautiful Gaurí,:: who knows the hearts of all, said to Úshá:

and gives the ten names of each set, with one or two exceptions.§§

---

* Corrected from "Vraja". See Vol. IV., pp. 112, 113.
† Corrected, here and everywhere below, from "Ushá", which, like-
wise, occurs, but not in our Puráńa.   ‡ See Vol. II., p. 69.
§ The original is जनिवत्तो रवे वस: ।
‖ The Sanskrit has Chakrin.   ¶ Hara, in the Sanskrit.
** कर्ष घर्ष च वाखद्द बाह्नलां ज्ञतधाम्हरि: ।
†† The original adds:
      महल्बीतृहलं आतं कर्षां मोतुनिमां हरि: ।
So reads Śrídhara. Ratnagarbha has:
      महल्बीतृहलं आतं कबयाप कबानिमाम् ।
:: The same as Párvatí. See Vol. I., p. 104, note 1.
§§ Vide supra, p. 79, notes *, †, §, ¶, and **; p. 81, notes * and †;
and p. 82, note ‖ ‖.

"Do not grieve. You shall have a husband."* "But when will this be?" thought Úshá to herself. "Or who will be my lord?" On which, Párvatí continued: "He who shall appear to you, princess, in a dream, on the twelfth lunation† of the light half of Vaiśákha, he will be your husband.": Accordingly, as the goddess had foretold, on that lunar day a youth appeared (to Úshá,) in a dream, of whose person she became enamoured. When she woke, and no longer perceived him, she was overcome with sorrow, and, unrestrained by modesty, demanded of her companion whither he had gone. The companion and friend of the princess was Chitralekhá, the daughter of Kumbhánda,§ the minister of Bána. "Of whom do you speak?" inquired she (of Úshá). But the princess, recollecting herself, was ashamed, and remained silent.‖ At length, however, Chitralekhá conciliated her confidence; and she related to her what had passed, and what the goddess had foretold; and she requested her friend to devise some means of uniting her with the person whom she had beheld in her dream.¶

Chitralekhá then delineated the most eminent gods,** demons,†† spirits,‡‡ and mortals, and showed them (to

---

* चलमलर्षतापेन भर्षा लमपि रंखवे ।

† By this word Professor Wilson intends, at variance with scientific precedent, and otherwise entirely without justification, 'lunar day'.

‡ In this sentence, and in the next, the Translator, with commendable taste, has not reproduced the grossness of the original.

§ Corrected from "Kubhánda".

‖ यदा लव्याकुला गारी कचयामास सा सखी ।

¶ देखा तथैव तन्माप्री योऽभुपायः कुरुख तम् ।

** Sura.　　†† Daitya.　　‡‡ Gandharva.

Úshá). Putting aside the portraits of gods, spirits, snake-gods,* and demons,† the princess selected those of mortals, and, amongst them, the heroes of the races of Andhaka and Vŕishńi.‡ When she came to (the likenesses of) Kŕishńa and Ráma, she was confused with shame.§ From (the portrait of) Pradyumna she modestly averted her eyes; but, the moment she beheld the picture of his son, the object of her passion, her eyes wide expanded, and all her bashfulness was discarded.‖ "This is he! This is he!" said she (to Chitralekhá). And her friend, who was endowed with magic power,¶ bade her be of good cheer, and set off, through the air, to Dwáraká.**

---

* *Uraga.*
† *Asura.*
‡ मनुष्येषु ददौ दृष्टिं तेष्वप्यन्धकवृष्णिषु ।
For Andhaka and Vŕishńi, see Vol. IV., pp. 71, *et seq.*
§ *Lajjá-jada.*
‖ दृच्यात्मर्षविकाशिन्या लज्जा क्वापि निराहता ।
¶ *Yoga-gámin.*
** Dwáravatí, in the original.

CHAPTER XXXIII.

Bána solicits Śiva for war: finds Aniruddha in the palace, and makes him prisoner. Krishna, Balaráma, and Pradyumna come to his rescue. Śiva and Skanda aid Bána: the former is disabled; the latter, put to flight. Bána encounters Krishna, who cuts off all his arms, and is about to put him to death. Śiva intercedes; and Krishna spares his life. Vishṇu and Śiva are the same.

BEFORE this took place, Bána had been engaged in the adoration of the three-eyed* (god), and had thus prayed to him: "I am humiliated,† O lord, by (the possession of) a thousand arms in a state of peace. Let some hostilities ensue, in which I may derive some advantage from their possession. Without war, what is the use of these arms? They are but a burthen to me.": Śankara replied: "When thy peacock-banner shall be broken, thou shalt have war,—the delight of the evil spirits that feast on the flesh of man."§ Bána, pleased (by this promise), proffered his thanks‖ to Śambhu, and returned to his palace, where he found his standard broken; at which his joy was increased.

At that time, the nymph Chitralekhá returned (from Dwáraká), and, by the exercise of her magic power, brought Aniruddha (along with her). The guards of

---

* Trilochana. See Vol. I., p. 141.
† Nirvinna.
: कविवर्मेषां बाह्नां साफ़जवनको रव: ।
भविष्यति विना युद्धं भारत मम किं भुवै: ॥
§ पिञ्चितान्विजनाष्ठं प्राप्स्यसि त्वं तदा रवम् ।
‖ The Sanskrit has simply प्रबन्ध ।

the inner apartments, discovering him there with
Úshá,* reported it to the king, who immediately sent
a body of his followers (to seize the prince). But the
valiant youth, taking up an iron club, slew his assailants;† on which, Báńa mounted his car, advanced
against him, and endeavoured to put him to death.
Finding, however, that Aniruddha was not to be subdued by prowess, he followed the counsel of his minister, and brought his magical faculties into the conflict,
by which he succeeded in capturing the Yadu prince,
and binding him in serpent-bonds. ‡

When Aniruddha was missed from Dwáravatí, and
the Yádavas were inquiring of one another whither he
had gone, Nárada came to them, and told them that
he was the prisoner of Báńa; having been conveyed,
by a female possessed of magic faculties, to Śońita-
pura.¹§ When they heard this, they were satisfied;

---

¹ The synonyms of Śońitapura, in the Trikáńda Śesha,‖ are
Devikoťa, Báńapura, Koťívarsha, and Ushávana.¶ The first is,
usually, considered to be the modern Devicotta, in the Carnatic,
which is commonly believed to be the scene of Báńa's defeat.
The name, however, occurs in other parts of India: in the Deccan,
on the banks of the Godávari,—according to Wilford, the capital
of Munja (Asiatic Researches, Vol. IX., p. 199); and in Assam,

---

* तं रममाणं सहोषया ।
† अचान परिचं बीहमाहाय परबीरहा ।
‡ ततखं पन्नगास्त्रेव बबन्ध यदुनन्दनम् ।
§ The translation, hereabouts, is rather free.
‖ II., I., 17.
¶ The better reading, it seems, is Umávana, as in the Haima-koša,
IV., 43, where, also, we find all the synonyms of Śońitapura which are
specified above.

for they had imagined he had been taken away by the
gods, (in reprisal for the Párijáta-tree).* Krishńa,†
therefore, immediately summoned Garuda, who came
with a wish;‡ and, mounting upon him, along with
Bala and Pradyumna, he set off for the city of Báńa.
On their approach to the city, they were opposed by
the spirits who attend on Rudra:§ but these were soon
destroyed by Hari; and he and his companions reached
the vicinity of the town.‖ Here, mighty Fever—an
emanation from Maheśwara,¶ having three feet and
three heads[1],—fought desperately with Vishńu,** in
defence of Báńa. Baladeva, upon whom his ashes were

near Gwálpára, as the city of the Daityas. Asiatic Researches,
Vol. XIV., p. 443. Hamilton†† notices the remains of a city, so
called, in Dinajpoor. In the Káĺiká Puráńa, Báńa is described as
the friend and, apparently, neighbour of Naraka, king of Prág-
jyotisha‡‡ or Assam.

[1] Alluding to the three stages of febrile paroxysms, or to the
recurrence of tertian ague. A contest with this enemy, in the
course of military operations, is an allegory which the British
armies in India too often illustrate.

* तं त्रोषितपुरे श्रुत्वा नीतं विद्याविद्ग्धया ।
त्रोषिता प्रव्रयं जग्मुर्यादृत्वा नामरेरिति ॥
† The Sanskrit has Hari.
‡ I. e., "at his wish".
§ The Translator takes from Śrídhara this explanation of pramatha.
पुरीमवेषे प्रमथैर्युक्तमासीन्महात्मनः ।
यदा बाण्रपुराभ्याग्रं नीला तामरषरं हरिः ॥
¶ Maheśwara is the word translated by "an emanation from Maheśwara."
** Śárnga-dhanwan, "armed with the bow Śárnga," is the term by
which Krishńa is here called, in the original.
†† History, &c. of Eastern India, Vol. II., p. 660.
‡‡ Vide supra, p. 54, note 1; p. 55, note ‡; and p. 88, note 1.

scattered, was seized with burning heat, and his eyelids trembled; but he obtained relief by clinging to the body of Kŕishńa.* Contending, thus, with the divine holder of the bow,† the Fever (emanating from Śiva) was quickly expelled from the person of Kŕishńa by Fever: which he himself engendered.§ Brahmá,‖ beholding the impersonated malady bewildered by the beating inflicted by the arms of the deity, entreated the latter to desist; and the foe of Madhu refrained, and absorbed into himself the Fever he had created.¶ The rival Fever then departed, saying to Kŕishńa: "Those men who call to memory the combat between us shall be (ever) exempt from febrile disease."**

Next, Vishńu overcame and demolished the five fires,[1]†† and, with perfect ease,‡‡ annihilated the army

---

[1] The Áhavaníya, Gárhapatya, Dakshińa, Sabhya, and Ávasathya are the five fires; of which the three first have a religious, and the other two, a secular, character. The first is a fire pre-

---

* तन्नस्त्रास्त्रार्च्संभूततापः क्ष्णाङ्गसंगमात् ।
  ध्वाप बखदेवोऽपि ध्ममामीजितेषः ॥

† To render Śárngin, as Kŕishńa is denominated from his bow spoken of in note ** in the preceding page.

‡ Vaishńava is the epithet given it in the Sanskrit.

§ Kŕishńa here figures as a practitioner of homoeopathy.

‖ Pitámaha, in the original.

¶ नारायणभुजाघातपरिपीड़नविह्वलम् ।
  तं वीच्य च्म्यतामस्त्याह देवः पितामहः ॥
  ततच्च चात्तमेवेति प्रोक्का तं वैष्णवं ज्वरम् ।
  चातम्बेव चयं निम्बे भगवाक्षमधुसूदनः ॥

** Vijwara.

†† "The protectors of that city",—namely, Bána's, says Ratnagarbha.

‡‡ लीलया ।

of the Dánavas. Then the son of Bali (Bána), with the whole of the Daitya* host, assisted by Śankara and Kárttikeya,† fought with Śauri. A fierce combat took place between Hari and Śankara. All the regions shook, scorched by their flaming weapons; and the celestials felt assured that the end of the universe was at hand. Govinda, with the weapon of yawning, set Śankara a-gape; and then the demons: and the demigods at-tendant upon Śiva § were destroyed on every side; for Hara, overcome with incessant gaping, sat down in his car, and was unable longer to contend with Krishńa, whom no acts affect.‖ The deity of war, Kárttikeya,¶ wounded in the arm by Garuda,** struck by the weapons of Pradyumna, and disarmed by the shout of

pared for oblations at an occasional sacrifice; the second is the household fire, to be perpetually maintained; the third is a sacri-ficial fire, in the centre of the other two, and placed to the south; the Sabhya is a fire lighted to warm a party; and the Ávasathya,†† the common domestic or culinary fire. Manu, III., 100, 185,‡‡ and Kullúka Bhatta's explanation. §§

* Daiteya, in the Sanskrit.
† See Vol. I., Preface, p. LXXXIX.; and Vol. II., p. 23.
‡ Daiteya.
§ In definition of pramatha.
‖ Aklishṭa-karman, "unweariable."
¶ For "the deity of war, Kárttikeya," the Sanskrit has, simply, Guha.
** Professor Wilson has followed the reading of Śrídhara, as it appears in the only copy of his commentary to which we, in common, have had access,—गरुडपतवाङः. Ratnagarbha adopts the ordinary lection, गरु-ड्पतवाङः l
†† Corrected from "Ávasatthya."
‡‡ Neither thence nor from Kullúka's comments is much to be gleaned touching the five fires.
§§ Also see Vol. III., p. 175, note §; and Vol. IV., p. 11, note 1.

8*

Hari,* took to flight. Báṅa, when he saw Śaṅkara disabled, the Daityas destroyed, Guha† fled, and Śiva's followers: slain,§ advanced, on his vast car,— the horses of which were harnessed‖ by Nandíśa,—¶ to encounter Kṛishṅa and his associates Bala and Pra-dyumna.** The valiant Balabhadra, attacking the host of Báṅa, wounded them, in many ways, with his ar-rows, and put them to a shameful rout;†† and their sovereign beheld them dragged about by Ráma,‡‡ with his ploughshare, or beaten, by him, with his club, or pierced, by Kṛishṅa,§§ with his arrows. He, therefore, attacked Kṛishṅa; and a fight took place between them. They cast at each other fiery shafts, that pierced through their armour: but Kṛishṅa intercepted, with his arrows, those of Báṅa, and cut them to pieces. Báṅa, nevertheless, wounded Keśava; and the wielder of the discus wounded Báṅa; and both, desirous of victory, and seeking, enraged, the death of his antag-onist, hurled (various) missiles at each other. When

---

* The original has Kṛishṅa.
† *l. e.*, Kárttikeya.
‡ To render *pramatha-sainya*.
§ शार्ङ्गधन्वना, "by the bearer of the bow Śárṅga", the original par-ticularizes.
‖ Read 'driven',—*saṅgṛihíta*.
¶ Also called Nandi and Nandin. Generally he is represented as a follower of Śiva. See Vol. I., Preface, p. LXXXIX., and p. 122.
** The Sanskrit here calls him by his patronym, Kárshṅi.
†† बलभद्रो महावीर्यो बाणसैन्यमनेकधा ।
विव्याध बाणैः प्रधम्य धर्मैतत्सत्यलायत ॥

Ratnagarbha ends the second verse with धर्मैतस्यापलायतः: and some MSS. give, with this reading, संहृष्ट:, instead of प्रधम्य।
‡‡ Bala, in the original.
§§ The Sanskrit has Chakrin.

an infinite number of arrows* had been cut to pieces,
and the weapons began to be exhausted,† Kŕishńa:
resolved to put Báńa to death. The destroyer§ of the
demon-host, therefore, took up his discus, Sudarśana,
blazing with the radiance of a hundred suns As he‖
was in the act of casting it, the mystical goddess Ko-
tavi,¶ the magic lore of the demons, stood, naked,
before him.[1]** Seeing her before him, Krishńa,†† with
unclosed eyes, cast Sudarśana, to cut off the arms‡‡ of
Báńa. The discus, dreaded, in its flight, by the whole
of the weapons of the demons, lopped off, successively,

---

[1] Koŧaví (कोटवी) is said to be an eighth portion of Rudráńi,
and the tutelary goddess of the Daityas, composed of incantations
(मन्त्रमयी).§§ The Hari Vaṁśa calls her, also, Lambá, and in-
timates her being the mother of Báńa, and as identical with
Durgá. The word, in the lexicons, designates a naked woman,
and is, thence, applicable to Durgá, in some of her forms.

---

* The Sanskrit yields "all the arrows".

† अस्त्रे च सीदति माधवेन । Ratnagarbha explains this as follows:
माधवेनास्त्रे सीदति चीर्ष सति ।

‡ Hari, in the original.

§ Read "enemy",—ari.

‖ Here called, in the original, by his epithetical appellation, Madhu-
dwish, or Madhuvidwish, according to various copies.

¶ Variant: Kodavi. And Ratnagarbha, in my best MSS., has Koŧŧavi.

** नग्ना दैतेयविद्याभूत्कोटवी पुरतो हरेः ।
Ratnagarbha says: कोटुवी दैतविद्या मन्त्रमयी दैत्यकुलदेवता ।
Also see note §§, below.

†† The Sanskrit has Hari.

‡‡ बाहुवनं, according to Śridhara. बाहुवनं is Ratnagarbha's reading.

§§ This is from Śridhara, who says: कोटवी नाम दैतेयानां विद्या-
मन्त्रमयी कुलदेवता रुद्राखा अष्टमांग्रः ।

‖‖ Śl. 10722.

the numerous arms of the Asura. Beholding Kríshńa
with the discus again in his hand, and preparing to
launch it once more, for the total demolition of Báńa,
the foe of Tripura * (Śiva,) respectfully addressed him.†
The husband of Umá,‡ seeing the blood streaming from

---

* In the Eighth Chapter of the *Revd-máhátmya*, it is said, that Tripuri-
kshetra, where Śiva flung down Tripura, the Asura, lies to the north of
the Narmadá. The Twenty-ninth Chapter of the same work somewhat
discordantly relates as follows. The demon Báńa, in reward of his austerities as a votary of Śiva, received from him the gift of a city. Brahmá
and Vishńu adding, each, another, he obtained the epithet of Tripura, or
Τρίπολις. When slain by Śiva, as he was traversing the heavens, a
part of his carcase fell near the well-known mountain Śriśaila, in Siddha-
kshetra; another fragment, not far from Amarakáńtaka; and the remainder,
in the vicinity of Gangáságara. The weapon, Aghorástra, with which
he was demolished, reached the earth at a point of the Narmadá hard
by Jaleśwaratirtha, and sank to Rasátala, the nethermost of the infernal
stages.

Where this tale is briefly rehearsed in the *Gańeśa Upapuráńa*,— Prior
Section, Chapter LXXI.,— Báńa carries off Pradyumna, whose father,
Kríshńa, attacks the giant, and, after propitiating Gańeśa, overcomes the
monster, and takes possession of his city, Sońitapura. Some ten chapters
of the first half of the *Gańeśa Upapuráńa*, beginning with the thirty-eight.
are taken up with Tripura or Báńa.

Tripuri, the capital of the Chedis,—a place connected with the preceding
legends,— I discovered, while exploring the banks of the Narmadá, in the
insignificant village of Tewar. See the *Journal of the American Oriental
Society*, Vol. VI., p. 516.

† The Translator has strangely misunderstood the import of the following stanzas:

क्रमेव तनु बाह्लनां बाषक्षान्धुतनोदितम् ।
छेदं चक्रेऽसुरापाक्तयुक्लीषपधावृतम् ॥
छिन्ने बानुसहस्ते तु करखं मधुसूदनः ।
सुमुसुर्बाखनाग्राय विषातस्तिपुरद्विषा ॥

Ratnagarbha reads -नोदितं, for -गोदितं; -चेपव°, for -चपव°;
and बाज्रवने तख, for बानुसहस्ते तु. One other variant which I find is
बाज्रवने तख; and my Ajmere MS. interpolates, after the first verse of
the extract:

चिच्छेद चक्रं बाह्लनां सहस्रमतिवेगवत् ।

‡ Umápati.

the dissevered arms of Bána, approached Govinda, to solicit a suspension of hostilities,[*] and said to him: "Kŕishńa, Kŕishńa, lord of the world, I know thee, first of spirits,[†] the supreme lord, infinite felicity, without beginning or end, and beyond all things.[‡] This sport of universal being, in which thou takest the persons of god, animals, and men, is a subordinate attribute of thy energy.[§] Be propitious, therefore, O lord, (unto me). I have given Bána assurance of safety. Do not thou falsify that which I have spoken. He has grown old in devotion[‖] to me. Let him not incur thy displeasure. The Daitya has received a boon from me; and, therefore, I deprecate thy wrath." When he had concluded, Govinda, dismissing his resentment against the Asura, looked graciously on the lord of Umá,[¶] the wielder of the trident,[**] and said to him: "Since you, Śankara, have given a boon unto Bána, let him live. From respect to your promises, my discus is arrested.[††] The assurance of safety granted by you is granted (also,) by me. You are fit to apprehend that you are not distinct from me.[‡‡] *That* which I am thou art; and

---

[*] सामपूर्वम् ।
[†] *Purushottama.*
[‡] "Beyond all things" is to render *para.*
[§] देवतिर्यङ्मनुष्येषु शरीरेष्वङ्गलिका ।
    लीलेयं सर्वभूतस्य तव चेष्टोपलक्षणा ॥
[‖] *Saṁśraya.*
[¶] *Umápati.*
[**] *Śúla-páńi.*
[††] त्वद्वाक्यगौरवादेतमया चक्रं निवर्तितम् ।
[‡‡] मत्तोऽविभिन्नमात्मानं द्रष्टुमर्हसि शंकर ।
"You must perceive," &c.

that, also, is this world, with its gods, demons,* and
mankind. Men contemplate distinctions, because they
are stupified by ignorance," So saying, Kŕishńa went
to the place where the son of Pradyumna† was confined. The snakes that bound him were destroyed,
being blasted by the breath of Garuḍa; and Kŕishńa,
placing him,: along with his wife, upon the celestial
bird, § returned, with Pradyumna and Ráma, to Dwáraká. ¹‖

---

¹ There can be little doubt that this legend describes a serious
struggle between the Śaivas and Vaishńavas, in which the latter,
according to their own report, were victorious: and the Śaivas,
although they attempt to make out a sort of compromise between
Rudra and Kŕishńa, are obliged to admit his having the worst
of the conflict, and his inability to protect his votary. The Bhágavata tells the story much as the text. The Hari Vaṁśa ampli-
fies, even more than usual; the narrative occupying nearly se-
venty pages of the French translation. The legend is to be found,
to the same purport, but in various degrees of detail, in the Agni
Puráńa, Kúrma Puráńa, Padma Puráńa (Uttara Khaṇḍa), Vámana Puráńa, and Brahma Vaivarta Puráńa, (Kŕishńa Janma
Khaṇḍa).

* *Asura*.
† In the original, Prádyumni.   Aniruddha is intended.
: The Sanskrit has Aniruddha.
§ To represent Garutmat.
‖ बाअरमुर्वारकां रामकार्ष्णिदामोदरः पुरीम् ।
"Ráma, Kárshńi, and Dámodara went to the city of Dwáraká."

CHAPTER XXXIV.

Paundraka, a Vásudeva, assumes the insignia and style of Krishna, supported by the king of Kási. Krishna marches against and destroys them. The son of the king sends a magical being against Krishna: destroyed by his discus, which also sets Benares on fire, and consumes it and its inhabitants.

MAITREYA.—Of a truth, the divine Śauri, having assumed a mortal body, performed great achievements in his easy victories over Śakra, and Śiva,* and all their attendant divinities.† I am now desirous to hear from you, illustrious (sage), what other mighty exploit the humiliator of the prowess of the celestials performed.

PARÁŚARA.—Hear, excellent Brahman, ‡ with reverent attention, an account of the burning of Váránasí§ by Krishna, in the course of his relieving the burthens of the earth.∥

There was a Vásudeva who was called Paundraka,[1]

---

[1] From being, the commentator ¶ says, king of Pundra.** The

---

* Śarva, in the original.

† चक्रे कर्म महच्छौरिर्विधायो मानुषीं तनुम् ।
विगाय शर्म धर्मं च सर्वदेवांश्च लीलया ॥

‡ Viprarshi; the same as Brahmarshi, for which term see Vol. III., p. 68, text and note 1.

§ Corrected, here and everywhere below, from "Varánaśí" or "Varánaśí."

∥ भारावतारे । Variant: नरावतारे ।

¶ The two commentators have identically the same explanation of the name in question: पौंड्रदेशज:, "born in the country of the Paundras." They do not call Paundraka a king.

** See Vol. II., p. 170, note 5.

and who, though not *the* Vásudeva, was flattered, by ignorant people, as the descended deity, until he fancied himself to be the Vásudeva[1] who had come down upon earth.* Losing all recollection (of his real character), he assumed the emblems of Vishńu, and sent an ambassador to the magnanimous Krishńa, with this message: "Relinquish, thou foolish fellow, the discus. Lay aside all my insignia, my name, and the character of Vásudeva, and come and do me homage; and I will vouchsafe thee means of subsistence."† At which, Janárdana laughed, and replied: "Go, messenger, back to Pauńdraka, and say to him, from me: 'I will despatch: to thee my emblem the discus, without fail. Thou wilt rightly apprehend my meaning, and consider what is to be done; for I shall come to

Bhágavata§ calls him chief of the Kárúshas;‖ the Padma, king of Kási; but the Bhágavata, as well as our text, makes the king of Kási¶ his friend and ally.

[1] According to the Padma Puráńa, he propitiates Śiva, and obtains from him the insignia which constitute a Vásudeva. The different authorities for this legend all use the term Vásudeva in the sense of a title.

* पौण्ड्रको वासुदेवस्तु वासुदेवोऽभवन्भुवि ।
   जयतीर्थास्त्वमिश्रुको अभैरज्ञानमोहितः ॥
   स मेने वासुदेवोऽहमवतीर्णो महीतले ।

† वासुदेवात्मकं मूढ मुक्ता सर्वं विशेषतः ।
   आत्मनो जीवितार्थाय ततो मे प्रणतिं व्रज ॥

सर्वं, for सर्वं, is the reading of some MSS.

: समुत्स्रक्षे ।

§ X., Latter Section, Chapter XVI.
‖ See Vol. III., p. 240, notes 1, *etc.*
¶ In all such cases, read "king of the Kásis."

thy city, bringing the discus with me, and shall, un-doubtedly, consign* it to thee. If thou wilt command me to come, I will immediately obey, and be with thee to-morrow. There shall be no delay. † And, having sought thy asylum, I will so provide, O king, that I shall never more have anything to dread from thee.'"

So saying, he dismissed the ambassador, (to report these words to his sovereign), and, summoning,‡ Garuḍa,§ mounted him, and set off for the city (of Paundraka¹).

---

¹ The Hari Vaṁśa and Padma Puráṅa send Pauṅdraka to Dwáraká. According to the latter, Nárada incites Pauṅdraka to the aggression, telling him he cannot be a Vásudeva till he has overcome Kṛishṅa. He goes, and is killed. The former work, as usual, enters into particulars of its own invention. Kṛishṅa is absent on a visit to Śiva at Kailása; and, during his absence, Pauṅdraka, assisted by Ekalavya, king of the Nishádas, makes a night-attack upon Dwáraká. They are resisted by the Yádavas, under Sátyaki and Balaráma; by the former of whom Pauṅdraka is repeatedly overthrown, and all but slain. He requires so much killing, however, that he is likely to obtain the victory; when Kṛishṅa comes to the aid of his kinsmen, and, after a protracted encounter, described in language employed a hundred times before, kills his competitor. The whole of the sections called the Kailása Yátrá—or Kṛishṅa's Journey to Kailása,—must have been wanting in the copy used by M. Langlois, as they are not included in his translation. The chapters of the Hari Vaṁśa,

---

* समुत्सृजामि ।

† आज्ञापूर्वं च यदिदमानच्छेति लयोदितम् ।
संपादयिष्ये स्वभुजं तद्विषोऽविलम्बितम् ॥

‡ संयुज्य, "calling to mind."

§ In the Sanskrit, Garutmat.

‖ See Vol. IV., p. 113, note 1.

When the king of Káśi* heard of the preparations of
Keśava, he sent his army (to the aid of Pauńdraka),
himself bringing up the rear;† and, with the force of
the king of Káśi,: and his own troops, Pauńdraka, the
(false) Vásudeva, marched to meet Kŕishńa. § Hari
beheld him afar off, standing in his car, holding a discus, a club, a mace,‖ a scimitar, and a lotos, in his
hands; ornamented with a garland of flowers; bearing
a bow; and having his standard made of gold. He had,
also, the Śrívatsa¶ mark delineated on his breast; he
was dressed in yellow garments, and decorated with
ear-rings and a tiara.** When the god whose standard
is Garuda beheld him, he laughed with a deep laugh,
and engaged in conflict with the hostile host of cavalry
and elephants, fighting with swords,†† scimitars,::

according to his enumeration of them, are 261: my copy
has 316. §§

---

* *Káśi-pati.* See note :, below.
† सर्वसैन्यपरीवारः पार्ष्णिग्राह उपाययौ ।
Ratnagarbha defines पार्ष्णिग्राहः by सहायः, 'ally.' Compare Vol. IV.,
p. 2, text and note ¶.
: *Káśi-rája.* See Vol. IV., p. 344, supplementary note on p. 87.
§ The original has Keśava.
‖ Probably the Translator forgot to strike out this word, after inserting
'club'. Kŕishńa has only four insignia, named, in the original, as
follows:
चक्रहस्तं गदाखड्गबाणं पार्ष्णिगताम्बुजम् ।
For Kŕishńa's complete equipment of weapons, *vide infra,* p. 149.
¶ *Vide supra,* p. 13, text and note :. For the *śrívatsa* of the Jainas,
see Colebrooke's *Miscellaneous Essays,* Vol. II., p. 210.
** *Kirita.*   †† *Nistriṁśá.*   :: *Ŕishti.*
§§ The Calcutta edition has 326; the Bombay edition, 317, in three
Sections of 55, 128, and 134, severally.

maces, tridents,* spears,† and bows. Showering upon
the enemy the shafts from his Śárnga: bow, and hurl-
ing at them his mace and discus, he § quickly destroyed
both the army of Pauṅdraka and that of the king of
Káśi.| He then said to the former, who was foolishly
wearing his emblems: "Pauṅdraka, you desired me, by
your envoy, to resign to you all my insignia. I now
deliver them to you. Here is my discus. Here I give
up my mace. And here is Garuḍa:¶ let him mount upon
thy standard." Thus speaking, he let fly the discus
and the mace, by which Pauṅdraka was cut to pieces,
and cast on the ground; whilst the Garuḍa (on his
banner) was demolished by the Garuḍa (of Vishṇu).
The people, beholding this sight, exclaimed "Alas!
alas!" But the valiant king of Káśi,** adhering to the
imposture of his friend, continued the conflict,†† till
Sauri‡‡ decapitated him with his arrows, shooting his
head into the city of Káśi,§§ to the marvel of all the
inhabitants. Having, thus, slain Pauṅdraka and the
king of Káśi,||| with all their followers, Sauri returned

* Śúla, 'pikes'.
† Śakti.
‡ Corrected from "Śáranga", a mistake found in Professor Wilson's
Hindu-made version.
§ Janárdana, in the original.
|| Káśi-rája.
¶ Garutmat, in the Sanskrit; and so twice, just below.
** काशीनामधिप:, "king of the Káśis," literally.
†† युयुधे वासुदेवेन मिन्नव्यापचिन्ती स्थित: ।
The two commentators remark, in the same words: व्यपचिन्ती ।
व्यावृत्ते स्थित: सन्युयुधे ।
‡‡ This name does not appear in the original.
§§ Káśi-puri, "the city of the Káśis."
||| Káśi-rája.

to Dwáraká,* where he lived in the enjoyment of heavenly delights.†

When the inhabitants of Kási: saw the head of their king§ shot into their city, they were much astonished, and wondered how it could have happened, and by whom the deed could have been done.‖ Having ascertained that the king had been killed by Kríshńa,¶ the son of the monarch (of Kási),[1] together with the priest of the family, propitiated Śankara; and that deity, well pleased to be adored in the sacred place** Avimukta,†† desired the prince to demand a boon. On which he prayed, and said: "O lord, mighty god, through thy favour, let thy mystic spirit‡‡ arise to destroy Kríshńa, the murderer of my father." "It shall be so," answered Śankara. And from out of the southern fire§§ upsprang a vast and formidable female,[2] like flame out of

---

[1] The Bhágavata‖‖ names him Sudakshiná; the Padma, Dańdapáńi.

[2] A personified Krityá, a magical creation. The Padma has

---

* The Sanskrit has Dwáravatí.

† पुनर्द्वारवतीं प्राप्तो रेमे स्वर्गनतो यथा ।

‡ Not literal.

§ Kási-pati.

‖ तच्छिरः पतितं दृष्ट्वा तथ काश्यिपतेः पुरे ।
अग्रः किमेतदिलाह केनेत्यब्रत्तविस्मितः ॥

¶ Vásudeva, in the original.

** Mahá-kshetra.

†† This name of Benares is found in the Kási-khańda, as well. It occurs, also, in the Jábála Upanishad. See my Benares, &c., p. 4, note 2.

‡‡ "Thy mystic spirit" is to translate krityá, for which see note 2 in the present page.

§§ Dakshińágni. Vide supra, p. 114, note 1.

‖‖ X., Latter Section, XVI., 27.

fire, blazing with ruddy light, and with fiery radiance streaming amidst her hair.* Angrily she called upon Krishña, and departed to Dwáraká;† where the people, beholding her, were struck with dismay, and fled, for protection, to Madhusúdana, the refuge of all worlds. The wielder of the discus,‡ knowing that the fiend § had been produced by the son of the king of Kási,‖ through his adoration of the deity whose emblem is a bull, and being engaged in sportive amusements, and playing at dice, said to the discus: "Kill this fierce creature, ¶ whose tresses are of plaited flame." Accordingly, Sudarsana, the discus of Vishñu, immediately attacked the fiend,** fearfully enwreathed with fire, and wearing tresses of plaited flame.†† Terrified at the might of Sudarsana, the creation of Mahes'wara‡‡ awaited not his attack, but fled with speed, pursued by him with equal velocity, until she reached Váráñasí, repelled by the superior might of the discus of Vishñu.

the same. The Bhágavata makes the product of the sacrificial fire a male, and sends him to Dwáraká, accompanied by a host of Bhútas, Śiva's attendant goblins.

* My MSS. present a great variety of readings in the epithets applied to the being under description.
† Dwáravatí, in the Sanskrit.
‡ Chakrin.
§ Mahá-kritydá.
‖ Kási-rája.
¶ Krityá.
** Krityá.
†† This is far from literal; and the same may be said of the remainder of the paragraph.
‡‡ ज्ञ्या माहेश्वरी ।

The army of Kási,* and the host of the demigods attendant upon Śiva,† armed with all kinds of weapons, then sallied out, to oppose the discus; but, skilled in the use of arms, he consumed (the whole of) the forces by his radiance, and then set fire‡ to the city, in which the magic power of Śiva§ had concealed herself.[1] Thus was Váráńasí burnt, with all its princes and their followers, its inhabitants, horses, elephants, and men, treasures and granaries, houses, palaces,‖ and markets.¶ The whole of a city that was inaccessible to the gods** was, thus, wrapped in flames by the discus of Hari, and was totally destroyed. The discus, then, with unmitigated wrath, and blazing fiercely, and far from satisfied with the accomplishment of so easy a task, returned to the hand of Vishńu.[2]††

---

[1] According to the Bhágavata, the magical being, himself, destroys Sudakshińa and his priest; but Sudarśana consumes the people and the city. The Padma ascribes the destruction of the king and all his city to the discus. The Hari Vaṁśa closes its narrative with the death of Paundraka, and makes no mention of the destruction of Benares. The circumstance‡‡ is alluded to, in a preceding section (s. 159), by Nárada, when detailing the exploits of Kṛishńa.

[2] In this legend, again, we have a contest between the followers

---

* Káśi-bala; which may mean either "the army of the Káśis" or "the army of the king of the Káśis."

† This phrase is to represent pramatha.

‡ हरधा implies combustion.

§ "The magic power of Śiva" is to render kṛityá.

‖ Prákára.　　　　　　　　¶ Chatwara.

** दुर्निरीधां दुरैरपि ।

†† The latter portion of this paragraph is translated very freely.

‡‡ Namely, of the burning of Benares.

of Vishńu and Śiva intimated; as, besides the assistance given, by the latter, to Pauńdraka, Benares—Váráńasí or Avimuktu, *
—has been, from all time, as it is at present, the high place of the Śaiva worship.† There is, also, an indication of a Vaishńava schism, in the competition between Pauńdra and Krishńa for the title of Vásudeva and the insignia of his divinity.

---

* Corrected from "Atimukti". *Vide supra*, p. 126, text and note ††.

† See my *Benares*, &c., p. 18, note 2.

CHAPTER XXXV.

Sámba carries off the daughter of Duryodhana, but is taken prisoner. Balaráma comes to Hastinápura, and demands his liberation: it is refused: in his wrath, he drags the city towards him, to throw it into the river. The Kuru chiefs give up Sámba and his wife.

MAITREYA.—I have a (great) desire to hear, (excellent) Brahman, some further account of the exploits of Balaráma.* You have related to me his dragging the Yamuná,† and other mighty deeds; but you can tell me, venerable sir,‡ some other of his § acts.

PARÁSARA.- Attend, Maitreya, to the achievements performed by Ráma, who is the eternal, illimitable Śesha, the upholder of the earth. At the choice of a husband by the daughter‖ of Duryodhana, the princess was carried off by the hero Sámba, the son of Jámbavatí.¶ Being pursued by Duryodhana,** Karña,†† Bhíshma,‡‡ Drona, and other celebrated chiefs, who were incensed at his audacity, he was defeated and taken prisoner.§§ When the Yádavas heard of the oc-

---

* Balabhadra, in the Sanskrit.
† Vide supra, pp. 65—68.
‡ Mahábhága.
§ Bala's, according to the original.
‖ Her name was Lakshmaná, according to the Bhágavata-puráńa, X., Latter Section, XVIII., 1.
¶ Vide supra, p. 79, note ¶; and p. 107.
** See Vol. IV., p. 158.
†† Ibid., pp. 102 and 126.
‡‡ Ibid., p. 157.
§§ ततः कुड्डा महावीर्याः कर्णदुर्योधनादयः ।
भीष्मद्रोणादयश्वैनं वबन्धुर्युधि निर्जितम् ॥
The translation of this stanza, as will be seen, is considerably interpolated.

currence, their wrath was kindled against Duryodhana
and his associates; and they prepared to take up arms
against them.* But Baladeva,† in accents interrupted
by the effects of ebriety,: forbade them, and said: "I
will go, alone, to the sons of Kuru.§ They will liberate
Sámba, at my request." Accordingly, he went to the
elephant-styled city‖ (Hastinápura), but took up his
abode in a grove without the town, which he did not
enter. When Duryodhana and the rest heard that he ¶
had arrived there, they sent him a cow, a present of
fruits and flowers, and water.** Bala received the offering in the customary form, and said to the Kauravas:
"Ugrasena†† commands you to set Sámba at liberty."
When Bhíshma, Drona, Karna, Duryodhana, and the
others heard this, they were (very) angry; and Báhlíka:: and other (friends of the) Kauravas, who looked
upon the Yadu race as not entitled to regal dignity,
said to the wielder of the club:§§ "What is this, Balabhadra, that thou hast uttered? What Yádava shall
give orders to the chiefs of the family of Kuru?‖‖ If
Ugrasena issues his mandates to the Kauravas, then

---

* चबुच ताबिहनुं महोबमम् ।

† The Sanskrit has Bala.

: मद्सोलकक्ताचरम् ।

§ *Kaurava.*

‖ I find two readings,— नगरं गागसाङ्ूर्यं and नगरं गजसाङ्ूयम् ।
For Hastinápura or Hástinapura, see Vol. IV., p. 139.

¶ Bala, in the original.

** गामर्घ्यमुद्कं चैव रामाय प्रत्यवेद्यन् ।

†† See Vol. IV., p. 98; also, *supra*, p. 45.

:: See Vol. IV, p. 154, where correct "Váhlika".

§§ *Musaláyudha.* Vide *supra*, p. 67, note **.

‖‖ See Vol. IV., pp. 148 and 152.

we must take away the white umbrella that he has usurped, and which is fit only for kings.* Depart, therefore, Balaráma.† You are entitled to our respect: but Sámba has been guilty of improper conduct; and we will not liberate him, either at Ugrasena's commands, or yours. The homage that is due to us, their superiors, by the Kukura‡ and Andhaka§ tribes, may not be paid by them. But who ever heard of a command issued by a servant to his master?‖ Elevation to an equal seat has rendered you arrogant. We have committed a great mistakě, in neglecting, through our friendship for you, the policy (that teaches the danger of treating the abject with deference).¶ Our sending you (to-day,) a respectful present** was an intimation

---

* तद्दलं पाण्डुरैरछवैर्नृपयोर्ग्यिर्विडम्बिते: ।

So reads Śrídhara, from whom Ratnagarbha differs, in ending the verse with अलंक्षते: ।

† Bala, in the Sanskrit.

‡ Corrected from "Kukkura". For Kukura, see Vol. IV., p. 97.

§ See Vol. IV., p. 96. Instead of the ordinary reading, कुकुराम्बकै:, my oldest and best MSS. of Ratnagarbha's text have कुरबाम्बवे:, "titular Kurus."

‖ प्रयातिर्या क्रताक्राकमार्याणां कुकुराम्बकै: ।
न नाम सा क्रता केयमाच्या स्वामिनि भृत्वत: ॥

This is Śrídhara's reading. Ratnagarbha substitutes मान्वानां for आर्याणां, and भृत्ववत् for भृत्वत: । Also see note §, above. It is scarcely worth while to dwell on the Translator's misapprehension of this unimportant passage.

In the couplet cited occurs the word árya, in connexion with which the reader will, perhaps, pardon a digression. The reverse of árya, anárya, 'disreputable', has, in Hindi, become corrupted into anári, 'inexpert', 'artless', 'stupid'. It being assumed, further, by popular etymology, that anári is compounded of a and nári, we have, by the prefixing of su, 'good', to the latter, sunári, 'expert', 'knowing', 'clever'.

¶ को दोषो भवतां नीतिर्यत्नीत्वा नावलोकिता ।

** Argha.

of (personal) regard, which it was neither fit for our race to have proffered, nor for yours to have expected."

Having thus spoken, the Kuru chiefs, unanimously refusing to set the son of Hari at large, immediately returned into the city.* Bala, † rolling about with intoxication, and the wrath which their contemptuous language had excited, struck the ground furiously with his heel, so that it burst to pieces with a loud sound that reverberated through the regions of space. ‡ His eyes reddened with rage, and his brow was curved with frowns, as he exclaimed: "What arrogance is this, in such vile and pithless creatures! The sovereignty of the Kauravas, as well as our own, is the work of fate, § whose decree it, also, is, that they now disrespect or disobey the commands of Ugrasena. Indra ‖ may, of right, give his orders to the gods; and Ugrasena exercises equal authority with the lord of Sachí. Fie upon the pride that boasts a throne the leavings of a hundred mortals! ¶ Is not he the sovereign of the earth, the wives of whose servants adorn themselves with the blossoms of the Párijáta-tree? Ugrasena shall be the undisputed king of kings; for I will not return to his capital, until I have rid the world wholly of the sons of Kuru.** I will destroy Karṇa,

---

* विविगुर्गजसाङ्कूयम् ।   † The original has Haláyudha.
‡ A free rendering; and so is the rest of the Chapter, generally.
§ Kála.   ‖ Sachípati, in the Sanskrit.

¶ धिग्गुगुष्यातोच्छिष्टे तुष्टिरेषां नृपासने ।

So reads Śrídhara. Ratnagarbha begins the verse with धिग्गुगुषा-
यामुच्छिष्टे ।

** समस्तभूर्ज्जां नाथ उग्रसेनः स तिष्ठतु ।

अथ निज्कौरवामुर्वीं कृत्वा यास्यामि तत्पुरीम् ॥

Duryodhana, Droṅa, Bhíshma, Báhlíka, Duḣsásana,* Bhúriśravas,† Somadatta,‡ Śala,§ Bhíma, Arjuna, Yudhishṭhira, ‖ the twins,¶ and all the other vile descendants of Kuru, with their horses, elephants, and chariots. I will rescue the hero Sámba from captivity, and carry him, along with his wife, to Dwáraká, where I shall again behold Ugrasena and the rest of my kin. Or, authorized by the king of the gods to remove the burthens of the earth, I will take this capital of the Kauravas,** with all the sons of Kuru, and cast the city of the elephant†† into the Bhágírathí."‡‡

So saying, the wielder of the club, §§ (Baladeva), his eyes red with rage, plunged the blade of his ploughshare ‖‖ downwards, beneath the ramparts of the city, ¶¶ and drew them towards him. When the Kauravas beheld Hastinápura tottering, they were much alarmed, and called loudly (on Ráma), saying: "Ráma, Ráma! Hold, hold! Suppress your wrath! Have mercy upon us! Here is Sámba, and his wife, also, delivered up to

---

* See Vol. IV., p. 158.

† Ratnagarbha's text introduces both Bhúri and Bhúriśravas.

‡ For Somadatta and his sons, Bhúri, Bhúriśravas, and Śala, see Vol. IV., p. 157.

§ Corrected from "Śalya", for which I find no authority. See note ‡, above‖; also, *supra*, p. 70, text and note **.

‖ For these three personages, see Vol. IV., pp. 102 and 159.

¶ According to the commentators, Nakula and Sahadeva. See, for them, Vol. IV., pp. 103 and 159.

** Kauravádháni.

†† नगरं नागसाह्वयम् ।

‡‡ See Vol. III., p. 303.

§§ Musaldyudha. Vide supra, p. 87, note **.

‖‖ "The blade of his ploughshare" is to render hala. Vide supra, p. 51, note ‖.

¶¶ Prákára-vapra.

thee. Forgive our sins, committed in ignorance of thy
wondrous power."* Accordingly, issuing, hurriedly,
from the city, the Kauravas delivered Sámba and his
bride to the mighty Balaráma, who, bowing to Bhíshma, Dróna, and Kŕipa,† who addressed him in concil-
iatory language, said "I am satisfied," and so desisted.
The city bears the marks of the shock it received, even
to the present day,—such was the might of Ráma,—
proving both his strength and prowess. The Kauravas,
then, offering homage to Sámba and to Bala,‡ dismissed the former, with his wife and a bridal portion.[1]

---

[1] This adventure is related in the Bhágavata, and very briefly
noticed in the Hari Vaṁśa; but I have not found any mention
of it in the Mahábhárata. It may have been suggested, originally,
by Hastinápura having sustained some injury, either from an
earthquake, or from the encroachments of the river, which, as is
recorded, compelled the removal of the capital to Kauśámbí
(Vol. IV., p. 164).

---

* अविज्ञातप्रभावार्हां यभ्तामपराधिनाम् ।
† See Vol. IV., p. 147.
‡ Halin, in the Sanskrit. *Vide supra*, p. 84, note ९. Halin means
the same as Haláyudha, for which *vide supra*, p. 63, text and note ‖.

CHAPTER XXXVI.

The Asura Dwivida, in the form of an ape, destroyed by Balaráma.

HEAR, also, Maitreya, another exploit performed by the mighty Balaráma.* The great Asura,† the foe of the friends of the gods, Naraka,‡ had a friend, of exceeding prowess, in the monkey named Dwivida, who was animated by implacable hostility against the deities, and vowed to revenge on the whole of them the destruction of Naraka by Kríshńa, at the instigation of the king of the celestials, by preventing sacrifices, and effecting the annihilation of the mortal sphere. Blinded by ignorance, he, accordingly, interrupted all religious rites, subverted all righteous observances, and occasioned the death of living beings. He set fire to the forests, to villages, and to towns; sometimes he overwhelmed cities and hamlets with falling rocks; or, lifting up mountains in the waters,§ he cast them into the ocean: then, taking his place amidst the deep, he agitated the waves, until the foaming sea rose above its confines, and swept away the villages and cities situated upon its shores. Dwivida, also, who could assume what shape he would, enlarged his bulk to an immense size: and, rolling, and tumbling, and trampling amidst the cornfields, he crushed and spoiled

---

* Bala, in the original.
† Asurendra.
‡ Vide supra, pp. 87, et seq.
§ तोयेषु । Some MSS. have पोतेषु,—"in boats",—a reading noticed by Ratnagarbha.

the harvests.* The whole world, disordered by this iniquitous monkey, was deprived of sacred study† and religious rites.: and was greatly afflicted.

On one occasion, Haláyudha§ was drinking in the groves of Raivata, along with the illustrious Revatí‖ and other beautiful females; and the distinguished Yadu, in whose praises songs were sung, and who was preeminent amidst graceful and sportive women, resembled Kubera, the god of riches, in his palace.¶ Whilst thus engaged, the monkey (Dwivida) came there, and, stealing the ploughshare** and the club of Baladeva,†† grinned at and mocked him,‡‡ and laughed at the women, and threw over and broke the cups filled with wine.§§ Balaráma,‖‖ becoming angry at this,

---

* कामरूपी महारूपं कृत्वा सस्वान्यषेषतः ।
गुल्मस्थमवसंमर्दैः संपूर्षयति वानरः ।

† Swádhyáya.

‡ Vashatkára. See Vol. II., p. 29, note §; and Vol. III., p. 122, note †.

§ Vide supra, p. 63, note ‖.   ‖ See Vol. III., p. 264.

¶ उपगीयमानो विलसज्जनानामौलिमधग्रः ।
रेमे यदुवरश्रेष्ठः कुबेर एव मन्दिरे ॥

So reads Śrídhara, according to the only copy of his commentary at my command. Both the scholiasts give the first line hypermetrical, as above; but Ratnagarbha has -लोक°, instead of -मौलि°. In lieu of Śrídhara's मन्दिरे, at the end of the stanza, I find, everywhere else, मन्दरे, "on Mandara". On this mountain was Chaitraratha, the garden of Kubera. See Vol. II., p. 110, note *; and Vol. IV., p. 6.   ** Hala.

†† The Sanskrit has Śírin. See Vol. IV., p. 82, note †; and Vol. III., p. 332, note ¶. Śírin is the same as Halin, &c. Vide supra, p. 135, note ‡.

‡‡ चकाराख संमुखं च विडम्बनम् ।

§§ पानपूर्णांश्च करकांश्चिक्षेपाहृतष वै पृहा ।

For आहृतष, some MSS. have आहृतष ।

‖‖ Bala, in the original.

threatened the monkey: but the latter disregarded his
menaces, and made a chattering noise;* on which,
Bala, starting up, seized his club, in wrath; and the
monkey† laid hold of a large rock, which he hurled
at the hero. Bala, casting his club at it, as it neared .
him, broke it into a thousand fragments, which, together with the club, fell upon the ground.‡ Beholding
the club prostrate, the monkey sprang over it, and
struck the Yádava violently on the breast with his
paws. Bala replied with a blow of his fist upon the
forehead§ of Dwivida, which felled him—vomiting
blood, and lifeless,—to the earth. The crest of the
mountain on which he fell was splintered into a hundred pieces by (the weight of) his body, as if the
Thunderer‖ had shivered it with his thunderbolt. The
gods threw down a shower of flowers upon Ráma, and
approached him, and praised him for the glorious feat
he had performed. "Well has the world been freed,"
said they, "by thy prowess, O hero, of this vile ape,
who was the ally of the enemy of the gods!"¶ Then
they and their attendant spirits** returned, well pleased,

---

* चक्रे किलिकिलाध्वनिम् । Variants: किलकिल॰ and किलिकिला॰ ।
† Plavaga.
‡ चिक्षेप च स तां चिन्तां मुसलेन सहस्रधा ।
   बिभेद यादवश्रष्ठः सा पपात महीतले ॥
   चापतन्मुसलं चासौ समुह्र्त्य अभ्यगमः ।
   वेगेनागम्य रोषेण तलेनोरस्यताडयत् ॥
§ Múrdhan.
‖ Vajrin, i. e., Indra.
¶ Daitya-pakshopakárin.
** "Attendant spirits" is to render guhyaka. The Guhyakas attended
on Kubera. See Vol. I., p. 122; Vol. III., p. 116, note †.

to heaven. Many such inimitable* deeds were wrought
by the illustrious† Baladeva, (the impersonation of)
Śesha, the supporter of the earth.[1]

---

[1] This exploit of Balaráma is, also, similarly, but more vul-
garly, related in the Bhágavata. It is simply said, in the Hari
Vaṁśa,‡ — and erroneously, — that Mainda§ and Dwivida were
conquered by Kṛishṅa.

* *Aparimeya.*
† *Dhimat.*
‡ *Śl.* 9802.
§ Corrected from "Menda".

CHAPTER XXXVII

Destruction of the Yádavas. Sámba and others deceive and ridicule the Ŕishis. The former bears an iron pestle: it is broken, and thrown into the sea. The Yádavas go to Prabhása, by desire of Kŕishńa: they quarrel and fight, and all perish. The great serpent Śesha issues from the mouth of Ráma. Kŕishńa is shot by a hunter, and again becomes one with universal spirit.

IN this manner did Kŕishńa, assisted by Baladeva, destroy demons* and iniquitous monarchs, for the good of the earth; and, along with Phálguna,[1]† also, did he: relieve earth of her load, by the death of innumerable hosts.§ Having, thus, lightened the burthens of the earth, and slain many (unrighteous princes), he exterminated, by the pretext of an imprecation denounced by Brahmans, his own (Yádava) race. Then, quitting Dwáraká, and relinquishing his mortal being,

---

[1] A name of Arjuna, the great friend of Kŕishńa, to whom the latter served as charioteer, in the war between the Pándus and Kurus.

---

* *Daitya.*

† For the various names of Arjuna, and their origin, see the *Mahábhárata, Viráta-parvan, śl.* 1375, *et seq.*

‡ The original here names Hari.

§ समस्ताचौहिणीवधात् । For *akshauhińi, vide supra,* p. 50, notes 2 and **.

‖ My Arrah MS. here inserts as follows:

त्यक्ता मानुष्यकं भावं देवदेवो जनार्दनः ।
कृत्वा चान्यानि कार्याणि देवानां हितकाम्यया ॥
दुर्योधनस्य विग्रहे युधिष्ठिरपुरोगमैः ।
पाण्डवैर्भेदमुत्यन्नमुपेच्छत विभुस्तदा ॥

the self-born reentered, with all his emanations,[1] his own sphere of Vishńu. *

MAITREYA.—Tell me how Janárdana effected the destruction of his own race, under the plea of Brahmanical imprecation; and in what manner he relinquished his mortal body.[2]

PARÁŚARA.—At the holy place† Pindáraka,[3]: Viswámitra,§ Kańwa,‖ and the great sage Nárada were

---

[1] With Balaráma, Pradyumna, Aniruddha, and the rest.

[2] The legend of the destruction of the Yádava race and the death of Kŕishńa appears, probably, in its earliest extant form, in the Mausala Parvan of the Mahábhárata. It forms the narrative portion of the Eleventh Book of the Bhágavata; having been previously briefly adverted to in the First and Third Books; and it is summarily told in the Uttara Khańda of the Padma Puráńa,

[3] The village of Pindáraka, still held in veneration, is situated in Gujerat, about twenty miles from the north-west extremity of the Peninsula. Hamilton, Vol. I., p. 664.

अन्वमोद्गतः छ्ण्बतो वैरमकारयत् ।
तच हला कुरुसर्वान्याछ्दवैदैः परस्परम् ।
जगाम निर्वृतिं देवो जगतां पतिरीश्वरः ।
अथौहिको हतान्तान्व अष्टादश महामुने ॥

A second of my copies gives the same verses, with the variation of only three words.

It is not palpable that this passage is an interpolation. The first line of it does not repeat the sense of what immediately precedes it,—Professor Wilson's "relinquishing his mortal body",—the Sanskrit of which is त्वत्का मानुष्यं, i. e., according to both the commentators, मनुष्यभावं, "personation of man."

* सांग्रो विष्णुमयं खागं प्रविवेश पुनर्निजम् ।

† Mahá-tírtha.

: Connected, perhaps, with Pindáraka, son of Vasudeva and Robińi. See Vol. IV., p. 109, text and note ::.

§ See Vol. III., p. 14, note 1, near the end.

‖ Ibid., p. 57.

observed by some boys of the Yadu tribe. Giddy with youth, and influenced by predestined results,* they dressed and adorned Sámba, the son of Jámbavatí, as a damsel; and, conducting her to the sages, they addressed them with the usual marks of reverence, and said: "What child will this female, the wife of Babhru,† who is anxious to have a son, give birth to?" The sages, who were possessed of divine wisdom, were very angry to find themselves thus tricked by the boys, and said: "She will bring forth a club, that shall crush the whole of the Yádava race." The boys, thus spoken to by the sages, went and related all that had occurred to Ugrasena; and (as foretold,) a club was produced from the belly of Sámba. Ugrasena had the club—which was of iron,—ground to dust, and thrown into the sea; but the particles of dust (there) became rushes.¹ There

¹ The term is Eraká (एरका), which is explained, in some medical lexicons, "a kind of grass." The commentator‡ also calls it a kind of grass; and, in the text of the Mahábhárata, the term subsequently used, and as synonymous with it, is Triña (तृण), 'grass.' The Mahábhárata, when describing the affray which follows, mentions, that the grass, or rushes, on being plucked by Krishńa and the Yádavas, turn to clubs. The text, and that of the Bhágavata, here say, that the powdered particles, floating on the sea, became rushes. Or the latter may imply, that they fastened upon grass or weeds. The commentator, however, explains, that, the particles of iron being borne to land, they were so transformed. The Mahábhárata says nothing of the piece

* भाविकार्यमचोदिताः ।
† See Vol. IV, p. 72.
‡ एरका: । धारानयोपेतातृणभेदाः । Śridhara. एरका: । विधार-
तृषविशेषा: । Ratnagarbha.

was one part of the iron club which was like (the blade
of) a lance,* and which the Andhakas could not
break.† This, when thrown into the sea, was swallowed by a fish: the fish was caught, the iron spike
was extracted from its belly, and was taken by a hunter
named Jaras.‡ The all-wise§ and glorious Madhusúdana did not think fit to counteract what had been
predetermined by fate.

Then there came to Keśava, when he was private
and alone, a messenger from the gods, who addressed
him with reverence, and said: "I am sent to you, O
lord, by the deities. And do thou hear what Indra,∥
together with the Viśwas,¶ Aświns,** Maruts, Ádityas,
Rudras, and Sádhyas, respectfully represents. "More
than a hundred years have elapsed since thou, in
favour to the gods,†† hast descended upon earth, for

---

which could not be pounded; and this seems to be an embellishment, either of our text or the Bhágavata. The Mahábhárata,
however, adds another precaution, which the two others have left
unnoticed. Ugrasena causes a proclamation to be made, that none
of the inhabitants of Dwáraká shall, thenceforth, drink wine, on
pain of being impaled alive; and the people, for some time, observe the prohibition.

---

* *Tomara.*

† The original yields 'triturate': चूर्षयितुं शेकुर्न ।

‡ Corrected from "Jará". *Vide infra*, p. 152, note ‡.

§ विज्ञातपरमार्थः ।

∥ Śakra, in the Sanskrit.

¶ *Vide supra*, p. 101, note *. Ratnagarbha reads 'Vasus'. My Ajmere
MS. yields "Ádityas, Rudras, Sádhyas, Aświns, Vasus, Agnis, Maruts, &c.,"
and in this order.

** I have inserted this word, inadvertently omitted by the Translator.

†† विद्मे: संमसादितः ।

the purpose of relieving it of its load. The demons[*] have been slain, and the burthen of earth has been removed. Now let the immortals once again behold their monarch in heaven.[†] A period exceeding a century has passed. Now, if it be thy pleasure, return to Swarga. This is the solicitation of the celestials. But, should such not be thy will, then remain here as long as it may be desirable to thy dependants."[1]: To this, Kŕishńa replied:[§] "All that thou hast said I am well aware of. The destruction of the Yádavas by me has commenced. The burthens of the earth are not removed, until the Yádavas are extirpated. I will effect this, also, in my descent, and quickly; for it shall come to pass in seven nights. When I have restored the land of Dwáraká to the ocean, and annihilated the race of Yadu, I will proceed to the mansions of the immortals. Apprise the gods, that, having abandoned my human body, and accompanied by Sankarshańa, I will then return to them. The tyrants that oppressed the earth,

---

[1] Nothing of this kind occurs in the Mahábbárata. Our text, therefore, offers an embellishment. The Bhágavata, again, improves upon the text; for, not content with a messenger, it makes Brahmá (with the Prajápatis), Śiva (with the Bhútas), Indra (with the other divinities), all come, in person; indicating, evidently, a

---

[*] Daitya.

[†] तथा सगाथाखिद्मा भवन्तु विदिवे पुन: ।

[:] देवैर्विज्ञाप्ते चेदमवाषीव रतिक्षव ।
तत्खीयतां यथाकालमाख्येयमनुशीविभि: ॥

[§] श्रीभगवानुवाच ।

मानुषं देहमुत्सुज्य संकर्षणसहायवान् ।
प्राम एवाक्षि मक्ताम्बो देवेन्द्रेव तथा सुरै: ॥

—Jarásandha and the rest,—have been killed; and a youth, even, of the race of Yadu, is, no less than they, an incumbrance. When, therefore, I have taken away this great weight upon earth, I will return to protect the sphere of the celestials.* Say this to them." The messenger of the gods, having received this reply, bowed, and took his heavenly course to the king of the gods.

The mighty (Krishńa) now beheld signs and portents,† both in earth and heaven, prognosticating, day and night, the ruin of Dwáraká.¹ Showing these to the

----

later date, as plainly as the addition of the text shows it to be subsequent to the date of the legend in the Mahábhárata.

¹ The Mahábbárata, which delights in describing portents and signs, does not fail to detail them here. A dreadful figure, death personified, haunts every house, coming and going no one knows how, and being invulnerable to the weapons by which he is assailed. Strong hurricanes blow; large rats multiply, and infest the roads and houses, and attack persons in their sleep; Sárikás (or starlings,) utter inauspicious screams in their cages; storks imitate the hooting of owls; and goats, the howling of jackals; cows bring forth foals; and camels, mules; food, in the moment of being eaten, is filled with worms; fire burns with discoloured flames; and, at sunset and sunrise, the air is traversed by headless and hideous spirits. There is more to the same effect, which neither our text nor the Bhágavata has ventured to detail. The whole passage has been published in Maurice's Ancient History of Hindustan, Vol. II., p. 463; translated, apparently, by the late Sir Charles Wilkins. The names have been much disfigured either by the copyist or compositor.

----

* *Amara-loka.*
† "Signs and portents" is to render *utpáta*.

Yádavas, he said: "See! Behold these fearful phenomena! Let us hasten to Prabhása, to avert these
omens."* When he had thus spoken to the eminent
Yádava,† the illustrious Uddhava: saluted and said to
him: "Tell me, O lord, what it is proper that I should
do. For it seems to me, that thou wilt destroy all this
race. The signs (that are manifest) declare (nothing
less than)the annihilation of the tribe." Then Krishńa §
replied to him: "Do you go by a celestial route, which
my favour shall provide you, to the holy (place) Ba-
darikásrama,‖ in the Gandhamádana mountain, the
shrine of Naranáráyańa;¶ and, on that spot, sanctified
by them, thou, by meditating on me, shalt obtain perfection,** through my favour. When the race (of Yadu)
shall have perished, I shall proceed to heaven; and the
ocean shall inundate Dwáraká, when I have quitted it."
Accordingly, Uddhava, thus instructed†† by Keśava,
saluted him with veneration, and departed to the shrine
of Naranáráyańa.[1]

---

[1] In the Mahábhárata, it is said, merely, that Uddhava, who
was versed in Yoga, foreseeing the destruction of the Yádavas,

---

* सुमाचीषां प्रभासं याम मा चिरम् ।

† एवमुक्ते तु कृष्णेन याद्ववमवरक्षतः ।

This verse is recognized by Śrídhara, but not by Ratnagarbha; and
the sense is complete without it. My Ajmere MS. gives it; my Arrah
MS. omits it.

: See Vol. IV., p. 113, notes 1 and :.

§ Bhagavat, in the original.

‖ Ratnagarbha calls this hermitage by its shorter name, Badari, instead
of Badariká, the form preferred by Śrídhara.

¶ We have already had mention of it. *Vide supra*, p. 62.

** *Siddhi.*

†† *Anumodita.*

Then the Yádavas ascended their rapid cars, and drove to Prabhása,[1] along with Kríshńa, Ráma, and the rest of their chiefs.[2] They bathed there; and, excited* by Vásudeva, the Kukuras† and Andhakas indulged in liquor. As they drank, the destructive flame of dissension was kindled amongst them by mutual collision, and fed with the fuel of abuse. Infuriated by the divine influence, they fell upon one another with missile weapons;‡ and, when those were expended, they had recourse to the rushes § growing nigh. The rushes in their hands became like thunderbolts; and they struck one another, with them, fatal∥ blows.

---

went away; that is, according to the commentator, he practised penance, and went to heaven: अगाम योगमास्थाय परलोकम् ।
The Bhágavata, taking the hint, makes much more of it than our text, and expands it into a long course of instruction, given by Kríshńa to Uddhava, occupying 150 leaves.

[1] Vide supra, p. 47, note 2. By sending the Yádavas to Prabhása, (the commentator asserts,) Kríshńa prevented, purposely, the Yádavas from obtaining Mukti, 'final liberation', which would have been the consequence of dying at Dwáraká. Death at Prabhása conferred only Indra's heaven.

[2] The Mahábhárata describes them as going forth with horses, elephants, and cars, and their women and abundance of good cheer, and varieties of wine and meat:
बहुनानाविधं चत्रुमेव मांसमनेकश: ।

---

* Anumodita.
† Corrected, here and frequently elsewhere, from "Kukkuras".
‡ Śastra, which almost always signifies an edged weapon, in contradistinction from astra, 'a missile weapon'.
§ Eraká. Vide supra, p. 142, note 1.
∥ Sudáruńa.

Pradyumna, Sámba, Kŕitavarman,* Sátyaki,† Aniruddha, Pŕithu, Vipŕithu, ‡ Cháruvarman, § Cháruka, ǁ
Akrúra, and many others struck one another with the
rushes, which had assumed the hardness of thunderbolts[1]. Keśava interposed, to prevent them; but they
thought that he was taking part with each, severally,

[1] The Bhágavata, like the text, adverts only in this general
manner to the conflict; but the Mahábhárata gives the particulars.
Yuyudbána¶ reproaches Kŕitavarman with having aided Aśwat-
thámen** in his night-attack on the Páńdu camp, and killing warriors in their sleep. Pradyumna joins in the abuse. Kŕitavarman
retorts. Kŕishńa looks at him angrily. Sátyaki repeats the story
of the Syamantaka gem, by which he accuses Kŕitavarman of
being an accomplice in the murder of Sattrájita†† (See Vol. IV.,
pp. 75, et seq.). Satyabhámá,‡‡ the daughter of the latter, then
mixes in the quarrel, and incites Kŕishńa to avenge her; but Sátyaki anticipates him, and murders Kŕitavarman. Śaineya§§ and
the Bhojas attack Sátyaki; the Andhakas defend him; and the
affray becomes general. Kŕishńa attempts to part the combatants,
until Pradyumna is killed; and, then, taking up a handful of
rushes, which become an iron club, he kills, indiscriminately, all
that come in his way. The conflict continues, until the greater
part of the combatants have fallen, including all Kŕishńa's sons;
and he then, in wrath, sweeps off all the survivors, except Babbru
and Dáruka, with his discus.

* See Vol. IV., p. 99.
† Ibid., p. 93.
‡ For these two brothers, see Vol. IV., p. 96.
§ I know nothing of him. In Vol. IV, p. 113, we have a Sucháru.
One of my MSS. has Chárudharman.
ǁ The same as Cháru, for whom see p. 78, supra.
¶ The same as Sátyaki. See Vol. IV., p. 93.
** See Vol. IV., p. 147.
†† Corrected from "Satrajit".
‡‡ See Vol. IV., p. 80.
§§ Was this Satyaka, Sátyaki's father? See Vol. IV., p. 92.

and continued the conflict. Kríshńa, then, enraged, took up a handful of rushes, to destroy them; and the rushes became a club of iron. And with this he slew many of the murderous Yádavas; whilst others, fighting fiercely, put an end to one another. The chariot of the holder of the discus,* named Jaitra, was quickly carried off by the (swift) steeds, and swept away by the sea, in the sight of Dáruka, (the charioteer). The discus, the club, the bow, the quiver, the shell, and the sword† (of Kesava), having circumambulated their lord,‡ flew along the path of the sun. In a short time there was not a single Yádava left alive, except the mighty Kríshńa and Dáruka.[1] Going towards Ráma, who was sitting at the root of a tree, they beheld a large serpent coming out of his mouth. Having issued from his mouth, the mighty § snake proceeded towards

[1] The Mahábhárata, as observed at the end of the last note, adds Babhru; but it presently gets rid of him. Kríshńa sends him to take care of the old people, the women, and children, in Dwáraká, whilst Dáruka goes to bring Arjuna to their aid. But, as he goes along,—overcome with grief for the loss of his kindred, and approaching separation from Kríshńa,—he is killed by a club that is cast from a snare, or trap, set by a hunter. Kríshńa then goes to Dwáraká, and desires Vasudeva to await the coming of Arjuna; after which, he returns to Ráma, and sees the phenomenon described in the text; the serpent being Sesha, of whom Balaráma was the incarnation. The Bhágavata does not mention this incident; merely observing, that Ráma, by the power of Yoga, returned into himself,—that is, into Vishńu.

* *Chakrin.*
† *Vide supra,* p. 124; also, a passage towards the end of Chapter VII. of Book VI.
‡ Hari, in the Sanskrit.   § *Mahábhoga.*

the ocean, hymned by saints, * and by other great serpents. Bringing an offering of respect, Ocean came to meet him; and, then, the majestic being, adored by attendant snakes, entered into the waters of the deep.† Beholding the departure of (the spirit of) Balabhadra,‡ Keśava said to Dáruka: "All this is to be related, by you, to Vasudeva and Ugrasena. Go and inform them of the departure of Balabhadra, and the destruction of the Yádavas; also, that I shall engage in religious meditation, and quit this body. Apprise Áhuka,§ and all the inhabitants of Dwáraká,¹ that the sea will inundate the town. Be ready, therefore, in expectation of the coming of Arjuna; and, when he‖ quits Dwáraká, no longer abide there, but go whithersoever that descendant of Kuru shall repair. Do you, also, go to the son of Kuntí,¶ and tell him, that it is my request that he will grant what protection he can to all my family.

---

¹ The women, the elders, and the children, amongst whom, as we shall presently see, was Vajra, the son of Aniruddha,** who was established as chief of the Yádavas at Indraprastha, and who, therefore, escaped the destruction which overwhelmed their kinsmen, the Vŕishńis, Kukuras, and Andhakas, of Dwáraká. This was a fortunate reservation for the tribes which, in various parts of Hindusthan,—both on the Ganges and in the Deccan,—profess to derive their origin from the Yádavas.††

---

* *Siddha.*
† प्रविवेश च तत्तोयं पूजितः पन्नगोत्तमैः ।
‡ Bala, in the original.
§ Father of Ugrasenu. See Vol. IV., p. 98.
‖ Hero called Páńdava, in the Sanskrit.
¶ Kaunteya; namely, Arjuna. See Vol. IV., pp. 101, 102, and 159.
** *Vide supra,* p. 108, text and note *.
†† See Vol. IV., p. 58, notes 2 and §.

Then depart, with Arjuua and all the people of Dwáravatí; and let Vajra be installed sovereign over the
tribe of Yadu."*

Dáruka, being thus instructed, prostrated himself,
again and again, before Kṛishḍa, and walked round him
repeatedly, and then departed, as he had been desired;
and, having conducted Arjuna to Dwáravatí,† the intelligent (servant of Kṛishḍa) established Vajra as king.
The divine Govinda, then, having concentrated in himself that supreme spirit: which is one with Vásudeva,
was identified with all beings.[1] Respecting the words
of the Brahman,—the imprecation of Durvásas,[2] §—the

---

[1] The process is explained by the commentator:‖ "By the
force of Dhyána (or abstraction), Kṛishḍa satisfies himself that he
is Brahma (ब्रह्मैवाहमिति आत्मा), or universal spirit; and is,
next, convinced, that he is, therefore, all things (सर्वभूतान्यहमेव);
by which his individuality ceases."

[2] The story is told in the Mahábhárata.¶ Durvásas was, on
one occasion, hospitably entertained by Kṛishḍa; but the latter
omitted to wipe away the fragments of the meal which had fallen
on the foot of the irascible sage, who, thereupon, foretold, that
Kṛishḍa should be killed as in the text.

---

* यत्र यदुराज्येऽभिषिच्यताम् । So Śrídhara. Ratnagarbha reads:
यत्र यदुराजो भविष्यति ।

† Corrected, here and just above, from "Dwárávatí". The original
has Dwáraká.

‡ परं ब्रह्म ।

§ दुर्वासा यदुवाच । See, for Durvásas, Vol. I., pp. 135 and 154.

‖ What follows is taken from Śrídhara, whose words are: आत्मनि
परं ब्रह्म समारोप्य ब्रह्मैवाहमिति आत्मा तमात्मानं सर्वभूतेष्वधार-
यत्सर्वभूतान्यहमेवेति दध्याविखर्षः । Ratnagarbha comments to the
same effect.

¶ And it is told briefly by both the commentators on the Vishṇu-purdṇa.

illustrious Krishńa* sat engaged in thought,† resting his foot upon his knee. Then came there a hunter, named Jaras,[1]‡ whose arrow was tipped with a blade made of the piece of iron of the club, which had not been reduced to powder;§ and, beholding, from a distance, the foot of Krishńa, he mistook it for part of a deer, and, shooting his arrow, lodged it in the sole.[2] ‖ Approaching (his mark), he saw the four-armed king, and, falling at his feet, repeatedly besought his forgiveness, exclaiming: "I have done this deed unwittingly, thinking I was aiming at a deer. Have pity upon me, who am consumed by my crime! For thou art able to consume me."¶ Bhagavat replied: "Fear

---

[1] This is an allegorical personage, however; for Jará signifies 'infirmity', 'old age', 'decay.'**

[2] The Bhágavata explains how this part of the foot became exposed. Krishńa had assumed one of the postures in which abstraction is practised. He had laid his left leg across his right thigh, by which the sole of the foot was turned outwards.

---

* This name and its epithet are supplied by the Translator.

† योगयुक्तः ।

‡ Corrected from "Jará", which the original cannot yield, as a huntress would be called lubdhakí. The original is as follows:

आययौ च अरा नाम स तदा तत्र लुब्धकः ।

Compare note ‡ in p. 143, supra. Also see the Mahábhárata, Mausala-parvan, śl. 126, et seq.

§ मुसलावशेषलौहिकसायकन्यस्ततोमरः ।

This compound is descriptive of लुब्धकः ।

‖ A free translation.

¶ क्षम्यतामात्मपापेन दग्धं मां दग्धुमर्हसि ।

Ratnagarbha begins this verse with the words क्षम्यतां आत्मपापेन ।

** To this speculation it is difficult to assent. See note ‡, above.

not, thou, in the least.* Go, hunter, through my favour, to heaven, the abode of the gods." As soon as
he had thus spoken, a celestial car appeared; and the
hunter, ascending it, forthwith proceeded to heaven.
Then the illustrious (Kŕishńa), having united himself
with his own pure, spiritual,† inexhaustible, inconceivable, unborn, undecaying, imperishable,‡ and universal spirit, which is one with Vásudeva, abandoned his
mortal body and the condition of the threefold qualities.[1]§

---

[1] He became Nirguńa, 'devoid of all qualities.'

---

* न तेऽस्ति भयमखिलपि ।
† Brahma-bhúta.
‡ The epithet aprameya, 'boundless', is here omitted.
§ तत्राज मानुषं देहमतील्य चिविधां गतिम् ।
॥ Thus explain both Śrídhara and Ratnagarbha.

CHAPTER XXXVIII

Arjuna comes to Dwáraká, and burns the dead, and takes away
the surviving inhabitants. Commencement of the Kali age.
Shepherds and thieves attack Arjuna, and carry off the women
and wealth. Arjuna regrets the loss of his prowess, to Vyása,
who consoles him, and tells him the story of Ashtávakra's
cursing the Apsarasas. Arjuna and his brothers place Parikshit on the throne, and go to the forests. End of the Fifth
Book.

ARJUNA, having found the bodies of Krishńa and
of Ráma, performed, for them and the rest (of the
slain), the obsequial rites.* The eight queens of
Krishńa, who have been named,† with Rukminí at
their head,: embraced the body of Hari, and entered
the (funeral) fire.[1] Revatí, also, embracing the corpse
of Ráma, entered the blazing pile, which was cool to
her, happy in contact with her lord.§ Hearing these
events, Ugrasena and Ánakadundubhi, with Devakí
and Rohińí, committed themselves to the flames.[2] The

---

[1] The Mahábhárata takes the wives of Krishńa, first, to Indraprastha; and there Rukminí and four others burn. But Satyabhámá and others become ascetics, going to perform Tapasya in
the forest.

[2] It is merely said, in the Mahábhárata, that Vasudeva ex-
pired; on which, four of his wives burnt themselves.

---

* "Obsequial rites" is to render *samskára*.
† *Vide supra*, pp. 78, *et seq.*, and p. 107.
: रुक्मिणीप्रमुखाः, "Rukminí and the rest."
§ विवेश ज्वलितं वह्निं तत्संगाद्ह्लादशीतलम् ।

last ceremonies* were performed, for all these, by Arjuna, who, then, made all the people leave the city, and took Vajra with him. The son of Kuntí† conducted the thousands of the wives of Kríshńa, with Vajra and all the people, from Dwáraká,‡ with tenderness and care, and travelled slowly away. The Sudharman § palace and the Párijáta-tree, which had been brought to earth by Kríshńa, both proceeded to heaven; and, on the same day that Hari departed from the earth, the powerful dark-bodied ‖ Kali (age) descended.[1] The ocean (rose and) submerged the whole of Dwáraká, except alone the dwelling of the deity of the race of Yadu.¶ The sea has not yet been able to wash that (temple) away; and there Kesava constantly abides, (even in the present day). Whoever visits that holy shrine—the place where Kríshńa pursued his sports,— is liberated from all his sins.[2]**

[1] The Kali age commenced from the death of Kríshńa, according to the usual notions; but it is commonly supposed to commence a little later, or with the reign of Parikshit. ††

[2] The Bhágavata agrees with the text, in excepting the temple of Dwáraká, and asserting that it still remains, in direct contradiction of the Mahábhárata, which declares, that the sea did not spare any part whatever. It is clear, therefore, that, when the latter was compiled, the temple was not standing, and that it was

* *Preta-kárya.*
† Kaunteya. *Vide supra*, p. 150, note ¶.
‡ Dwáravatí, in the Sanskrit.
§ *Vide supra*, p. 46, text and note *.
‖ *Kála-káya.* There are three unimportant variants. Ratnagarbha notes and elucidates two of them.

¶ यदुदेवगृहं, "the temple of the Yadus."
** This sentence greatly abridges the original.
†† See Vol. IV, p. 230, note *, and p. 233.

The son of Prithá* (Arjuna,) halted the people (he
had brought from Dwáraká,) in the Panchanada country,[1] in a rich and fertile spot. But the desires of the
robbers (of the neighbourhood) were excited, when
they observed so many widowed females,—also, such
great riches,—in the possession of Arjuna* alone.†

---

erected between the date of the compilation and that of the two
Puráńas. The present shrine, which is held in great repute,
stands at the extremity of the peninsula of Gujerat. It is still
an object of pilgrimage. It was so in the reign of Akbar (Ayeen
Akbaree); and has been so, no doubt, from a remote period.
The image formerly worshipped there was carried off 600 years
ago; and this was, most probably, subsequent to the date of both
the Puráńas: for the idol was a form of Kŕishńa, called Raña-
chhoŕ,—a popular divinity, unknown in the Pauráńik pantheon.
Another image was substituted in place of that which was taken
away. Notwithstanding the testimony of our text, and that of
the Bhágavata, the originality of the temple is disputed; and a
place thirty miles south from Poorbundur is said to be the spot
where Dwáraká was swallowed up by the ocean. Hamilton (from
Macmurdo, &c.), Vol. I., p. 662.

[1] "The country of the five rivers,"‡ the Punjab:—rather an
out-of-the-way route from Dwáraká to Dehli.

---

* Pártha, in the original. See Vol. IV., pp. 101, 102.

† ततो क्षोभः समभवद्धसूनां लिह्नतेश्वरा: ।
   वृद्धा स्त्रियो नीयमाना: पार्थेनैकेन धन्विना ॥

Ratnagarbha reads as follows:

   ततो क्षोभः समभवत्पार्थेनैकेन धन्विना ।
   वृद्धा स्त्रियो नीयमाना दस्सूनां लिह्नतेश्वरा: ॥

And herewith agree my Ajmere and Arrah MSS.
In no MS. do I find, in lieu of धन्विना, धनिना, which might suggest
Professor Wilson's "such great riches."

‡ The original is पञ्चनदे देशे. Most probably the tírtha called Panchanada is intended; for which see the Mahábhárata, Vana-parvan,
ll. 5025, 5086; and elsewhere.

Inflamed by their cupidity, they assembled the villainous Ábhiras, [1]* and said to them: "Here is this Arjuna,—immensely rich,† and having numerous women, whose husbands have been slain,—passing confidently amongst us; a disgrace to all brave men.‡ His pride is raised by the death of Bhíshma, Droṇa, Jayadratha, Karṇa, and others (whom he has slain). He does not know the prowess of (simple) villagers. Up! up! Take your long thick staves.§ This stupid fellow despises us. Why should we not lift up our arms?" So saying, they rushed, armed with cudgels and clods of earth,

---

[1] Ábhiras mean 'herds;' ¶ and they are, afterwards, called, by Arjuna, Gopálas, 'herdsmen.' The pastoral tribes of the west of India, and, particularly, those of Afghanistan, almost always combine the character of freebooter with that of shepherd.

तततो पापकर्मांणो लोभोपहतचेतसः ।
चाभीरा मन्त्रयामासुः समेत्यात्मनदुर्मदा ॥

† I find, everywhere, धन्वी, 'archer.' See note ‡ in the preceding page.

ः अयमेकोऽर्जुनो धन्वी स्त्रीजनं निहतेश्वरम् ।
नयत्यसागतिकम्य धिगेतन्ननवतां बलम् ॥

Instead of भवतां, क्रियतां is preferred by Ratnagarbha, according to my oldest copy of his commentary. And so reads my Arrah MS.

My Ajmere MS. gives, in the place of the verse beginning as above, a whole stanza, and one of very different import.

§ हे हे यष्टीर्महायामा गृह्णीत । Ratnagarbha has महामाया ।

|| Nothing to yield "clods of earth" is read in the text as alone I find it:

ततो यष्टिमहरबा दस्यवो लोष्टहारिणः ।
सहस्रशोऽभ्यधावन्त तं अनं निहतेश्वरम् ॥

Srídhara and Ratnagarbha: यष्टिमहरबा: । दण्डायुधा: । लोष्टहा-रिण: । परस्वग्राहिण: । Professor Wilson must have supposed that the reading was लोष्टहारिण: ।

¶ I know no authority for this meaning. For the Ábhiras, see Vol. II., p. 168, notes 4, etc.; p. 185, notes 2, etc.

upon the people, who were without their lord.* Arjuna† encountered: them, and said to them, in derision: "Retire, wretches, ignorant of what is right, unless ye are desirous of dying." But they disregarded his menaces, and seized his treasures, and his women,—the wives of Viśwaksena. Thereupon, Arjuna began to brace his heavenly bow, Gáńdíva, irresistible§ in battle. But it was in vain; for, in spite of all his efforts to tighten it, it continued flaccid. Neither could he call to recollection the incantations of the superhuman weapons. Losing all patience, he launched, as best he might, his shafts upon the enemy; but those shot from Gáńdíva merely scratched the skin. The arrows given him, by Agni,¶ to carry certain destruction,** now were, themselves, destroyed, and were fatal to Arjuna, in his contest with herdsmen. He endeavoured to recall the might of Kríshńa,—animated by which, his numerous arrows had overthrown mighty kings;—but he tried in vain: for, now, they were put aside by the peasants;†† or they flew at random, wide of their aim.‡‡ His arrows being expended, he§§ beat the ban-

---

* The widows above spoken of are intended.
† Kaunteya, in the Sanskrit. *Vide supra*, p. 150, note ¶.
‡ निवृत्त; implying that Arjuna desisted from encountering the Ábhiras.
§ *Ajara*.
‖ न सस्मार तथास्त्राणि चिन्तयन्नपि पाण्डवः ।
¶ In the original, Vahni.
** The epithet thus rendered is *akshaya*, 'indestructible.'
†† *Ábhíra*.
‡‡ अचिन्तयच्च कौन्तेयः कृष्णश्चैव हि तद्बलम् ।
यन्मया शरसंघातैः सकला भूभुजो जिताः ॥
मिषतः पाण्डुपुत्रस्य ततस्ताः समदोत्तमाः ।
आभीरैरयज्ञश्चन्ते कामाच्चान्याः प्रवव्रजुः ।
§§ Here Arjuna is called Dhananjaya, in the original.

ditti with the horn of his bow: but they only laughed at his blows; and the barbarians,* in the sight of Arjuna,† carried off all the women of the Vŕishńi and Andhaka tribes, and went their way.[1]

Then Jishńu: was sorely distressed, and lamented bitterly, exclaiming: "Alas! alas! I am deserted by my lord!" And he wept; and, in that instant, the bow and (heavenly) arms, his car and steeds, perished entirely, like a donation to an unlearned Brahman.§ "Resistless," said he, "are the decrees of fate, by whom feebleness has been inflicted upon me,—deprived of my illustrious friend,—and victory given to the base. These two arms are mine; mine is this fist; this is my place;¶ I am Arjuna: but, without that righteous aid, all these are pithless. The valour of Arjuna,** the strength of Bhíma,†† was, all, his work; and, without him, I am overcome by peasants::: it cannot be from any other

---

[1] The principal wives of Kŕishńa, however, according to the Mahábbhárata, escaped. The occurrence is described, there, much in the same way, but more briefly. It is not detailed in the Bhágavata.

---

* *Mlechchha.*

† *Pártha,* in the Sanskrit.

: Still another name of Arjuna. *Vide supra*, p. 156, note *.

§ हानमश्रोचिये यचा ।
   बाहोऽतिबलवईिवं विना तेन महात्मना ।
   यद्सामर्थ्ययुक्तेऽपि नीचवर्गे अयमद्म् ॥

¶ हानं तत् । His position as an archer, says Ratnagarbha: धानु-
ष्कसंस्थानविशेषः ।

** To render *Arjunatwa.*

†† भीमश्च भीमबलम् ।

:: *Abhíra.*

cause." So saying, Arjuna* went to the city of Mathurá,† and there installed the Yádava prince, Vajra,
as its king. There he: beheld Vyása, who was living
in a wood; and he approached the sage,§ and saluted
him respectfully. The Muni surveyed him for some
time, as he lay prostrate at his feet, and said to him:‖
"How is it that I see you thus shorn of your lustre?¶
Have you been guilty of illicit intercourse with
women?** Or of the death of a Brahman? Or have
you suffered some grievous disappointment, that you
are so dejected?†† Have your prayers for progeny, or
other good gifts, proved fruitless? Or have you indulged improper passions, that your lustre is so dim?‡‡
Or are you one that devours the meal he has given to
the Brahmans? Say, Arjuna, have you seized upon the
substance of the poor? Has the wind of a winnowing-
basket lighted upon you? Or has an evil eye gazed
upon you, Arjuna, that you look thus miserable?§§

---

* Jishńu, in the original. This is one of the many names or epithetical
designations of Arjuna.
† Śrídhara and Ratnagarbha notice a variant expressing that Arjuna
went from Indraprastha to Hastinápura. My Ajmere and Arrah MSS.
simply substitute Indraprastha for Mathurá.
: The Sanskrit has Phálguna.
§ *Mahábhága.*
‖ Pártha is the word here used.
¶ विच्छायः कथमत्यन्तमीदृशः ।
** This sentence is to render अवीरऽऽनुगमनम् । Both Śrídhara
and Ratnagarbha dwell at length on the first of these words and its
variant अवीरऽऽ ।
†† अष्टच्छायः ।
‡‡ सान्तानिकादयो वा ते याचमाना गिराह्नताः ।
  अगम्यस्त्रीरतिर्वा त्वं तेनासि विगतप्रभः ॥
§§ विच्छायः ।

Have you been touched by the water of a finger-nail?
Or has the water of a water-jar sprinkled you? Or,
what is, most probably, the case, have you been
beaten by your inferiors in battle?"*

Arjuna,† having sighed deeply, related to Vyása all
the circumstances of his discomfiture, and continued:
"Hari, who was our strength, our might, our heroism,
our prowess, our prosperity, our brightness, has left
us, and departed. Deprived of him, our friend, illustrious, and ever kindly speaking, we have become as
feeble as if made of straw.‡ Purushottama, who was
the living§ vigour of my weapons, my arrows, and
my bow,‖ is gone. As long as we looked upon him,
fortune, fame, wealth, dignity¶ never abandoned us.
But Govinda is gone from amongst us. That Kríshńa
has quitted earth, through whose power Bhíshma,
Drona, the king of Anga,** Duryodhana, and the rest
were consumed. Not I alone, but Earth, has grown
old, miserable,†† and lustreless, in the absence of the
holder of the discus.‡‡ Kríshńa, through devotion to
whom Bhíshma and other mighty men perished like

---

* The Translator has here somewhat departed from the order of the
original.

† Pártha, in the original.

‡ एतरेषेव महता क्षितपूर्वाभिभाषिषा ।
हीना वयं मुने तेन आतास्तृणमया एव ॥

Ratnagarbha begins this stanza with गौरवेण, *i. e.*, आदरेण, he says.

§ Múrtta.

‖ Substituted, by the Translator, for Gáńdíva.

¶ Unnati.

** Anga-rája. Karńa is intended.

†† षट्क्षाया ।

‡‡ Chakrin.

moths in the flame of my valour, is gone; and I am,
now, overcome by cowherds.* The bow Gándíva,
that was famed throughout the three worlds, has been
foiled, since he has departed, by the sticks of peasants.† The myriads of women over whom I was lord
have been carried off from me by thieves, armed but
with cudgels. The whole household: of Krishńa, O
Krishńa,[1] has been (forcibly) carried away by peasants,
who, with their staves, have put my strength to shame.
That I am shorn of my lustre I do not marvel: it is
wonderful that I live. Surely, grand-sire, I alone am
so shameless as to survive the stain of indignity inflicted by the vile."§

Vyása replied to Arjuna, and said: "Think no more,
my son,‖ of your disgrace. It does not become you to
grieve. Know that time subjects all beings to similar
vicissitude.¶ Time effects the production and dissolution of all creatures. All that exists is founded on time.
Know this, Arjuna, and retain your fortitude. Rivers,
seas, mountains, the whole earth, gods, men, animals,
trees, insects** are, all, created, and, all, will be de-

---

[1] A name of Vyása.††

* यस्यानुभावान्मोक्षादौर्मंव्यपौ भ्रळभाषितम् ।
विना तेनाव क्रप्खेन गोपालैरक्षि निर्जितः ॥

† Abhíra.

‡ Avarodhana. Ratnagarbha explains it to mean अन्तःपुरं स्त्रीवर्गं ।

§ निःश्रीकता न मे चित्रं यस्त्रीवामि तदुद्भुतम् ।
नीचापमान एकाकी निर्लज्जोऽक्षि पितामह ॥

‖ The original has Pártha.

¶ त्वेहि सर्वभूतेषु कालस्य गतिमीदृशीम् ।

** Sarishpa; 'reptiles.' Vide supra, p. 59, note ††.

†† So the scholiasts allege.

stroyed, by time. Knowing that all that is is the effect
of time, be tranquillized.* These mighty works† of
Krishńa, whatever they have been, have been performed to relieve earth of its burthens: for this he has
come down. Earth, oppressed by her load, has had
recourse to the assembly: of the immortals; and Janárdana, who is one with time, has descended on that
account. This object has been, now, accomplished.
All the kings (of the earth) are slain; the race of
Vŕishńi and Andhaka is destroyed: no more remained
for him to accomplish.§ Therefore has the lord de-
parted whither he pleased, his ends being, all, fulfilled.||
At the period of creation, the god of gods creates; in
that of duration. he preserves; and, at the end (of all),
he is mighty to annihilate.¶ Now all is done. Therefore,
Arjuna,** be not afflicted by thy defeat. The prowess
of mortals is the gift of time.†† Bhíshma, Dróna,::
Karńa. and other kings have been slain by thee alone.
This was the work of time: and why, therefore, should
not thy discomfiture, by those less than thou art,

---

* कालात्मकमिदं सर्वं ज्ञात्वा प्रममवासुहि ।
कालात्मकम् । कालाधीनम् । Ratnagarbha.

† "Mighty works" is to render *máhátmya*.

‡ *Samiti.*

§ Add "on earth": भूमितले ।

|| *Kŕitokŕitya*, 'satisfied,' 'happy.' .

¶ च्वताय समर्थः ।

** Pártha, in the original.

†† भवन्ति भवकालेषु पुरुषाणां पराक्रमाः ।

:: I have inserted this name, to conform the translation to Śrídhara's
text, which Professor Wilson, no doubt, hereabouts follows. Ratnagarbha's
reading yields Bhíshma and Dróna, omitting Karńa; and therewith my
Arrah MS. harmonizes.

occur?* In like manner as, through thy devotion to†
Vishńu, these were overthrown by thee, so, at last, has
thy defeat by miserable thieves been wrought by
time.‡ That divinity, assuming various bodies, preserves the world; and, in the end, the lord of creatures
destroys it. In the birth of thy fortunes,§ Janárdana
was thy friend; in their decline,‖ thy enemies have
been favoured by Keśava. Who would have believed
that thou shouldst slay all the descendants of Kuru,
and kindred of Gangá?¶ Who would have believed
that peasants** should triumph over thee? Be assured,
son of Pŕithá,†† that it is (but) the sport of the univer-
sal‡‡ Hari, that the Kauravas have been destroyed by
thee, and that thou hast been defeated by herdsmen.§§
With respect to the women whom thou lamentest, and
who have been carried off by the thieves, hear from
me an ancient story, which will explain why this has
happened.‖‖

"In former times, a Brahman, named Ashṭávakra,¹

---

¹ The story of Ashṭávakra is related in the Mahábhárata.¶¶ He
was the son of Kahoḍa,*** who, neglecting his wife, was rebuked

* तेषामर्जुन कालोत्यः किं न्यूनाभिमयो न सः ।
† Read "through the might of": अनुभावेन ।
‡ ततस्त्वैव भवतो दुःखभोऽन्ते तदुद्भवः ।
§ भवोद्भवे ।   ‖ भवान्ते ।
¶ To render Gángeya.   ** Abhíra.
†† Pártha is the original word.
‡‡ Sarva-bhúta. Vide supra, p. 34, text and note ††.
§§ Ábhira.
    ‖‖ तद्वयहं यथावृत्तं कथयामि तवार्जुन ।
¶¶ Ádi-parvan, śl. 10599, et seq.
*** Corrected from "Kahora".

was pursuing his religious penances, standing in water,
and meditating on the eternal spirit, for many years.[*]
In consequence of the overthrow of the Asuras, there
was a great festival on the summit of Meru; on their
way to which, Rambhá, Tilottamá,[†] and hundreds and
thousands of beautiful nymphs: saw the ascetic Ashtávakra; and they praised and hymned him (for his devotions). They bowed down (before him), and eulogized him, (as he was immersed) up to his throat in
water, his hair twisted in a braid. So they sang, in
honour of him, whatever they thought would be most
agreeable to that most eminent of Brahmans. Ashtávakra (at last,) said to them: 'I am well pleased with
you, illustrious damsels.[§] Whatever you wish for, ask
of me, and I will give it you, however difficult it may
be of attainment.' Then all those nymphs,[||] Rambhá,
Tilottamá, and others, recorded in the Vedas,[¶] replied:
'It is enough for us that thou art pleased. What need
we aught else, venerable Brahman?'[**] But some

for it by his yet unborn son. The father angrily cursed him, that
he should be born bent in every part; and he was, accordingly,
brought forth crooked (vakra) in eight limbs (ashían).[††] He became, nevertheless, a celebrated sage. See, also, Hindu Theatre,
Vol. I., p. 293, note.

[*] अष्टावक्रः पुरा विप्रो जलवासरतोऽभवत् ।
बह्वन्वर्षगणान्यार्थं गृणन्ब्रह्म सनातनम् ॥
[†] See, for them, Vol. II., p. 75, note 3.   [‡] वरस्त्रियः ।
[§] "Illustrious damsels" is to translate महाभागाः ।
[||] Apsaras.
[¶] For Apsarases mentioned in the Vedas, see Vol. II., pp. 80, 81.
[**] प्रसन्ने स्वय्यपर्यासं किमस्माकमिति द्विज ।
[††] With the name Ashtávakra compare Naikavakrá and Trivakrá, for
which vide supra, p. 21, note [†].

(amongst them) said: 'If, exalted sir, you are (indeed)
pleased with us, then grant us a husband, the best of
men,* and sovereign of the Brahmans.'† 'So be it,'
replied Ashťávakra, and, thereupon, came up from the
waters. When the nymphs beheld him coming out of
the water, and saw that he was (very) ugly, and crooked
in eight places, they could not restrain their merri-
ment, but laughed aloud. The Muni was (very) angry,
and cursed them, and said: 'Since you have been so
impertinent as to laugh at my deformity, I denounce
upon you this imprecation: through the grace I have
shown unto you, you shall obtain the first of males:
for your husband; but, in consequence of my curse,
you |shall (afterwards) fall into the hands of thieves.'
When the nymphs heard this uttered by the Muni,
they endeavoured to appease him; and (they so far
succeeded, that) he announced to them, they should
finally return to the sphere of the gods. It is in consequence, then, of the curse of the Muni Ashťávakra, that
these females, who were, at first, the wives of Keśava,
have, now, fallen into the hands of the barbarians;§
and there is no occasion, Arjuna, for you to regret
it in the least. All this destruction has been effected
by the lord of all; and your end is, also, nigh at hand,
since he has withdrawn from you strength, splendour,
valour, and preeminence.¶ Death is the doom of every

* Purushottama, i, e., Vishńu or Kŕishńa.
† According to all my MSS., the term here rendered "sovereign of
the Brahmans" is in the vocative, and applies to Ashťávakra.
‡ Purushottama, as above.
§ Dasyu.
|| Addressed, in the original, as Páńdava.
¶ Máhátmya.

one who is born; fall is the end of exaltation; union terminates in separation; and growth tends but to decay.* Knowing (all this), wise men are susceptible of neither grief nor joy; and those who learn their ways are even as they are,—(equally free from pleasure or pain). Do you, therefore, most excellent prince, understand this (truth), and, along with your brothers, relinquish everything, and repair to the holy forest. Go, now. and say, from me, to Yudhishthira,† that he, to-morrow, with his brethren, tread the path of heroes.":

Thus instructed by Vyása, Arjuna went and related to the other sons of Prithá all that he had seen, had experienced, and had heard.§ When he had communicated to them the message of Vyása. the sons of Pándu placed Parikshit on the throne, and went to the forest.

I have thus narrated to you, Maitreya, in detail, the actions of Vásudeva, when he was born in the race of Yadu.

---

* आतस्व नियतं मृत्युः पतनं च तथोन्नतेः ।
विप्रयोगावसानञ्च संयोग: संचयत्त्यय: ॥

Instead of संचयत्त्यय:, some MSS. give: संचयात्त्यय: ।

† Denominated, in the Sanskrit, by his epithet Dharmarája. Yama, also, is so called. See Vol. III., p. 118.

: परस्वो भ्रातृभि: सार्धं गतिं वीरपथा कुरु ।

The more ordinary reading ends the verse with the words यथा यासि तथा कुरु ।

§ रहुक्तोऽभेत्य पार्थाभ्यां यमाभ्यां चाह सौऽर्जुन: ।
वृहं चैवानुभूतं च कथितं तद्ग्रूपत: ॥

By the two Párthas here spoken of, Yudhishthira and Bhima are intended, in the opinion of Ratnagarbha.

The words च सहार्जुन: end the first verse, according to some MSS.

VISHŃU PURÁŃA.

BOOK VI.

CHAPTER I.

Of the dissolution of the world: the four ages: the decline of all
things, and deterioration of mankind, in the Kali age.

MAITREYA.—You have narrated to me, illustrious
sage, the creation (of the world), the genealogies (of
the patriarchs), the duration* of the Manwantaras, and
the dynasties† (of princes), in detail. I am now desirous to hear from you (an account of) the dissolution
of the world, the season of total destruction, and that
which occurs at the expiration of a Kalpa.[1]

PARÁŚARA.—Hear from me, Maitreya, exactly (the
circumstances of) the end of all things,‡ and the disso-

---

[1] Two kinds of great or universal dissolution are here intimated; one occurring at the end of a Kalpa, or day of Brahmá,
to which the term Upasaṁhṛiti is applied in the text, and Átyan-
tika-laya by the commentator;§ and the other taking place at
the end of the life of Brahmá, which is termed a great or elemental dissolution: Mahá-pralaya and Prákṛita-pralaya.

---

* *Sthiti.*
† *Vaṁśanucharita.*
‡ *Upasaṁhṛiti.*
§ Ratnagarbha.

lution that occurs either at the expiration of a Kalpa, or that which takes place at the close of the life of Brahmá.[*] A month (of mortals) is a day and night of the progenitors: a year (of mortals is a day and night) of the gods Twice a thousand aggregates of the four ages is a day and night of Brahmá.[1][†] The four ages are the Kŕita, Tretá, Dwápara, and Kali; comprehending, together, twelve thousand years of the gods. There are infinite: successions of these four ages, of a similar description, the first of which is (always) called the Kŕita, and the last, the Kali. In the first, the Kŕita, is that age§ which is created by Brahmá; in the last, which is the Kali age, a dissolution of the world occurs.||

MAITREYA.—Venerable sir, you are able to give me a description of (the nature of) the Kali age, in which four-footed virtue[2] suffers total extinction.

---

[1] These measures of time are more fully detailed iu the First Book. See Vol. I., pp. 46, et seq.

[2] This is an allusion to a popular notion, originating, probably, with Manu: "In the Kŕita age, the Genius of truth and right • • • • stands firm on his four feet; • • • • • but, in the

---

[*] "At the close of the life of Brahmá" is to translate प्रा्षते ।

[†] चतुर्युगसहस्ने तु ब्रह्मणो दे विजोत्तम ।

[‡] *Aśesha.*

§ Read "creation". Professor Wilson here went wrong from following his favourite MS., which, from the fault of the copyist, begins the verse with आबे क्षतयुगाँ ब्रह्मणा । See the next note. Besides, *yuga*, in the sense of 'age', is neuter.

|| आबे क्षतयुगे सर्गो ब्रह्मणा क्रियते यत: ।
क्रियते चोपसंहारस्तथाब्धे च कली युगे ॥

PARÁŚARA.—Hear, Maitreya, an account (of the nature) of the Kali age, respecting which you have inquired, and which is now close at hand.

The observance of caste, order, and institutes will not prevail in the Kali age:* nor will that of the ceremonial enjoined by the Sáma-, Rig-, and Yajur-Vedas. Marriages, in this age, will not be conformable to the ritual;† nor will the rules that connect the spiritual preceptor and his disciple be in force. The laws that regulate the conduct of husband and wife will be disregarded; and oblations to the gods with fire no longer be offered. In whatever family he may be born, a powerful and rich man will be held entitled to espouse maidens of every tribe. A regenerate man will be initiated in any way whatever; and such acts of penance as may be performed will be unattended by any results.[1]: Every text will be scripture, that people

---

following ages, • • • • he is deprived, successively, of one foot," &c.§ I., 81, 82.

[1] "Such an act is just what it is:" या सेव मायश्चित्तक्रिया
कसी।¶ That is, it may be attended by inconvenience to the individual, but is utterly inefficacious for the expiation of sin.

---

* वर्णाश्रमाचारवती प्रवृत्तिर्न कसौ नृणाम् ।

† *Dharmya.*

: धैव सेव च भैवेव मायश्चित्तक्रिया कसौ ।

§ From Sir William Jones's Translation.

| चतुष्पात्सकलो धर्म: सत्यं चैव कृते युगे ।
  नाधर्मेणागम: कश्चिन्मनुष्यान्प्रतिवर्त्ते ॥
  इतरेष्वागमाद्धर्म: पादशस्त्ववरोपित: ।
  चौरिकानृतमायाभिर्धर्मश्चापैति पादश: ॥

¶ This was suggested by the comment of Śrīdhara, who understands penance to be spoken of which is performed simply for popular applause,

choose to think so;[1] all gods will be gods to them that
worship them;[*] and all orders of life will be common
alike to all persons. In the Kali age, fasting, auste-
rity,[†] liberality, practised according to the pleasure of
those by whom they are observed, will constitute
righteousness. Pride (of wealth) will be inspired by
very insignificant possessions. Pride of beauty:[‡] will
be prompted by (no other personal charm than fine)
hair. Gold, jewels, diamonds,[§] clothes, will, all, have
perished; and then hair will be the only ornament with
which women can decorate themselves.[||] Wives will
desert their husbands, when they lose their property;
and they only who are wealthy will be considered, by
women, as their lords. He who gives away much
(money) will be the master of men; and family descent

---

[1] Whether it is conformable or contradictory to the Vedas and
the law. The passage ¶ may be rendered, also: "The doctrine
or dogma of any one soever will be scripture."

---

and not to wipe away sin. His words are एव सेवेति । प्रायश्चित्तक्रिया
लोकरञ्जनमानार्था न तु पापचयार्था । Ratnagarbha says: एव शेव ।
अनियतेत्यर्थः ।

[*] देवताश्च कली सर्वाः । This rather implies, that unaccredited gods
will receive honour. Ratnagarbha says: येन तेन कल्पिताः सर्वा
देवताः ।

[†] Áyása. Ratnagarbha explains it by penance, or pilgrimage: आयासः ।
कृच्छादि: । तीर्थयात्रादिर्वा ।

[‡] In women. The verse runs:
स्त्रीणां रूपमदश्चैव केशैरेव भविष्यति ।

[§] Ratna.

[||] कली स्त्रियो भविष्यन्ति तदा केशैरलंकृताः ।

[¶] सर्वमेव कली शास्त्रं यस्य यद्वचनं द्विज ।

will no longer be a title of supremacy.* Accumulated treasures will be expended on (ostentatious) dwellings. The minds of men will be wholly occupied in acquiring wealth; and wealth will be spent solely on selfish gratifications.† Women will follow their inclinations, and be ever fond of pleasure. Men will fix their desires upon riches, even though dishonestly acquired. No man will part with the smallest fraction of the smallest coin,[1] though entreated by a friend. Men of all degrees will conceit themselves to be equal with Brahmans. Cows will be held in esteem, only as they supply milk.[2] The people will be, almost always, in dread of dearth, and apprehensive of scarcity, ‡ and will, hence, ever be watching (the appearances of) the sky: they will, all, live, like anchorets,§ upon leaves, and roots, and fruit; and put a period to their lives, through fear of famine and want. || In truth, there will never be abun-

---

[1] He will not part with the half of the half of half a Pana,—that is, with ten Cowries: a Pana being equal to eighty Cowries (or small shells).¶ Five Panas are equal to one Anna, or the sixteenth of a Rupee; and, at two shillings the Rupee, ten Cowries are equal to about one-seventh of a farthing.

[2] They will be valued for their individual use only, not from any notion of their generic sanctity.

---

* स्वामित्वहेतुः संबन्धो भावी नाभिजनस्तदा ।

† गृहात्ता द्रव्यसंघाता द्रव्यात्ता च तथा मतिः ।
अर्थस्वात्मोपभोगात्ता भविष्यन्ति कलौ युगे ॥

Much that follows this is, likewise, freely rendered.

‡ *Kshudh*, 'hunger,' 'famine.'

§ *Tápasa*, 'ascetics.'

|| अवृष्ट्यादिदुःखिताः ।

¶ See Colebrooke's *Algebra, &c.,* p. 1.

dance, in the Kali age; and men will never enjoy pleasure and happiness.* They will take their food without previous ablution, and without worshipping fire,
gods, or guests, or offering† obsequial libations to
their progenitors. The women will be fickle,‡ short
of stature, gluttonous. They will have many children,
and little means. Scratching their heads with both
hands, they will pay no attention to the commands of
their husbands or parents. They will be selfish, abject,
and slatternly; they will be scolds and liars; they will
be indecent and immoral in their conduct, and will
ever attach themselves to dissolute men. Youths, although disregarding the rules of studentship, will study
the Vedas. Householders will neither sacrifice nor
practise becoming liberality. Anchorets§ will subsist
upon food accepted from rustics; and mendicants will
be influenced by regard for friends and associates.[1]
Princes, instead of protecting, will plunder, their subjects, and, under the pretext of levying customs, will

---

[1] The Bhágavata‖ has: "Religious students will be regardless
of vows and purification; householders will beg, not give alms;
anchorets will dwell in villages; and mendicants will be desirous
of riches."

* दुर्भिक्षमेव सततं तदा क्षेत्रमनीश्वराः ।
  प्राप्स्यन्ति व्याहतसुखप्रमोदा मानवाः कलौ ॥
† Read "and they will not offer", &c.
‡ *Lolupa*, 'covetous.'
§ *Vanavása*, 'hermits.' *Vánaprasthas* are meant; for whose duties,
see Vol. III., pp. 94—97.
‖ XII., III., 33:

अव्रता बटवोऽशौचा भिक्षवश्च कुटुम्बिनः ।
तपस्विनो ग्रामवासा न्यासिनो अर्थलोलुपाः ॥

rob merchants of their property. In the Kali age, every one who has cars, and elephants, and steeds will be a Raja;[1] every one who is feeble will be a slave.* Vaisyas will abandon agriculture and commerce, and gain a livelihood by servitude,† or the exercise of mechanical arts.‡ Súdras, seeking a subsistence by begging, and assuming the outward marks of religious mendicants, will become the impure followers of impious and heretical doctrines.[2]§

Oppressed by famine and taxation, men will desert their native lands, and go to those countries which are fit for coarser grains.[3] The path of the Vedas being

---

[1] That is, princes and warriors will be so no longer by virtue of their birth and caste.

[2] Most of the mendicant orders admit members without distinction of caste; but, probably, Buddhists, especially, are here intended. The Bhágavata repeatedly alludes to the diffusion of heretical doctrines and practices, the substitution of outward signs and marks for devotion, and the abandonment of the worship of Vishńu. The Śaiva mendicant orders are, probably, those especially in view. The same, probably, are intended, by our text, in the subsequent allusion to unauthorized austerities and sectarial marks.

[3] "Gavedhuka ‖ (Coix barbata) and other bad sorts of grain:" गवेधुककदमाद्यान्देशान् । Another reading is गोधूमाम्रयवाम्नान्देशान् । ¶ "Countries growing wheat, barley, and the like." But to place wheat and barley amongst inferior grains, and to

---

* Bhŕitya, 'servant.'
† Súdra-vŕitti.
‡ Káru-karman.
§ भैक्षव्रतास्तथा शूद्रा: प्रव्रज्यालिङ्गिनोऽधमा: ।
पाषण्डसंश्रयां वृत्तिमाश्रयिष्यन्तसंस्कृता: ॥
‖ For gavedhuká, the same grain, see Vol. I., p. 95.
¶ This is Ratnagarbha's reading.

obliterated, and men having deviated into heresy, iniquity will flourish, and the duration of life will (therefore,) decrease. In consequence of horrible penances, not enjoined by scripture, and of the vices of the rulers, children will die in their infancy. Women will bear children at the sage of five, six, or seven years; and men beget them, when they are eight, nine, or ten. A man will be grey, when he is twelve; and no one will exceed twenty years of life.[1] Men will possess little sense, vigour, or virtue, and will, therefore, perish in a very brief period. In proportion as heresy extends, so, Maitreya, shall the progress of the Kali age be estimated by the wise. In proportion as the number of the pious who adhere to the lessons of the Vedas diminishes, as the efforts of individuals who cultivate virtue relax, as the first of males becomes no longer the object of sacrifices,* as respect for the teachers of the Vedas declines, and as regard is acknowledged for the disseminators of heresy, so may wise men note the augmented influence of the Kali age.[2]†

---

rank them lower than rice, is a classification that could have occurred to a native of Bengal alone.

　[1] The Váyu says three and twenty; the Bhágavata,‡ from twenty to thirty.

　[2] The complaints of the prevalence of heterodox doctrines, and neglect of the practices of the Vedas, which recur in the

* यदा यदा न यज्ञानामीश्वर: पुरुषोत्तम: ।
　रज्यते पुरुषैर्यज्ञैसदा श्रेयं कलेर्बलम् ॥
† न भीतिर्वेदवादेषु पाषण्डेषु यदा रुचि: ।
　कलिवृद्धिसदा प्राधीरनुमेया द्विजोत्तम ॥
‡ XII., II., 11.

In the Kali age, Maitreya, men, corrupted by unbe-
lievers, will refrain from adoring Vishńu, the lord of
sacrifice,* the creator and lord of all, and will say:
"Of what authority are the Vedas? What are gods, or
Brahmans? What need is there of purification with
water?"† Then will the clouds yield scanty rain; then
will the corn be light in ear; and the grain will be
(poor and) of little sap. Garments will be, mostly,
made of the fibres of the San;¹‡ the principal of trees
will be the Śamí;² the prevailing caste will be the Śúdra. Millet will be the more common grain; the milk
in use will be, chiefly, that of goats; unguents will be
made of Uśíra-grass.§ The mother- and father-in-law
will be venerated in place of parents; and a man's
friends will be his brother-in-law, or one who has a

Bhágavata and our text, indicate a period of change in the condition of the Hindu religion, which it would be important to
verify. If reference is made to Buddhism,—to which, in some
respects, the allusions especially apply,—it would, probably, denote
a period not long subseqnent to the Christian era; but it is more
likely to be of a later date, or in the eighth and ninth centuries,
when Śankara‖ is said to have reformed a variety of corrupt
practices, and given rise to others. See Asiatic Researches, Vol.
XVI., p. 12.¶
    ¹ Crotalaria juncea.
    ² The silk cotton, Bombax heptaphyllum.**

    * *Yajnapati.* Variant: *jagatpati.*
    † किं वेदैः किं द्विजैर्देवैः किं शौचेनाम्बुअम्बगा ।
    ‡ *Śańi.* The word also means 'mere rags'.
    § Andropogon muricatum.
    ‖ See Vol. I., Preface, p. XVI.
    ¶ Or Professor Wilson's collected Works, Vol. I., pp. 14, 15.
    ** This is the *śálmali.* Read acacia suma.

wanton * wife. Men will say: "Who has a father?
Who has a mother? Each one is born according to his
deeds. "† And, therefore, they will look upon a wife's
or husband's parents as their own. : Endowed with
little sense, men, subject to all the infirmities of mind,
speech, and body, will daily commit sins; and everything that is calculated to afflict beings, vicious, impure, and wretched, will be generated in the Kali age.
Then shall some places follow a separate duty,[1]§ devoid

[1] The expression Kwachil lokah (क्वचिल्लोकः), 'a certain place,'
is explained, by the commentator,‖ 'Kikaṭa, &c.' (कीकटादी);
confirming the inference that Buddhism is especially aimed at in
the previous passages; for Kikaṭa,¶ or South Behar, is the scene
of Śákya's earliest and most successful labours.

* Hári, 'handsome.'

† यदा कर्मात्मकः पुमान् ।

: खगुरानुगता नरा: । This is the whole that the English is intended
to translate.

§ तदा प्रविरलो विप्र क्वचिल्लोको निवर्त्स्यति ।

‖ So it is explained by both Śrídhara and Ratnagarbha.

¶ The Kikaṭas are spoken of in the Ṛigveda, III., LIII., 14. In the
third volume of his Translation, Introduction, p. XX., Professor Wilson
speculates on their locality; and, again, in p. 86, note 4, commenting on
the passage adverted to, as follows: "The Kikaṭas are said, by Sáyaṇa,—
following Yáska, Nirukta, VI., 32,—to be countries inhabited by anáryas,
people who do not perform worship, who are infidels, nástikas. Kikaṭa
is usually identified with South Behar; showing, apparently, that Vaidik
Hinduism had not reached the province, when this was said. Or, as
Kikaṭa was the fountain-head of Buddhism, it might be asserted that the
Buddhists were here alluded to, if it were not wholly incompatible with
all received notions of the earlier date of the Vedas."

Père Vivien de Saint-Martin, in his Étude sur la Géographie, &c.,
pp. 138—144, is very full, if not conclusive, on the country of the Kikaṭas. It is by no means improbable that this name was borne by two
peoples, sundered by a very considerable interval of space, and belonging
to different periods. In the Bhágavata-puráṇa, I., III., 24, it is said
that Buddha, son of Anjana, will be born among the Kikaṭas.

* संदेहनिर्णयार्थाय वेदव्यासं महामुनिम् ।
ययुस्ते संशयं प्रष्टुं मैत्रेय मुनिपुङ्गवाः ॥

of holy study, oblations to fire,* and invocations of the gods.[1]† Then, in the Kali age, shall a man acquire, by a trifling exertion, as much eminence in virtue as is the result of arduous penance in the Kríta age (or age of purity).[2]

---

[1] Several of the Puráńas contain allusions to the degeneracy of the Kali age; but none afford more copious details. The description in the Bhágavata is much shorter; that of the Váyu is much the same, and employs many of the same verses and illustrations.

[2] This might be suspected of being said ironically, referring to what had been just observed of places where a religion prevailed that required neither study nor sacrifice. The commentator, however, understands it literally, and asserts, that allusion is here made to the Vaishńava faith, in which devotion to Vishńu or Kríshńa, and the mere repetition of his name, are equally efficacious, in the Kali age, with the penances and sacrifices of the preceding ages. Therefore, he concludes, the Kali, by this one property, is the best of all the ages: चुनेनेकेन गुबेन कलि: सर्वश्रेष्ठ रुक्ष्वं: । ‡ This interpretation is confirmed by the following Chapter.

---

* *Vashatkára.* See Vol. II., p. 29, notes 3 and §.
† *Swadhá* and *swáhá.* See Vol. III., p. 122, note ‡, *ad finem.*
‡ Both the commentators give this explanation

CHAPTER II.

Redeeming properties of the Kali age. Devotion to Vishńu sufficient to salvation, in that age, for all castes and persons.

UPON this subject, Maitreya, you shall hear what
the wise Vyása has related, as it is communicated truly
by me.

It was, once, a matter of dispute, amongst the sages,
at what season the least moral merit obtained the greatest reward, and by whom it was most easily displayed.
In order to terminate the discussion, they went to Veda
Vyása, to remove their doubts.* They found the
illustrious Muni, my son, half immersed in the water
of the Ganges;† and, awaiting the close of his ablu-
tions, the sages remained on the banks of the sacred‡
stream, under shelter of a grove of trees. As my son
plunged down into the water, and again rose up from
it, the Munis heard him exclaim: "Excellent, excellent
is the Kali age!" Again he dived, and, again rising,
said, in their hearing: "Well done, well done, Súdra!
Thou art happy." Again he sank down; and, as he
once more emerged, they heard him say: "Well done,
well done, women! They are happy. Who are more
fortunate than they?" After this, my son finished his
bathing; and the sages met him, as he approached to
welcome them. After he had given them seats, and

---

* संदेहनिर्णयार्थाय वेद्व्वासं महामुनिम् ।
  ययुस्ते संशयं प्रष्टुं भैरेय मुनिपुङ्गवाः ॥

† Jáhnavi, in the original.

‡ 'Great', according to the Sanskrit.

they had proffered their respects, the son of Satya-
vati* said to them: "On what account have you come
to me?" They replied: "We came to you to consult
you on a subject on which we entertain some doubt.
But that may be, at present, suspended. Explain to us
something else. We heard you say: 'Excellent is the
Kali age. Well done, Súdra! Well done, women!'
Now we are desirous to know why this was said, why
you called them, repeatedly, happy. Tell us the meaning of it, if it be not a mystery. We will then propose
to you the question that occupies our thoughts."

Being thus addressed by the Munis, Vyása smiled,
and said to them: "Hear, excellent sages, why I uttered
the words 'Well done! Well done!' The fruit of penance, of continence,† of silent prayer, and the like,
practised, in the Kŕita age, for ten years, in the Tretá,
for one year, in the Dwápara, for a month, is obtained,
in the Kali age, in a day and night. Therefore did I
exclaim: 'Excellent, excellent is the Kali age.' That
reward which a man obtains, in the Kŕita, by abstract
meditation, in the Tretá, by sacrifice, in the Dwápara,
by adoration, he receives, in the Kali, by merely reciting the name of Keśava. In the Kali age, a man dis-
plays the most exalted virtue by (very) little exertion:
therefore, (pious sages,) who know what virtue is, I
was pleased with the Kali age. Formerly, the Vedas
were to be acquired, by the twice-born, through the
diligent observance of self-denial;‡ and it was their
duty to celebrate sacrifices conformably to the ritual.

* See Vol. IV., p. 158.
† Brahmacharya.
‡ Vratacharyá.

Then idle prayers,* idle feasts, and fruitless ceremonies were practised but to mislead the twice-born; for,
although observed, by them, devoutly, yet, in consequence of some irregularity in their celebration, sin
was incurred in all their works; and what they ate or
what they drank did not effect the fulfilment of their
desires.† In all their objects the twice-born enjoyed
no independence; and they attained their respective
spheres only with exceeding pain. The Śúdra, (on the
contrary,) more fortunate than they, reaches his assigned station by rendering them service, and performing merely the sacrifice of preparing food, ‡ in
which § no rules determine what may or may not be
eaten, what may or may not be drunk. Therefore, most
excellent sages,‖ is the Śúdra fortunate.

"Riches are accumulated, by men, in modes not incompatible with their peculiar duties; and they are
then to be bestowed upon the worthy, and expended
in constant sacrifice. There is great trouble in their
acquisition; great care, in their preservation; great
distress, from the want of them;¶ and great grief, for

---

* *Kathá.* "Praise of Kŕishńa", the commentators say.

† A free rendering.

‡ पाकयज्ञाधिकारवान् ׀ This implies "possessing the privilege of
domestic sacrifices." For the *pákayajnas,* which have nothing to do with
ordinary cookery, see Vol. III., p. 114, notes ‡ and §.

§ This has not the connexion with what precedes that the Translator
supposed. For "in which", read "and for him", or the like,—to render
freely.

‖ *Muni-śárdúla.*

¶ It is, rather, implied, that there is difficulty in the proper application
of them:

तथा सद्विनियोगाय विद्धेयं गहनं नृणाम् ׀

their loss.* Thus, eminent Brahmans, through these
and other sources of anxiety, men attain their allotted
spheres of Prajápati† and the rest, (only by exceeding
labour and suffering). (This is not the case with
women.) A woman has only to honour her husband,
in act, thought, and speech, to reach the same region
to which he is elevated; and she, thus, accomplishes
her object without any great exertion. This was the
purport of my exclamation 'Well done!' the third time.
I have, thus, related to you (what you asked). Now
demand the question you came to put to me, in any
way you please; and I will make you a distinct reply."
The Munis then said (to Vyása): "The question we
intended to have asked you has been already answered,
by you, in your reply to our subsequent inquiry."
On hearing which, Kríshńa Dwaipáyana laughed, and said
to the holy persons: who had come to see him, whose
eyes were wide open with astonishment: "I perceived,
with the eye (of) divine (knowledge), the question you
intended to ask; and, in allusion to it, I uttered the
expressions 'Well done! Well done!' In truth, in the
Kali age, duty is discharged with very little trouble§
by mortals whose faults are, all, washed away by the
water of their individual merits; by Súdras, through
diligent attendance (only) upon the twice-born; and
by women, through the slight effort of obedience to
their husbands. Therefore, Brahmans, did I thrice ex-

---

* I find no Sanskrit for this clause.
† In the original, Prájápatya. For this heaven, see Vol. I., p. 98,
notes 1 and *.
‡ Tápasa.
§ Some MSS. yield 'time'.

press my admiration of their happiness; for, in the Kŕita and other ages, great were the toils of the regenerate to perform their duty. I waited not for your inquiry, but replied, at once, to the question you purposed to ask. Now, ye who know what virtue is, what else do you wish me to tell you?"

The Munis then saluted and praised Vyása, and, being freed, by him, from uncertainty, departed as they came. To you, also, excellent (Maitreya), have I imparted this secret,—this one great virtue of the (otherwise) vicious Kali age.* The dissolution † of the world, and the aggregation of the elements,‡ I will now describe to you.[1]

---

[1] The illustration of the efficacy of devotion to Vishńu, given in this Chapter, is peculiar to this Puráńa; but the doctrine is common to it and the Bhágavata. It is repeatedly inculcated in that work. The parallel passage, in the Twelfth Book, § is the following: "Purushottama, abiding in the hearts of men, takes

---

* Śrídhara seems to recognize the following verse, disregarded by the Translator:

कीर्त्तनादेव कृष्णस्य मुक्तबन्धः परं व्रजेत् ।

This verse is identical with one near the end of the passage cited, from the Bhágavata-puráńa, in note §, below.

† Upasaṁhṛiti.

‡ प्राक्षतामन्तराणाम् । Śrídhara: अन्तराणाम् । ब्रह्मणो दिने दिने भवाम् । Ratnagarbha: अन्तराणाम् । दैनंदिनीम् ।

§ Chapter III., 45—52:

पुंसां कलिकृतान्दोषान्द्रव्यदेशात्मसंभवान् ।
सर्वान्हरति चित्तस्थो भगवान्पुरुषोत्तमः ॥
श्रुतः संकीर्त्तितो ध्यातः पूजितश्चादृतोऽपि वा ।
नृणां धुनोति भगवान्हृत्स्थो जन्मायुताशुभम् ॥
यथा हेम्नि स्थितो वह्निर्दुर्वर्णं हन्ति धातुजम् ।
एवमात्मगतो विष्णुर्योगिनामशुभाश्रयम् ॥

away all the sins of the Kali age, produced by place or property. Bhagavat, abiding in the heart, and heard, repeated, read of, worshipped, or honoured, dissipates the ills of men for ten thousand births. As fire, entering into the substance of gold, purifies it from the alloy with which it is debased in the mine, so Vishńu, united with the devotee, is the refiner from all that is evil. . By learning, penance, suppression of breath, friendship, pilgrimage, ablution, mortification, gifts, prayer, the soul attains not that exceeding purity which it derives from the presence of Vishńu. Therefore, with all your soul, O king, hold Keśava ever present in your heart. Let one about to die be most careful in this; for so he goes to supreme felicity. Let the name of the supreme god, Vishńu, be repeated, diligently, by all, in their last moments; for he who desires liberation shall attain it by the frequent repetition of the name of Krishńa. Final felicity is derived, in the Krita age, from holy study; in the Tretá, from religious rites. In the Dwápara, it is attained by pious services; but, in the Kali age, it is secured by repeating the name of Hari." Similar doctrines are taught in the Gítá, and other Vaishńava works. See Asiatic Researches, Vol. XVI., p. 116. *

विवातपःप्रायनिरोधमैची-
तीर्थाभिषेकव्रतदानजन्यैः ।
नालभतग्रुद्धिं लभतेऽन्तराला
यथा हृदिस्थे भगवत्यनन्ते ॥
तस्मात्सर्वात्मना राजन्हृदिस्थं कुरुकेशवम् ।
म्रियमाणो ह्यवहितस्ततो यासि परां गतिम् ॥
म्रियमाणैरभिध्येयो भगवान्परमेश्वरः ।
आत्मभावं न यत्त्वङ्क सर्वात्मा सर्वसंश्रयः ॥
कलेर्दोषनिधे राजन्नस्ति ह्येको महागुणः ।
कीर्तनादेव कृष्णस्य मुक्तबन्धः परं व्रजेत् ॥
कृते यद्ध्यायतो विष्णुं त्रेतायां यजतो मखैः ।
द्वापरे परिचर्यायां कलौ तद्धरिकीर्तनात् ॥

Three different kinds of dissolution. Duration of a Parárdha.
The clepsydra, or vessel for measuring time. The dissolution
that occurs at the end of a day of Brahmá.

THE dissolution[*] of existing beings is of three
kinds,—incidental, elemental, and absolute.[1] The incidental is that which relates to Brahmá, and occurs at
the end of a Kalpa; the elemental is that which takes

---

[1] The first is called Naimittika,[†] 'occasional' or 'incidental,'
or Bráhmya, as occasioned by the intervals of Brahmá's days;
the destruction of creatures, though not of the substance of the
world, occurring during his night. The general resolution of the
elements into their primitive source, or Prakṛiti, is the Prákṛitika
destruction, and occurs at the end of Brahmá's life. The third,
the absolute or final, Átyantika, is individual annihilation; Moksha,
exemption for ever from future existence.[‡] The Bhágavata[§] here
notices the fourth kind, of which mention occurred in a preceding
passage (Vol. I., p. 113),—Nitya, or constant dissolution;—explaining it to be the imperceptible change that all things suffer
in the various stages of growth and decay, life and death. "The
various conditions of beings subject to change are occasioned by
that constant dissolution of life which is rapidly produced by the
resistless stream of time, taking everything perpetually away:"

कालस्रोतोअवेगायु त्रियमाणस्य निवद्या ।
परिणामिनामवस्नाद्या अव्यमलयहेतवः ॥

The Váyu describes but three kinds of Pralaya, omitting the
Nitya.

---

[*] *Pratisanchara.* See Vol. I., p. 52, note *.
[†] Corrected from "Naimittaka".
[‡] *Vide supra*, p. 61, note §, *ad finem*.
[§] XII., IV., 35.

place after two Parárdhas; the absolute is (final) liberation * (from existence).

MAITREYA.—Tell me, excellent master, what is the
enumeration of a Parárdha, the expiration of two of
which is the period of elemental dissolution.[1]

PARÁSARA.—A Parárdha, Maitreya, is that number
which occurs in the eighteenth place of figures, enumerated according to the rule of decimal notation.[2] At

---

[1] Maitreya has a rather indifferent memory (see Vol. I., pp. 46,
47); but the periods specified in the two places do not agree. In
the First Book, two Parárdhas, as equal to one hundred years
of Brahmá, are 311.040.000.000.000 years of mortals.

[2] Counting according to this mode of enumeration, a Parárdha
is represented by 100.000.000.000.000.000. The Váyu Puráṇa† has

---

* Moksha.
† Quoted by Śrídhara and Ratnagarbha, as follows:

कोटिकोटिसहस्राणि परार्धमिति कीर्त्यते ।
परार्धं द्विगुणं चापि परमाङ्कमणीषिणः ॥
ख्वानं दशगुणं विवादेकं दश शतं ततः ।
सहस्रमयुतं तक्षानियुतं प्रयुतं ततः ॥
अर्बुदं न्यर्बुदं चैव वृन्दं चैव ततः परम् ।
खर्वं चैव निखर्वं च प्राहुः पद्मस्तैव च ॥
समुद्रो मध्यमन्तश्च परार्धं परमेव च ।
एवमष्टादशैतानि पदानि गणनाविधौ ॥

The English of this is, in brief, as below, and corrects Professor Wilson's representation, in several particulars:

Eka	1
Daśa	10
Śata	100
Sahasra	1.000
Ayuta	10.000
Niyuta	100.000
Prayuta	1.000.000
Arbuda	10.000.000

the end of twice that period, elemental dissolution
occurs, when all the discrete products of nature are

---

a term for each of these decimal values: Daśa (दश), 10; Śata
(शत), 100; Sahasra (सहस्र), 1000; Ayuta (अयुत), 10.000; Niyuta
(नियुत), 100.000; Prayuta (प्रयुत), 1.000.000; Arbuda (अर्बुद),
10.000.000; Nyarbuda* (न्यर्बुद), 100.000.000; Vŕinda (वृन्द),
1.000.000.000; Para† (पर), 10.000.000.000; Kharva (खर्व),
100.000.000.000; Nikharva (निखर्व), 1.000.000.000.000; Śankha
(शङ्ख), 10.000.000.000.000; Padma (पद्म), 100.000.000.000.000; Samudra (समुद्र), 1.000.000.000.000.000; Madhyama‡ (मध्यम),
10.000 000.000.000.000;§ Parárdha (परार्ध), 100.000.000.000.000.000. ||

Nyarbuda 100.000.000
Vŕinda............... 1.000.000.000
Kharva 10.000.000.000
Nikharva 100.000.000.000
Śankha............1.000 000.000.000
Padma...........10.000.000.000.000
Samudra 100.000.000.000.000
Madhya 1.000.000.000.000.000
Anta......... 10.000.000.000.000.000
Parárdha.... 100.000.000.000.000.000
2 parárdhas, i. e., half-paras, = a para.

Our commentators' manuscripts of the Váyu-puráṇa must have differed
very noticeably, as to the foregoing passage, from those to which I have
access.

A niyuta denotes, according to different authorities, a hundred thousand,
a million, &c. More usually, however, it is a synonym of laksha; as in
the passage annotated supra, p. 92, note ‡. See Messrs. Böhtlingk and
Roth's Sanskrit-Wörterbuch, sub voce नियुत.

For a very learned article on Sanskrit numeration, from the pen of
Dr. Albrecht Weber, see the Zeitschrift der Deutschen morgenländischen
Gesellschaft, Vol. XV., pp. 132—140.

  * Corrected from "Nyurvuda", and the Sanskrit similarly.

  † The original word is not, here, a technicality.

  ‡ Read "Madhya". See note † in the preceding page.

  § Anta is here omitted.

  || In the Lilávati, Chapter II., Section I., the parárdha is arrived at
differently, in this wise:

withdrawn into their indiscrete source. The shortest period of time is a Mátrá, which is equal to the twinkling of the human eye.* Fifteen Mátrás make a Káshthá; thirty Káshthás, one Kalá; fifteen Kalás, one Nádiká. A Nádiká is ascertained by a measure of water, with a vessel made of twelve Palas and a half of copper, in the bottom of which there is to be a hole made with a tube of gold, of the weight of four Máshas, and four inches long.¹† According to the Mágadha measure,

In the First Book, the Parárdha, as the half of Brahmá's life, is but 155.520.000.000.000,—fifteen, instead of eighteen, places of figures.

¹ The description of the Clepsydra is very brief, and wanting

Eka	1
Dasa	10
Sata	100
Sahasra	1.000
Ayuta	10.000
Laksha	100.000
Prayuta	1.000.000
Koti	10.000.000
Arbuda	100 000.000
Abja	1.000.000.000
Kharva	10.000.000.000
Nikharva	100.000.000.000
Mahápadma	1.000.000.000.000
Sanku	10.000.000.000.000
Jaladhi	100.000.000.000.000
Antya	1.000.000.000.000.000
Madhya	10.000.000.000.000.000
Parárdha	100.000.000.000.000.000

As words, *abja* is a synonym of *padma*; and *jaladhi*, of *samudra*.

* निमेषो आगुषो योऽयं मात्रामात्र: प्रमाणत: ।

† तन्मानेनाक्षस: सा तु पलान्यर्धचयोद्श ।

इममाषे: कृतच्छिद्र चतुर्भिस्तुरङ्गुलि: ॥

The expression अर्धचयोद्श is explained, by the commentators, to mean "twelve and a half". The *Bhágavata-puráńa* has *dwádasárdha*.

the vessel should hold a Prastha (or sixteen Palas) of water. Two of these Nádikás make one Muhúrtta,— thirty of which are one day and night. Thirty such periods form a month; twelve months make a year, or a day and night of the gods; and three hundred and sixty such days constitute a year of the celestials. An aggregate of four ages contains twelve thousand divine years; and a thousand periods of four ages complete a day of Brahmá. That period is, also, termed a Kalpa, during which fourteen Manus preside; and, at the end of it, occurs the incidental or Brahmá dissolution. The nature of this dissolution is very fearful. Hear me describe it, as well as that which takes place at the elemental dissolution, which I will, also, relate to you.

At the end of a thousand periods of four ages, the earth is, for the most part, exhausted. A total dearth then ensues, which lasts a hundred years; and, in conse-

---

in precision. One of the commentaries* is more explicit: "A vessel made of twelve Palas and a half of copper, and holding a Prastha, (Mágadha measure) of water, broad at top, and having, at bottom, a tube of gold, of four Máshas weight, four fingers long, is placed in water; and the time in which the vessel is filled by the hole in the bottom is called a Nádiká:" साधैवाट्यपलताम्र-
मयं मागधं प्रस्थं संमितमूर्ध्वायतं पात्रं चतुर्माषचतुरङ्गुलहेमशलाकया छताधरिछद्रं जले स्थापितं तेन छिद्रेण यावता कालेन पूर्यते ताव-
त्कालो नाडिकेति। The term Saláká generally means a needle or stake; but it must, here, denote a pipe. The common measure of the Nádí is a thin shallow brass cup, with a small hole in the bottom. It is placed on the surface of water, in a large vessel, where nothing can disturb it, and where the water gradually fills the cup, and sinks it. Asiatic Researches, Vol. V., p. 87.

---

* Śrídhara's. Ratnagarbha enters into further particulars.

quence of the failure of food, all beings become languid and exanimate, and, at last, entirely perish.* The eternal† Vishńu then assumes the character of Rudra, the destroyer, and descends to reunite all (his) creatures with himself. He enters into the seven rays of the sun,[1]: drinks up all the waters (of the globe), and causes all moisture whatever, in living bodies or in the soil, to evaporate; thus drying up the whole earth. The seas, the rivers, the mountain torrents, and springs are, all, exhaled; and so are all the waters of Pátála,§ (the regions below the earth). Thus fed, through his intervention,‖ with abundant moisture, the seven solar rays dilate to seven suns,[2] whose radiance glows above,

---

[1] See Vol. II., p. 297, note 1.

[2] These, also, have their several appellations. The commentator¶ quotes the Vedas,** as the authority: Áraga.†† Bhrája, Paíala, Patanga, Swarńabháj,‡‡ Jyotishmat, and Savibhása.§§

---

* ततो यान्वल्करारागि तानि सत्त्वान्वषेतः ।
  षयं यान्ति मुनिश्रेष्ठ पार्श्विवान्वप्रपीडमात् ॥

† *Avyaya.* See Vol. I., p. 17, note *.

‡ See the *Taittiríya-áranyaka*, I., VII., I. The seven suns are there called Ároga, Bhrája, Paíara, Patanga, Swarńara, Jyotishmat, and Vibhása.

§ "The Pátálas", according to the Sanskrit. For these domains, see Vol. II., pp. 209, *et seq.*

‖ *Anubháva.*

¶ Both the commentators give the names following.

** Hereon the commentators cite a stanza: Ratnagarbha gives it as anonymous; but Śrídhara refers it to the *Kúrma-puráńa.* The seven rays are there said to be Sushumná, Harikeśa, Viśwakarman, Viśwavyarchas (?), Varchas, Vasu, Sampadvasu (?).

Compare the particulars in notes 1 and † to p. 297 of Vol. II.

†† So reads Ratnagarbha. Śrídhara has Ároga.

‡‡ Corrected from "Swamábhák". Śrídhara's reading, in my one MS., seems to be Swarńaroman.

§§ Vibhávasu, according to Śrídhara.

below, and on every side,* and sets the three worlds
and Pátála† on fire. The three worlds, consumed by
these suns, become rugged and deformed,‡ throughout
the whole extent of their mountains, rivers, and seas;
and the earth, bare of verdure, and destitute of moisture, alone remains, resembling, in appearance, the back
of a tortoise. The destroyer of all things, Hari, in the
form of Rudra, who is the flame of time, § becomes the
scorching breath of the serpent Śesha, and thereby re-
duces Pátála ‖ to ashes. The great fire, when it has
burnt all the divisions of Pátála, proceeds to the earth,
and consumes it, also. ¶ A vast whirlpool of eddying
flame then spreads to the region of the atmosphere,**
and the sphere of the gods,†† and wraps them in ruin.
The three spheres show like a frying-pan, amidst the
surrounding flames that prey upon all moveable or
stationary things. The inhabitants of the two (upper)
spheres, having discharged their functions,‡‡ and being
annoyed by the heat, remove to (the sphere above, or)
Mahar-loka. When that becomes heated, its tenants,
who, after the full period of their stay, are desirous of

* There is no Sanskrit for "on every side".
† The plural is better.
‡ For "rugged and deformed" the original has *nissneha*, "deprived of moisture."
§ *Kálágni.* See Vol. I., p. 128, text and note ‡.
‖ The original has the plural.

¶ पाताळानि समस्तानि स दग्ध्वा ज्वलनो महान् ।
भूमिमभ्येत्य सकलं बभक्ति वसुधातळम् ॥

** *Bhuvar-loka.* Variant: *Bhuvo-loka.*
†† *Swar-loka.*
‡‡ *Kŕitádhikára.* Variant: *hŕitádhikára,* "deprived of office."

ascending to higher regions, depart for the Jana-loka.[1*]

Janárdana, in the person of Rudra, having consumed the whole world, breathes forth heavy clouds; and those called Samvartaka,[†] resembling vast elephants, in bulk, overspread the sky,—roaring, and darting lightnings. Some are as black as the blue lotos; some are (white) as the water-lily; some are dusky, like smoke; and some are yellow; some are (of a dun colour,) like (that of) an ass; some, like ashes sprinkled on the forehead;[‡] some are (deep blue,) as the lapis lazuli; some

---

[1] The passage§ may, also, be understood: "Those go to Jana-loka, who are desirous of obtaining Brahma, or final liberation, through the ten stages of perfection,—devotion, penance, truth, &c." In the Váyu Puráṇa, more details are specified. Those sainted mortals who have diligently worshipped Vishṇu, and are distinguished for piety, abide, at the time of dissolution, in Mahar-loka, with the Pitṛis, the Manus, the seven Ṛishis, the various orders of celestial spirits, and the gods. These, when the heat of the flames that destroy the world reaches to Mahar-loka, repair to Jana-loka, in their subtile forms, destined to become reem-bodied, in similar capacities as their former, when the world is renewed, at the beginning of the succeeding Kalpa. This continues throughout the life of Brahmá. At the expiration of his life, all are destroyed; but those who have then attained a residence in the Brahma-loka, by having identified themselves, in spirit, with the Supreme, are, finally, resolved into the sole-existing Brahma.[‖]

---

[*] तस्मादपि महातापतप्ता लोकास्तत: परम् ।
गच्छन्ति जनलोकं ते दग्धावृत्या परीषिण: ॥

[†] Corrected from "Samvartta". See Vol. I., p. 53, note 3.

[‡] I find लाचारसनिभा: ।

[§] Both the commentaries dwell on it at length.

[‖] For the various Lokas and their denizens, see Vol. II., pp. 225, et seq.

(azure), like the sapphire; some are (white) us the
conch or the jasmine; and some are (black) as collyrium; some are (of bright red), like the lady-bird;[*]
some are of the fierceness of red arsenic;[†] and some
are like the wing of the (painted) jay. (Such are these
massy clouds, in hue.) In form, some resemble towns;
some, mountains: some are like houses and hovels;[‡]
and some are like columns. [§] Mighty in size, and loud
in thunder, they fill all space.[||] Showering down tor-
rents of water, these clouds quench the dreadful fires
which involve the three worlds; and then they rain,
uninterruptedly, for a hundred years, and deluge the
whole world. Pouring down, in drops as large as dice,
these rains overspread the earth, and fill the middle
region,[¶] and inundate heaven. The world is now enveloped in darkness; and, all things, animate or inanimate, having perished, the clouds continue to pour
down their waters for more than a hundred years.

---

* *Indragopa.* See Vol. IV., p. 284, note *.

† मनःशिलनिभाखचा ।

‡ "Houses and hovels" is to render *kúṭágára*, which denotes a super-
structure on the roof of a house.

§ Śrīdhara reads *sthúla*, 'a heap', 'a tent'; Ratnagarbha, *úrṇa*, 'wool'.
Other lections which I find are *sthala* 'a mound', 'a tent'; and *sthaṅa*,
of unascertained signification.

|| *Nabhas-tala.*

¶ *Bhuvo-loka.*

CHAPTER IV.

Continuation of the account of the first kind of dissolution. Of the second kind, or elemental dissolution; of all being resolved into primary spirit.

WHEN the waters have reached the region of the seven Rishis,* and the whole of the three worlds is one ocean, they stop. The breath of Vishńu becomes a (strong) wind, which blows for more than a hundred years, until all the clouds are dispersed. The wind is then reabsorbed; and he of whom all things are made, the lord by whom all things exist,† he who is inconceivable, without beginning, beginning of the universe,‡ reposes, sleeping upon Śesha, in the midst of the deep. The creator,§ Hari, sleeps (upon the ocean), in the form of Brahmá,—glorified by Sanaka‖ and the saints ¶ who had gone to the Jana-loka, and contemplated by the holy inhabitants of Brahma-loka, anxious for final liberation,—involved in mystic slumber, the celestial personification of his own illusions, and meditating on his own ineffable spirit, which is called Vásudeva.**

* See Vol. II., p. 226, and p. 230, note †.

† भूतभावनः ।

‡ Corrected from the printer's error "without beginning of the universe." The original is अनादिरादिर्विश्वस्य ।

§ *Ádikŕit.*

‖ See Vol. I., p. 59, and p. 77, note 1; also, Vol. II., p. 200, note ‡.

¶ *Siddha.*

** आत्ममायामयीं दिव्यां योगनिद्रां समास्थितः ।
आत्मानं वासुदेवाख्यं चिन्तयन्परमेश्वरः ॥

For Yoganidrá, which the Translator here renders by "mystic slumber", see Vol. IV., p. 260, note 1.

13*

This, Maitreya, is the dissolution* termed incidental; because Hari, in the form of Brahmá, sleeps there, as its incidental cause. †

When the universal spirit wakes, the world revives; when he closes his eyes, all things fall upon the bed of mystic slumber.‡ In like manner as a thousand great ages constitute a day of Brahmá, § so his night consists of the same period,—during which the world is submerged by a vast ocean. Awaking at the end of his night, the unborn, Vishńu, in the character of Brahmú, creates the universe anew, in the manner formerly related to you.[1]

I have, thus, described to you the intermediate dissolution‖ of the world, occurring at the end¶ of every Kalpa. I will now, Maitreya, describe to you elemental dissolution. When, by dearth and fire, all the worlds and Pátálas are withered up, and the modifications of Mahat and other products of nature are, by the will of Krishńa, destroyed, the progress of elemental dissolution is begun. Then, first, the waters swallow up the property of earth, (which is the rudiment of smell);

---

[1] The Naimittika Pralaya is described in the Váyu, Bhágavata, Kúrma, and other Puránas, to the same effect, and, very commonly, in precisely the same words.

---

* Pratisanchara.
† "Incidental cause" is for nimitta. See Vol. I., p. 65, note †, ad finem.
‡ निमीषत्वेतद्रिवलं योगयब्रायमे ऽच्युते ।
§ The original has Padmayoni, the same as Abjayoni, for which see Vol. I., p. 17, note †.
‖ Pralaya.
¶ Samhára.

and earth, deprived of its property, proceeds to destruction. Devoid of the rudiment of odour, the earth becomes one with water.* The waters, then, being much augmented, roaring, and rushing along, fill up all space, whether agitated or still. † When the universe is, thus, pervaded by the waves of the watery element, its rudimental flavour is licked up by the element of fire; and, in consequence of the destruction of their rudiments, the waters themselves are destroyed.‡ Deprived of (the essential rudiment of) flavour, they become one with fire; and the universe is, therefore, entirely filled with flame, § which drinks up the water on every side, and gradually overspreads the whole of the world. While space is enveloped in flame, above, below, and all around, the element of wind seizes upon the rudimental property, or form, which is the cause of light; ‖ and, that being withdrawn, ¶ all becomes of the nature of air. The rudiment of form being destroyed, and fire** deprived of its rudiment, air extinguishes fire, and spreads, resistlessly, over space, which is deprived of light, when fire merges into air. Air, then, accompanied by sound, which is the source of ether, extends

---

* Śrídhara, like several independent MSS., here interposes the following verse:

रसाज्वलं समुभूतं तदाज्वातं रसात्मकम् ।

† तिष्ठति विचरति च ।

‡ अपामपि गुणो यस्तु ज्योतिषा पीयते तु सः ।
तस्मात्तापक्षतत्वाच्च रसतत्त्वाच्चयाचात् ॥

§ तारभवस्ते तु सलिले तेजसा सर्वतो वृते ।

‖ ज्योतिषोऽपि परं रूपं वायुरत्ति प्रभाकरम् ।

¶ Pralína.

** Vibhávasu.

everywhere throughout the ten regions of space,[*] until
ether seizes upon contact,[†] its rudimental property, by
the loss of which, air is destroyed, and ether[‡] remains
unmodified: devoid of form, flavour, touch,[§] and smell,
it exists unembodied[||] and vast, and pervades the
whole of space. Ether,[¶] whose characteristic property
and rudiment is sound, exists alone, occupying all the
vacuity of space.[**] But then the radical element[††]
(egotism,) devours sound; and all the elements and
faculties are, at once, merged into their original.[‡‡] This
primary element is consciousness,[§§] combined with the
property of darkness,[||||] and is, itself, swallowed up by
Mahat, whose characteristic property is intelligence;[¶¶]
and earth and Mahat are the inner and outer boun-
daries of the universe. In this manner, — as (in the
creation,) were the seven forms of nature (Prakṛiti),
reckoned from Mahat to earth,[1][***]—so, at the (time of

---

[1] See Vol. I., p. 29.

---

[*] ततस्तु मूलमासाद्य वायुः संभवमात्मनः ।
अर्धं चाधस्व तिर्यक्तु दीधवीति दिग्रो दश ॥
[†] *Sparśa.*
[‡] *Kha.*
[§] *Sparśa.*
[||] I find no reading but *múrttimat*, which means 'embodied'.
[¶] *Ákáśa.* See Vol. I., p. 34, note *.
[**] परिमण्डलं तत्सुधिरमाकाशम् ।
[††] *Bhútádi.* See Vol. I., p. 33, note *.
[‡‡] भूतेन्द्रियेषु युगपन्नूतादौ संस्थितेषु वै ।
[§§] अभिमानात्मकः । See Vol. I., p. 33, note ‡.
[||||] This phrase is to render *támasa*, for which see Vol. I., p. 34, note 1,
and p. 35, note *.
[¶¶] *Buddhi.*
[***] एवं सप्त महानुद्धेः क्रमात्प्रकृतयस्तु वै ।

elemental) dissolution,* these seven successively re-
enter into each other. The egg of Brahmá† is dissolved
in the waters that surround it, with its seven zones,‡
seven oceans, seven regions, and their mountains. The
investure of water is drunk up by fire; the (stratum
of) fire is absorbed by (that of) air; air blends itself
with ether; the primary element§ (of egotism) devours
the ether, and is (itself,) taken up by intellect,‖ which,
along with all these, is seized upon by nature (Prakŕiti).
Equilibrium of the (three) properties, without excess
or deficiency, is called nature (Prakŕiti), origin (Hetu),
the chief principle (Pradhaṅa),¶ cause (Káraṅa), supreme (Para). This Prakŕiti is, essentially, the same,
whether discrete or indiscrete; only that which is
discrete is, finally, lost or absorbed in the indiscrete.**
Spirit,†† also, which is one, pure, imperishable, eternal,
all-pervading, is a portion of that supreme spirit which
is all things. That spirit‡‡ which is other than (embodied) spirit, in which there are no attributes of name,

---

The seven *prakŕitis*, or productive productions, are, in the pure Sánkhya
philosophy, *mahat*, *ahaṁkára*, and the five *tanmátras*. See the *Sánkhya-
kárihá*, III., and the commentaries.

With the statements in the text, which counts the seven *prakŕitis*
from *mahá-buddhi*—the same as *mahat*,—compare Vol. I., p. 40.

* *Pratyáhára*.
† *Sarva-maṅdala*.
‡ *Dwípa*.
§ *Bhútádi*.
‖ *Mahat*.
¶ See Vol. I., p. 20, note ●.
** एिषा प्रक्रति: सर्वा बाह्याबह्मस्वरूपिणी ।
    व्यक्तं सह्यपमव्यक्ते तद्विज्ञेय विलीयते ॥
†† *Puṁs*.
‡‡ *Sarveṣa*.

species,* or the like,—which is one with (all) wisdom, and is to be understood as (sole) existence,†—that is Brahma, infinite glory,‡ supreme spirit, supreme power,§ Vishńu, all that is; from whence the (perfect) sage‖ returns no more. Nature (Prakŕiti)—which I have described to you as being, essentially, both discrete and indiscrete,—and spirit¶ (which is united with body), both resolve into supreme spirit. Supreme spirit is the upholder of all things, and the ruler of all things,** and is glorified, in the Vedas and in the Vedánta, by the name of Vishńu.

Works, as enjoined by the Vedas, are of two kinds, active (Pravŕitta) and quiescent (Nivŕitta), by both of which the universal person†† is worshipped by mankind. He, the lord of sacrifice,‡‡ the male of sacrifice, §§ the most excellent male, ‖‖ is worshipped, by men, in the active mode, by rites enjoined in the Rig-, Yajur-, and Sáma-Vedas. The soul of wisdom, the person of wisdom,¶¶ Vishńu, the giver of emancipation, is worshipped, by sages, *** in the quiescent form, through medi-

---

* *Náman* and *játi.* *Vide supra,* p. 15, note ∗.
† *Sattá.*
‡ पर धाम ।
§ "Supreme power" is to render *íswara.*
‖ *Yati.*
¶ *Purusha.*
** This expression is to translate *parameśwara.*
†† *Sarva-múrtti.*
‡‡ *Yajneśwara.*
§§ *Yajna-puṁs.*
‖‖ *Purushottama.*
¶¶ *Jnána-múrtti.*
*** *Yogin.*

tative devotion.* The exhaustless† Vishṇu is whatever thing that is designated by long, short, or prolated syllables, or that which is without a name. He is that which is discrete, and that which is indiscrete: he is exhaustless spirit, supreme spirit, universal spirit,‡ Hari, the wearer of universal forms. Nature, whether discrete or indiscrete, is absorbed into him; and (detached) spirit, § also, merges into the all-diffusive, and unobstructed spirit.¶ The period of two Parárdhas, as I have described it to you, Maitreya, is called a day of that potent Vishṇu; and, whilst the products of nature are merged into their source, nature into spirit, and that into the Supreme, that period is termed his night, and is of equal duration with his day.** But, in fact, to that eternal supreme spirit there is neither day nor night; and these distinctions are only figuratively applied to the Almighty.†† I have, thus, explained to you the nature of elemental dissolution, and will now expound to you which is final.[1]

---

[1] The Bhágavata notices the Prákṛita pralaya much more briefly; and it is omitted in the Váyu.

---

* *Jnána-yoga.*
† *Ayvaya.* See Vol. I., p. 17, note *.
‡ *Viśwátman.*
§ *Purusha.*
∥ *Vyápin.*
¶ *Átman.*

** बन्धे च प्रकृती लीने प्रकलतां पुद्धे तथा ।
तथ क्षिते लिग्ना भान्वा तत्प्रमाणा महामुने ॥

†† उपचारस्वथाचैष तस्रोग्रस्त द्विजोत्तमे ।

CHAPTER V.

The third kind of dissolution, or final liberation from existence. Evils of worldly life. Sufferings in infancy, manhood, old age. Pains of hell. Imperfect felicity of heaven. Exemption from birth desirable by the wise. The nature of spirit or god. Meaning of the terms Bhagavat and Vásudeva.

THE wise man, having investigated the three kinds of worldly pain, *—or mental and bodily affliction, and the like,[1]—and having acquired (true) wisdom, and detachment (from human objects), obtains final dissolution. The first of the three pains, or Ádhyátmika, is of two kinds, bodily and mental. Bodily pain is of many kinds, as you shall hear. Affections of the head, catarrh, fever, cholic, fistula, spleen, hemorrhoids,† intumescence, sickness, ophthalmia, dysentery, leprosy, and many other diseases constitute bodily affliction. Mental sufferings are love, anger, fear, hate, covetousness, stupefaction,: despair, § sorrow, malice,|| disdain, jealousy, envy, and many other passions which are engendered in the mind. These and various other

---

[1] The three kinds of affliction,¶ inseparable, incidental, and superhuman, are fully described, in the commentary on the first verse of the Sánkhya Káriká, p. 8, in a similar strain as that which is adopted in the text.

* *Tápa-traya.*
† Here the original inserts *śwdsa*, 'asthma' (?).
: *Moha.*
§ *Vishádda.*
|| *Asúyá.*
¶ *Vide supra*, p. 80, note *.

(afflictions, mental or corporeal,) are comprised under the class of (worldly) sufferings, which is called Ádhyátmika (natural and inseparable). That pain to which, excellent Brahman, the term Ádhibhautika (natural, but incidental,) is applied, is every kind of evil which is inflicted * (from without,) upon men by beasts, † birds, men, goblins, : snakes, fiends, § or reptiles; and the pain that is termed Ádhidaivika (or superhuman,) is the work of cold, heat, wind, rain, ¶ lightning, and other (atmospherical phenomena). Affliction, Maitreya, is multiplied in thousands of shapes, in (the progress of) conception, ** birth, decay, disease, death, and hell. The tender (and subtile) animal exists in the embryo, †† surrounded by abundant filth, floating in water, :: and distorted in its back, neck, and bones; enduring severe pain, even in the course of its development, §§ as disordered by the acid, acrid, bitter, ¶¶ pungent, *** and saline articles of its mother's food; incapable of extending or contracting its limbs, reposing amidst the slime of ordure and urine, every way incommoded, unable to breathe, endowed with conscious-

---

* There is free interpolation here.
† Mŕiga.
: Piśácha.
§ Rákshasa.
|| Sarísŕipa.
¶ Insert 'water', ambu.
** Garbha.
†† Garbha, again.
:: I find no Sanskrit for these words.
§§ वर्धमानातिवेदन: ।
|||| Kaṭu.
¶¶ Tikshńa.
*** Ushńa.

ness,[*] and calling to memory many hundred (previous)
births. Thus exists the embryo, in profound affliction,
bound (to the world) by its (former) works.

When the child is about to be born, its face is be-
smeared by excrement, urine, blood, mucus,[†] and
semen; its attachment to the uterus is ruptured: by
the Prájápatya§ wind; it is turned head downwards,
and violently expelled from the womb by the powerful
and painful winds of parturition; and the infant, losing,
for a time, all sensation, when brought in contact with
the external air, is immediately deprived of its intel-
lectual knowledge.[||] Thus born, the child is tortured
in every limb, as if pierced with thorns, or cut to pieces
with a saw, and falls from its fetid lodgement, as from
a sore, like a crawling thing, upon the earth.¶ Unable
to feel[**] itself, unable to turn itself, it is dependent
upon the will of others for being bathed[††] and nourished. Laid upon a dirty bed,[::] it is bitten by insects
and musquitoes,[§§] and has not power to drive them
away. Many are the pangs attending birth; and (many
are those) which succeed to birth; and many are the

---

* Sachaitanya.
† There is no word for "mucus", in the original.
‡ पीड्यमानास्त्रिबन्धनः ।
§ Corrected from "Prájápati".
|| "Intellectual knowledge" is to render vijnána.
¶ कष्टवैरिव तुमागः कवचैरिव दारितः ।
पूतिमयानिष्पतितो धरखां कमिको यथा ॥
** The original, कण्डूयने चाख्यात्रः, denotes scratching.
†† A variant yields 'drinking milk'.
:: Srastara, with prastara as a variant. See Vol. III., p. 131, note *,
and p. 150, note *.
§§ Daṁśa, 'gadflies.'

sufferings which are inflicted by elemental and superhuman agency, in the state of childhood.* Enveloped
by the gloom of ignorance, and internally bewildered,
man knows not whence he is, who he is, whither he
goeth, nor what is his nature; by what bonds he is
bound; what is cause, and what is not cause; what is
to be done, and what is to be left undone;† what is to
be said, and what is to be kept silent; what is righteousness, what is iniquity; in what it consists, or how;
what is right, what is wrong;‡ what is virtue, what is
vice. Thus, man, like a brute beast, addicted only to
animal gratifications, suffers the pain that ignorance
occasions.§ Ignorance, darkness, inactivity influence
those devoid of knowledge, so that pious works are
neglected;‖ but hell is the consequence of neglect of
(religious) acts, according to the great sages; and the
ignorant, therefore, suffer affliction both in this world
and in the next.

When old age arrives, the body is infirm; the limbs
are relaxed; the face is emaciate and shrivelled;¶ the
skin is wrinkled, and scantily covers the veins and

---

* बालभावे यदाप्नोति चाधिभौतादिकानि च ।

† किं कार्यं किमकार्यं वा । I should prefer "what is effect, and what
is not effect", considering what we meet with just below. See the next note.

‡ किं कर्त्तव्यमकर्त्तव्यं किम् । "What is to be done, and what is not
to be done."

§ एवं पशुसमैर्मूढैरज्ञानप्रभवं महत् ।
  अवाप्यते नरैर्दुःखं जिह्वोदरपरायणैः ॥

‖ अज्ञानं तामसो भावः कार्योरम्भप्रवृत्तयः ।
  अज्ञानिनां प्रवर्त्तन्ते कर्मलोपास्ततो द्विज ॥

¶ Rather, "the teeth decay and fall out:" विनष्टदशीर्यदशनः । This
is the only good reading that I find.

sinews;* the eye discerns not afar off, and the pupil
gazes on vacuity; the nostrils are stuffed with hair; the
trunk trembles (as it moves); the bones appear (beneath the surface); the back is bowed, and the joints are
bent; the digestive fire is extinct, and there is little ap-
petite and little vigour;† walking. rising, sleeping, sitting are (all,) painful efforts; the ear is dull; the eye
is dim; the mouth is disgusting with dribbling saliva;:
the senses no longer are obedient to the will; and, as
death approaches, the things that are perceived even
are immediately forgotten.§ The utterance of a single
sentence is fatiguing; and wakefulness is perpetuated
by (difficult) breathing, coughing, and (painful) exhaust-
ion. The old man is lifted up by somebody else; he
is clothed by somebody else; he is an object of con-
tempt to his servants, his children, and his wife. Incapable of cleanliness, of amusement, or food, or desire,
he is laughed at by his dependants, and disregarded by
his kin; and, dwelling on the exploits of his youth, as
on the actions of a past life,‖ he sighs deeply, and is
sorely distressed. Such are some of the pains which
old age is condemned to suffer. I will now describe to
you the agonies of death.

The neck droops; the feet and hands are relaxed;
the body trembles; the man is, repeatedly, exhausted,

---

* वलिखायुयिरावृतः ।

† *Cheshťita*, 'activity.'

: स्रवज्ञानाविलाननः ।

§ अनायतिः समतीव करषिमंरबोमुखः ।
तत्वणेऽप्यनुभूतानामसतोखिलवनुनाम ॥

‖ "Past life," in the sense of previous state of existence. The original
expression is अन्वकिज्ञनानि ।

subdued, and visited with interrupted knowledge.[*]
The principle of selfishness afflicts him, and he thinks:
"What will become of my wealth, my lands,[†] my children, my wife, my servants, my house?" The joints of
his limbs are tortured with severe pains, as if cut by
a saw, or as if they were pierced by the sharp arrows
of the destroyer;[:] he rolls his eyes, and tosses about
his hands and feet; his lips and palate are parched and
dry; and his throat, obstructed by foul humours and
deranged vital airs,[§] emits a rattling sound; he is afflicted with burning heat, and with thirst, and with
hunger; and he, at last, passes away, tortured by the
servants of the judge of the dead,[‖] to undergo a renewal of his sufferings in another body. These are the
agonies which men have to endure, when they die. I
will now describe to you the tortures which they suffer
in hell.

Men are bound, when they die, by the servants of
the king of Tartarus,[¶] with cords, and beaten with
sticks, and have, then, to encounter the fierce aspect
of Yama, and the horrors of their terrible route. In
the different hells there are various intolerable tortures
with burning sand,[**] fire, machines, and weapons: some

---

[*] सत्त्रीवाजिगृहक्षोऽथ व्राम्रो वेपथुना नरः ।
मुहुर्ग्लानिः परवशो मुक्तश्चाभववान्वितः ॥

[†] *Dhánya*, 'grain.'

[:] The Sanskrit has Antaka, the same as Yama. *Vide supra*, p. 16, note §§.

[§] This is a free rendering.

[‖] याम्यकिङ्करपीडितः ।

[¶] याम्यकिङ्कर॰ ।

[**] कारखवाखुका: । Compare the *Laws of the Mánavas*, XII., 76.

are severed with saws; some, roasted in forges;* some
are chopped with axes; some, buried in the ground;
some are mounted on stakes; some, cast to wild beasts,†
(to be devoured); some are gnawed by vultures; some,
torn by tigers;‡ some are boiled in oil; some, rolled in
caustic slime;§ some are precipitated from great
heights; some, tossed (upwards) by engines. The number of punishments inflicted in hell, which are the consequences of sin, is infinite.[1]

But not in hell alone do the souls of the deceased
undergo pain: there is no cessation, even in heaven;
for its temporary inhabitant is ever tormented with the
prospect of descending again to earth.‖ Again is he
liable to conception and to birth; he is merged again
into the embryo, and repairs to it, when about to be
born; then he dies, as soon as born, or in infancy, or
in youth, or in old age. Death, sooner or later, is inevitable.¶ As long as he lives, he is immersed in manifold afflictions, like the seed of the cotton amidst the
down** that is to be spun into thread. In acquiring,

---

[1] Some further particulars of the different hells, and the punishments inflicted in them, have been given before. See Vol. II.,
pp. 214, et seq.

* Múshá, 'crucibles.'
† व्याघ्रवक्त्रे ।
‡ Dwípin, 'ounces', or 'panthers'.
§ चारकर्दमे ।
‖ न केवलं द्विजश्रेष्ठ नरके दुःखपद्यति ।
  स्वर्गेऽपि पातभीतस्य क्षयिष्णोर्नास्ति निर्वृतिः ॥
¶ This sentence is to render ध्रुवा मृतिः ।
** Pakshman, 'filaments.'

losing, and preserving wealth, there are many griefs; and so there are in the misfortunes of our friends.* Whatever (is produced that) is (most) acceptable to man, that, Maitreya, becomes a seed whence springs the tree of sorrow. Wife, children, servants, house, lands, riches contribute much more to the misery, than to the happiness, of mankind. Where could man, scorched by the fires of the sun of this world,† look for felicity, were it not for the shade afforded by the tree of emancipation? Attainment of the divine being is considered, by the wise, as the remedy of the three-fold class of ills that beset the different stages of life, —conception, birth, and decay,—as characterized by that only happiness which effaces all other kinds of felicity, however abundant, and as being absolute and final.[1]:

It should, therefore, be the assiduous endeavour of wise men to attain unto God.[2] The means of such at-

---

[1] All this is conformable to the Sánkhya doctrines, in particular, although the same spirit pervades all Hindu metaphysics.

[2] Tasmát Tat práptaye yatnah kartavyah paṅditair naraiḥ:

तस्मात्तत्प्राप्तये यत्नः कर्तव्यः पण्डितैर्नरैः ।

The expression Tat-práptaye, "for the obtaining of *that*," refers to the phrase immediately preceding,—Bhagavat-práptili, "obtaining of," or "attaining to, Bhagavat," the Lord.

---

* तथैवेष्टविपत्तिषु ।
† Saṁsára.

: तदुक्तं त्रिविधस्यापि दुःखजातस्य पण्डितैः ।
गर्भजन्मजरादीषु स्थानेषु प्रभविष्यतः ॥
निरस्तातिशयाह्लादसुखभावैकलक्षया ।
भेषजं भगवत्प्राप्तिरेकान्तात्यन्तिकी मता ॥

V.   14

tainment are said, great Muni, to be knowledge and
works. Knowledge is of two kinds,—that which is derived from scripture, and that which is derived from
reflection.* Brahma that is the word is composed of
scripture; Brahma that is supreme is produced of reflection.[1] Ignorance is utter darkness, in which knowledge obtained through any sense (as that of hearing,)
shines like a lamp; but the knowledge that is derived
from reflection breaks upon the obscurity like the sun.†
What has been said by Manu, when appealing to the
meaning of the Vedas, with respect to this subject, I
will repeat to you.‡ There are two (forms of) spirit
(or God),—the spirit which is the word, and the spirit
which is supreme. He who is thoroughly imbued with
the word of God obtains supreme spirit.[2] The Atharva
Veda, also, states that there are two kinds of know-

---

[1] Brahma is of two kinds; Śabda-Brahma,—spirit, or God, to
be attained through the word (that is, the Vedas,) and the duties
they prescribe; and Para-Brahma,—spirit, or God, to be attained
through reflection, by which the difference between soul and matter is ascertained.

[2] This seems intended as a quotation from Manu; but it has
not been found in the code. It is:

द्वे ब्रह्मणी वेदितव्ये शब्दब्रह्म परं च यत् ।
शब्दब्रह्मणि निष्णातः परं ब्रह्माधिगच्छति ॥ §

---

* Viveka.

† अन्धं तम इवाज्ञानं दीपवद्वेन्द्रियोद्भवम् ।
यथा सूर्यस्तथा ज्ञानं यद्विप्रैर्षे विवेकजम् ॥

‡ मनुरप्याह वेदार्षं कुत्वा यत्तुनिसत्तम ।
तद्देतच्छूयतामत्र संबन्धे महतो मम ॥

§ This stanza appears in the *Maitri-upanishad*, VI., 22; and it occurs
in the *Mahábhárata*, *Śánti-parvan*, śl. 8550, 8551.

ledge. By (the one which is) the supreme, God* is attained; the other is that which consists of the Rich and other Vedas. [1] That which is imperceptible, undecaying, inconceivable, unborn, inexhaustible, † indescribable; which has neither form, nor hands, nor feet; ‡ which is almighty, § omnipresent, eternal; the cause of all things, and without cause; permeating all, itself unpenetrated, and from which all things proceed,—that is the object which the wise behold, that is Brahma, that is the supreme state, that is the subject of contemplation to those who desire liberation, that is the thing spoken of by the Vedas, the infinitely subtile, supreme condition of Vishńu.‖ That essence of the Supreme ¶ is de-

---

[1] The commentator quotes other passages from the Vedas, of a similar tendency; intimating, however, the necessity of performing acts prior to attaining knowledge; as: कषाये कर्मभि: पक्वे ततो ज्ञानं तु परमा गति: । ** "The decoction (preparatory process) being digested by rites, thereafter knowledge is the supreme resource."

अविद्यया मृत्युं तीर्त्वा विद्ययामृतमश्नुते ।
"Having crossed the gulf of death by ignorance (ceremonial acts), man obtains immortality by (holy) knowledge."

---

* Akshara.
† Avyaya. See Vol. I., p. 17, note *.
‡ Compare Vol. IV., p. 253.
§ Vibhu.
‖ श्रुतिवाक्योदितं सूक्ष्मं तद्विष्णो: परमं पदम् ।
¶ Paramátman.
** This seems to be a selection from the following stanza, cited by the commentator Ratnagarbha:

कषायपङ्क्ति: कर्माणि ज्ञानं तु परमा गति: ।
कषाये कर्मभि: पक्वे ततो ज्ञानं प्रवर्तते ॥

fined by the term Bhagavat.[1] The word Bhagavat is
the denomination of that primeval and eternal god;*
and he who fully understands the meaning of that expression is possessed of holy wisdom,—the sum and
substance of the three Vedas.† The word Bhagavat
is a convenient form to be used in the adoration of
that supreme being: to whom no term is applicable;
and, therefore, Bhagavat expresses that Supreme Spirit,
which is individual, almighty, and the cause of causes
of all things. § The letter *Bha* implies the cherisher and
supporter (of the universe). By *ga* is understood the
leader, impeller, or creator. The dissyllable *Bhaga* indicates the six properties,—dominion, might, glory,
splendour, wisdom and dispassion.‖ The purport of

---

[1] According to the comment, allusion is here made to the
twelve-syllable Mantra (or mystic formula) addressed to Vishńu:
"Oṁ Bhagavate Vásudeváya namah;¶ 'Om! Salutation to Bhagavat Vásudeva:' the repetition of which, by those devoted (bhakta)
to Vishńu, is the easy mode of securing their liberation." The
mysticism is, however, no doubt, older than the worship of
Vishńu; and the term Bhagavat is defined, in the text, according
to the interpretation of the Vedas.

---

* *Átman.*

† एवं निगदितार्थस्य शतलं तस्य तस्वतः ।
  ग्रायते येन तच्चानं परमं यत्तधीमयन् ॥

: *Brahma.*

§ शुद्धे महाविभूत्याखे परे ब्रह्मणि वर्तते ।
  मैनेय भगवच्छब्द: सर्वकारणकारणे ॥

‖ ऐश्वर्यस्य समयस्य धर्मस्य यशसः श्रिय: ।
  ग्रानवैराग्ययोश्चैव षण्णां भग इतीङ्गना ॥

¶ See Vol. I., p. 99, note *.

the letter *va* is that elemental spirit in which all beings exist, and which exists in all beings.[1*] And, thus, this great word Bhagavat is the name of Vásudeva,—who is one with the supreme Brahma,—and of no one else. This word, therefore, which is the general denomination of an adorable object, is not used, in reference to the Supreme, in a general, but a special, signification. When applied to any other (thing or person), it is used in its customary or general import.[†] In the latter case, it may purport one who knows the origin, and end, and revolutions of beings, and what is wisdom,[:] what ignorance. In the former, it denotes wisdom,[§] energy, power, dominion, might, glory, without end, and without defect.[||]

The term Vásudeva means, that all beings abide in that Supreme Being, and that he abides in all beings;[2] as was formerly explained by Keśidhwaja to Khándi-

---

[1] The commentator says, these interpretations are from the Nirukta,—the glossary of the Vedas. The more etymological derivation of the term is: Bhaga, 'power,' 'authority,' and vat, possessive affix.

[2] From the root Vas (वस्), 'abiding,' 'dwelling.' See Vol. I., pp. 1 and 17.

---

* वसन्ति यत्र भूतानि भूतात्मन्यखिलात्मनि ।
  सर्वभूतेष्वशेषेषु वकारार्थस्ततोऽव्ययः ॥

† तत्र पूज्यपदार्थोक्तिपरिभाषासमन्वितः ।
  ब्रह्मोऽयं नोपचारेण जन्म यत्रोपचारतः ॥

: *Vidyá.*

§ *Jnána.*

|| विना हेयैर्गुणादिभिः ।

kya, called Janaka,[*] when he inquired of him an explanation of the name of the immortal,[†] Vásudeva.
He said: "He dwelleth internally in all beings; and all
things dwell in him; and, thence, the lord Vásudeva is
the creator and preserver: of the world. He, though
one with all beings, is beyond and separate from material nature (Prakṛiti), from its products, from properties, from imperfections; he is beyond all investing
substance; he is universal soul. All the interstices of
the universe are filled up by him.[§] He is one with all
good qualities; and all created beings are endowed
with but a small portion of his individuality.[||] Assum-
ing, at will, various forms, he bestows benefits on the
whole world, which was his work.[¶] Glory, might, dominion, wisdom,[**] energy, power, and other attributes
are collected in him. Supreme of the supreme, in whom
no imperfections[††] abide, lord over finite and infinite,[‡‡]

---

god in individuals and universals,* visible and invisible, omnipotent, omnipresent, omniscient, almighty. The wisdom, perfect,† pure, supreme, undefiled, and one only, by which he is conceived, contemplated, and known,—that is wisdom: all else is ignorance."

---

* व्यष्टिसमष्टिरूप: । See Vol. IV., p. 255, note §. The commentators concrete *vyashti* into Sankarshańa, &c., and *samashti* into Vásudeva.

† *Ashta-dosha.*

CHAPTER VI.

Means of attaining liberation. Anecdotes of Khándikya and Keśidhwaja. The former instructs the latter how to atone for permitting the death of a cow. Keśidhwaja offers him a requital; and he desires to be instructed in spiritual knowledge.

HE, Purushottama, is, also, known by holy study[*] and devout meditation;[†] and either, as the cause of attaining him, is entitled Brahma. From study let a man proceed to meditation,[‡] and from meditation to study:[1] by perfection in both, supreme spirit becomes manifest. Study is one eye, wherewith to behold it; and meditation is the other. He who is one with Brahma sees not with the eye of flesh.[§]

MAITREYA.—Reverend teacher, I am desirous of being informed what is meant by the term meditation (Yoga), by understanding which I may behold the Supreme Being, the upholder of the universe.

---

[1] Both study of the Vedas (Swádhyáya) and abstraction (Yoga) are to be practised. When a man is weary of one, he may apply to the other. The Yoga,[||] however, limits the practical part to silent prayer.

अपाक्ष्रान्तः पुनर्ध्यायेद्ध्यानाक्ष्रान्तः पुनर्बपेत् ।

"Wearied of meditation, let him pray inaudibly: weary of prayer, let him repeat meditation."

अपध्यानाभियोगेन पश्येदात्मानमात्मनि ।

"By the union of prayer and meditation let him behold soul in himself."

---

[*] *Swádhyáya. Vide infra*, p. 229, note §.   [†] *Saṁyama.*   [‡] *Yoga.*

[§] न मांसचक्षुषा द्रष्टुं ब्रह्मभूतः स युज्यते ।

[||] The verses quoted by the Translator are given by both the commentators, and as from the *Yoga-śástra.*

PARÁŚARA.—I will repeat to you (Maitreya,) the explanation formerly given by Keśidhwaja to the magnanimous Khándikya, also called Janaka. *

MAITREYA,—Tell me, first, Brahman, who Khándikya was, and who was Keśidhwaja; and how it happened, that a conversation relating to (the practice of) Yoga occurred between them.

PARÁŚARA.—There was Janaka, (named) Dharmadhwaja, who had two sons, Mitadhwaja and Kṛitadhwaja; and the latter was a king ever intent upon existent supreme spirit:† his son was the celebrated Keśidhwaja. The son of Mitadhwaja was Janaka, called Khándikya.¹: Khándikya was diligent in the way of works, and was renowned, on earth, for religious rites. Keśidhwaja, on the other hand, was endowed with spiritual knowledge. These two were engaged in hostilities; and Khándikya was driven from his principality by Keśidhwaja. Expelled from his dominions, he wandered, with a few followers, his priest, and his counsellors, amidst woods and mount-

---

¹ No such names occur amongst the Maithila kings of the Vishńu Puráńa (see Vol. III., pp. 330, *et seq.*); but, as there noticed (p. 333, note 2§), the Bhágavata inserts them. Janaka is used as a title. Kṛitadhwaja, in some of the copies, is read Ṛitadhwaja.

* That is to say, Janaka, son of Khándika. In the *Bhágavata-puráńa*, IX., XIII., 20, he is called son of Mitadhwaja; and, the original of the *Vishńu-puráńa* being ambiguous, I have corrected accordingly Professor Wilson's "Amitadhwaja", just below. Mitadhwaja was patronymically called Khándika; and his father must have been called Khándika, with other names.   † सद्राष्ट्रार्तिर्नृप: ।

: Here, as in p. 214, *supra*,'the original does not yield "Janaka, called Khándikya", but Khándikyajanaka. Also see note •, above.

§ But also see note •••, in the page referred to.

ains, where, destitute of true wisdom, he performed many sacrifices, expecting, thereby, to obtain divine truth, and to escape from death by ignorance.[1]*

Once, whilst the best of those who are skilled in devotion† (Keśidhwaja,) was engaged in devout exercises,‡ a fierce tiger slew his milch-cow,[2] in the lonely forest. When the Raja heard that the cow had been killed, he asked the ministering priests what form of penance would expiate the crime. They replied, that they did not know, and referred him to Kaśeru. Kaśeru, § when the Raja consulted him, told him that he knew not, but that Śunaka would be able to tell him. Accordingly, the Raja went to Śunaka; but he replied: "I am as unable, great king, to answer your question as Kaśeru has been; and there is no one now, upon earth, who can give you the information, except your enemy Khándikya, whom you have conquered."

Upon receiving this answer, Keśidhwaja said: "I will go, then, and pay a visit to my foe. If he kill me, no

---

[1] The performance of rites, as a means of salvation, is called ignorance, in the Vedas (*vide supra*, p. 211, note 1). Works arc recommended as introductory to the acquirement of knowledge: it is ignorance to consider them as finite.

[2] Tasya dhenum (तस्य धेनुम्). One copy has Homa-dhenum, 'cow of sacrifice;' another, Dharma-dhenum, ‖ 'cow of righteousness.' The commentator explains the terms as importing the same thing,—a cow yielding milk for holy purposes, or for the butter which is poured, in oblations, upon the sacrificial fire.

---

* ब्रह्मविद्यामभिप्रेत्य तं मृत्युमविद्यया ।

† All my MSS. have the vocative योगविदां वर ।   ‡ *Yoga*.

§ The original calls him a Bhárgava, or descendant of Bhṛigu.

‖ *Dharma-dogdhrim* is the only variant noticed by Śrídhara or Ratnagarbha; and the former explains it by *homa-dhenum.*

matter; for, then, I shall obtain the reward that attends
being killed in a holy cause.* If (on the contrary,) he
tell me what penance to perform, then my sacrifice
will be unimpaired in efficacy." Accordingly, he ascended his car, having clothed himself in the deer-skin
(of the religious student), and went to the forest where
the wise Khándikya resided. When Khándikya beheld
him approach, his eyes reddened with rage, and he
took up his bow, and said to him: "You have armed
yourself with the deer-skin, to accomplish my destruction; imagining, that, in such an attire, you will be safe
from me. But, fool, the deer upon whose backs this
skin is seen are slain, by you and me, with sharp arrows. So will I slay you: you shall not go free, whilst
I am living. You are an unprincipled felon, who have
robbed me of my kingdom, and are deserving of
death."† To this, Keśidhwaja answered: "I have come
hither, Khándikya, to ask you to solve my doubts, and
not with any hostile intention. Lay aside, therefore,
both your arrow and your anger." Thus spoken to,
Khándikya retired, awhile, with his counsellors and
his priest, and consulted with them what course to
pursue. They strongly urged him to slay Keśidhwaja,
who was now in his power, and by whose death he
would again become the monarch of the whole earth.
Khándikya replied to them: "It is, no doubt, true, that,
by such an act, I should become the monarch of the
whole earth. He, however, would, thereby, conquer

* स चाह तं मयाम्येष मद्दुमाल्लरिएं मुने ।
प्राप्र एव मया यज्ञो यदि मां स हनिष्वति ॥

† The translation is free hereabouts, as throughout the rest of the
Chapter.

the world to come; whilst the earth would be mine. Now, if I do not kill him, I shall subdue the next world, and leave him this earth. It seems to me, that this world is not of more value than the next: for the subjugation of the next world endures for ever; the conquest over this is but for a brief season. I will, therefore, not kill him, but tell him what he wishes to know." Returning, then, to Keśidhwaja, Kháńdikya* desired him to propose his question, which he promised to answer; and Keśidhwaja related to him what had happened,—the death of the cow,†—and demanded to know what penance he should perform. Kháńdikya, in reply, explained to him, fully, the expiation that was suited to the occasion; and Keśidhwaja then, with his permission, returned to the place of sacrifice, and regularly fulfilled every necessary act. Having completed the ceremony, with its supplementary rites, Keśidhwaja accomplished all his objects. But he then reflected thus: "The priests whom I invited to attend have, all, been duly honoured; all those who had any request to make have been gratified by compliance with their desires; all that is proper for this world has been effected by me. Why, then, should my mind feel as if my duty had been unfulfilled?" So meditating, he remembered that he had not presented to Kháńdikya the gift that it is becoming to offer to a spiritual preceptor; and, mounting his chariot, he immediately set off to the thick forest where that sage abode. Kháńdikya, upon his reappearance, assumed his weapons, to kill him. But Keśidhwaja exclaimed: "Forbear,

---

* The original has Kháńdikyajanaka.　　　† Dharma-dhenu.

venerable sage. I am not here to injure you, Khándikya. Dismiss your wrath; and know that I have come
hither to offer you that remuneration which is due to
you, as my instructor. Through your lessons I have
fully completed my sacrifice; and I am, therefore, desirous to give you a gift. Demand what it shall be."

Khándikya, having once more communed with his
counsellors, told them the purpose of his rival's visit,
and asked them what he should demand. His friends
recommended him to require his whole kingdom back
again; as kingdoms are obtained, by prudent men,
without conflicting hosts. The reflecting king Khándikya laughed, and replied to them; "Why should a
person such as I be desirous of a temporary earthly
kingdom? Of a truth, you are able counsellors in the
concerns of this life; but of those of the life to come
you are, assuredly, ignorant." So speaking, he went
back to Kesidhwaja, and said to him: "Is it true that
you wish to make me a gift, as to your preceptor?"
"Indeed, I do," answered Kesidhwaja. "Then," rejoined
Khándikya, "as it is known that you are learned in the
spiritual learning that teaches the doctrine of the soul,
if you will communicate that knowledge to me, you
will have discharged your debt to your instructor.
Declare to me what acts are efficacious for the allevia-
tion of human affliction." *

---

* वाडमिलेय तेनोहः खाखिखखसमचाप्रचीत् ।
भवानभाल्मविन्नानपरमार्थविचचथः ॥
यदि चेह्रीयते मह्यं भवता गुरनिक्षयः ।
तत्लेयप्रयमायालं यत्कर्म तडुद्रीरय ॥

CHAPTER VII.

Keśidhwaja describes the nature of ignorance, and the benefits of the Yoga or contemplative devotion. Of the novice and the adept in the performance of the Yoga. How it is performed. The first stage, proficiency in acts of restraint and moral duty: the second, particular mode of sitting: the third, Pránáyáma, modes of breathing: the fourth, Pratyáhára, restraint of thought: the fifth, apprehension of spirit:* the sixth, retention of the idea. Meditation on the individual and universal forms of Vishńu. Acquirement of knowledge. Final liberation.

"BUT," said Keśidhwaja, "why have you not asked of me my kingdom, now free from all annoyance? What else except dominion is acceptable to the warrior race?" "I will tell you," replied Khándikya, "why I did not make such a demand, nor require that territory which is an object of ignorant ambition. It is the duty of the warrior to protect his subjects (in peace), and to kill, in fight, the enemies of his sway. It is no fault, that you should have taken my kingdom from one who was unable to defend it, to whom it was a bondage, and who was, thus, freed from the incumbrance of ignorance. My desire of dominion originated in my being born to possess it. The ambition of others, which proceeds from (human) frailties, is not compatible with virtue. To solicit gifts is not the duty of a prince and warrior; and, for these reasons, I have not asked for your kingdom, nor made a demand which ignorance

---

* By referring to note † in p. 240, *infra*, it will be seen that *yama* and *niyama* are the first and second stages, while "apprehension of spirit", *bhávaná*, should not be counted as a stage.

alone would have suggested.* Those only who are
destitute of knowledge, whose minds are engrossed by
selfishness, † who are intoxicated with the inebriating
beverage of self-sufficiency,‡ desire kingdoms,—not
such as 1 am."

When King Keśidhwaju heard these words, he was
much pleased, and exclaimed: "It is well-spoken." §
Then, addressing Khándikya‖ affectionately, he said:
"Listen to my words. Through desire of escaping death
by the ignorance of works, I exercise the regal power,
celebrate various sacrifices, and enjoy pleasures sub-
versive of purity. Fortunate is it for you, that your
mind has attached itself to the dominion of discrimi-
nation. Pride of your race! now listen to the real
nature of ignorance. The (erroneous) notion that self
consists in what is not self, and the opinion that property consists in what is not one's own, ¶ constitute the
double seed of the tree of ignorance. The ill-judging
embodied being, bewildered by the darkness of fascination, situated in a body composed of the five elements, loudly asserts 'This is I.' But who would ascribe
spiritual individuality to a body in which soul is distinct from the ether, air, fire, water, and earth, (of

---

* न याद्या वयवन्यूनां धर्मो द्येतत्सतां मतम् ।
  यतो न याचितं राज्यमविद्यान्तर्गतं तव ॥

The translation of the a large part of the present Chapter is not at
all close.

† *Mamatwa.*

‡ *Aham-mána.*

§ 'Enough!' सार्थीति प्राह । A sacred license of grammar is here
taken, as is remarked by the commentators.

‖ The original has Khándikyajanaka.

¶ च्स्ते खमिति या मति: ।

which that body is composed)?[1] What man of understanding assigns to disembodied* spirit corporeal fruition, or houses, lands, and the like, that it should say
'These are mine'? What wise man entertains the idea
of property in sons or grandsons, begotten of the body,
after the spirit has abandoned it?† Man performs all
acts, for the purpose of bodily fruition; and the consequence of such acts is another body; so that their result is nothing but confinement to bodily existence.‡
In the same manner as a mansion of clay is plastered
with clay and water, so the body, which is of earth, is
perpetuated by earth and water, (or by eating and
drinking). The body, consisting of the five elements,
is nourished by substances equally composed of those
elements. But, since this is the case, what is there in
this life that man should be proud of?§ Travelling the
path of the world‖ for many thousands of births, man
attains only the weariness of bewilderment, and is smoth-
ered by the dust of imagination.¶ When that dust is

---

[1] The text is somewhat obscure; but it is, in some degree,
cleared up by the next illustration. No one would think of applying the property of self—the idea of possession, or personality,
—to soul separated from body. But the objection is equally
applicable to soul in the body; for, whilst there, it is as distinct,
in its nature, from the materials of body, as if it was disembodied,
and quite as incapable of individual personal fruition.

---

* *Adeha.*
† This clause is to render अनात्मनि कलेवरे ।
‡ देहवान्यो यदा पुंस्वदा वन्याच तत्परम् ।
§ I find no Sanskrit answering to this sentence.
‖ *Saṁsára.*
¶ *Vásaná.*

washed away by the bland * water of (real) knowledge, then the weariness of bewilderment sustained by the wayfarer through repeated births is removed. When that weariness is relieved, the internal man is at peace, and he obtains that supreme felicity which is unequalled and undisturbed.† This soul is (of its own nature,) pure, and composed of happiness: and wisdom. The properties of pain, ignorance, and impurity are those of nature (Prakṛiti), not of soul. There is no affinity between fire and water; but, when the latter is placed over the former, in a caldron, it bubbles, and boils, and exhibits the properties of fire.§ In like manner, when soul is associated with Prakṛiti, it is vitiated by egotism‖ and the rest, and assumes the qualities of grosser nature, although essentially distinct from them, and incorruptible.¶ Such is the seed of ignorance, as I have explained it to you. There is but one cure of worldly sorrows,—the practice of devotion: no other is known."**

"Then," said Khāṇḍikya, "do you, who are the chief of those versed in contemplative devotion, explain to me what that is: for, in the race of the descendants of Nimi,[1]†† you are best acquainted with the sacred writ-

---

[1] That is, in the race of princes of Mithilā.

* Ushṇa.
† अनन्यातिप्रयावाधं परं निर्वाणमृच्छति ।
‡ Nirodha-maya.
§ अलस्य नापिसंसर्गः स्वालीसंगात्तथापि हि ।
यद्वोद्रेकादिकान्धर्मांस्तत्करोति यथा मुने ॥
‖ Ahaṁ-mānă.
¶ Avyaya. See Vol. I., p. 17, note *.
** क्लेशानां च चयकरं योगादन्वन्न विद्यते ।
†† See Vol. III., pp. 259 and 327.

ings in which it is taught." "Hear," replied Keśidhwaja, "the account of the nature of contemplative devotion,[1] which I impart to you, and by perfection in which the sage attains resolution into Brahma, and never suffers birth again.[*] The mind of man is the cause both of his bondage and his liberation: its addiction to the objects of sense is the means of his bondage; its separation from objects of sense[†] is the means of his freedom. The sage who is capable of discriminative knowledge must, therefore, restrain his mind from all the objects of sense, and therewith meditate upon the Su-

---

[1] The term Yoga (योग), which is that used in the text, in its literal acceptation signifies 'union,' 'junction,' from युज् 'to join': in a spiritual sense, it denotes "union of separated with universal soul;" and, with some latitude of expression, it comes to signify the means by which such union is effected. In the Bhagavad Gítá, it is variously applied, but, ordinarily, denotes the performance of religious ceremonies as a duty, and not for interested purposes. Thus, Kŕíshńa says to Arjuna:

योगस्थः कुरु कर्माणि संगं त्यक्त्वा धनंजय ।
सिद्ध्यसिद्ध्योः समो भूत्वा समत्वं योग उच्यते ॥

"Engaging in Yoga, perform rites, Dhananjaya, being indifferent to success or failure. Such indifference is called Yoga." II., verse 48. It is elsewhere defined "exemption from the contact of pain:" दुःखसंयोगवियोगं योगसंज्ञितम् । VI., verse 23. The word has been, accordingly, rendered 'devotion', by Wilkins, and 'devotio', by Schlegel, in their translations of the Gítá. In this place, however, it is used in a less general sense, and signifies, as is subsequently explained, reunion with spirit, through the exercises necessary to perfect abstraction, as they are taught and practised by the followers of Patanjali.

---

[*] यतः क्षितो न च्यवते प्राप्य ब्रह्मत्वं मुनिः ।

[†] Nirvishaya.

preme Being,—who is one with spirit,—in order to attain liberation.* For that Supreme Spirit† attracts (to itself) him who meditates upon it, and who is of the same nature; as the loadstone attracts the iron by the virtue which is common to itself and to its products.[1]: Contemplative devotion is the union with Brahma, effected by that condition of mind which has attained perfection through those exercises which complete the control of self;[2] and he whose contemplative devotion

---

[1] This illustration is, however, only to a limited extent explanatory of the nature of Yoga; for, though the loadstone and iron unite, by virtue of a community of kind, yet the union that takes place is only that of contiguity, Saṁyoga (संयोग), not that of identification or unity, Tad-aikya (तदैक्य). Some further explanation, therefore, is required.

[2] The first stage is the Átma-prayatna, the practice of moral and religious restraint,—Yama, Niyama,§ &c. When the novice is perfect in these, then he is fit to attain the perfectibility of an adept, through the especial practices which treatises on the Yoga prescribe. When the mind has attained the state which can alone be attained through them, then the union with Brahma, which is the consequence, is called Yoga:

आत्मप्रयत्नसापेषा विशिष्टा या मनोगतिः ।
तस्या ब्रह्मणि संयोगो योग इत्यभिधीयते ॥ ‖

The Átma-prayatna is defined¶ to be that which has Yama, &c.

---

* विषयेभ्यः समाहृत्य विज्ञानात्मा मनो मुनिः ।
चिन्तयेन्मुक्तये तेन ब्रह्मभूतं परेश्वरम् ॥
† "Supreme Spirit" is for Brahma.
: विकार्यमात्मनः शक्त्या लोहमाकर्षको यथा ।
§ *Vide infra*, p. 230, notes * and †.
‖ This is the original of the passage to which the Translator's note is attached.
¶ By the commentator Śrídhara, whom Ratnagarbha here closely follows.

is characterized by the property of such absolute perfection is, in truth, a sage, expectant of final liberation from the world.*

"The sage (or Yogin), when first applying himself to contemplative devotion, is called the (novice or) practitioner (Yoga-yuj); when he has attained spiritual union,† he is termed (the adept, or) he whose meditations are accomplished.[1] Should the thoughts of the

---

for its object, यमनियमादिविषय: । The next phrase, तत्सायेषा, is explained तद्धीना 'depending upon, or relating to, such control.' मनोमति; is the same as मनोवृत्ति:, condition or state of mind which is विशिष्ट, 'perfected:' of that state of mind union with Brahma is Yoga. Union with Brahma is the abstraction that proposes the identity of the living with the supreme spirit, — of the Jívátman‡ with Brahma: जीवात्मब्रह्मकविषयत्वम् । And Yoga is understanding of the identity of the contemplator and the object contemplated: ध्यातृध्येयैकबुधी: । A text of Yájnavalkya§ is quoted to this effect: ‖

ज्ञानं योगाबलं विद्धि योगद्वाष्टाङ्गसंयुतः ।
संयोगो योग इत्युक्तो जीवात्मपरमात्मनोः ॥

"Know holy wisdom to be the same with Yoga, (the practice of) which has eight divisions. That which is termed Yoga is union of the living with the supreme soul."

[1] Vinishpanna-samádhi¶ is the expression of the text, which can scarcely be regarded as an appellative. The commentator terms the adept Brahma-jnánin, "he who knows Brahma."

---

* स वै योगी मुमुक्षुरभिधीयते ।
† परब्रह्मोपलब्धिमान् ।
‡ See Vol. IV., p. 253, note *.
§ Corrected from "Yajnyawalkya". With reference to Yájnavalkya, *vide infra*, p. 230, note ‖ .
‖ By Ratnagarbha.
¶ *Samádhi* is rendered "abstraction", in Vol. II., p. 315.

former be unvitiated by any obstructing imperfection, he will obtain freedom,* after practising devotion through several lives.[1] The latter speedily obtains liberation in that existence (in which he reaches perfection), all his acts being consumed by the fire of contemplative devotion. The sage who would bring his mind into a fit state for (the performance of) devout contemplation must be devoid of desire,† and observe (invariably,) continence, compassion, truth, honesty, and disinterestedness:‡ he must fix his mind intently on the supreme Brahma, practising holy study,§ purification, contentment, penance, and self-control.‖ These

---

[1] After three lives, according to the Váyu Saṁhitá, as quoted in the comment.¶

---

* *Mukti.*

† *Nishkáma.*

‡ Compare Vol. III., p. 77, note 1; also, Vol. IV., p. 294, notes 1 and ‡. *Ahiṁsá, asteya*, and *aparigraha* I should render 'not killing', 'not thieving', and 'not coveting', rather than "compassion", "honesty", and "disinterestedness".

§ *Swádhyáya*, "the murmuring of sacred texts." In the *Rája-mártaṅḍa* we find the following definition, in explanation of the *Yoga-śástra*, II., 1: स्वाध्यायः । प्रणवपूर्वाणां मन्त्राणां जपः । The *Sútrártha-chandriká* has: स्वाध्यायः । ओंकारपूर्वकमन्त्राणां जपः ।

‖ स्वाध्यायशौचसंतोषतपांसि नियतात्मवान् ।
कुर्वीत ब्रह्मणि तथा परस्मिन्प्रवणं मनः ॥

The Translator should not have rendered नियतात्मवान् as if it denoted "self-control". The fifth observance is प्रवणं मनः,—the Translator's "mind intently",—which is equivalent, the scholiasts say, to *praṇidhána*, 'persevering devotion.' See the *Yoga-śástra*, II., 32.

¶ By Ratnagarbha, as follows:

अल्पाभ्यासोऽपि यो मार्गः सोऽपि अनवधात्मरम् ।
न योनियन्त्रपीडाद्यै पुनरेति न संशयः ॥

(virtues), respectively termed the five acts of restraint* (Yama), and five of obligation† (Niyama), bestow excellent rewards, when practised for the sake of reward, and eternal liberation, when they are not prompted by desire (of transient benefits).‡ Endowed with these merits, the sage,§ self-restrained, should sit in one of the modes termed Bhadrásana, &c., and engage in contemplation.¹ Bringing his vital airs, called Práńa, under subjection, by frequent repetition, is, thence, called Práńáyáma, which is, as it were, a seed with a seed.² In this, the breath of expiration

---

¹ There are various postures in which the Yogin is directed to sit, when he engages in meditation. In the Bhadrásana,‖ he is directed to cross his legs underneath him, and to lay hold of his feet, on each side, with his hands.

² सबीजो बीज एव च ।¶ It is, itself, figuratively, the seed of the fruit, which is meditation; but it is to be accompanied with what is also technically called Bíja (or seed),—inaudible repe-

---

* 'Forbearance' is more exact.　† 'Religious observance' is preferable.

‡ विशिष्टफलदाः काम्या निष्कामानां विमुक्तिदाः ।

§ Yati.

‖ The commentators cite, in description of this posture, a stanza from Yájnavalkya. Perhaps it is taken from the *Yájnavalkya-gítá*, for which see my *Contribution towards an Index to the Bibliography of the Indian Philosophical Systems*, p. 14.

Besides the *bhadrásana*, the Yoga philosophy prescribes postures denominated *padmásana*, *swastikásana*, *vajrásana*, and *vírásana*. These seem to be the principal out of an aggregate said to consist of eighty-four, among which are the *siddhásana*, *kamalásana*, *dańdásana*, &c.

¶ Correctly, सबीजोऽबीज एव च, "with a seed, and also without a seed." The term 'seed' is here, of course, a technicality.

Samádhi, as *sabíja* and as *nirbíja*, is spoken of in the *Yoga-śástra*, I., 46 and 50. The abstract meditation referred to is, in other words, divided into that in which there is distinct recognition of an object, and that in which there is not such recognition.

See, further, note ‡ in the following page.

and that of inspiration* are alternately obstructed, constituting the act twofold; and the suppression† of both (modes of breathing) produces a third.[1] The exercise of the Yogin, whilst endeavouring to bring before his thoughts the gross form of the eternal, is denominated Álambana.[2]: He is then to perform the

tition of certain prayers, and meditation on the visible form of the deity,—termed, likewise, Álambana, and presently mentioned.§

[1] Práńáyáma is performed by three modifications of breathing. The first act is expiration, which is performed through the right nostril, whilst the left is closed with the fingers of the right hand: this is called Rechaka. The thumb is then placed upon the right nostril, and the fingers raised from the left, through which breath is inhaled: this is called Púraka. In the third act, both nostrils are closed, and breathing suspended: this is Kumbhaka. And a succession of these operations is the practice of Práńáyáma. ||

[2] Álambana is the silent repetition of prayer. ¶

* *Práńa* and *apána*.	† *Saṁyama*.

: तस्य बालम्बनवतः स्थूलं रूपं द्विजोत्तम । -
आलम्बनममलस्त्र योगिनोऽभ्यसतः कुतम् ॥

"And, as regards the Yogin practising *meditation* with a rest *for his thoughts, as he feels after the Supreme*, the gross aspect of the Infinite— i. e., *Hiraṅyagarbha, etc.*,—is prescribed as the rest, O best of Bráhmans."

See the beginning of annotation ¶ in the preceding page. On the words there quoted Ratnagarbha says: सबीजः । सालम्बनः । मनवप- ध्यानसहित: । And Śrídhara writes to the same effect. It is now evident how the Translator came to misunderstand the sense of *bíja* and *álambana*. The commentators begin their gloss on the stanza cited above with the words: तत्र सबीजस्रालम्बनमाह ।

§ This view of the meaning of *bíja* and *álambana* is quite a misapprehension. See the preceding note.

|| Both Śrídhara and Ratnagarbha have the substance of this note. The Translator has previously rendered *práńáyáma* by "suppression of breath," "austerity", and "ascetic practices". See Vol. II., pp. 89 and 272; Vol. III., p. 55. Its exact meaning is 'regulation of the breath'.

The third division of the *práńáyáma*, the *kumbhaka*, has its name from *kumbha*, 'a jar'; inasmuch as, on its taking place, the vital airs are stationary, like water in a jar.	¶ See note :, above.

Pratyáhára, which consists in restraining his organs of
sense * from susceptibility to outward impressions, and
directing them entirely to mental perceptions. By
these means the entire subjugation of the unsteady
senses is effected; and, if they are not controlled, the
sage will not accomplish his devotions. When, by the
Práńáyáma, the vital airs are restrained, and the senses
are subjugated by the Pratyáhára, then the sage will
be able to keep his mind steady in its perfect asylum."†

Kháńdikya then said (to Keśidhwaja): "Illustrious
sage, inform me what is that perfect asylum of the
mind,‡ resting on which, it destroys all the products
of (human) infirmity." To this, Keśidhwaja replied:
"The asylum of mind is spirit (Brahma), which, of its
own nature, is twofold, as being with, or without,
form; and each of these is supreme and secondary.[1]

---

¹ आश्रयश्चेतसो ब्रह्म द्विधा तच्च स्वरूपतः§ ।
  भूप मूर्त्तममूर्त्तं ‖ च परं चापरमेव च ॥

The Brahma that is without form (Amúrtta) may be Para or Apara.
Supreme formless spirit is without attributes of any kind. Secondary formless spirit is invested with the attributes of power,
glory, truth, perfection. Spirit embodied, or with form in his
highest state, is, according to our text. Vishńu and his manifestations. Spirit, in an inferior or secondary series of bodily forms,
is Brahmá and all other living beings. ¶

---

  * Akaśa.
  † ततः कुर्यादिखरं चेतः शुभाश्रये ।
  ‡ Chetas, as above; and so below.
  § The ordinary reading is स्वभावतः ।
  ‖ Variant: भूतमूर्त्तममूर्त्तम् ।
  ¶ This note is gleaned, with additions and variations, from the com-
mentaries.

Apprehension of spirit,[1] again, is threefold. I will explain the different kinds to you. They are: that which is called Brahma, that which is named from works, and that which comprehends both. That (mental apprehension) which consists of Brahma is one; that which is formed of works is another; and that which comprehends both is the third: so that mental apprehension* (of the object or asylum of the thoughts) is threefold. Sanandana and other (perfect sages) were endowed with apprehension of the nature† of Brahma. The gods and others, whether animate or inanimate, are possessed of that which regards acts.‡ The apprehension that comprehends both works and spirit exists in Hiraṅyagarbha§ and others, who are possessed of contemplative knowledge, of their own nature, and who, also, exercise certain active functions, as creation and the rest. Until all acts, which are

---

[1] The term is Bhávaná, defined to be "function to be engendered by knowledge," ज्ञानजन्यः संस्कारः ¶, the mental impression or apprehension following upon knowledge. Here it implies, in particular, the formation of a fixed idea, by the Yogin, of the object of his contemplations. It is also termed Bháva-bhávaná, "apprehension of the being, the existence, or substantiality, of the object; the thing contemplated:" भावभावना । भावो वस्तु तद्वि-षया भावना । **

* भावभावना ।
† Here, "apprehension," &c. is to render भावभावना ।
‡ कर्मभावना ।   § A name of Brahmá.
    हिरण्यगर्भादिषु च ब्रह्मकर्मात्मिका द्विधा ।
    बोधाधिकारयुक्तेषु विषते भावभावना ॥
¶ Ratnagarbha.
** Śrídhara.

the causes of notions of individuality, are discontinued,
spirit is one thing, and the universe is another, to
those who contemplate objects as distinct and various.*
But that is called true knowledge, or knowledge of
Brahma, which recognizes no distinctions, which con-
templates only simple existence, which is undefinable
by words, and is to be discovered solely in one's own
spirit.† That is the supreme, unborn, imperishable
form of Vishńu, who is without (sensible) form, and is
characterized as a condition of the supreme soul, which
is variously modified from the condition of universal
form.‡ But this (condition) cannot be contemplated
by sages in their (early) devotions;§ and they must,
therefore, direct their minds to the gross form of Hari,
which is of universal perceptibility.‖ They must meditate upon him as Hirańyagarbha, as the glorious¶
Vásava, as Prajápati, as the winds,** the Vasus, the
Rudras, the suns, stars, planets, Gandharvas, Yakshas,
Daityas, all the gods and their progenitors,†† men,
animals,‡‡ mountains, oceans, rivers, trees, all beings,
and all sources of beings, all modifications whatever

---

* अषीणेषु समस्तेषु विशेषज्ञानकर्मसु ।
विश्वमेतत्परं चान्यद्दभिमन्यूयां नृप ॥

† प्रत्वक्षामितभेदं यत्सत्तामाचमगोचरम् ।
वचसामात्मसंवेयं तज्ज्ञानं ब्रह्मसंज्ञितम् ॥

‡ विश्वस्वरूपवैरूप्यलक्षणं परमात्मनः ।

§ This expansion is to represent *yoga-yuj*, for which see p. 228, *supra*.

‖ *Viśwa-gochara.*

¶ *Bhagavat.*

** *Marut.*

†† सकला देवयोनयः ।

‡‡ *Paśu.*

of nature and its products, * whether sentient or unconscious, one-footed, two-footed, or many-footed.†
All these are the sensible: form of Hari, to be appre-
hended by the three kinds of apprehension. All this
universal world, this (world) of moving and stationary
beings, is pervaded by the energy of Vishńu, who is
of the nature of the supreme Brahma. This energy is
either supreme, or, when it is that of conscious embodied spirit,§ it is secondary. Ignorance, or that
which is denominated from works, is a third energy,[1]
by which the omnipresent energy of embodied spirit
is ever excited, and whence it suffers all the pains of
repeated worldly existence. Obscured by that (energy
of ignorance or illusion), the energy that is denominated from embodied spirit is characterized by different degrees of perfection, in all created beings. In
things without life, it exists in a very small degree;

---

[1] The term used, throughout, is Śakti (शक्ति), 'power,' 'ability,' 'energy.' By the first kind. or Pará, is understood knowledge able to appreciate abstract truth, or the nature of universal
soul; by the second, ability to understand the nature of embodied
soul; and, by the third, inability to discern one's own nature,
and reliance on moral or ceremonial merit. These different kinds
are called energies, because they are the energies or faculties of
the Supreme Spirit, or, according to the Vaishńavas, of Vishńu,
accompanying soul in all its various conditions of existence.

---

* प्रधानादिविषयानकम् ।
† Add "or footless": अपाद्कम् ।
‡ Múrtta.
§ चेषग्राज्ञा ।
‖ As stones and the like, Ratnagarbha says.

it is more, in things that (have life, but) are without
motion;* in insects,† it is still more abundant; and
still more, in birds; it is more in wild animals;‡ and,
in domestic animals, § the faculty is still greater. Men
have more of this (spiritual) faculty than animals; and
thence arises their authority over them:‖ the faculty
exists, in an ascending degree, in Nágas, Gandharvas,
Yakshas, gods, Śakra, Prajápati, and Hiraṅyagarbha,
and is, above all, predominant in that male (Vishṅu)
of whom all these various creatures are but the diver-
sified forms, penetrated universally by his energy,—as
all-pervading as the ether.¶

"The second¹ state of him who is called Vishṅu,
and which is to be meditated upon by the (advanced)
sage, is that (imperceptible,) shapeless** form of
Brahma, which is called, by the wise 'That which is,'²
and in which all the before-described energies re-
side. Thence proceeds the form of the universal form,
the other great form of Hari, which is the origin of

---

¹ The first, which has been intended to be described in the
foregoing passages, was the universal, visible form of Vishṅu;
the second is his formless or imperceptible condition.

² Sat (सत्). "what is being."

---

* Sthávara. Ratnagarbha explains that trees, &c. are intended.
† Sarísṛipa, which the Translator generally renders "reptiles". Vide
supra, p. 59, note ††; and p. 94, note ††.
‡ Mṛiga.
§ Paśu.
‖ पशुभ्यो मनुजाश्चातिप्रसुख्या पुंसः प्रभावितः ।
¶ एतान्येषरूपाणि तस्य रूपाणि पार्थिव ।
यतस्तच्छक्तियोगेन पुतानि नभसा यथा ॥
** Amúrtta.

those manifested forms (or incarnations) that are endowed with every kind of energy, and which, whether
the forms of gods, animals, or men, are assumed by
him (Hari,) in his sport. This active interposition of
the undefinable god, all-comprehending and irresistible,
is for the purpose of benefiting the world, and is not
the necessary consequence of works.* This form of
the universal form is to be meditated upon by the
sage,† for the object of purification; as it destroys all
sin. In the same manner as fire, (blazing) in the wind,
burns dry grass,‡ so Vishńu, seated in the heart, consumes the sins of the sage: and, therefore, let him
(resolutely) effect the fixation of his mind upon that
receptacle of all the (three) energies, (Vishńu); for that
is (the operation of the mind which is called) perfect
Dhárana:[1] and, thus, the perfect asylum § of individual,
as well as universal, spirit, that which is beyond the
three modes of apprehension,‖ is attained, for the
(eternal) emancipation of the sage. The minds of other
beings, which are not fixed upon that asylum, are
altogether impure, and are all the gods and the rest,
who spring from acts.¶ The retention or apprehen-

---

[1] Retention, or holding of the image or idea formed in the
mind by contemplation: from Dhŕi (धृ), 'to hold,' literally or
figuratively.

---

* These two sentences are a very free rendering.
† Read 'the novice'; the original being *yoja-yuj*. *Vide supra*, p. 228.
‡ *Kaksha*, 'dry wood.'
§ शुभाश्रयः ।   ‖ भावभावना ।
¶ अन्ये तु पुरुषव्याघ्र चेतसो ये व्यपाश्रयाः ।
   अगुड़ास्ते समस्तासु देवाद्याः कर्मयोनयः ॥

sion, by the mind, of that visible form of Vishńu,
without regard to subsidiary forms, is, thence, called
Dháraná;* and I will describe to you the perceptible†
form of Hari, which no mental retention will manifest,
except in a mind that is fit to become the receptacle
of the idea.[1]: The meditating sage must think (he beholds internally the figure) of Vishńu, as having a
pleased and lovely countenance, with eyes like the
leaf of the lotos, smooth cheeks,§ and a broad and
brilliant forehead; ears of equal size, the lobes of which
are decorated with splendid pendants; a painted neck; ||
and a broad breast, on which shines the Śrívatsa¶
mark; a belly falling in graceful folds, with a deep-
seated navel;** eight long arms, or else four; and firm
and well-knit thighs and legs, with well-formed feet
and toes. Let him, with well-governed thoughts, con-

---

[1] The explanation of Dháraná given in the text is rendered
unnecessarily perplexed by the double doctrine here taught, and
the attempt to combine the abstractions of Yoga theism with the
sectarian worship of Vishńu.

---

* मूर्ति भगवतो रूपं सर्वापाश्रयनिस्पृहम् ।
एषा वै धारणा ज्ञेया यच्चित्तं तत्र धारयेत् ॥

In *dháraná*, or 'fixed attention', no mediate rest is required, such as
is spoken of in note ‡ to p. 231, *supra*.

† *Múrtta.*

‡ तत्र मूर्तिं हरे रूपं यादृक्चिन्त्यं नराधिप ।
तच्छ्रूयतामनाधारे धारणा नोपपद्यते ॥

§ *Su-kapola.*

|| ? The original has कम्बुग्रीवम् । Śrídhara and Ratnagarbha say:
रेखात्रयाङ्कितकण्ठम् ।

¶ See p. 6, and p. 124, note ¶, *supra*.

** वलीविभक्तिना मग्नाभिना चोदरेण वै ।

template, as long as he can persevere in unremitting
attention, Hari,[*] as clad in a yellow robe, wearing a
(rich) diadem (on his head), and brilliant armlets and
bracelets[†] (on his arms), and bearing (in his hands)
the bow, the shell, the mace, the sword, the discus, the
rosary,[‡] the lotos, and the arrow.[1][§] When this image
never departs from his mind, whether he be going, or
standing, or be engaged in any other voluntary act,
then he may believe his retention to be perfect. The
sage[||] may then meditate upon the form of Vishńu[¶]
without (his arms, — as) the shell, mace, discus, and
bow,—and as placid, and bearing (only) his rosary.[**]
When the idea of this image is firmly retained, then[††]
he may meditate on Vishńu without his diadem, bracelets,[‡‡] or other ornaments. He may, next, contemplate
him as having but one single limb, and may then fix
his whole thoughts[§§] upon the body to which the
limbs belong. This process of forming a lively image
in the mind, exclusive of all other objects, constitutes

---

[1] The two last implements are from the comment: the text
specifies only six.

[*] चिन्तयेत्तमना योगी समाधायात्ममानसम् ।
    तावद्भावबुद्धीभूता तथैव नृप धारणा ॥

[†] *Keyúra* and *kaṭaka.*

[‡] *Aksha-valaya.*

[§] *Vide supra,* pp. 124 and 149.

[||] *Budha.*

[¶] *Bhagavat,* in the original.

[**] *Aksha-sútraka.*

[††] सा यदा धारणा तद्द्रव्यज्ञानवती ततः ।

[‡‡] *Keyúra.*

[§§] प्रतिधानपरो भवेत् ।

Dhyána (or meditation), which is perfected by six stages;[1] and, when an accurate knowledge of self, free from all distinction, is attained by this mental meditation, that is termed Samádhi.[2]*

---

[1] They are :† 1. Yama, &c., acts of restraint and obligation;‡ 2. Ásana, sitting in particular postures;§ 3. Práńáyáma, modes of breathing;‖ 4. Pratyáhára, exclusion of all external ideas;¶ 5. Bhávaná, apprehension of internal ideas;** 6. Dháráná, fixation or retention of those ideas.††

[2] The result of the Dhyána or Samádhi‡‡ is the absence of all idea of individuality, when the meditator, the meditation, and the thing or object meditated upon are, all, considered to be but one. According to the text of Patanjali: "Restraint of the body, retention of the mind, and meditation, which, thence, is exclusively confined to one object, is Dhyána. The idea of identification with the object of such meditation, so as if devoid of individual nature. is Samádhi:' देहबन्धचित्तधारणा तन्मयत्वैकतानता ध्यानम् । तदे-कार्थमात्रनिर्भासं खरूपशून्यमिव समाधिः । §§

तद्रूपमत्रयये चैका संततिख्यान्यनिःस्पृहा ।
तख्यानं प्रथमैरङ्गैः षड्भिर्निष्पाद्यते नृप ॥
तख्येव कल्पनाहीनं खरूपग्रहणं हि यत् ।
मनसा ध्याननिष्पाद्यं समाधिः सो ऽभिधीयते ॥

† I do not know whence this classification is taken; and I doubt its correctness exceedingly. According to the Yoga-śástra, II., 29, the six stages preceding dhyána are yama, niyama, ásana, práńáyáma, pratyáhára, and dháráná. Yama and niyama can scarcely, from their very nature, be taken as parts of a whole; and bhávaná is not at all a stage subservient to the attainment of yoga.

‡ Vide supra, p. 230, notes * and †.

§ Ibid., note ‖.

‖ Ibid., p. 231, note ‖.

¶ Ibid., p. 232.

** Ibid., p. 233, note 1.

†† Ibid., p. 238, note *.

‡‡ These, 'contemplation' and 'meditation', are never to be considered as synonyms. See note †, above.

§§ Here we have an extract from the Yoga-śástra,—III., 1—3. These

"(When the Yogin has accomplished this stage, he acquires) discriminative knowledge, which is the means of enabling living soul. when all the three kinds of apprehension are destroyed, to attain the attainable supreme Brahma.[1][*] Embodied spirit is the user of the instrument, which instrument is true knowledge; and, by it, that (identification) of the former (with Brahma) is attained.[2] Liberation, which is the object to be effected, being accomplished, discriminative knowledge ceases. When endowed with the apprehension of the nature of the object of inquiry,[†] then

---

[1] The expressions of the text are somewhat obscure; nor does the commentator[‡] make them much more intelligible, until he cuts the matter short, by stating the meaning to be, that "discriminative knowledge enables the living spirit to attain Brahma:" विज्ञानं जीवात्मानं ब्रह्म प्रापयतीत्यर्थ: ।

[2] The text is very elliptical and obscure. Having stated that embodied spirit (Kshetrajna) is the Karanin, the possessor or user of the Karana, which is knowledge, it adds तेन तस्य तत्, literally, "by that, of that, that;" i. e., Tat, "that which is;" and Brahma, or supreme spirit, is the attainment of that spirit which abides in body by that instrument, or discriminative knowledge, of which it has become possessed through perfect meditation:

चेन्नः करणी ज्ञानं करणं तेन तस्य तत् ।
निष्पाद्य मुक्तिकार्यं वै ज्ञतद्धयात्रिवर्तते ॥
विज्ञानं निवर्तते ।

---

aphorisms are read as follows: देशबन्धश्चित्तस्य धारणा । तत्र प्रत्यये-
कतानता ध्यानम् । तदेवार्थमात्रनिर्भासं स्वरूपशून्यमिव समाधि: ।
Thus we have definitions of *dháraná*, *dhyána*, and *samádhi*.

[*] विज्ञानं प्रापकं प्राप्ये परब्रह्मणि पार्थिव ।
प्रापणीयस्तथैवात्मा प्रचीणामेषभावनः ॥

[†] तन्नावभावना ।
[‡] Ratnagarbha.
V.   16

there is no difference between it (individual,) and supreme spirit:* difference is the consequence of the absence of (true) knowledge. When that ignorance which
is the cause of the difference between individual and
universal spirit† is destroyed, finally and for ever,
who shall (ever) make that distinction (between them)
which does not exist? Thus have I, Kháńdikya, in
reply to your question, explained to you what is meant
by contemplative devotion, both fully and summarily.
What else do you wish to hear?"

Kháńdikya replied (to Keśidhwaja, and said): "The
explanation which you have given me of the real nature of contemplative devotion has fulfilled all my
wishes, and removed all impurity from my mind. The
expression 'mine', which I have been accustomed to
use, is untruth,: and cannot be otherwise declared by
those who know what is to be known. The words
'I' and 'mine' constitute ignorance; but practice is
influenced by ignorance. Supreme truth § cannot
be defined; for it is not to be explained by words.
Depart, therefore, Keśidhwaja. You have done all that
is necessary for my (real) happiness,|| in teaching me
contemplative devotion,—the inexhaustible bestower
of liberation from existence."¶

Accordingly, King Keśidhwaja, after receiving suitable homage from Kháńdikya, returned to his city.

---

* Five kinds of emancipation are enumerated in the *Bhágavata-pu-
ráńa*, III, XXIX., 13: *sálokya, sárshti, sámipya, sárúpya*, and *ekatwa*.
† The original words are *átman* and Brahma.
: *Asat.*
§ *Paramártha.*
|| *Śreyas.*
¶ *Vimukti.* Vide *supra*, p. 61, note §.

Khándikya, having nominated his son Raja,[1] retired to the woods, to accomplish his devotions; his whole mind being intent upon Govinda. There, his entire thoughts being engrossed upon one only object, and being purified by practices of restraint, self-control, and the rest,[*] he obtained absorption into the pure and perfect spirit[†] which is termed Vishńu. Keśidhwaja, also, in order to (attain) liberation, became averse from his own perishable works, and lived amidst objects of sense (without regarding them), and instituted religious rites without expecting therefrom any advantages to himself.[‡] Thus, by pure and auspicious fruition, being cleansed from (all) sin, he, also, obtained that perfection which assuages all affliction for ever.

---

[1] The commentator, in order to explain how Khándikya should have given what he did not possess, states that it is to be understood that Keśidhwaja relinquished to him the kingdom. Or the term Raja may denote merely "master of, or acquainted with, mystic prayers, or Mantras:" यद्वा राजानं मन्त्रादिखामिनं कृत्वा ।

---

[*] यमादिगुणयोषितः ।
[†] This is to render Brahma.
[‡] केशिध्वजोऽपि मुक्त्यर्थं खकर्मफलपर्णोमुखः ।
बुभुजे विषयान्कर्म चक्रे चानभिसंहितम् ॥

CHAPTER VIII.

Conclusion of the dialogue between Parásara and Maitreya. Recapitulation of the contents of the Vishńu Puráńa: merit of hearing it: how handed down. Praises of Vishńu. Concluding prayer.

I HAVE now explained to you, Maitreya, the third kind of worldly dissolution, or that which is absolute and final, which is liberation and resolution into eternal spirit.[1] I have related to you primary and secondary creation, the families (of the patriarchs), the (periods of the) Manwantaras, and the genealogical histories* (of the kings). I have repeated to you, (in short,) who were desirous of hearing it, the imperishable Vaishńava Puráńa, which is destructive of all sins, the most excellent of all holy writings, and the means of attaining the great end of man. If there is anything else you wish to hear, propose your question, and I will answer it.

MAITREYA.—Holy teacher,† you have, indeed, related to me all that I wished to know; and I have listened to it with pious attention.‡ I have nothing further to inquire. The doubts inseparable from the

---

[1] The term is Layo Brahmańi (लयो ब्रह्मणि), which means 'a melting away,' 'a dissolution', or 'fusion;' from the root Lí (ली), 'to liquefy,' 'to melt,' 'to dissolve.'

---

* Vamśánucharita.
† Bhagavat.
‡ Bhakti.

mind of man have, all, been resolved by you;* and, through your instructions, I am acquainted with the origin, duration, and end† of all things; with Vishńu, in his collective fourfold form;[1] his three energies;[2] and with the three modes of apprehending the object of contemplation.[3]: Of all this have I acquired a knowledge, through your favour; and nothing else is worthy to be known, when it is once understood that Vishńu and this world are not (mutually) distinct. Great Muni, I have obtained, through your kindness, all I desired,—the dissipation of my doubts;§ since you have instructed me in the duties of the several tribes, and in other obligations; the nature of active life, and discontinuance of action: and the derivation of all that exists from works.‖ There is nothing else, venerable Brahman, that I have to inquire of you. And forgive me, if your answers to my questions have imposed upon you any fatigue. Pardon me the trouble

---

[1] Or with Vishńu in the four modifications described in the First Book,¶—spirit, matter, form, and time. See Vol. I., pp. 18, 19.

[2] Or Śakti, noticed in the last Chapter;—p. 235, *supra*.

[3] Or Bhávanás, also described in the preceding Chapter;¶— p. 233, *supra*.

---

* विचिन्ना: सर्वसंदेहा वैमर्ख मनस: क्षतम् ।

† *Saṁyama.* See Vol. I., p. 26, note *.

: जातचतुर्विधो राशि: शक्तिश्च चिविधा गुरो ।
विज्ञाता चापि कार्त्स्न्येन चिविधा भावभावना ॥

§ *Apasandeha.*

‖ सर्वधर्मादयो धर्मा चिदिता यदग्रेषत: ।
प्रवृत्तं च निवृत्तं च जातं कर्म मयाखिलम् ॥

¶ Substituted for "section".

that I have given you, through that amiable quality of
the virtuous which makes no distinction between a
disciple and a child.*

PARÁSARA.—I have related to you this Puráńa,
which is equal to the Vedas (in sanctity), and by hearing which, all faults and sins whatever are expiated.
In this have been described to you the primary and
secondary creation, the families (of the patriarchs),
the Manwantaras, the regal dynasties;† the gods,
Daityas, Gandharvas, serpents,‡ Rákshasas, Yakshas,
Vidyádharas, Siddhas, and heavenly nymphs;§ Munis
endowed with spiritual wisdom, and practisers of devotion;‖ the (distinctions of the) four castes, and the
actions of the most eminent amongst men;¶ holy
places on the earth, holy rivers and oceans, sacred
mountains, and legends ** of the (truly) wise; the duties
of the different tribes, and the observances enjoined by
the Vedas.†† By hearing this, all sins are, at once, obliterated. In this, also, the glorious‡‡ Hari has been re-
vealed,—the cause of the creation, preservation, and destruction of the world; the soul of all things, and, himself, all things;§§ by the repetition of whose name man

* यद्स कथनायासेर्योजितोऽसि मया गुरो ।
तत्सम्यतां विशेषोऽसि न सतां पुत्रशिष्ययोः ॥
† Vamśánucharita.
‡ Uraga.
§ Apsaras.
‖ मुनयो भावितात्मानः कथ्वते तपसान्विताः ।
¶ पुंसां विशिष्टचरिता नराः ।
** Charita.
†† वर्णधर्मादयो धर्मा वेदधर्माश्च शाश्वताः ।
‡‡ Bhagavat.
§§ Sarva-bhúta.

is, undoubtedly, liberated from all sins, which fly like wolves that are frightened by a lion. The repetition of his name with devout faith* is the best remover of all sins; destroying them, as fire purifies the metal (from the dross). The stain of the Kali age, which ensures to men sharp punishments in hell, is, at once, effaced by a single invocation of Hari.† He who is all that is—,the whole egg of Brahmá, with Hiranyagarbha, Indra,‡ Rudra, the Ádityas, the Aswins, the winds, the Kimnaras, the Vasus, the Sádhyas, Viswadevas, the (celestial) gods,§ the Yakshas, serpents, ‖ Rákshasas,¶ the Siddhas, Daityas, Gandharvas, Dánavas, nymphs,** the stars, asterisms, planets, the seven Rishis,†† the regents and superintendents of the quarters,‡‡ men, Brahmans, and the rest, animals tame and wild,§§ insects,‖‖ birds, ghosts and goblins,¶¶ trees, woods, mountains, rivers, oceans, the subterrene regions,***

---

* *Bhakti.*

† कलिकलुषमलुयं नरकार्तिमदं नृणाम् ।
प्रयाति विलयं सद्यः सङ्गयानुसंस्मृते ॥

‡ *Devendra*, in the original.

§ *Sura.*

‖ I do not find them named in the Sanskrit.

¶ The original yields *Rakshases*.

** *Apsaras.*

†† See Vol. II., p. 226.

‡‡ "The quarters and superintendents of the quarters: धिष्ण्यधिष्णा-
धिपतिभिः । The term Dhishnyádhipati is synonymous with Dikpála;
for which, see Vol. III., 170, note §.

Srídhara—if I may judge from the single MS. of his commentary
which is accessible to me,—has धिष्ण्य°, with reference to the like of
which, see Vol. IV., p. 164, note §.

§§ *Pasu* and *mriga.*

‖‖ *Sarisripa. Vide supra,* p. 236, note †; also, Vol. I., p. 84, note §.

¶¶ These two terms are to render भूतानि: ।

*** Corrected from "legions".

the divisions of the earth, and all perceptible objects,—
he who is all things, who knoweth all things, who is
the form of all things, being without form himself,
and of whom whatever is, from (Mount) Meru to an
atom, all consists,—he, the glorious Vishńu, the destroyer of (all) sin,—is described in this Puráńa. By
hearing this (Puráńa) an equal recompense is obtained
to that which is derived from the performance of an
Aśwamedha sacrifice, or from fasting at (the holy
places) Prayága,* Pushkara,† Kurukshetra,‡ or Arbuda.§ Hearing this (Puráńa) but once is as efficacious as the offering of oblations in a perpetual fire
for a year. The man who, with well-governed passions, bathes at Mathurá, on the twelfth day ‖ of (the
month) Jyeshtha,¹ and beholds (the image of) Hari,
obtains a great recompense:¶ so does he who, with
mind fixed upon Keśava, attentively recites this Pu-

---

¹ This month is also called Jyeshtha-múla,** which the commentator ††explains to mean the month of which the root or cause
(Múla) of being so called is the moon's being full in the constel-
lation Jyeshtha. But it may be so termed, perhaps, from the
lunar asterism Múla,—which is next to Jyeshthá,—falling, also,
within the moon's passage through the same month.

---

* See Vol. III., p. 246, note 2; and Vol. IV., p. 218, note ‡.
† See Vol. I., Preface, p. XXX.; and Vol. II., p. 96.
‡ See Vol. II., p. 133, note 1; and p. 142, note 4.
§ For this mountain, *vide ibid.*, p. 131, note 1, and p. 141, note 2;
also, Vol. IV., p. 222, note ‡.
‖ Insert "of the light fortnight".
¶ प्राप्नोति परमां गतिम् । This means, that he obtains emancipation.
** See note † in the next page.
†† Both the commentators give the ensuing explanation. See, further,
Nílakańṭha on the *Mahábhárata, Anuśásana-parvan, śl.* 4609.

ráńa. The man who bathes in the waters of the Yamuná, on the twelfth lunation* of the light fortnight
of the month in which the moon is in the mansion
Jyeshthá,† and who fasts and worships Achyuta in
(the city of) Mathurá, receives the reward of an uninterrupted Aśwamedha. Beholding the (degree of)
prosperity (enjoyed by others) of eminence, through
(the merits of) their descendants, a man's paternal ancestors, his parents, and their parents exclaim:‡ "Who-
soever of our descendants, having bathed in the Yamuná,§ and fasted, will worship Govinda in Mathurá,
in the light fortnight of Jyeshtha, will secure for us
eminent exaltation;¶ for we shall be elevated by the
merits of our posterity." A man of good extraction
will present obsequial cakes to his fortunate (ancestors)
in the Yamuná, having worshipped Janárdana in the
light fortnight of Jyeshtha.** But the same degree of
merit that a man reaps from adoring Janárdana†† at
that season, with a devoted heart, and from bathing
in the Yamuná, and effecting the liberation of his progenitors by offering to them (on such an occasion,)
obsequial cakes, he derives, also, from hearing, with
equal devotion, a section of this Puráńa.‡‡ This Pu-

---

* _Vide supra_, p. 109, note †.
† "The month", &c. is to translate _Jyeshthá-múla._
‡ The extract is said, by Śrídhara, to be from the _Pitŕi-gítá._ See
Vol. III., p. 66, note §; and p. 170, text and note ‖.
§ Kálindí, in the original. See Vol. IV., p. 286, note *.
‖ The original is _Jyeshthá-múla._
¶ _Riddhi._
** _Jyeshthá-múla_, in the Sanskrit.
†† The original has Kŕishńa.
‡‡ मूलाख्यायं तदाप्नोति पुराणस्याङ्ग भक्तिमान् ।

ráńa is the best of all preservatives for those who are afraid of worldly existence,* a certain alleviation of the sufferings of men,† and remover of all imperfections. This (Puráńa), originally composed by the Rishi (Náráyańa), was communicated, by Brahmá,‡ to Ribhu;§ he related it to Priyavrata,|| by whom it was imparted to Bháguri.¶ Bháguri recited it to Tamasitra;[1]** and he, to Dadhícha,†† who gave it to Sáraswata.‡‡ From the last Bhŕigu§§ received it, who imparted it to Purukutsa;|||| and he taught it to Narmadá. The goddess¶¶ delivered it to Dhŕitaráshtŕa,***

---

[1] This name is also read Tambamitra. ††† One copy has Tava mitráya,‡‡‡ "to thy friend." as if it was an epithet of Dadhícha: but the construction of the verse requires a proper name. "Bháguri gave it to Tambamitra; and he, to Dadhícha:'§§§

भागुरिस्तम्बमित्राय दधीचाय स चोक्तवान् ।

* *Samsára.*

† Literally, "a cure for men's bad dreams": दुःस्वप्ननाशनं पुंसाम् ।

‡ Called, in the original, by his epithet Kamalodbhava,—the same as Abjayoni. See Vol. I., p. 17, note †.

§ See Vol. I., p. 77, note 1; and Vol. II., p. 330.

|| Ibid., pp. 107, et seq.

¶ For a Bháguri, see Vol. II., p. 113, note 1.

** This reading I find nowhere. See, further, note †††, below.

†† Correct from "Dadicha". See Vol. I., p. 124; also, Professor Wilson's Translation of the *Ŕigveda*, Vol. I., p. 216, note a, and p. 310, note a.

‡‡ See Vol. I., p. 17.

§§ Ibid., p. 100.

|||| Ibid., p. 17; Vol. III., p. 268, text and note ‡, and p. 283.

¶¶ Literally, Narmadá.

*** See Vol. I., p. 188, note 1; and Vol. II., p. 74.

††† So reads, like, my Ajmere MS., my oldest MS. of all. Ratnagarbha has Tambhamitra; and my Arrah MS. yields Stambamitra.

‡‡‡ This is Śrídhara's lection.

§§§ Corrected from "Dadhichi".

the Nága king,* and to Apúrańa,† of the same race,‡ by whom it was repeated to their monarch,§ Vásuki. Vásuki communicated it to Vatsa;¶ and he, to Aśwatara, from whom it successively proceeded to Kambala and Elápatra.** When the Muni Vedaśiras descended to Pátála,†† he there received the whole (Puráńa) from these Nágas,‡‡ and communicated it to Pramati.§§ Pramati consigned it to the wise Játúkarńa;‖‖ and he taught it to many other holy persons. Through the blessing of Vasishťha¶¶, it came to my knowledge§ and I have, now, Maitreya, faithfully imparted it to you. You will teach it, at the end of the Kali age, to Samíka.[1]*** Whoever hears this great mystery, which

---

¹ A different series of narrators ††† has been specified in the First Book,—Vol. 1., p. 17.

* The original has only Nága.

† Corrected from "Puráńa". See Vol. II., p. 288. From note * to *ibid.*, p. 290, it seems that other Puráńas read Varuńa and Aruńa (?).

‡ The original is भूतरात्राय नागाधापूरणाय च । Apúrńa is not, then, said to be "of the same race". In the passages referred to in the preceding note, he figures as a Grámańi or Yaksha.

§ Literally, "to the king of the Nágas", नागराजाय ।

See Vol. II., p. 74, and p. 86, note 1.

¶ For the Nága called Vatsa, see Vol. II., p. 287, note *.

** For Aśwatara, Kambala, and Elápatra, see Vol. II., p. 74.

†† The original seems to denote that Vedaśiras became master of Pátála:
पातालं समनुप्राप्तवानो वेद्यिरा मुनिः ।

‡‡ By the word तेन, immediately following the mention of Elápatra, it is implied that from him alone the Puráńa passed to Vedaśiras.

§§ Variant: Pramita.

‖‖ Some of my best MSS. give Játúkarńya. For both names, see Vol. III., p. 36, text and note *.

¶¶ Pulastya, according to my Ajmere MS.

*** Variants: Śaniku, Sanika, and Śinika. For Śamika, see Vol. I., Preface, p. LV.

††† On which Ratnagarbha remarks: अथ संप्रदायानरमेदं कथमिद्-अवस्थितः ।

removes the contamination of the Kali, shall be freed from all his sins. He who hears this every day, acquits himself of his daily obligations to ancestors, gods, and men.* The (great and) rarely attainable merit that a man acquires by the gift of a brown cow,† he derives from hearing ten chapters of this (Puráña).[1] He who hears the entire (Puráña), contemplating, in his mind, Achyuta,—who is all things, and of whom all things are made; who is the stay of the whole world, the receptacle of spirit; who is knowledge, and that which is to be known; who is without beginning or end, and the benefactor of the gods,:—obtains, assuredly, the reward that attends the uninterrupted celebration of the Aśwamedha rite. § He who reads, and retains with faith this (Puráña), in the beginning, middle, and end of which is described the glorious Achyuta, the lord of the universe in every stage,‖ the master of all that is stationary or moveable, composed of spiritual knowledge,¶ acquires such purity as exists not in any world,—the eternal state of perfection,** (which is) Hari. The man who fixes his

---

[1] This seems to be an injudicious interpolation: it is not in all the copies. ††

---

* पितृयज्ञमनुष्येभ्यः समस्तामरसंस्तुतिः ।
  ज्ञाता तेन भवेदेतष: शृणोति दिने दिने ॥

† Kapilá. According to Colebrooke, "when applied to a cow, this term signifies one of the colour of lac dye, with black tail and white hoofs." Two Treatises on the Hindu Law of Inheritance, p. 131, note.

: Amara.   § Vájimedha, in the original.

‖ अखिलजगन्मध्यान्तसर्गप्रभुः ।

¶ ब्रह्मज्ञानमयः ।   ** एकान्तसिद्धि: ।

†† Śridhara ignores it; otherwise it seems to be recognized.

mind on Vishńu goes not to hell. He who meditates upon him regards heavenly enjoyment only as an impediment; and he whose mind and soul are penetrated by him thinks little of the world of Brahmá: for, when present in the minds of those whose intellects are free from soil, he confers upon them eternal freedom. What marvel, therefore, is it, that the sins of one who repeats the name of Achyuta should be wiped away? Should not that Hari be heard of whom those devoted to acts worship with sacrifices, continually, as the god of sacrifice;* whom those devoted to meditation† contemplate as primary and secondary, composed of spirit;‡ by obtaining whom, man is not born, nor nourished,§ nor subjected to death; who is all that is, and that is not, (or both cause and effect); who, as the progenitors, receives the libations‖ made to them; who, as the gods, accepts the offerings¶ addressed to them; the glorious being who is without beginning or end; whose name is both Swáhá** and Swadhá;¹** who is the abode of all spiritual power; in whom the limits of finite things cannot be measured; and who, when he enters the ear, destroys all sin?²

---

¹ The words or prayers employed in presenting oblations with fire.

² The text has:

यस्मिन्नङ्गानि सर्वमूर्तिनिलये मानानि गो मानिनाम् ।
जिह्वादौ प्रभवन्ति इति कलुषं श्रोषं स यातो हरि: ॥

Mána commonly means 'pride;' but here it seems most appro-

---

* *Yajneśwara.*   † *Yogin.*   ‡ *Brahma-maya.*
§ The original has गो वर्धते रीयते चैव ।
‖ *Kavya.*   ¶ *Havya.*
** See Vol. IIL, p. 122, note ‡, ad finem.

I adore him, that first of gods, Purushottama,* who
is without end and without beginning, without growth,
without decay,† without death;‡ who is substance that
knows not change. I adore that ever inexhaustible
spirit,§ who assumed sensible qualities;‖ who, though
one, became many; who, though pure, became as if
impure, by appearing in many and various shapes;
who is endowed with (divine) wisdom, and is the
author of the preservation of all creatures.¶ I adore
him, who is the one conjoined essence and object of
both meditative wisdom and active virtue; who is
watchful in providing for human enjoyments; who is
one with the three qualities; who, without undergoing
change, is the cause of the evolution of the world;
who exists of his own essence, ever exempt from
decay.** I constantly adore him, who is entitled
heaven,†† air, fire, water, earth, and ether;‡‡ who is the

priately rendered by its radical import, 'measure.' The measures
which are for the determination of measurable things are not
applicable to Vishńu.

* जतोऽस्मि पुरुषोत्तममाबमीषुज् ।   † Parińáma.   ‡ Apakshaya.
§ तबी जतोऽस्मि पुरुषाय सदाब्ययाय ।
For avyaya, see Vol. I., p. 17, note *.
‖ अनुगुबभुज् ।   ¶ सकलतत्त्वविभूतिकर्ता ।
** ज्ञानप्रवृत्तिनियमैकमयाय पुंस: ।
भोगप्रदानपटवे त्रिगुबाक्षकाय ॥
अव्याहताय भवभावनकारणाय ।
वन्दे स्वरूपभवाय सदाबराय ॥
†† Vyoman, the same as ákáśa, which is generally rendered 'ether'.
See Vol. I., p. 34, note *.
‡‡ The only reading which I find is
वोमानिलाविश्वभुवनामयाय ।
We have had "ether" just above, in the Translator's "heaven"; and

bestower of all the objects which give gratification to the senses; who benefits mankind with the instruments of fruition; who is perceptible, who is subtile, who is imperceptible. May that unborn, eternal Hari, whose form is manifold, and whose essence is composed of both nature and spirit,* bestow upon all mankind that blessed state which knows neither birth nor decay!

---

there is no sixth element.

In the MS. which Professor Wilson used in preference to any or all others, the letters •र्ख- in this passage look very like ख, for which he probably took them, not noticing the two letters following, makiug up •र्खनी-; and *kha* is one of the words for "ether". *Vide supra*, p. 198, text, with notes ‡ and ¶.

* यत्र रूपं प्रकृतिपरात्ममयम् ।

APPENDIX.

[No one among the contemporaries of Professor Wilson is known to have qual'fied himself more adequately than Colonel Vans Kennedy for discussing the subject of the Puránas; and it has, therefore, been considered that the following correspondence must, with all its defects, possess, to the readers of these volumes, sufficient interest to justify its republication in this place. The seven letters of which it consists—namely, five entitled *On Professor Wilson's Theory respecting the Puránas*, the Professor's Reply, and the Colonel's Rejoinder,—originally appeared in the London *Asiatic Journal* for 1840 and 1841, addressed to its editor. F. H.]

SIR: In the learned and ingenious remarks contained in the Preface to his Translation of the *Vishńu Puráńa*, Professor Wilson remarks that the Puráńas "may be acquitted of subservience to any but sectarial imposture. They were pious* frauds for temporary purposes;"† and that they "are, also, works of evidently different ages, and have been compiled under different circumstances, the precise nature of which we can but imperfectly conjecture from internal evidence, and from what we know of the history of religious opinion in India. It is highly probable that, of the present popular forms of the Hindu religion, none assumed their actual state earlier than the time of Śankara Áchárya, the great Śaiva reformer, who flourished, in all likelihood, in the eighth or ninth century. Of the Vaishńava teachers, Rá-

---

* Colonel Kennedy omitted this word.   † Vol. I., Preface, p. XI.

mánuja dates in the twelfth century; Madhwáchárya, in
the thirteenth; and Vallabha, in the sixteenth; and the
Puráṇas seem to have accompanied, or followed, their
innovations; being obviously intended to advocate the
doctrines they taught."* He further observes that
"a very great portion of the contents of many [of the
Puráṇas], some portion of the contents of all, is genuine and old. The sectarial interpolation, or embellishment, is always sufficiently palpable to be set aside
without injury to the more authentic and primitive
material; and the Puráṇas, although they belong especially † to that stage of the Hindu religion in which
faith in some one divinity was the prevailing principle,
are, also, a valuable record of the form of Hindu
belief which came next in order to that of the Vedas." ‡ And yet Professor Wilson, at the same time,
maintains that religious instruction is not one of the
five topics which are treated of in a genuine Puráṇa,
and that its occurrence in the Puráṇas now extant is
a decisive proof that these are not the same works, in
all respects, that were current, under the denomination
of Puráṇas, in the century prior to Christianity.

These, however, and similar remarks contained in
that Preface, seem to be inconsistent and inconclusive;
for, if the Puráṇas, in their present form, are of so
modern a date, and if the ancient Puráṇas are no
longer extant, by what means can it be ascertained
that any portion of the contents of the works now
bearing the name of Puráṇas is genuine and old?

---

* Vol. I., Preface, p. XVI.
† Colonel Kennedy—a very heedless quoter,—had "essentially".
‡ Vol. I., Preface, pp. XI., XII.

Professor Wilson rejects, as not belonging to the Puránas, in the time of Amara Simha (B. C. 56), all those parts of the present Puránas which relate to the rites and observances and to the theology of the Hindus; but it is those parts only which admit of being compared with other Hindu works, and with all that is known of the Hindu religion. It is, also, unquestionable that certain works denominated Puránas have been immemorially considered, by the Hindus, as sacred books;* and it must be evident that, unless the doctrines of the Hindu religion were inculcated in those works, they could contain nothing which could communicate to them a sacred character. The opinion, therefore, of Professor Wilson, that the genuine Puránas treated of profane subjects only, is, obviously, incompatible with that profound reverence with which the Puránas are regarded by all Hindus, even at the present day. The only argument, also, which he has adduced in support of this opinion depends entirely upon the use and meaning of the term *pancha-lakshaṅa*, as applied to a Puráṅa. But the passage in Sanskrit, quoted in the note in page VII., does not admit of the restricted sense which Professor Wilson has given to it; because the first of the five topics[1] there mentioned, or *sarga*, is inadequately expressed† by "primary creation, or cosmogony." This will be at once evident by a reference

---

[1] The five topics, as explained by Professor Wilson, are: "1. Primary creation, or cosmogony; 2. Secondary creation, or the destruction and renovation of worlds, including chronology; 3. Genealogy of gods and patriarchs; 4. Reigns of the Manus, or periods called Manwantaras; and, 5. History."

* ?? † But see what the Colonel says in p. 299, note 2, *infra*.

to the contents of the Translation of the *Vishńu Puráńa*, where, under *sarga*, are enumerated: * Vishńu, the origin, existence, and end of all things; his existence before creation; his first manifestations; description of Pradhána, of Prakŕiti, of the active cause; development of effects, of the mundane egg. For the description of all that precedes the appearance of the mundane egg, which occurs in the *Vishńu* and other Puráńas, is the most abstruse and sacred part of Hindu theology; as it explains the real nature of the Supreme Being, and of those manifestations of his divine essence which lead men to believe in the actual existence of a material world. The first, therefore, of the five topics treated of in a genuine Puráńa, according to Professor Wilson, necessarily includes religious instruction; because the antecedents to creation could not have been described without, at the same time, explaining the distinction between the one sole-existing spirit and those illusive appearances which seem to be composed of matter. The second, also, of those topics is, equally, of a religious nature; for an account of the destruction and renovation of worlds must, necessarily, include a description of the means and agents employed, by the Supreme Being, for those purposes. Under the first two topics, consequently, is comprised a great part of what is contained in the Puráńas, as at present extant: namely, a description of the real essence of the Supreme Being, and of the illusive nature of the universe; of the production of Brahmá, Vishńu, Śiva, and their female energies; of the origin of angelic beings and holy sages; and of all the circumstances relating

* This is not a fair representation.

to the repeated creation, destruction, and renovation of the world; and it may, therefore, be justly concluded, that these subjects were also treated of in the eighteen Puránas, as originally committed to writing, and that the term *pancha-lakshana* affords no grounds for the conclusion which Professor Wilson has deduced from its use and meaning.

But those parts of the present Puránas which relate to festivals, rites, and observances, and to the worship of particular deities, may appear to support this remark of Professor Wilson: "They [the Puránas] are no longer authorities for Hindu belief, as a whole: they are special guides for separate and, sometimes, conflicting branches of it; compiled for the evident purpose of promoting the preferential, or, in some cases, the sole, worship of Vishńu, or of Śiva."* It is not clear what is here meant by the "Hindu belief, as a whole;" for there are, I believe, no traces, now extant, of the Hindu religion having ever existed as one uniform system of belief in one and the same deity. But the antiquity of the Upanishads is not disputed; and, in one or other of them, the attributes of the Supreme Being are distinctly ascribed to Brahmá, Vishńu, Śiva, Deví, Súrya, and Gańeśa; and, consequently, when the Upanishads were composed, there must have been some Hindus who paid a preferential worship to one or other of those deities. These, however, are precisely the same deities to whom the attributes of the Supreme Being are ascribed in one or other of the Puránas; and, therefore, if the antiquity

* Vol. I., Preface, p. V.

of the Upanishads be admitted, the variety of deities
proposed for worship in the Puráńas now extant can
be no proof that these works were recently compiled,
for sectarian purposes. The Vedas, indeed, have not
yet been so examined as to admit of its being determined whether the same distinction is to be found in
them; but Mr. Colebrooke has stated that the whole
of the Indian theology is founded on the Upanishads,
and that several of them, which he has described, were
extracts from the Vedas. The six deities, therefore,
just mentioned, were, most probably, objects of worship,
when the religious system of the Vedas flourished;
and it must, in consequence, be altogether improper
to consider the worshippers of one of those deities,
in preference to the others, as sectarians, if, by this
term, is intended such sectarians as have existed in
India in later times. For, according to the principles
of the Hindu religion, there is unity in diversity; and,
hence, it is held that these apparently different deities
are merely variant forms of one and the same Supreme
Being, and that, consequently, the worship of any one
of them is equally holy and effective,—as it is, in fact,
the adoration of the Supreme Being in that particular
form. Sectarianism, at the same time, consists in the
exclusive, and not merely preferential, worship of a
particular deity; but in not one of the Puráńas is there ·
a single intimation, or injunction, which, virtually, or
expressly, sanctions the rejection of the worship of
Vishńu, or Śiva, or of any of the other six deities. The
orthodox Hindus, therefore, are, even at the present
day, votaries, but not sectaries, of either Vishńu or
Śiva; and such they appear to have been from the

remotest time,—as the particular worship of Brahmá has long ceased, and, though particular worshippers of Súrya and Gańeśa have existed, and, perhaps, still exist, in India, they have never been numerous, and the worship of Deví has degenerated into rites and ceremonies which, though practised by many Hindus, are, generally, considered to be contrary to the tenets and ritual of the Hindu religion.[1]

Professor Wilson also has not explained the sectarian purposes to promote which he thinks the works at present bearing the names of Puráńas were compiled in a period so comparatively modern as that between the eighth and seventeenth centuries. But he cannot mean to contend that Vishńu and Śiva were not objects of worship in the earliest times of the Hindu religion, or that they were worshipped with the same rites and ceremonies; and, if not, the mere ascribing, in those works, preeminence to either Vishńu or Śiva, and a superior excellence to the worship of either of those gods,—which is all that occurs of them,—can be no proof that the Puráńas, as now extant, are mere modern works, compiled for sectarian purposes; because in not one of the eighteen Puráńas is it, in any manner, intimated that Vishńu or Śiva ought not to be worshipped; and, on the contrary, numerous passages occur in them, in which precisely the same rewards are promised to the worshipper of either god. So far, indeed, is any one of the Puráńas from inculcating the exclusive worship of either Vishńu or

---

[1] I here merely allude to the worship of Deví by the sacrifice of auimals, and not to the abominable worship described in the Tantras.

Śiva, that Vishńu is introduced, in some of them, teaching the worship of Śiva, and, in others, Śiva, teaching the worship of Vishńu. The only distinction which appears to exist between these gods is, that, in particular Puráńas, each is represented as the Supreme Being, when the other becomes, in a certain sense, inferior, without, however, detracting from his divine excellence. It is, also, remarkable that it is not in separate Puráńas only that preeminence is ascribed to either Vishńu or Śiva, or even to Brahmá; but this ascription occurs in the very same Puráńa. For, as far as I have observed, there are only five Puráńas in which the supremacy is uniformly ascribed to the same god: namely, the *Linga* and *Skanda*, in which Śiva is identified with the Supreme Being; the *Vishńu* and *Bhágavata*, in which this honour is attributed to Vishńu; and the *Brahma Vaivarta*, in which Kŕishńa is represented as the Supreme Being, and his favourite mistress, Rádhá, as his *śakti* or energy. When, therefore, in the Puráńas as now extant, equal reverence is given not only to Vishńu and Śiva, but to four other deities, and when nothing occurs, in them, which in the least sanctions the rejection of the worship of those deities, or in any manner condemns or disparages it, it seems evident that such works could not have been composed for the sectarian purpose of promoting the exclusive worship of either Vishńu or Śiva, or of any other god.[1]

---

[1] I should except the *Brahma Vaivarta Purána* (for I have not met with any Upanishad in which Kŕishńu is represented as the Supreme Being); but this Puráńa appears to me to be of

It is, as the same time, impossible to understand
why Professor Wilson should have been so anxious
to establish, in that Preface, that the Puránas now
extant are mere modern compilations, and that a
genuine Purána treats of profane subjects only, when,
in p. XCVII., he makes these remarks: "That Brahmans unknown to fame have remodelled some of the
Hindu scriptures, and, especially, the Puránas, cannot
reasonably be contested, after dispassionately weighing
the strong internal evidence, which all of them afford,
of the intermixture of unauthorized and comparatively
modern ingredients. But the same internal testimony
furnishes proof, equally decisive, of the anterior existence of ancient materials; and it is, therefore, as idle
as it is irrational, to dispute the antiquity or authenticity of the gieater portion of the contents of the Puránas, in the face of abundant positive and circumstantial evidence of the prevalence of the doctrines which
they teach, the currency of the legends which they
narrate, and the integrity of the institutions which they
describe, at least three centuries before the Christian
era." For the natural conclusion from such premisses
must, necessarily, be, that the Puránas now extant are
the very same works which were known, under that
denomination, three centuries before the Christian era,
but that they, at the same time, afford strong internal
testimony of an intermixture of unauthorized and
comparatively modern ingredients. But, to invert this
conclusion, and to suppose that, because some parts

a much more ancient date than that ascribed to it by Professor
Wilson.

of the present Puráńas are, perhaps, modern, therefore these works must be modern compilations, is, obviously, contrary to every principle of just reasoning;
because, as it is admitted that ancient materials existed
anterior to the supposed compilation of the present
Puráńas, and as no cause can be assigned for their disappearance — if such existed, — in the tenth or eleventh
century, it is most reasonable to conclude that the
Puráńas now extant do, actually, consist of those very
materials, and that they are, in fact, the very same
works which were current, under that denomination,
in the time of Amara Siṅha. Professor Wilson, however, seems to have given more weight to the internal
testimony arising from those passages of the Puráńas
which he thinks have a modern appearance, than to
that which results from those parts which the Puráńas
must have contained from their first composition, in
order to entitle them to a sacred character and to that
reverence with which these works have been always
regarded by the Hindus. But the fixing the precise
date when the Puráńas received their present form is
a question of little or no consequence, when it is admitted that there is "abundant positive and circumstantial evidence of the prevalence of the doctrines
which they teach, the currency of the legends which
they narrate, and the integrity of the institutions which
they describe, at least three centuries before the
Christian era."

The Puráńas, therefore, cannot be—as also remarked
by Professor Wilson, in p. XI.,—pious frauds, written
for temporary purposes, in subservience to sectarial
imposture. But these are the principal grounds on

which he rests his opinion, that the Puráńas now extant did not receive their present form until a thousand
years after the birth of Christ. Professor Wilson, however, does not explain in what this imposture con-
sisted, or for what sectarian purpose it was intended.
That there are, at this day, and may have been, for
many centuries, exclusive worshippers of Vishńu, or
Śiva, is undoubted; but, as I have before observed,
this exclusive worship is not sanctioned by anything
that is contained in the Puráńas now extant; nor do
they, in any manner, countenance those more obscure
sects which have existed in India in later times. The
opinion, also, of Professor Wilson, that "the designation of Śakti may not be correctly applicable to the
whole [of the *Rájasa* division of the Puráńas], although
it is to some of the series; for there is no incompatibility in the advocacy of a Tántrika modification of
the Hindu religion by any Puráńa,"* is, unquestionably, erroneous; because, in not one of the eighteen
Puráńas is there the slightest indication of the Tántrika
worship, or the slightest allusion to it; for the worship
of Deví, in the form of Durgá or Kálí, by blood, flesh,
and spirituous liquors, is essentially different from
that of Deví as Śakti: in the one, it is her image which
is worshipped, and, in the latter, it is a naked virgin.[1]
Had, however, imposture for sectarian purposes been
the object for which the Puráńas were written, it must
have been evident in every part of them; but, on the

---

[1] Strictly speaking, not the virgin, but the κτείς of the virgin.

* Vol. I., Preface, pp. XXI., XXII.

contrary, I have no doubt that, were they carefully
and dispassionately examined, it would satisfactorily
appear that they contain nothing which is incompatible
with those principles of the Hindu religion which are
universally acknowledged by all Hindus. The argument, consequently, deduced from the assumption that
the Puránas, as now extant, are pious frauds, and,
therefore, modern compilations, is refuted by the whole
scope and tendency of those works; nor, were it even
proved that interpolations and additions have taken
place in them, would this circumstance detract from
the authenticity of such portions of them as afford
strong internal evidence of their antiquity. But what
more conclusive evidence of their antiquity can be required than — as is admitted by Professor Wilson himself,—their containing a correct description of the doctrines, the legends, and the institutions of the Hindu
religion which were prevalent in India three centuries
before the Christian era? For it is, obviously, much
more probable that the present Puránas are works
which were then extant, than that eighteen different
persons should, each, have conceived, thirteen hundred
years afterwards, the design of writing a Purána, and
should have been able to compile or compose, so ac-
curately, eighteen different works which correspond
so exactly in numerous essential and minute particulars.

The eighteen Puránas, also, as Professor Wilson
states, consist of 400.000 *slokas*, or 1.600.000 lines;
and it must, therefore, be evident that nothing but
the most attentive examination of the whole of such
extensive works, and a thorough knowledge of the

exact state of India, and of all the changes which may
have taken place, in the country and amongst the
people, during the last two thousand years, could
enable any person to fix, with any degree of certainty,
from the internal evidence of the Puránas, the date
when each of them was composed. A name, a circumstance, or even a legend may have a modern appearance; but its recentness, or antiquity, can only be determined by there being some known facts with which
it can be compared; and it is the want of such facts,
in the present state of our knowledge of Hindu history,
that renders all reasoning, with respect to the dates of
the events mentioned in the Puránas, so completely
inconclusive. Most of the legends, also, are of a miraculous nature; and no date, therefore, can be inferred
from them. Professor Wilson, however, undeterred by
such considerations, has not hesitated to fix the time
when each Purána was composed, and to place the
compilation of the Puránas, as now extant, between
the eighth and seventeenth centuries. But his reasons
for assigning so modern a period to the compilation
of those works appear to rest, principally, if not entirely, on the contents of the different Puránas not corresponding with his preconceived opinion of what a
Purána ought to be. For Professor Wilson thus observes, with respect to the *Brahma Vaivarta Purána*:
"The character of the work is, in truth, so* decidedly
sectarial, and the sect to which it belongs, so distinctly
marked,—that of the worshippers of the juvenile
Kŕishńa and Rádhá, a form of belief of known modern
origin,—that it can scarcely have found a notice in a

---

* Colonel Kennedy omitted the words "in truth, so".

work to which, like the Matsya, a much more remote
date seems to belong. Although, therefore, the Matsya
may be received in proof of there having been a Brahma Vaivarta Puráńa at the date of its compilation, dedicated especially to the honour of Kŕishńa, yet we
cannot credit the possibility of its being the same we
now possess."[1] * Thus, Professor Wilson decides,
not only that "the Brahma Vaivarta has not the
slightest title to be regarded as a Puráńa,"† but, also,
that the Puráńa which bore that name is no longer
extant; and yet he adduces neither argument nor proof
in support of this decision, and of his gratuitous assumption that this Puráńa owes its origin to the modern
sect of the worshippers of the juvenile Kŕishńa. He
admits, also, that the first three Books (or nearly two-
thirds,) of this Puráńa are occupied in the description
of the acts of Brahmá, Deví, and Gańeśa; but he does
not explain why the supposed sectarian writer, instead
of composing a work solely in honour of Kŕishńa, and
in support of his sect, has dedicated so great a part of
the Puráńa to the celebration of other deities. In the
same manner, Professor Wilson remarks, with respect
to the Vámana Puráńa: "It is of a more tolerant

---

[1] The object of this Puráńa is to represent Kŕishńa as the
Supreme Being, and Rádhá, as his energy; and it is, therefore,
altogether improbable that it should have been compiled for the
purpose of promoting the modern worship of the juvenile Kŕishńa,
or that a modern work should have been written, and substituted
in the place of the Brahma Vaivarta Puráńa mentioned in the
Matsya.

character than the Puránas, and divides its homage
between Śiva and Vishńu with tolerable impartiality.
It is not connected, therefore, with any sectarial principles, and may have preceded their introduction. It
has not, however, the air of any antiquity; and its
compilation may have amused the leisure of some
Brahman of Benares three or four centuries ago."[1*]
But this, surely, is not the manner in which the question whether the Puránas, as now extant, are ancient
and original compositions, or mere modern compilations, ought to be discussed,—far less, decided. On the
contrary, the particular passages of the Puránas which
are supposed to be modern ought to be adduced, or
referred to; and it should, then, be shown that the circumstances and events, or the doctrines and legends,
mentioned in them could not be of an ancient date,
because they had occurred, or had been introduced, in
modern times, or that they were posterior to modern
events of known dates; and, as, therefore, Professor
Wilson has not followed this method, but trusted to
conjecture and inferences deduced from erroneous premisses, it seems evident that his speculations respecting the modern period in which the present Puránas
were composed must be considered to be either groundless or not yet supported by the requisite proof.

---

[1] As, however, Professor Wilson places the introduction of
sectarial principles in the eighth or ninth century,† the date of the
Vámana Puráńa, if compiled previous to their introduction, must
be the eighth century, at least, and not the fourteenth or fifteenth.

---

* Vol. I., Preface, p. LXXVI.
† *Vide supra*, p. 257.

The preceding observations will have, perhaps,
evinced that the remarks contained in Professor Wilson's Preface to his Translation of the *Vishńu Puráńa*
have been written under the impression of two conflicting opinions: for he is obliged to admit that the
Puráńas now extant were compiled from ancient materials, and that they are "a valuable record of the
form of Hindu belief which came next in order to that
of the Vedas"; and yet he contends that those works
are pious frauds, written for temporary purposes, in
subservience to sectarial imposture. But both these
opinions cannot be correct; and it must, therefore, be
most accordant with probability to conclude that,
although interpolations and additions may, possibly,
have taken place in the Puráńas, as now extant, they
are, still, in all essential respects, the very same works
which have been, from remote times, held sacred by
the Hindus. That, however, alterations have been
made in the present Puráńas is a mere supposition,
which has never yet been supported by any clear and
satisfactory proof; and the inconsistent and inconclusive reasoning, employed by a person so well acquainted with the Puráńas as Professor Wilson, to
prove that they are mere modern compilations, must,
alone, evince that the internal evidence of the Puráńas, even in their present form, affords such incontrovertible proof of their antiquity, that even those who
wish to contest this are obliged to admit it, and to explain it by having recourse to the conjecture, that ancient materials existed, from which those parts of the
extant Puráńas which are, most probably, ancient, were
compiled. But, as this conjecture is altogether gra-

tuitous, and unsupported by proof, it may be much
more reasonably concluded that the Puránas now extant are the very same works which have been always
known, under that denomination, from the remote time
when they were originally composed;* and Professor
Wilson himself remarks that "they never emanated
from any impossible combination of the Brahmans to
fabricate for the antiquity of the entire Hindu system
any claims which it cannot fully support;"† and that
"the origin and development of the doctrines, traditions, and institutions [described in the Puránas now
extant,] were not the work of a day; and the testimony
that establishes their existence three centuries before
Christianity carries it back to a much more remote
antiquity,–to an antiquity that is, probably, not surpassed by any of the prevailing fictions, institutions,
or beliefs of the ancient world.":

VANS KENNEDY.

Bombay, 28th August, 1840.

SIR: In the letter which I addressed to you on the
28th ult., I confined myself to such observations as
seemed to evince that the remarks contained in Professor Wilson's Preface to his Translation of the *Vishńu
Puráńa* were written under the impression of two
conflicting opinions, which could not, both, be correct.
As my attention has, thus, been again directed to the
question whether the eighteen Puráńas, as now extant,

---

* Of this untenable position Colonel Kennedy nowhere offers any proof
† Vol. I., Preface, p. XI. ‡ *Ibid.,* p. XCIX.

V. 18

are ancient compositions, or modern compilations, I am induced to enter into a further discussion of this subject. For it is evident that, if the works now known under that denomination were written between the eleventh and seventeenth centuries, for temporary purposes, in subservience to sectarial imposture, they cannot be a valuable record of the form of Hindu belief which came next in order to that of the Vedas. Nor can they, indeed, afford any authentic information with respect to the state of the Hindu religion previous to the twelfth century; because, even admitting that those works may have been partly compiled from ancient materials, there are no means now available by which what is genuine and old that may be contained in them can be distinguished from what is supposed to be spurious and modern.

The limits of a preface may have prevented Professor Wilson from fully discussing this question; but, as that Preface extends to seventy-five quarto pages, it is most probable that he has, at least, stated, in it, the principal reasons which induce him to consider the Puráńas to be modern compositions. To me, however, it appears that those reasons, instead of supporting Professor Wilson's opinion, should lead to a directly contrary conclusion. The arguing, in particular, that, because not one of the present Puráńas corresponds with the term *pancha-lakshańa*, or "treatises on five topics",—which is given as a synonym to a Puráńa, in the vocabulary of Amara Siṁha,—therefore it is decidedly proved "that we have not, at present, the same works, in all respects, that were current, under the denomination of Puráńas, in the century

prior to Christianity,"* is, certainly, altogether inconclusive. For a mere descriptive term cannot be received as proof, when the argument itself admits that
the works which it was intended to describe are no
longer extant, and that, consequently, there are no
means of determining whether the term did, or did
not, apply strictly to those works. On the supposition,
also, that the Puráńas now extant are modern compositions, written in imitation of the ancient Puráńas, it
must be evident that those works could not have been
restricted to the treating only of the five topics mentioned by Professor Wilson; for he himself observes
that the description of a Puráńa, included in the term
pancha-lakshańa, is utterly inapplicable to some of the
present Puráńas, and that to others it only partially
applies. But, though it may be supposed that the Brahmans might possibly recompose their sacred books,
it is altogether improbable that they would so alter
them, as to leave no resemblance between the original
and its substitute; and, consequently, had the prescribed form for the composition of a Puráńa required the treating of five topics only, in that precise form would the present Puráńas (if modern compilations,) have, no doubt, been written. As, therefore,
they do not exhibit that form, and as they could not
have succeeded to the reverence in which the ancient
Puráńas were held, unless they resembled those works,
(at least in form,) it is most reasonable to conclude that
a Puráńa, as originally composed, was not "a treatise
on five topics." The miscellaneous nature, consequently, of the contents of the present Puráńas cannot

* Vol. I., Preface, p. XI.

be admitted as a valid objection to their antiquity, on
a mere supposition, which is not only improbable in
itself, but which is, also, disproved by the sacred
character that has been immemorially ascribed to the
Puráńas, which, it is obvious, they could not have received, had they treated only of the profane topics
mentioned by Professor Wilson.

The argument also supposes that the original eighteen Puráńas were current prior to the Christian era;
and, before, therefore, the conclusion can be granted,
the time and manner in which those works have become extinct should be proved: for, as numerous
Sanskrit works which were, unquestionably, extant
at the commencement of the Christian era, have been
preserved until the present day, nothing but satisfactory proof can establish that the Puráńas alone, although held to be sacred books, have completely disappeared. It requires to be particularly considered
that the Puráńas consist of eighteen distinct works,
comprising an aggregate of 1.600.000 lines,[*] and that
India, more than one million of square miles in extent,
has been, during the last two thousand years, divided
into at least ten distinct regions,[†] differing in language
and in local customs and prejudices. Were it, therefore, even conceded that the Brahmans, since the
Christian era, had succeeded in suppressing the whole
of the eighteen Puráńas, and in substituting other
works in their place, in some one or other region of
India, still copies of the original Puráńas would have

---

[*] See Vol. I., Preface, p. XXIV.
[†] For the particulars of this unscientific classification, see Colebrooke's
Miscellaneous Essays, Vol. II., p. 179.

been preserved in the other regions. Nothing but the entire extirpation of the Brahmanical religion, throughout the whole of so extensive a country, could have effected the complete destruction of such voluminous works,—the more especially, as their sacred character would have rendered their preservation an object of constant solicitude. But, until a complete suppression of the ancient Puránas had been effected, other works could not have been substituted in their place; and, thus, the objection to the supposition that the Puránas, as now extant, were not written until between the eleventh and seventeenth centuries becomes insuperable. For, admitting the dates assigned to each of the Puránas by Professor Wilson, it may be asked: Was the ancient Purána, bearing the same name, extant until it was superseded by the modern one, or was it not? In the first case, in what manner was its supersession accomplished? Professor Wilson extends the period during which he supposes the Puránas to have received their present form, to eight centuries; and he, thus, admits that the replacing of the ancient Puránas by new works did not proceed from a combination of the Brahmans to remodel the Hindu religion on new but premeditated principles. It becomes, therefore, impossible to understand how any individual could, without the consent and assistance of the Brahmans, effect the suppression of an ancient Purána, and the substitution, in its place, of a work of his own composition or compilation, throughout the whole of India. If, for instance, the *Bhágavata* was written by Bopadeva, at Doulutabad, in the twelfth century, was the original *Bhágavata* then in existence, or not? If it

was, what reason, consistent with probability, can be
assigned for supposing that the Brahmans of all India
would have suppressed one of their sacred books, to
which they ascribed a divine origin, and received, as
entitled to the same reverence, the acknowledged composition of an obscure grammarian? The supposition
is, evidently, absurd. It is strange, also, that Mr. Colebrooke should have remarked that "Bopadeva, the
real author of the Śrí Bhágavata, has endeavoured
to reconcile all the sects of Hindus, by reviving the
doctrines of Vyása. He recognizes all the deities, but
as subordinate to the Supreme Being, or, rather, as
attributes or manifestations of God:"[1] for, with the
omission of the word "attributes", this is precisely
the same doctrine which is invariably taught in each
and all of the eighteen Puráńas. The Bhágavata, therefore, as now extant, could not have been written for
the purpose of inculcating a new doctrine; for, in that
respect, it entirely corresponds with the other Puráńas: nor is the representation, in it, of Vishńu as the
Supreme Being inconsistent with the principles of the
Hindu religion as explained in the other Puráńas. It,
in consequence, does not afford the slightest internal
evidence of its having been written for the purpose
of sectarial imposture; nor have I observed, in it, any
passage which indicates that this Puráńa could not
have been written prior to the twelfth century. If,
however, the original Bhágavata was not then in

---

[1] *Asiatic Researches*, Vol. VII., p. 280.*

---

* Or *Miscellaneous Essays*, Vol. I., p. 197.

existence, the objection still remains insuperable; for nothing can render it in the least probable that the Brahmans of all India would receive the composition of an obscure individual as a sacred book entitled to their reverence. It must, also, be evident that, if the Puránas which were current in the century prior to the Christian era have not been suppressed, there can be no reason for supposing that they have not been preserved until the present day. But it seems unquestionable that the Puránas then current could not have been subsequently suppressed, and other works substituted in their place, unless the Brahmans of all India had combined together in order to effect that object; and Professor Wilson, himself, remarks that the Puránas, in their present form, "never emanated from any impossible combination of the Brahmans to fabricate for the antiquity of the entire Hindu system any claims which it cannot fully support."* A combination, therefore, of the Brahmans being considered to be impossible, it must appear most probable that the eighteen Puránas have been preserved, during the last eighteen hundred years, in the same manner as other Sanskrit works of the same period have been preserved, and that the present Puránas are, in fact, in all essential respects, the same works which were current, under that name, in India in the century prior to the Christian era.†

Another argument adduced by Professor Wilson, in

---

* Vol. I., Preface, p. XI.

† Throughout this critique, Colonel Kennedy seems to ignore the predictive sections of the Puránas,—a very essential feature in almost all of them.

support of his opinion, is the sectarian tendency of the
Puráńas. But he does not clearly explain what he
means by that term; and, in his "Sketch of the Religious
Sects of the Hindus," he has observed: "This is not
the case, however, with the first two on the list, the
Saurapátas and Gáńapátas: these are usually, indeed,
ranked with the preceding divisions, and make, with
the Vaishńavas, Śaivas, and Śáktas, the five orthodox
divisions of the Hindus."[1] In this passage, however,
some inadvertency must have occurred: for, according
to Professor Wilson's own account, the Śáktas cannot
be included among the orthodox divisions of the Hindus; and I suppose, therefore, that the worshippers of
Deví were here intended. But Vishńu, Śiva, Deví,
Súrya, and Gańapati are the very deities, and the only
ones, whose worship is described or mentioned in the
Puráńas; and, as this is admitted to be orthodox, it
must follow that the Puráńas could not have been
written for sectarian purposes. What are the sects,
therefore, to which Professor Wilson alludes, in that
Preface, is not apparent. But his notion of a sect would
seem to originate in this singular opinion, which he
has expressed with respect to the Pauráńik account
of the Hindu religion: "The different works known
by the name of Puráńas are, evidently, derived from
the same religious system as the Rámáyańa and Mahábhárata, or from the mytho-heroic stage of Hindu
belief."[*] For, in both those poems, the passages which

---

[1] *Asiatic Researches*, Vol. XVII., p. 230.[†]

[*] Vol. I., Preface, p. V.
[†] Professor Wilson's collected Works, Vol. I., pp. 265, 266.

relate to the legends and tenets of the Hindu religion
are merely incidental, and do not form a principal part
of those works; while, on the contrary, the legends and
tenets of the Hindu religion are not only the principal,
but the sole, subject of the Puránas. It is much more
probable, therefore, that such incidental notices of
those topics as occur in the two poems were derived
from the Puránas, than that such extensive works as
the Puránas—which embrace all the details of Hindu
mythology, and all the abstruse doctrine of Hindu
theology,—were derived from poems which are, principally, of an historical character. To conclude, consequently, that, because those topics are treated of at
much greater length in the Puránas than in the *Rámáyana* and *Mahábhárata*, therefore the Puránas were
written at a later period than those poems, is, evidently, erroneous. At the same time, on what grounds
does Professor Wilson suppose that there ever was a
"mytho-heroic stage of Hindu belief"? He merely says
that Ráma and Kŕishńa "appear to have been, originally, real and historical characters," who have been "elevated to the dignity of divinities,"* and that the Puránas
belong, essentially, to that stage of Hindu belief "which
grafted hero-worship upon the simpler ritual"† of the
Vedas. But Professor Wilson adduces neither argument nor quotation in support of this opinion; and it
is, therefore, sufficient to observe that, in the Puránas,
the *Rámáyana*, and *Mahábhárata*, Ráma and Kŕishńa
are invariably described, not as mere men, but as in-

* Vol. I., Preface, p. IV.
† *Ibid.*, p. XII.

carnate forms of Vishńu, and that not a single passage
can be produced, from those works, which inculcates
hero-worship.

Professor Wilson, however, not only remarks that
"Śiva and Vishńu, under one or other form, are almost the sole objects that claim the homage of the
Hindus, in the Puráńas,"* but also rests much of his
reasoning, with respect to the date when each Puráńa,
as at present extant, was composed, and to its having
been written for sectarian purposes, on the character of
Kŕishńa as a hero-god. For, in describing the *Brahma
Puráńa,* he observes: "Then come a number of chapters
relating to the holiness of Orissa, with its temples and
sacred groves dedicated to the Sun, to Śiva, and Jagannátha, ¹—the latter, especially. These chapters are characteristic of this Puráńa, and show its main object to be
the promotion of the worship of Kŕishńa as Jagannátha."²† With regard, also, to the *Vishńu Puráńa,* he remarks: "The fifth book of the Vishńu Puráńa is exclusively occupied with the life of Kŕishńa. This is one of
the distinguishing characteristics of the Puráńa, and is
one argument against its antiquity.":‡ And this objection
he explains, in speaking of the *Brahma Vaivarta Puráńa,* where he observes that the decidedly sectarial

¹ A name of Kŕishńa.

² Professor Wilson states, at the same time, that the legend
of Jagannátha occupies one-third only of this Puráńa; from which
it would be more just to conclude that its main object could not
be the promotion of the worship of Jagannátha.

* Vol. I., Preface, p. V.
† *Ibid.,* p. XXVIII.
‡ *Ibid.,* p. CLX.

character of that Puráńa shows that it belongs to the
sect, of known modern origin, which worship the juvenile Kŕishńa and Rádhá.* But Professor Wilson
does not specify the forms of Śiva, the worship of
which is mentioned in the Puráńas, as he states; and,
on the contrary, it is unquestionable that, in those
works, it is strictly enjoined that Śiva should be worshipped under no other figure or type than that of the
Linga; and, as Śiva was never incarnate, there could
be no form under which he could be worshipped.
With regard, also, to Vishńu, Professor Wilson confines his remarks to the eighth incarnation only, that
of Kŕishńa. But the Puráńas contain long details relating to the incarnation of Vishńu in the human forms
of Rámachandra and Paraśuráma; and why, therefore, should Kŕishńa alone be considered as a real
historical character who has been elevated to the
dignity of divinity? The answer is obvious. There is
a sect, of known modern origin, who worship the juvenile Kŕishńa and Rádhá; and it may, in consequence,
be concluded that the Puráńas in which Kŕishńa is
mentioned were written for the purpose of promoting
the extension of that sect. But, as no sect has selected
Rámachandra or Paraśuráma as the peculiar object of
their worship, no argument could be founded on the
mention of their names in the Puráńas; and, therefore,
it was unnecessary to notice them. But they were,
both, greater heroes than Kŕishńa, and lived several
centuries before him;† and, had, consequently, hero-

---

* Vol. I., Preface, p. LXVI.
† The Colonel is precise, here, beyond all reasonable warrant.

worship ever prevailed in India, it must seem most probable that it would have originated with Ráma-chandra,—whose expedition to Lanká is the subject of a celebrated and revered poem,—had the Hindus ever considered him to be merely a mortal prince. It is, however, needless to continue these observations; for Professor Wilson has, himself, refuted his own opinion; as he has also remarked that Kŕishńa is not represented in the character of Bála Gopála (the object of worship of the modern sect,) in the *Vishńu* and *Bhá-gavata Puráńas,** and that the life of Kŕishńa in the *Brahma Puráńa* "is, word for word, the same as that of the Vishńu Puráńa;"† to which I add, that Kŕishńa is not represented in that character in the *Brahma Vaivarta Puráńa*: for it is in those Puráńas only that the life of Kŕishńa is described at length; and, in them, Kŕishńa invariably appears and acts as a human being, except on occasions when he exerts his divine power; but he is, at the same time, frequently acknowledged and adored as Vishńu in the incarnate form of Kŕishńa.[1]

---

[1] I do not exactly understand what Professor Wilson means by this remark: "Ráma, although an incarnation of Vishńu, commonly appears [in the *Rámáyańa*,] in his human character alone."‡ I suppose he means, that Ráma is seldom described, in that poem, as exerting his divine power; for he always appears, in it, as a man, even when he acts as a god. Nor can I understand what the notion is which Professor Wilson has formed of a divine incarnation; for he observes that the character of Kŕishńa is very *contradictorily* described in the *Mahábhárata*,—usually,

---

* Vol. I., Preface, p. XXII. Colonel Kennedy here misrepresents.
† *Ibid.*, p. XXIX.
‡ *Ibid.*, p. XV.

All suppositions, therefore, that hero-worship ever prevailed in India, or that it is inculcated in the Puráñas, or that Vishñu and Śiva have ever been worshipped under any other figure or type than such as exist at the present day, are entirely groundless.

It will hence appear that this remark of Professor Wilson must be erroneous: "The proper appropriation of the third [*Rájasa*,[1]] class of the Puráñas, according to the Padma Puráña[2] appears to be the worship of Kŕishña .... as the infant Kŕishña, Govinda, Bála Gopála, the sojourner in Vŕindávana, the companion of the cowherds and milkmaids, the lover of Rádhá, or as the juvenile master of the universe, Jagannátha."[*] But, in the same manner as Professor Wilson thus appropriates, on no grounds whatever, one class of the Puráñas to the worship of Kŕishña, he also appropriates another class, the *Támasa*, to the Tántrika worship. For he remarks: "This last argument is of weight in regard to the particular instance specified; and the designation of Śakti may not be correctly applicable to the whole class, although it is to some of the series: for there is no incompatibility in the advocacy of a Tántrika modification of the Hindu religion by any Puráña."[†] That is, that there is no incompati-

---

as a mere mortal, though frequently as a divine person. But is not that precisely the character of an incarnation,—a man, occasionally displaying the powers of a god?

[1] The Puráñas are divided into three classes,—named *Sáttwika*, *Támasa*, and *Rájasa*,—consisting, each, of six Puráñas.

[2] No passage in the *Padma Puráña* authorizes this remark.

[*] Vol. I., Preface, p. XXII.
[†] *Ibid.*, pp. XXI., XXII.

bility in the Puráńas—which have immemorially been held to be sacred books,—inculcating a worship not only directly contrary to the Vedas, but which even requires, for its due performance, flesh, fish, wine, women, and which is attended "with the most scandalous orgies amongst the votaries." The mere mention, however, of such an opinion is, alone, sufficient to show its improbability; and Professor Wilson correctly observes: "The occurrence of these impurities is, certainly, countenanced by the texts which the sects regard as authorities, and by a very general belief of their occurrence. The members of the sect are enjoined secrecy,—which, indeed, it might be supposed they would observe on their own account,—and, consequently, will not acknowledge their participation in such scenes."¹ It is, therefore, surprising that, notwithstanding his own previous account of the Sáktas, he should remark, in the Preface to his Translation of the *Vishńu Puráńa*: "The date of the Kúrma Puráńa cannot be very remote; for it is, avowedly, posterior to the establishment of the Tántrika, the Sákta, and the Jaina sects. In the twelfth chapter it is said: 'The Bhairava, Váma, Árhata, and Yámala Sástras are intended for delusion.'"* The passage here referred to is, at length, as follows: "Certain acts have been prescribed to Brahmans and others; and for those who do

---

¹ These three quotations will be found in Professor Wilson's "Sketch of the Religious Sects of the Hindus," in the *Asiatic Researches*, Vol. XVII., pp. 223, 224, 225.†

* Vol. I., Preface, pp. LXXIX., LXXX.

† Or Professor Wilson's collected Works, Vol. I., pp. 256—260.

not perform these acts are prepared the lowest hells.
But there is no other Śástra than the Vedas which de-
serves the name of virtuous; and Brahmans, therefore,
ought not to delight in reciting the *Yoni Śástras*, which
are of various kinds in this world; because they belong
to the quality of darkness, and are contrary to the
Śruti and Smṛiti: of these are the Kapála, the Bhairava, the Yámala, the Váma, and the Árhata. Thus,
for the purpose of deception, are there many such
Śástras; and by these false Śástras are many men deceived." This passage, it is evident, condemns these
sects, and could not, therefore, have been written by
a person who belonged to some one of them. But I
have quoted it in order to show the manner in which
allusions to philosophical and religious sects occur, in
a few instances, in some of the Puráñas; for, in all
such passages, the name only is mentioned, and the
doctrine of the sect is never in the least explained.
Before, therefore, it is concluded that the name applies
to a sect of modern origin, it should, surely, be first
proved that no sect existed in India, under that name,
until the establishment of the modern sect. In the
above quotation, the worship of Śiva in his terrific
character, and of Deví as Śakti, is, no doubt, clearly
intimated; but it affords no indication of the date when
such worship commenced, or of the period during
which it may have been prevalent. But it is stated,
in more than one Puráña, that the Kapála sect was
coeval with the institution of the worship of the Linga;
and its antiquity is, further, rendered probable by its
having long become extinct in India; and it is evident
that, as the Árhata is here distinctly called a *Yoni*

(that is, a *Śákta*,) *Śástra*, this term can have no reference whatever to the Jaina sect. Were, also, the
Tántrika doctrines really inculcated in the Puráṅas,
the passages relating to them would be so numerous
and explicit as to attract attention; and yet, in my
examination of those works, I have never met with a
single Tántrika passage; and Professor Wilson adduces only the above-quoted text of the *Kúrma Pu-*
ráṅa, which can prove nothing, until the sects alluded
to, in it, are satisfactorily ascertained. To found, consequently, any argument with respect to the date when
the Puráṅas, as now extant, were written, or their
sectarian tendency, on a few obscure passages which
occur in them, the precise meaning of which it is now
impossible to determine, is, surely, a mode of reasoning which may be justly pronounced to be altogether
futile and fallacious.

Professor Wilson also states, in too decided and unqualified a manner, that, "In a word, the religion of
the Vedas was not idolatry:"* for he, at the same
time, correctly remarks that "It is yet, however,
scarcely safe to advance an opinion of the precise†
belief or philosophy which they inculcate.": But it
unquestionably appears, from several of the Upanishads,—which are admitted § to be portions of the Vedas,—that the principal deities have always been represented by images; and it may, therefore, be justly
inferred that image-worship has always formed part
of the Hindu religion. In its purest form, however, it

---

* Vol. I., Preface, p. III.   † The word 'precise' was here omitted.
‡ Vol. I., Preface, p. II.
§ Not with any scientific accuracy.

is probable that the worship of images was practised particularly by the inferior castes, and not, generally, by the Brahmans and Kshattriyas; but that, when the strict observance of the system of religious worship prescribed by the Vedas began to decline, then idolatry gradually assumed that form under which it appears in India at the present day. That such a change has taken place in the Hindu religion is clearly shown in the Puránas; for, in those works, though the worship of particular deities by various rites and observances is principally inculcated, they still contain numerous passages in which it is explicitly declared that such worship is not the adoration which is most acceptable to the Supreme Being, or the most effectual for obtaining final beatitude.

But the following remarks may appear to fix a modern character on the eighteen Puránas, as now extant: "It is a distinguishing feature of the Vishnu Puráña, and it is characteristic of its being the work of an earlier period than most of the Puránas, that it enjoins no sectarial or other acts of supererogation; no Vratas, occasional self-imposed observances; no holydays, no birthdays of Kríshña, no nights dedicated to Lakshmí; no sacrifices or modes of worship other than those conformable to the ritual of the Vedas. It contains no Máhátmyas or golden legends, even of the temples in which Vishñu is adored."* In these remarks, however, it is *assumed* that sacrifices and modes of worship which are not conformable to the ritual of the Vedas are prescribed in the Puránas: but

* Vol. I., Preface, pp. XCIX., C.

V.   19

this is precisely the question which requires to be proved. It is probable that the worship of images is not authorized by the Vedas; and so far, therefore, the Puráńas inculcate a mode of worship which is not conformable to the ritual of the Vedas. But idolatry has, unquestionably, existed, in India, from the remotest times; and, consequently, its being inculcated in the Puráńas cannot be admitted as any proof of their being modern compositions. The invocations, also, and prayers to the different deities, contained in the Puráńas appear to be in strict accordance with such as are contained in the Vedas; for they are composed of the *Gáyatrí* and, apparently, of other texts of the Vedas; and, although the rites and offerings with which the deities are directed to be worshipped may, probably, differ from the ritual of the Vedas, they still have been, evidently, intended to conform to it, as far as the difference of image-worship would admit of. [1] Sacrifices are not prescribed in the Puráńas; and the description of such as are mentioned in them is, no doubt, conformable to the ritual of the Vedas. It is not, therefore, the modes of worship which the Puráńas prescribe, upon which any argument to prove the remodelling of the Hindu religion in modern times can be validly founded; for their simplicity, and their

---

[1] It is unnecessary to except, expressly, the worship of Devi by the sacrifice of animals; for Professor Wilson has remarked (*Asiatic Researches*, Vol. XVII., p. 219):* "This practice, however, is not considered as orthodox, and approaches rather to the ritual of the *Vámácharins*; the more pure *Bali* [sacrifice] consisting of edible grain, with milk and sugar."

* Or Professor Wilson's collected Works, Vol. I., pp. 251, 252.

accordance, in all essential respects, with the ritual of
the Vedas must render it most probable that such
modes of worship were practised long prior to the
Christian era. Nor will the other acts specified by
Professor Wilson afford support to his opinion. I do
not, indeed, understand what is here intended by
"sectarial or other acts of supererogation:" but the
fourth order, or that of the ascetic, is mentioned in the
Institutes of Manu; and the Yogin is frequently mentioned in the Upanishads; and, surely, the sufferings
and deprivations to which the ascetic and Yogin subject themselves, for the purpose of obtaining beatitude,
are, decidedly, acts of supererogation. The inculcating,
therefore, in the Puránas, the advantage to be derived
from such acts can be no proof that those works were
written in modern times, for sectarian purposes. There
then remain to be considered only self-imposed observances, holydays, birthdays of Kríshńa, and nights
dedicated of Lakshmí. But Professor Wilson has in-
validated his argument by the mention of Lakshmí;
for, most certainly, that goddess has not been an object of peculiar worship in modern times; and her festival, therefore, must have been derived from the ancient calendar. It is singular, also, that the description
of holydays and festivals should be adduced as an argument against the antiquity of a religious work; for
these have been coeval with the institution of every
religion; and such self-imposed observances as fasts and
vows are too common, in all religions, to admit of their
mention in a religious work being considered as a valid
argument against its antiquity. Such description and
mention, therefore, are, in themselves, no proof of the

period when the Puráńas were composed; and Professor Wilson has not proved (nor can he, I am convinced, prove,) that the deity to whose honour a festival is ascribed in the Puráńas, or in whose propitiation a fast or vow is directed to be performed, was
not worshipped prior to the eighth or ninth century,
or that the preceding mode of worship has been since
altered. But, until either of these assumptions is
proved, it must be evident that the mention of the festival, the fast, or the vow, in any of the Puráńas, in no
manner proves, or even renders it probable, that that
Puráńa did not exist prior to the Christian era, in precisely the same state as that in which it is now extant.

I admit, however, that doubts may be reasonably
entertained with respect to the antiquity of some of
the legends relating to temples and places of pilgrimage, which are contained in the Puráńas; for the miscellaneous nature, the want of arrangement, and the
humility of style of the Puráńas would easily admit
of an account of a particular temple or place of pilgrimage being interpolated, without the interpolation
being liable to detection from the context. * It is, therefore, possible that, when those works are further examined, such interpolations may be discovered in them;
but, were it, for instance, even proved that the legend
of Jagannátha in the *Brahma Puráńa* was an interpolation, this would be no proof that that Puráńa was
written for the promotion of the worship of Jagannátha: for it would be much more reasonable to suppose that the Brahmans of that temple had availed

---

* Contrast what is said in p. 311, note 1, *infra*.

themselves of the original Puráña, to introduce into it,
and to circulate under the sacredness of its name, the
legend which they had composed in honour of their
god. When, therefore, a passage occurs in any Puráña,
which has a modern appearance, it should not, at once,
be concluded that the Puráña is a modern composition;
but it should first be ascertained whether the passage
is really modern, and, if so, whether it may not be an
interpolation which does not necessarily affect the antiquity of the Puráña itself.[1] Nothing, however, is so
difficult as to decide satisfactorily on the existence of
a supposed interpolation in any work; and, with respect
to the Puráñas, this difficulty, from the reasons just
mentioned, and from our almost entire ignorance of
the history of India during the centuries immediately
preceding and following the Christian era, becomes so
insuperable as clearly to evince how completely er-

---

[1] In forming, however, an opinion of the genuineness and
entireness of the Puráñas, as now extant, it should þe recollected
that these works are written in Sanskrit, and that the Brahmans
have always been, alone, acquainted with that language.[*] The Puráñas, therefore, circulated amongst the Brahmans only; and it,
consequently, seems in the highest degree improbable that the
Brahmans of all India would admit into their copies of these
sacred books interpolations which were merely intended to serve
some local purpose. It is, at least, certain that the manuscripts
of the Puráñas which are, at this day, spread over India, from
Cashmere to the extremity of the southern peninsula, and from
Jagannátha to Dwáraká, contain precisely the same works; and
it is, therefore, most probable that the Puráñas have always been
preserved in precisely the same state as that in which they were
first committed to writing.

---

[*] Never, in all probability, has this been the case.

roneous it must be to conclude, from their internal
evidence, that "the Puráńas are works of evidently
different ages, and have been compiled under different
circumstances."*
But it is impossible to ascertain, from this Preface,
Professor Wilson's precise opinion with respect to
what a work ought to be, in order to entitle it to the
character of a Puráńa; for, in speaking of the *Linga*,
he remarks: "Data for conjecturing the era of this work
are defective. But it is more of a ritual than a Puráńa;
and the Pauráńik chapters which it has inserted, in
order to keep up something of its character, have been,
evidently, borrowed for the purpose."† In considering,
however, the age and the scope and tendency of the
Puráńas, Professor Wilson has entirely overlooked the
sacred character which has immemorially been ascribed
to those works; and yet he could not intend to deny
so indisputable a fact; in which case it must be evident
that the more a Puráńa is occupied in "narrating legends, and enjoining rites, and reciting prayers,"† the
more it maintains its proper character. Professor Wilson, on the contrary, is of opinion that the religious
instruction which is contained in the present Puráńas
is a decisive proof that they have undergone some
material alteration, and that they are not the same
works which were current in the century prior to
Christianity. He admits, at the same time, the accuracy of this description of the Puráńas, as they are:[1]
The principal object of the Puráńas is the moral and

---

[1] In my work on Ancient and Hindu Mythology, p. 150.

* Vol. I., Preface, p. XVI.   † *Ibid.*, p. LXIX.

religious instruction which is inculcated in them, and
to which all the legends that they contain are rendered
subservient. In fact, the description of the earth and
of the planetary system, and the lists of royal races,
that occur in them are, evidently, extraneous, and not
essential, circumstances; as they are omitted in some
Puránas, and very concisely discussed in others; while,
on the contrary, in all the Puránas, some or other of
the leading principles, rites, and observances of the
Hindu religion are fully dwelt upon, and illustrated,
either by suitable legends, or by prescribing the ceremonies to be practised, and the prayers and invocations to be employed, in the worship of different
deities. It will, I think, be admitted that these are
precisely the topics which ought to occupy a sacred
book intended for the religious instruction of the Hindus; and that, consequently, so far from its being supposed that the present Puránas have undergone some
material alteration in consequence of these topics being
their principal subject, this very circumstance should
be considered as a conclusive argument in support of
their genuineness and antiquity. As, also, the religious
instruction contained in the Puránas is perfectly uniform, and entirely consistent with the principles of
the Hindu religion, and as it, consequently, betrays not
the slightest indication of novelty or sectarianism, it
must be most consistent with probability to conclude
that the eighteen Puránas, as now extant, are ancient
compositions, and not, as Professor Wilson supposes,
an "intermixture of unauthorized and comparatively
modern ingredients" with "ancient materials."[*]

_____

[*] Vol. I., Preface, p. XCIX.

I have, thus, examined the arguments adduced, by
Professor Wilson, to prove that the books now extant
under the name of Puráńas are not the original eighteen Puráńas which have been immemorially held to
form part of the sacred literature of the Hindus, but
works which have been compiled, within the last eight
hundred years, from ancient and modern materials,
and written in subservience to sectarial imposture.
The remarks, however, contained in this and my former
letter will, perhaps, evince that those arguments are
much too inconsistent and inconclusive to render the
antiquity and genuineness of the present Puráńas in
the least questionable. The admission, indeed, that the
original Puráńas were extant in the century prior to
the Christian era, is, alone, sufficient to invalidate all
suppositions of their being, now, no longer in existence; and, unless, therefore, the time and manner of
their becoming extinct are proved, it must be evident
that inferences resting merely on their internal evidence cannot be received as any proof that the original
Puráńas have not been preserved until the present
day. For all reasoning founded on the internal evidence which the Puráńas may afford on any point can
be of no avail; as there are, I believe, scarcely any persons competent to decide upon its correctness; and
the different conclusions which Professor Wilson and
myself have drawn from this internal evidence must
show that the impression received from it depends entirely on the disposition of mind and the spirit of re-
search with which the Puráńas are perused. I read
them with a mind perfectly free from all preconceived
opinion, and with the sole object of making myself

acquainted with the mythology and religion of the
Hindus; and I did not observe, in them, the slightest
indication of their having been written in modern
times, for sectarian purposes; but, on the contrary, their
perusal irresistibly led me to conclude that they must
have been written at some remote period. Even Professor Wilson has not been able to resist this impression of their antiquity; for he declares that it is "as
idle as it is irrational, to dispute the antiquity or authenticity of the greater portion of the contents of * the
Puráńas."† Why, therefore, he should have endeavoured—particularly, in his account of each of the Puráńas,—to demonstrate that those works are modern
compilations, and that, in consequence, "they are no
longer authorities for Hindu belief, as a whole," but
"special guides for separate and, sometimes, conflicting
branches of it,"‡ I pretend not to conjecture.

But it is very evident that Professor Wilson examined the Puráńas with a preconceived opinion of their
being modern compilations, and of their containing an
account of the sects which have originated in India in
modern times;[1] for it is only from the influence of
such a preconceived opinion that can have proceeded

---

[1] I cannot avoid observing, with reference to Professor Wilson's account of the manner in which his analyses of the Puráńas are made, contained in No. IX. of the *Journal of the Royal
Asiatic Society*, p. 61, § that it appears to me that no series of
indices, abstracts, and translations of particular parts of the Puráńas will ever enable any person either to form, himself, or to

* The words "the contents of" were omitted by the Colonel.
† Vol. I., Preface, p. XCIX.   ‡ *Ibid.*, p. V.
§ Or Professor Wilson's collected Works, Vol. III., p. 2. Also see
Vol. III. of the present Work, p. 225, last foot-note.

the contradictory and fallacious reasoning, with respect to the age and the scope and tendency of the Puráńas, which is contained in the Preface to his Translation of the *Vishńu Puráńa*. Because that reasoning rests entirely on two assumptions, neither of which is proved nor can be proved: the one, that a genuine Puráńa should treat of profane subjects only; and the other, that the works now extant under the name of Puráńas were written in modern times, for sectarian purposes. Thus, in the account of each of the Puráńas, it is pronounced that the main object of the *Brahma* is the promotion of the worship of Jagannátha (Kŕishńa), and that there is little, in it, which corresponds with the definition of a Puráńa; that the different portions of the *Padma* "are, in all probability, as many different works, neither of which approaches to the original definition of a Puráńa;" that the *Linga* "is more a ritual than a Puráńa;" that the *Brahma Vaivarta* "has not the slightest title to be regarded as a Puráńa;" that the date of the *Kúrma* "cannot be very remote, for it is, avowedly,

communicate to others, "a correct notion of the substance and character of those works." The Puráńa must not only be read from beginning to end, but examined over again more than once, before any person can be qualified to pronounce a decided judgment upon its age, scope, or tendency. The most ample index of its contents will never suggest or supply those reflections which necessarily arise during its perusal, and which, alone, can produce a correct opinion with respect to the connexion which the different parts of the Puráńa bear to each other, and with respect to the principal or accessory objects of its composition. A more attentive consideration of the context, for instance, would, perhaps, have prevented Professor Wilson from quoting the line of the *Kúrma Puráńa*, on which I have remarked in this letter.

posterior to the establishment of the Tántrika, the Śákta, and the Jaina sects;"* and so with respect to the other Puránas. It will not, however, be denied that nothing but the most attentive and repeated actual perusal of the whole of each and all of the Puránas would warrant such positive and unqualified assertions, and that nothing but satisfactory proof of such perusal would entitle them to the least credit; and yet Professor Wilson has stated that the Puránas comprehend a quantity of lines which any European scholar could scarcely expect to peruse with care and attention, unless his whole time were devoted, exclusively, for very many years, to the task.[1] Professor Wilson, therefore, is not, according to his own admission, qualified to decide *ex cathedrá* on the age, or the scope and tendency, of the Puránas. His reasoning, also, in support of the opinions which he had expressed on these points is singularly illogical; for he, first, assumes that a genuine Puráńa ought to treat of such and such topics only, and then—as not one of the present Puránas conforms to the definition[2] assumed,—he at once concludes that those works are modern compilations. But, as the definition fails in eighteen instances, it must appear most

---

[1] *Journal of the Royal Asiatic Society*, No. IX., p. 61.†

[2] Professor Wilson, also, has not translated this definition literally from the Sanskrit; and he, thus, argues, not on it, but on the meaning which he has, himself, thought proper to give to the definition. Literally translated, it can mean nothing more than "creation,‡ repeated creation, races or families, *manwantaras*,§ and

---

* Vol. I., Preface, pp. XXVIII., XXXIII., LXIX., LXVII., and LXXIX.
† *Vide supra*, p. 297, note §.
‡ See the Colonel's remark on *sarga*, in p. 259, *supra*.
§ This is transliteration, not translation.

probable that it was never intended to be understood
in the very restricted sense which Professor Wilson
applies to it; and, in my former letter, I have shown
that two of the topics, at least, comprise much more
than what he has included under them. The non-conformity, however, of the contents of the present Puráńas to this assumed definition—the precise extent and
meaning of which are not ascertained,—is, in fact, the
only argument which is adduced, by Professor Wilson,
to prove that the works now bearing the name of Puráńas are not the original Puráńas, and the only ground
on which he pronounces that this or that one of those
works does not correspond with the definition of a
genuine Puráńa. But the mere statement of such an
argument is, surely, quite sufficient to expose its total
invalidity. The other assumption is not only equally
groundless, but it is even disproved by Professor Wilson himself; for he has rested his argument, in support
of it, entirely on Kŕishńa being, as the juvenile Kŕishńa,
the peculiar object of worship of a sect of known
modern origin; and yet he is obliged to admit that

what accompanies races." To found, therefore, an argument
against the genuineness and antiquity of the Puráńas, as now
extant, on such a definition, is, surely, a most singular and futile
mode of reasoning. *

---

* This is hypercriticism. For the original terms referred to, see Vol. I.,
Preface, p. VII., note 1; also, Vol. III., p. 67, and p. 71, note; and *supra*,
pp. 169 and 244. Professor Wilson's expansions, to be found in Vol. I.,
Preface, p. VII., are fully authorized. Colebrooke, in his edition of the
Amara-kośa, p. 33, following the authority of scholiasts, defines a Puráńa to be "theogony, comprising past and future events, under five
heads: the creation; the destruction and renovation of worlds; genealogy
of gods and heroes; the reigns of Manus; and the transactions of their
descendants."

Kríshṅa is not represented in that character in three of the Puráṇas in which his life is related at length. The only proof, also, of the Tántrika doctrines being inculcated in the Puráṇas, which is adduced, is a single obscure line of the *Kúrma Puráṇa.** But, were that the case, there could have been no difficulty in quoting numerous Tántrika passage from some one or other of the Puráṇas; and, as, therefore, Professor Wilson has not supported his opinion by producing such passages, it may be justly concluded that not one of the Puráṇas in any manner advocates "a Tántrika modification of the Hindu religion."†

The more, therefore, that I consider the remarks contained in the Preface to his Translation of the *Vishṅu Puráṇa*, the more am I at a loss to understand how Professor Wilson could express such contradictory opinions. For he maintains, for instance, "that Brahmans unknown to fame have remodelled some of the Hindu scriptures, and, especially, the Puráṇas, cannot reasonably be contested;": but he equally contends that the internal evidence of the Puráṇas furnishes decisive proof "of the anterior existence of ancient materials; and it is, therefore, as idle as it is irrational, to dispute the antiquity or authenticity of the greater portion of the contents of the Puráṇas."§ On the contrary, it would, surely, be irrational to admit either, after Professor Wilson has proved—as he supposes,— that the works now bearing the name of Puráṇas are "an intermixture of unauthorized and comparatively

---

* See Vol. I., Preface, pp. LXXIX., LXXX.
† *Ibid.*, pp. XXI, XXII. ‡ *Ibid.*, pp. XCVIII., XCIX.
§ *Ibid.*, p. XCIX.

modern ingredients,"* and that not one of those works conforms to the definition of a genuine Puráńa. It becomes, therefore, requisite either to deny the antiquity and authenticity of the present Puráńas, or to contest the assumption that the Brahmans have remodelled their sacred books,—a supposition so totally improbable, that nothing but the most clear and incontrovertible proof could render it at all credible. Until, consequently, Professor Wilson produces such proof, it must appear most rational and reasonable to conclude that the Brahmans have never remodelled their sacred books (as no motive for their doing so can be conceived), and that the Puráńas now extant, having been preserved in the same manner as other Sanskrit manuscripts of the same period, are, in all essential respects, precisely the same works which were current in India in the century prior to the Christian era.

Bombay, 29th Sept., 1840.

VANS KENNEDY.

SIR: Notwithstanding my two former letters, there are still one or two points on which I would wish to offer a few remarks, in order to complete my observations on Professor Wilson's objections to the genuineness and antiquity of the Puráńas, as now extant. For it will, I think, be admitted that this question is discussed in a very unsatisfactory manner in the Pre-

* See Vol. I., Preface, p. XCIX. Only Professor Wilson makes no such assertion. His words are quoted correctly in p. 295, *ad calcem*, *supra*.

face to his Translation of the *Vishńu Puráńa*; as that
Preface contains merely the conclusions which Professor Wilson has drawn from certain circumstances that
are represented solely according to the view which he
has taken of them; and, thus, the reader is not afforded
the means of judging whether this view is correct, or
otherwise. But an inquirer into the real character of
the mythology and religion of the Hindus would, no
doubt, wish to know the grounds on which Professor
Wilson states: "It is not possible to conjecture when
this more simple and primitive form of adoration [of
the Vedas,] was succeeded by the worship of images
and types, representing Brahmá, Vishńu, Śiva, and
other imaginary beings, constituting a mythological
pantheon of most ample extent; or when Ráma and
Kŕishńa, who appear to have been, originally, real and
historical characters, were elevated to the dignity of
divinities."* In that Preface, however,—and in all, I
believe, that Professor Wilson has yet published respecting the Puráńas,—the most questionable assertions
are made in the most positive manner; but they remain unsupported by either argument or authority;
and, consequently, not even the deference which is
justly due to Professor Wilson, as an accomplished
Sanskrit scholar, should preclude an examination of
his opinions, or the rejection of such as are inconsistent
in themselves, or contrary to probability and evidence.

It is particularly remarkable that, in that Preface,
Professor Wilson has passed over a material fact,—the
sacred character of the Puráńas,—without a due consideration of which it is impossible to form a correct

* Vol. I., Preface, p. IV.

judgment with respect to their age, and their scope and tendency. But it is undeniable that certain works named Puráńas have immemorially been held, by the Hindus, to be sacred books of divine origin, and, therefore, entitled to the greatest veneration. Even at the present day, those works are regarded with the same reverence, and are, in consequence, considered to be incommunicable to Súdras, women, and barbarians:* and, on this account, a Brahman in my employment declined to read the Puráńas with me; while another Brahman, though he conversed with me on the subjects treated of in those works, and even gave me hints where to find particular passages, would not open the Puráńa in which they were contained, in my presence, and show me the passages.† In judging, therefore, whether the Puráńas now extant have been preserved, to the present day, in precisely the same state as that in which they were first committed to writing, the sacred character of those books should, most assuredly, be taken into consideration, and not passed over as of no consequence; for this circumstance, alone, renders it, in the highest degree, improbable that the Brahmans would allow the Puráńas to be lost, and utterly incredible that they would suppress any one of those sacred books, and substitute, in its place, another work of the same name. On this incredible supposition, however, Professor Wilson's opinion, that the present Puráńas are modern compilations, entirely rests. But he has not attempted to explain the manner in which the replacing of the original Pu-

* A grosser error than this was never committed to paper.
† Colonel Kennedy's Bráhmaus must have been very peculiar.

ránas by new works was effected; and, consequently,
his positive and unqualified statement, that the date
of the earliest of the present Puránas is not prior to
the ninth century, is a mere gratuitous assertion, which
is not only contrary to probability, but which is even
left unsupported by any proof whatever. But every
principle of reasoning requires that, before the conclusion is drawn, the premisses of the argument should
be, first, established; and, as, therefore, Professor Wilson
has neither proved nor rendered probable the premisses
from which he draws the startling and questionable
conclusion, that the present Puránas have no title to
be regarded as genuine Puránas, it must be evident
that his opinion on this point must be considered to
be totally groundless.

Another point essential to the proper discussion of
this question is, the ascertaining what it is that should
be held to constitute a genuine Purána; although it
might be supposed that no difference of opinion could
exist respecting it: for, the Puránas being sacred books,
their contents should, of course, relate, principally, to
the rites, ceremonies, offerings, prayers, and invocations
with which the deities mentioned in them are to be worshipped, and to the legends and doctrines of the Hindu
religion. Professor Wilson, on the contrary, has stated
that "The earliest inquiries into the religion, chronology, and history of the Hindus ascertained that there existed a body of writings especially devoted to those subjects.... These were the Puránas of Sanskrit literature."[1][*]

---

[1] In the Analysis of the *Brahma Purána*, contained in No. IX.

[*] Professor Wilson's collected Works, Vol. III., p. 1.

But this statement is altogether erroneous; for not a single Puráña contains chronology and history, in the meaning usually given to these terms; and, in the description of a Puráńa, given in that Analysis, are omitted that essential part of all the Puráńas which treats of the mythology and religion of the Hindus, and that part which has induced Professor Wilson to pronounce that the *Linga* is more of a ritual than a Puráńa. In his examination, therefore, of the Puráńas, he has, avowedly, overlooked topics the due consideration of which is indispensable for the forming a correct opinion of their age, object, and tendency. But this will be best rendered evident by a few remarks on his Analysis of the *Brahma Puráńa*, contained in No. IX. of the *Journal of the Royal Asiatic Society.*

In my last letter I was unavoidably led to observe that Professor Wilson had, evidently, examined the Puráńas under the influence of preconceived opinion; and this Analysis completely confirms that remark: for, at its very commencement, he states that "the first verses of the Brahma Puráńa" .... "sufficiently declare its sectarial bias, and indicate it to be a Vaishńava work."[*] But, in his "Sketch of the Religious Sects of the Hindus",[†]

_____

of the *Journal of the Royal Asiatic Society.* In this: it is also said that a genuine Puráńa "should treat of the creation and renovation § of the universe, the division of time, the institutes of law and religion, the genealogies of the patriarchal families, and the dynasties of kings." But no other topics than these are mentioned.

_____

[*] Professor Wilson's collected Works, Vol. III., p. 8, 9.
[†] *Ibid.,* Vol. I., pp. 3 and 30.   [‡] *Ibid,,* Vol. III., p. 1.
§ General Kennedy omitted the words "and renovation".

Professor Wilson admits that the preferential worship of Vishńu is perfectly orthodox; and, in the Preface to his Translation of the *Vishńu Puráńa*, he states that one-third only of the *Brahma Puráńa* is dedicated to Vishńu's incarnation as Jagannátha.* Consequently, it is evident that this Puráńa is neither sectarian nor exclusively dedicated to the legend of Jagannátha. But this erroneous impression has, evidently, led him to affirm, as erroneously, (unless my copy of this Puráńa differs from his), that "the first chapter of the Puráńa describes the creation, which it attributes to Náráyańa or Vishńu, as one with Brahmá or Íśwara." For the only verse to which he can refer will bear no other meaning than this: "Comprehend, O reverend Munis, Brahmá, of boundless splendour, the creator of all beings, Náráyańa, the all-pervading."[1] But this error is of material importance; because, in this Puráńa, Brahmá is represented as the Supreme Being; and, had it, therefore, been composed after the general worship of Brahmá had entirely ceased,—as it did in remote times,—and the preeminence (as at this day,) of either Vishńu or Śiva had been established, it seems altogether improbable that such a distinction would have been ascribed to Brahmá by any writer. The representing, consequently, Brahmá as the Supreme Being, in four of the Puráńas,—the *Brahma,*

---

[1] तं बुध्यध्वं मुनिश्रेष्ठा ब्रह्माणममितौजसम् ।
सष्टारं सर्वभूतानां नारायणं परायणम् ॥

It is quite clear that *Náráyańam* is here placed in apposition with *Brahmáńam*, and that it is, therefore, an epithet of Brahmá, and not of Vishńu.

---

* Not so. See Vol. I., Preface, p. XXVIII., note 1.

Váyu, Kúrma, and *Brahmáńda,*—was a circumstance
which, certainly, deserved particular attention; because
it corresponds with the character in which Brahmá is
represented in several of the Upanishads and in the
Institutes of Manu. When, therefore, a circumstance
so indicatory of the antiquity of the Puráńas is passed
over by Professor Wilson, it must be evident that his
conjectures respecting the dates when those works, as
now extant, were compiled, are not entitled to the
slightest consideration.

Professor Wilson also attaches no importance to
the long account of the Sun and his worship, which is
contained in the *Brahma Puráńa*; although this, undoubtedly, indicates that it cannot be a modern composition. And a similar description of the worship of
the Sun, contained in the *Linga Puráńa,* is not even
noticed by him, notwithstanding that it contains the
Gáyatrí and, apparently, other verses of the Vedas.
But it seems unquestionable that, if the Sun was ever
an object of popular worship in remote antiquity, this
worship had assumed a mysterious character at the
time that the Vedas received their present form, and
had become restricted to the Brahmans; for Mr. Ward
has correctly observed that "the Brahmans consider
Súrya as one of the greatest of the gods; because, in
glory, he resembles the one Brahma, who is called *te-
jomaya,* or 'the glorious'. In the Vedas, also, this god
is much noticed. The celebrated invocation called the
Gáyatri, and many of the forms of meditation, prayer,
and praise, used in the daily ceremonies of the Brahmans, are addressed to him."[1] The descriptions, there-

---

[1] Ward's *View of the Hindus,* Vol. I., p. 50.

fore, of a worship so ancient and so celebrated in the Vedas, contained in at least two of the Puránas,[1] should not, surely, have been overlooked by Professor Wilson, when deciding upon the period when the present Puránas were compiled; for these descriptions clearly prove that those works must be ancient, and not modern, compositions.

In the same manner, Professor Wilson takes no notice of the identification, in the *Brahma Puráńa*, of Brahmá, Vishńu, Śiva, and Súrya with the Supreme Being; but, on the contrary, he contends that its main object is the promotion of the worship of Jagannátha. This conclusion, however, is directly contradicted by the contents of that Puráńa; because it appears, from them, that the legend of Jagannátha occupies one-third only of the work, and that, in it, preeminence is not attributed exclusively to Vishńu. It is, hence, evident that the view taken by Professor Wilson of the object and tendency of the Puráńas cannot possibly be correct; since he, thus, discovers a sectarial bias in a Puráńa which so clearly illustrates that predominant principle of the Hindu religion which inculcates that the preferential worship of particular deities is equally meritorious; for it is, in fact, the worship of the Supreme Being under those forms. But Professor Wilson is not content with pronouncing that the *Brahma Puráńa* is a Vaishńava work; for he, at the same time, states that it "is referred to the Śákta class, in

---

[1] This worship is also mentioned in the *Garuda Puráńa*; but I do not immediately recollect whether it is mentioned in any other of the Puráńas.

which the worship of Śakti, the personified female principle, is more particularly inculcated."* It is not for
me to explain how any composition can be both a
Vaishṅava and a Tántrika work; but the assumption
that there is a class of Puráńas denominated *Sákta* is
totally unfounded. The division of the Puráńas into
three classes is mentioned in the *Padma Puráńa* alone;
and all that is said, in it, is, that such and such Puráńas
—naming them,—are included in the *Sáttwika, Rájasa,*
or *Támasa* class.[1] Nothing, therefore, contained in the
Padma Puráńa in the least authorizes the remark just
quoted; and in not one of the Puráńas is Deví ever
represented under the same character as the Śakti of
the Tántrika sect. It, hence, unquestionably appears
that Professor Wilson has completely mistaken the
object and tendency of the very Puráńa which he professes to have carefully analysed; and it must, therefore, follow that indices and abstracts of the Puráńas
will never enable any person to form, himself, or to
communicate to others, "a correct notion of the substance and character of these works."†

Professor Wilson, however, hesitates not to pronounce that "It is, nevertheless, obvious that such a
Brahma Puráńa as has been here described cannot have
any pretension to be considered as an ancient work,
as the earliest of the Puráńas, or even as a Puráńa at

---

[1] This division, also, is entirely fanciful; for there is nothing
contained in any one of the Puráńas which at all justifies it; as
the subjects treated of in those works are of precisely a similar
nature, and, in all of them, the same tenets and doctrines are inculcated.

---

* Professor Wilson's collected Works, Vol. III., p. 9.   † *Ibid.*, p. 6.

all."* He, thus, first gives a completely erroneous account of the real nature of the contents of this Puráńa, and then concludes that it is not even a Puráńa at all! The question, also, recurs: What is a Puráńa? Professor Wilson contends that it is a work which "should treat" only "of the creation and renovation of the universe, the division of time, the institutes of law and religion, the genealogies of the patriarchal families, and the dynasties of kings:" but the Sanskrit authority to which he refers, and which occurs at the commencement of several of the Puráńas, says, merely, "creation, repeated creation, families, *manwantaras*, and what accompanies families."† From such a definition as this it is obvious that no opinion can be formed with respect to the subjects which should, alone, be treated of in a Puráńa; and yet Professor Wilson's objections to the genuineness of the Puráńas, as now extant, rests principally on their non-conformity to this unintelligible definition. For this appears to be the only reason that has led him to pronounce that the *Brahma* is not even a Puráńa at all; because "the greater portion of the work belongs to the class of Máhátmyas,¹—

---

¹ There is no class of Máhátmyas; but passages, bearing that name, the authenticity of which cannot be contested,—as, for instance, the *Deví Máhátmya*‡ in the *Márkańdeya Puráńa*, — have been extracted from the Puráńas, and circulated as distinct works; and there seems to be no doubt that, in later times, works have been written in imitation of the authentic Máhátmyas; but their

---

* Professor Wilson's collected Works, Vol. III., pp. 16, 17.
† *Vide supra*, p. 299, note 2, and p. 300, note •
‡ It would be curious to know why the Colonel excepted it.

legendary and local descriptions of the greatness or
holiness of particular temples, or individual divinities."* But, as usual, he does not explain why the description of a particular temple, or an individual divinity, should be considered as incompatible with the
ancient and original composition of the Puráńa in
which it is contained. He merely assumes that the
temple of Kanárka, mentioned in this Puráńa, is the
same as the Black Pagoda, built A.D. 1241, and that
the temple of Jagannátha of the Puráńa is the same
as that which was built in A.D. 1198; and hence concludes that the *Brahma Puráńa* was written in the
course of the thirteenth or fourteenth century.† But
he adduces neither argument nor proof in support of
this assumption; although, in order to warrant it, it
was indispensable to prove that no temple of Kanárka
or Jagannátha ever existed in the same situations until the present temples were erected. For it may be
equally assumed that the temples mentioned in this
Puráńa were built, and had attained celebrity, several
centuries prior to the Christian era: and in what manner is this assumption to be disproved? The history
of India during the centuries immediately preceding
and following the Christian era is almost unknown; and
consequently, there are, now, no means available for
determining the dates when the temples were erected,
when the places of pilgrimage acquired holiness, when

spuriousness can always be detected by their not being to be
found in the Puráńas; to which they are ascribed.

---

* Professor Wilson's collected Works, Vol. III., p. 17.   † *Ibid.*, p. 18.
‡ And the *Máhátmyas* therein found are, in all likelihood, later than
their contexts.

the kings and distinguished personages lived,* or when
the events occurred which are mentioned in the Puráńas. To all these works this remark of Professor
Wilson applies: "The Vishńu Puráńa has kept very
clear of particulars from which an approximation to
its date may be conjectured."† For, as far as I have observed, not one of the Puráńas contains a single circumstance from which it would be possible to determine even the period when it may have been composed. The mere supposition, therefore, that the
temples mentioned in the *Brahma Puráńa* are the
same as those built in A.D. 1198 and 1241 cannot be
admitted as a sufficient ground for deciding that that
Puráńa is of modern date; for there is nothing improbable in concluding that other temples of the same
names, and in the same situations, may have existed
long before those erected in modern times were in
existence.

The only reason, also, that can have led Professor
Wilson to suppose that descriptions of temples and
places of pilgrimage should not be contained in the
Puráńas, is the above-mentioned definition; as it, certainly, does not include such a topic. But it is highly
probable that pilgrimages to sacred places, and the
visiting of temples, was practised, in remote times, by
the Hindus, as they are practised by them at the
present day; and no subject, therefore, could be more
adapted to such a sacred book as a Puráńa, than de-

---

* Inscriptions have brought us acquainted with not a few facts tending
to fix the age of later Pauráńik celebrities. And, inscriptions apart,
could Colonel Kennedy doubt our knowing the age of Chandragupta?

† Vol. I., Preface, p. CXI.

scriptions of those celebrated places and temples a
pilgrimage to which was deemed to be a pious and
meritorious act.* The legends, also, relating to temples
and places of pilgrimage, which occur in the Puráńas,
are of precisely the same kind as those which have
found a place in all religions, and cannot, consequently,
be considered, in themselves, to be any proof against
the antiquity of the Puráńa in which they are contained. Many of those places of pilgrimage are not
frequented at the present day, and some of them cannot, now, be even ascertained; which circumstances
must render it highly probable that they are of a remote period, and that they would not have been mentioned in a particular Puráńa, had they not been held
in reverence at the time when it was composed. I admit that this is an unsatisfactory mode of arguing; but,
in this instance, to supposition supposition can alone
be opposed; for, as I have just observed, the internal
evidence of the Puráńas affords no means of determining the date of any circumstance mentioned in
them.

In his Analysis, therefore, of the *Brahma Puráńa,*
Professor Wilson has, evidently, not only omitted circumstances which are essential to the forming a correct judgment of its object and tendency, but he has,
also, under the obvious influence of preconceived
opinion, found, in it, *that which it does not contain,*
and attached an undue importance to an unintelligible
definition, and to one-third only of the work, without
taking the other two-thirds into his consideration.

---

* Temples and pilgrimages were not Hindu institutions "in remote
times."

But nothing can more clearly evince the disposition of mind, and the attention with which Professor Wilson has examined the Puráńas, than this elaborate passage, contained in p. LIX. of the Preface to his Translation of the *Vishńu Puráńa:* "A considerable portion [of the *Agni Puráńa*] is then appropriated to instructions for the performance of religious ceremonies, many of which belong to the Tántrika ritual, and are, apparently, transcribed from the principal authorities of that system. Some belong to mystical forms of Śaiva worship, little known in Hindusthán, though, perhaps, still practised in the south. One of these is the Díkshá, or initiation of a novice; *by which, with numerous ceremonies and invocations, in which the mysterious monosyllables of the Tantras are constantly repeated, the disciple is transformed into a living personation of Siva, and receives, in that capacity, the homage of his Guru.*[1]" For, throughout this passage, some one or other of the names of Vishńu continually occurs; and it is evident, therefore, that the passage relates to Vishńu, and not to Śiva. In regard, also to the *díkshá,* these verses, contained in the 27th Chapter, will be sufficient to prove that this initiation is in the name of Vishńu, and not of Śiva: "Having propitiated Fire, sacrifice to Vishńu; and, then, having called the novices, initiate them standing near."[2] This *díkshá* is

---

[1] Nothing contained in the passage of the *Agni Puráńa* here referred to in any manner authorizes the words which I have placed in italics. Mysterious monosyllables, also, are perfectly orthodox; for they occur in the *Upanishads.*

[2] मखड्डीऽथ यजेद्विष्णुं ततः संतर्प्य पावनम् ।
श्राह्व दीषयेच्छिष्यानदुपन्यासनस्थितान् ॥

also mentioned in the *Garuda Puráńa*, in which it is equally said that the initiation is in the name of Hari or Vishńu; and not one of the prayers and invocations contained in those two passages is taken from the Tántrika ritual. It is, indeed, surprising that, after having written the accurate account[1] of the Śákta sect, contained in his "Sketch of the Religious Sects of the Hindus," Professor Wilson should state that the *Garuda Puráńa* contains prayers from the Tántrika ritual, addressed to the Sun, Śiva, and Vishńu; for he must be well aware that the Tántrika sect do not worship either Vishńu or the Sun. As, however, Professor Wilson has, in that Sketch, confined himself principally to the description of its distinguishing characteristics, — the *kumárí-pújá*, or worship of the virgin, — I add these remarks of Mr. Ward, in order to evince how totally impossible it must be to find such doctrines in the Puráńas: "The Tantras either set aside all these ceremonies [of the Vedas], or prescribe them in other

---

[1] I, of course, except this passage: "The adoration of Prakṛiti or Śakti is, to a certain extent, authorized by the Puráńas, particularly the Brahma Vaivarta, the Skanda, and the Kálíká:"* the erroneousness of which I have, perhaps, demonstrated in these letters. I am, indeed, strongly inclined to suspect that Professor Wilson's employment of indices and abstracts for the examination of the Puráńas has often led him to conclude that the term Śakti, which occurs so frequently in those works, denoted Deví in her character of Śakti, as worshipped by the Śáktas. But, in the Puráńas, this term means power and energy in general; and, when it does not, it invariably denotes the energy of the Supreme Being, or Máyá, or the impersonified energies of the three principal gods.

* Professor Wilson's collected Works, Vol. I., pp. 247, 248.

forms." The Tántrika prayers, even for the same
ceremony, differ from those of the Veda; and, in certain
cases, they dispense with all ceremonies; assuring men
that it is sufficient for a person to receive the initiatory
incantation from his religious guide, to repeat the
name of his guardian deity, and to serve his teacher.
They actually forbid the person called *púrńábhishikta*
to follow the rules of the Veda."[1]

In that Preface,[*] also, Professor Wilson observes:
"Colonel Vans Kennedy, however, objects to the application of the term Śákta to this last division of the Puráńas [the *Rájasa*]; the worship of Śakti being the
especial object of a different class of works, the Tantras; and no such form of worship being particularly
inculcated in the Brahma Puráńa. This last argument
is of weight in regard to the particular instance specified; and the designation of Śakti may not be correctly
applicable to the whole class, although it is to some
of the series: for there is no incompatibility in the advocacy of a Tántrika modification of the Hindu religion
by any Puráńa." Professor Wilson is, thus, obliged
to admit that he had completely mistaken the tendency
of a Puráńa which he had analysed; and yet he not
only adheres to his opinion, that some of the Puráńas
belong to his imaginary Śákta class, but he has even
advanced, in that Preface,[†] these extraordinary assertions: "The term Rájasa, implying the animation
of passion, and enjoyment of sensual delights, is appli-

---

[1] Ward's *View of the Hindus*, Vol. IV., p. 365.

[*] Pp. XXI., XXII.
[†] P. XXII.

cable not only to the character of the youthful divinity
[Kŕishńa], but to those with whom his adoration in
these forms seems to have originated,—the Gosains of
Gokul and Bengal, the followers and descendants of
Vallabha and Chaitanya, the priests and proprietors of
Jagannáth and Srínáthdwár, who lead a life of affluence
and indulgence, and vindicate, both by precept and
practice, the reasonableness of the Rájasa property,
and the congruity of temporal enjoyment with the
duties of religion." All this, however, is not only totally erroneous, but it rests entirely on certain fanciful
inferences which Professor Wilson has drawn from the
meaning of the term *Rájasa*; which is, certainly, a most
singular mode of reasoning. He is, here, also in direct
contradiction with himself; for, in one part of the paragraph from which this quotation is taken, he says that
the *Rájasa* Puráńas "lean to the Sákta division of the
Hindus, the worshippers of Sakti, or the female principle;" and, in conclusion, he speaks of persons vindi-
cating "the reasonableness of the Rájasa property, and
the congruity of temporal enjoyment with the duties
of religion." But Professor Wilson attempts not to explain how it can be possible that the same class of Puráńas should inculcate the pecular worship of both
Kŕishńa and Sakti; nor what the leading a life of affluence and indulgence has to do with worshipping the
yoni of a naked virgin; nor what resemblance there
can be between the scandalous and abominable orgies
of the Sáktas, and the calm though sensual enjoyment
of life by the votaries of Kŕishńa, as above described.
Nothing, indeed, can be more dissimilar than the worship of the juvenile Kŕishńa and that of Sakti; and,

when, therefore, Professor Wilson is of opinion that, in some of the Puránas, both of these dissimilar worships are peculiarly enjoined, it must be evident that he has as much mistaken the object and tendency of the *Brahmáṅḍa*, the *Brahma Vaivarta*, the *Márkaṅ-deya*, the *Bhavishya*, and *Vámana Puráńas*, as he admits he was mistaken in placing the *Brahma Puráńa* in the Śákta class. I have also remarked, above, that this division of the Puráńas into three classes is mentioned in the *Padma Puráńa* alone; and that this Puráńa does not explain the reason why a particular Puráńa is assigned to a particular class. But, admitting this classification, it appears clearly, from it, that the Puráńas relating to Śiva are placed in the *Támasa* class; and, consequently, as Tántrika works are dedicated to Śiva and Deví, if the *Rájasa* class of Puráńas inculcate Tántrika doctrines,—as Professor Wilson supposes,—they ought, according to the principle of classification in the *Padma Puráńa*, to have been included in the *Támasa*, and not in the *Rájasa*, class. The writer, however, of that Puráńa has not so classed them; and, thus, all the reasoning which Professor Wilson has founded on the meaning of the term *Rájasa* is refuted by the very authority that he has adduced in support of it.

It is, at the same time, obvious that all the arguments adduced by Professor Wilson against the genuineness of the Puráńas, as now extant, presuppose that descriptions of rites and ceremonies, injunctions for the preferential worship of particular deities, legends, tenets and doctrines, and moral and religious instruction should not find a place in a genuine Puráńa; for

he takes no notice of those parts of the present Puráńas which relate to these subjects, and, thus, rejects at
least two-thirds of the whole of the eighteen Puráńas
now extant, as being spurious and modern. But it is
evident that it is only from a due consideration of
these subjects, and a careful comparison of what is said,
respecting them, in one Puráńa, with what is said in
the other Puráńas, that a correct opinion can possibly
be formed with respect to whether those works exhibit
one uniform religious system, or whether they indicate that heterodox doctrines have been introduced into
them; for, if an undeniable uniformity exists—as I have
no doubt it does,—in an aggregate of 1.600,000 lines,
in the general description of rites, ceremonies, legends,
and doctrines, no stronger internal evidence is, surely,
requisite, to prove that the present Puráńas cannot be,
as Professor Wilson supposes, an intermixture of ancient
and modern ingredients.† Professor Wilson also avows
that he has not read the Puráńas, and that the notices
which he has given of their contents must have been
taken from indices and abstracts, the accuracy of which
I have never questioned. [1] But I am convinced that

---

[1] In his Analysis of the *Brahma Puráńa*, Professor Wilson
has observed* that the manner in which he effected his examination of the Puráńas has been misconceived; and he may, possibly, refer to a letter which I addressed to you, and which appeared in the number of your Journal of March, 1837. In that
letter I remarked, in a note: "Was any precaution adopted in
order to ascertain that all the chapters of each Puráńa, or even
all the subjects treated of, in it, were actually included in it?

* Collected Works, Vol. III., p. 6.
† Vol. I., Preface, p. XCIX.

such a manner of examining the Puráñas will never
enable any person to form any but an erroneous judgment of the real nature and genuineness of their contents. Had, for instance, Professor Wilson actually
read even that division of the *Brahma Vaivarta Puráña* which is dedicated particularly, *but not exclusively*, to the life of Kríshña, he would have found, in
it, several conversations between Kríshña and Rádhá,
in which Kríshña relates, in the most orthodox manner, several legends and particulars of Hindu mythology, and instructs Rádhá in the abstruse doctrines of
Hindu theology; and, even in one of those conversations, is contained a long orthodox account of Śiva,
Satí, and Párvatí. The ritual, also, prescribed, in it,
for the celebration of Kríshña's annual festival, is perfectly orthodox; for it directs that, in performing it,
texts of the *Sáma Veda* should be recited; besides
which, three divisions of this Puráña are dedicated to
Brahmá, Deví, and Gañeśa; so that, in fact, there is
not, perhaps, more than one-sixth of the whole work
that is occupied with descriptions of Kríshña. Yet
this is the work the character of which Professor
Wilson pronounces to be, "in truth, so decidedly secta-

For any omission of them would, obviously, prevent an accurate
opinion being formed of its contents." The indices and abstracts
may be quite correct, as far as they go; but the question is,
Are they full and complete? And, as it cannot be supposed
that Professor Wilson has omitted, in his notices of the Puráñas,
those particulars, contained in them, which were contrary to his
view of the subject, these letters will sufficiently show that no
precaution was adopted to render those indices and abstracts full
and complete, and that omissions of essential importance have,
in consequence, taken place in them.

rial," as to give it "not the slightest title to be regarded as a Purāṅa."*

I shall pursue the subject in a succeeding letter.

Bombay, 30th October, 1840.

VANS KENNEDY.

SIR: I proceed—with reluctance, however,—to consider another of Professor Wilson's arguments, in which he infers that the present Purāṅas must be modern compilations, because the Jainas are mentioned in them. But, in my last letter,† I have shown that, had Professor Wilson read the chapter of the *Kúrma Puráṅa* from which he has made a mutilated quotation, he would have observed, from the context, that the term *Árhata*, contained in it, could not possibly apply to Jina; and, in the passage which he quotes from the *Bhágavata*,‡ there is neither proof nor probability that *Árhata* means either Jina or the Jaina sect.§ It is, also, expressly said, in the *Vishṅu Puráṅa*, Vol. III., p. 209, the Buddhists "were called Árhatas, from the phrase he (Buddha,)‖ had employed, of 'Ye are worthy (Arhatha) of this great doctrine.'" It is singular, there-

---

* Vol. I., Preface, pp. LXVI. and LXVII.

† The Colonel should have written "my last letter but one". *Vide supra*, pp. 286, 287.

‡ Vol. II., p. 104, note 1. Arhat, a proper name, occurs there.

§ Árhata, according to circumstances, may denote either a follower of Buddha or a follower of Jina.

‖ *Vide infra*, p. 348, text and note 1, for a lame apology for this interpolation.

fore, that Professor Wilson should assume, in direct
opposition to the authority of the Puráńa which he
has, himself, translated, that the term *Árhata*, when it
occurs, as a proper name, in the Puráńas, should be
considered to apply to Jina, and not to Buddha.* But
it has been sufficiently proved that Buddha lived in
the sixth century B. C.; and no argument, therefore,
could be founded upon the mention of his name in the
Puráńas, to prove that not one of the works now
extant under the name of Puráńas was written prior
to *the year* 900 *A. D.*; and, on that account, Professor
Wilson has — too evidently, for the support of his
opinion,—transferred the term *Árhata* from Buddha (to
whom, alone, it is applied, in the Puráńas,) to Jina.
Professor Wilson, therefore, has not yet proved that
the Jainas are mentioned in the Puráńas.† But the
Buddhists are frequently mentioned in those works;
and it is, therefore, a strange mode of reasoning, to
infer that anything contained in the Puráńas relates to
Jina, when it may apply, with so much more probability, to Vishńu's incarnation, Buddha, from whom the
Buddhists, according to the Puráńas, originated.

The preceding remarks, and those contained in my
former letters, will evince that Professor Wilson's
examination of the Puráńas has been much too incom-
plete, and that the conclusions which he has drawn
from it are much too erroneous to authorize him to
state so positively: "That Brahmans unknown to fame
have remodelled some of the Hindu scriptures, and,
especially, the Puráńas, cannot reasonably be con-

---

* *Vide infra*, p. 362, text and note §.
† This is quite a mistake. See Vol. IV., p. 43, note 1.

tested,"* and that "It is possible¹ .. that there may
have been an earlier class of Puráńas, of which those
we now have are but the partial and adulterated representatives."† This opinion has been maintained by
Lieut. Col. Wilford and Mr. Bentley, and, in some
measure, countenanced by Mr. Colebrooke; but it still
remains unsupported by any proof whatever. Professor
Wilson argues thus: In the vocabulary of Amara Simha,
written 56 B.C., it is said that a Puráńa is "a treatise
on five topics," and, in several of the Puráńas, it is,
further, explained what these five topics are: but not
one of the Puráńas now extant conforms to that definition: therefore, the present Puráńas cannot be the
works which were current, under that name, in the
time of Amara Simha. This conclusion is, further,
supported by his affirming only, but not proving, that
the present Puráńas inculcate the doctrines of sects of
known modern origin, and that "circumstances are
sometimes mentioned, or alluded to, [in the Puráńas],
or references to authorities are made, or legends are
narrated, or places are particularized, of which the
comparatively recent date is indisputable.":

Such is the state of the question. On the first two
of these points I have, perhaps, already said more than
sufficient; and the only point, therefore, which re-

---

¹ This "it is possible" is singular; for much of Professor
Wilson's reasoning depends on the fact, that the original Puráńas
were current in the time of Amara Simha.

* Vol. I., Preface, pp. XCVIII., XCIX.
† Ibid., p VI.
‡ Ibid., p. XI.

mains to be considered is, whether there is any internal evidence, contained in the Puránas now extant, which proves that each and all of those works are modern compilations. I cannot place so much reliance on my own examination of the Puránas, as to affirm that there is not; but no passages containing such internal evidence have been yet produced; and, were even passages bearing a modern appearance produced, the dates of the circumstances mentioned in them could not be determined. For the Puránas contain no dates; and there exists not any biographical, topographical, chronological, or historical work which would afford the means of fixing the date when, in India, a place of pilgrimage first acquired sacredness, when a temple was first erected, when a distinguished character lived, when a king reigned,* or when an ancient sect, philosophical or religious, was founded, or when it became extinct. All the circumstances and events mentioned in the Puránas, from which an inference with respect to their date might be drawn, are of precisely the same kind as the temples in Orissa, from the mention of which, in the *Brahma Purána*, Professor Wilson infers the modern date of that work; for it is not only necessary to prove that those temples were built in modern times, but it must be, further, proved that, previous to their erection, no temples ever existed, in India, of the same names, and in the same situations. In the quotation, also, from the *Kúrma Purána*, contained in my second letter,† is mentioned a *Váma Sástra*; and there is, at this day, a sect

---

* *Vide supra*, p. 313, note *.   † *Vide supra*, pp. 286, 287.

named Váma Yamáchárin; but, as the Puráńa gives
no description of the *Váma Sástra*, on what grounds
can it be reasonably supposed that this is, actually, the
same as the *Tantras* of the *left-handed* sect of the
Śáktas? In all such cases, it is evident that coin-
cidence merely in name is no proof that the name
must necessarily apply to the modern temple or sect;
and, consequently, its applicability must be proved, before a mere name can be admitted as any proof that
the Puráńas are modern compilations. It is equally
evident that, as the Puráńas contain no dates, and as
there are no books to refer to for an illustration of
their contents, so far is the recent date of any particular circumstance mentioned in them from being indisputable, that, on the contrary, every adaptation of
an occurrence or event, mentioned in the Puráńas, to a
date must depend solely and entirely on conjecture.
No circumstances, therefore, are mentioned in the Puráńas, the precise or even approximate date of which
can be indisputably fixed, or even fixed at all; and it
must, hence, follow that those works do not contain
any internal evidence which proves their recent composition. *

Professor Wilson's supposition, however, that the
Puráńas have been remodelled by the Brahmans, rests
entirely on the further supposition, that circumstances
are mentioned, in those works, of which the comparatively recent date is indisputable. But I have examined
in vain the remarks contained in the Preface to the
Translation of the *Vishńu Puráńa*, in order to ascertain

---

* That the Puráńas are not ancient is evident from their very Sanskrit. How, too, as regards their prophetic parts?

what the precise opinion is which Professor Wilson
means to express with respect to the genuineness and
antiquity of the Puráñas, as now extant. He maintains
that the whole of the *Bhágavata* was written by Bopadeva; that the compilation of the *Vámana* "may have
amused the leisure of some Brahman of Benares"; that
the *Agni* and *Brahma Vaivarta* have no claims to be
regarded as Puráñas; and that the *Linga* "is more a
ritual than a Puráña":* and he, thus, gives approximate
dates to nine of the Puráñas, the dates of the other
nine being nearer to, or remoter from, the earliest date
mentioned:

Márkañdeya . . . 9th or 10th century.
Linga . . . . 9th or 10th „
Vishñu. . . . . . . 11th or 12th „
Padma[1] . . . . . . 12th — 16th „
Varáha . . . . . . 12th „
Bhágavata . . . . 12th „
Brahma . . . . . . 13th or 14th „
Vámana . . . . . . 14th or 15th „
Náradíya . . . . . 16th or 17th† „

But, although Professor Wilson thus expressly ascribes
the original composition of two of the Puráñas to two
individuals, and seems to intimate that several of the
other Puráñas were composed in the same manner, he

---

[1] Professor Wilson remarks that the different portions of this
Puráña "are, in all probability, as many different works"; and the
above dates, therefore, apply to different portions of the whole
work.

* Vol. I., Preface, pp. L., LXXVI., LX., LXVII., LXIX.
† *Ibid.*, pp. LVIII., LXX., CXI., XXXIV., LXXI., LI., XXIX., LXXVI.,
LIII.

yet seems to suppose that the groundwork of the present Puráńas was the eighteen ancient Puráńas; for he speaks of "the strong internal evidence, which all of them afford, of the intermixture of unauthorized and comparatively modern ingredients."* He even remarks that "the identity of the legends in many of them [the Puráńas], and, still more, the identity of the words,—for, in several of them, long passages are, literally, the same,†—is a sufficient proof that.....they must be copied either from some other similar work, or from a common and prior original.": To argue against such inconsistencies and contradictions is quite out of the question; but it is evident that, if the composition and compilation of the present Puráńas by eighteen different persons occupied eight centuries, those works could not also have been remodelled by the Brahmans, for sectarian purposes; and that, if their groundwork was the ancient Puráńas, not one of them could be the original composition of a modern writer; and that, if such was not their groundwork, it is utterly incredible that eighteen different persons, living at long intervals of time from each other, and while the Muhammadans were extending their dominions over the greatest part of India, should produce eighteen works in which the legends are identical, and long passages are, literally, the same. The supposition, also, that an aggregate of 1.600.000 lines, spread over an extent of a million of square miles, should have been remodelled, whether by the Brahmans or any

* Vol. I., Preface, p. XCIX.

† This is, I believe, greatly an overstatement. It is a rare thing, at least in my experience, to find even a single couplet precisely the same in any two Puráńas. See Vol. I., p. 57, note *. ‡ Vol. I., Preface, p. VI.

other persons, on one uniform plan, seems to be an
absolute impossibility: and the motive assigned for
such remodelling,—sectarial imposture,—is at once disproved by the simple facts, that not one of the Puráñas inculcates sectarian doctrines, and that the *exclusive* worshippers of Vishñu, or of Śiva, or of any
other deity, have always formed, in India, but a small
portion of the whole population.

There is, however, a difficulty which embarrasses
the decision of this question; for, not only in several
of the Puráñas are the names of all the eighteen specified, but, in most of them, the narrator is requested to
repeat the Puráña about to be related, expressly by
name. Professor Wilson, therefore, correctly remarks
that "the identity of the legends in many of them [the
Puráñas], and, still more, the identity of the words,—for,
in several of them, long passages are, literally, the same,
—is a sufficient proof that, in all such cases, they must be
copied either from some other similar work, or from
a common and prior original." The internal evidence,
however, of the Puráñas fully proves that they have
not been copied from each other; and this identity,
therefore, must have been derived from one common
original. But there is nothing improbable in supposing
that, previous to the Puráñas being committed to
writing in their present state, *four or five centuries
prior to the Christian era*, numerous legends and traditions relating to the modes of worship and the doctrines of the Hindu religion had, in remote times, been
formed, preserved, and transmitted by oral communication only.[1] When, therefore, eighteen different per-

[1] Such is the manner in which instruction is communicated

sons, in different parts of India, collected together
those legends and traditions, and committed them to
writing, the greatest similarity would, necessarily, exist
in the eighteen works, and the same legend and traoi-
tion would often be selected for insertion, and, consequently, often expressed in the same, or nearly the same,
words. The existence, therefore, of "a common and
prior original", so far from being an argument against
the genuineness and antiquity of the present Puráńas,
should, on the contrary, be considered as a decisive
proof that those works are, essentially, in the same
state as that in which they were first committed to
writing. Because, in their present state, each of the
Puráńas is a collection of legends, traditions, and
rituals, and not a work systematically written; and it
must, hence, be evident that such collections could have
been made only at a time when such traditionary lore
was fresh in the memory of the Brahmans. The present state, therefore, of the Puráńas now extant, in
which the most important legends, and even the origin
of the deities, are related in a discordant manner,—
though not in such a manner as in the least affects the
perfect homogeneity of the Hindu religion,—is, alone,
a strong proof that those works have undergone no

amongst the Brahmans, even at this day; and it is an immemo-
rial tradition, that the Puráńas were thus transmitted. In the
Vishńu Purdńa, for instance, Parásara thus replies to Maitreya:
"Now truly all that was told me formerly by Vasishtha, and by
the wise Pulastya" .... "I will relate to you the whole, even
all you have asked." *

---

* Vol. I., p. 11.

alteration since they were first committed to writing; for, as those discordancies have been allowed to remain, it is most probable that religious scruples have prevented the Brahmans from subsequently giving uniformity to their religious system.

But, to the supposition, that the present Puránas are modern compilations, written between the eighth and seventeenth centuries, the existence of "a common and prior original" becomes an insuperable objection; for it is highly improbable that such legends and traditions as are contained in the Puránas were then current; and, even admitting that they were, it is quite incredible that, in the disturbed state of India, and decay of Sanskrit learning, during that period, eighteen different persons should produce eighteen works in which not only the legends are identical, but long passages literally the same. It may, however, be said that the eighteen ancient Puránas were then extant, or, at least, that fragments of them were still preserved. I shall not here repeat what I have already said respecting the incredibility of the suppositions that the Brahmans have suppressed the ancient Puránas, and substituted, in their place, the works now bearing that name, or that the Brahmans of all India have received, in the place of the ancient Puránas, the acknowledged works of eighteen obscure individuals. On this point, also, it is impossible to ascertain what the opinion of Professor Wilson is: for, in one part of that Preface, he appears to admit, distinctly, that each of the ancient Puránas was extant until it was superseded by the present Purána; but, in other parts, he has argued at length, to prove that the present Purá- ·

ńas cannot be the same works which were current in
the time of Amara Simha. Since, therefore, Professor
Wilson has, thus, adopted 'two contradictory suppositions, in order to account for what he supposes to be
the spuriousness of the present Puráńas, it must be
evident that he has completely failed in proving that
the present Puráńas are not genuine. But the levity
and irreflection with which Professor Wilson has decided against the genuineness and antiquity of those
works will be best judged of from these remarks:
"No weight can be attached to the specification of the
eighteen names; for they are, always, complete: each
Puráńa enumerates all. Which is the last? Which had
the opportunity of naming its seventeen predecessors,
and adding itself? The argument proves too much.
There can be little doubt that the list has been inserted, upon the authority of tradition, either by some
improving transcriber, or by the compiler of a work
more recent than the eighteen genuine Puráńas."[1]*
Professor Wilson extends the compilation of the present

---

[1] Professor Wilson observes that the objection to the modern
composition of the Śri Bhágavata is rebutted by there being another Puráńa to which the name applies,—the Deví Bhágavata.
But all his remarks on this point are entirely misplaced and unnecessary; because the mere perusal of the Deví Bhágavata† will
at once show that it is, decidedly and avowedly, a Tántrika work:
for, in the 26th chapter of the 3rd skandha, is contained a description of the Kumári-pújá, or worship of the virgin. I possess
a copy of this work, in twelve skandhas, which appears to be
complete.

What, also, does Professor Wilson here mean by genuine Puráńas? He denies that the Puráńas current in the time of Amara

* Vol. I., Preface, p. XLV.   † Ibid., p. LXXXVIII., note †.

Puránas over eight centuries; and, therefore, in order
to get rid of the objection to this supposition, which
results from each Puráńa containing the names of all
the eighteen, he thinks it quite sufficient to observe
that this specification has been inserted by some improving transcriber,—he must mean, of course, after
the last of the present Puránas was written, that is,
after the seventeenth century. Thus, supposition is
supported by supposition; and, thus, all Professor Wilson's reasoning, to prove that the present Puránas are
modern compilations, depends entirely on gratuitous
assumptions and groundless assertions.

Whether, however, complete works, bearing the same
names, existed previous to the present Puránas being
committed to writing, is a question which admits not
of decision. That the names of all the eighteen Puráńas were previously known seems unquestionable;[*] and
it would, therefore, appear most probable that these
names had belonged to works which had preceded the
present Puránas. But the internal evidence of the present Puránas proves that they are, rather, collections
of legends, traditions, and rituals, than works systematically written; for they are entirely deficient in
arrangement, and the subjects treated of in them have

Simha are now extant; but he has not attempted to explain how
long it was that they continued current after that time, nor the
time and manner in which they subsequently became extinct; and
yet, in discussing a point relating to the present Puránas, he
seems to speak of them as if they were the genuine Puránas.
To elicit, therefore, either meaning or consistency out of such
remarks is, evidently, quite impossible.

* What proof is there of this assertion?

no further connexion with each other than that they all contribute to inculcate and illustrate some of the tenets and doctrines of the Hindu religion. It is possible, however, that more ancient Puráńas may have existed, which, from various circumstances during their transmission by oral communication only, were no longer in a complete state, when the present Puráńas were committed to writing; and that such fragments of them as were at that time preserved have been incorporated in the present Puráńas, to which, also, the names of the ancient works have been given. But the decision of this question is of no importance; because it is proved that works bearing the names of the Puráńas were current in India in the century prior to the Christian era;* and there is not the slightest reason for supposing that those works have not been preserved until the present day, in the same manner as other Sanskrit manuscripts of the same period have been preserved. From the notices, also, which occur in Greek writers, it appears highly probable that the very same system of religion which is described in the Puráńas prevailed in India at the time of Alexander's invasion; and it may, therefore, be justly concluded that the Puráńas had received their present form† four or five centuries prior to the Christian era. Even Professor Wilson remarks: "But the same internal testimony furnishes proof, equally decisive, of the anterior existence of ancient materials; and it is, therefore, as idle as it is irrational, to dispute the antiquity or authenticity of the greater portion of the contents of the Puráńas, in the face of abundant posi-

---

* This has never been proved.   † As to their predictions and all?

tive and circumstantial evidence of the prevalence of
the doctrines which they teach, the currency of the
legends which they narrate, and the integrity of the
institutions which they describe, at least three centuries before the Christian era."* But it must be evident that these remarks are totally irreconcileable with
what Professor Wilson elsewhere observes: "At the
same time, they [the Puránas,] may be acquitted of
subservience to any but sectarial imposture. They
were pious frauds for temporary purposes."†

It, hence, clearly appears that, in contending for the
modern compilation of the present Puránas, Professor
Wilson was influenced by a preconceived opinion, the
erroneousness of which he would not admit; but that,
in thus forcibly maintaining the antiquity of the greater
portion of the contents of those works, he was irresistibly compelled to yield to the convincing proof,
which their internal evidence presents, of the genuineness and antiquity of the Puránas, as now extant.
I have, also, sufficiently shown, in these letters, that
the present Puránas do neither inculcate sectarian doctrines nor indicate, in any manner, that they are an
intermixture of ancient and modern ingredients; but
that, on the contrary, they exhibit, throughout an aggregate of 1.600.000 lines, the utmost uniformity in
the general description of legends, traditions, modes
of worship, and doctrines.‡ It must, consequently, be
most reasonable to conclude that the Puránas now
extant received their present form four or five centuries prior to the Christian era, and that, since then,

---

* Vol. I., Preface, p. XCIX.   † Ibid., p. XI.
‡ One is at a loss to see where all this has been shown.

they have undergone no alteration whatever; rather
than that they are works which, for the purpose of
sectarial imposture, either have been remodelled by
the Brahmans since the Christian era, or which have
been written by eighteen obscure individuals, between
the eighth and seventeenth centuries.

Bombay, 30th October, 1840.

VANS KENNEDY.

Sir: As the eighteen Puráňas are, undoubtedly, the
only source from which a knowledge of the mythology
and popular religion of the Hindus can be derived, it
becomes of importance to determine whether those
works are ancient compositions, or mere modern compilations; and I trust, in consequence, that you will
have no objection to my offering a few further remarks
on this subject, previous to closing its discussion. In
my last letter, however, I observed that the Puráňas
contain no dates, and that there is no biographical,
topographical, geographical, or historical work which
would afford the means of fixing the date when, in
India, a place of pilgrimage first acquired sacredness,
when a temple was first erected, when a king or distinguished personage lived,* or when a philosophical
or religious sect was founded, or when it became
extinct. It would, hence, seem that, as the date of the
circumstances mentioned in the Puráňas cannot be determined, the question whether they are ancient or

* *Vide supra*, p. 313, note *.

modern cannot be decided; as all opinions respecting
the period when they may have been written must
depend, principally, if not entirely, on conjecture. But
the internal evidence of those works affords the strong-
est proof that they cannot be modern compilations;
for the legends, and descriptions of scenery, and of
men and manners, contained in them, bear such an
unquestionable impression of antiquity, and such a
dissimilarity to all that is known of India since the era
of Vikramáditya (B. C. 56),* that they irresistibly lead
to the conclusion that the Puránas must have been
written at some remote period. When, therefore, the
Professor of Sanskrit in the University of Oxford
published his opinion, that the works now bearing that
name were compiled between the eighth and seventeenth centuries, it might have been expected that he
would have supported so startling a statement by the
clearest and most conclusive arguments and authorities.
But he has, on the contrary,—as I have, perhaps sufficiently shown,—formed that opinion from an imperfect
examination of the Puránas, and maintained it solely
by having recourse to gratuitous assumptions and
groundless assertions.

The whole, indeed, of the remarks contained in the
Preface to the Translation of the *Vishńu Puráńa* appear to have been written for the purpose of demon-
strating that, "of the present popular forms of the
Hindu religion, none assumed their actual state earlier
than the time of Śankara Áchárya, the great Śaiva

---

* In p. 312, *supra*, Colonel Kennedy pronounces that "The history
of India during the centuries immediately preceding and following the
Christian era is almost unknown." Also see p. 293, *supra*.

reformer, who, flourished, in all likelihood, in the eighth
or ninth century. Of the Vaishńava teachers, Rámánuja dates in the twelfth century; Madhwáchárya, in
the thirteenth; and Vallabha, in the sixteenth; and the
Puráńas seem to have accompanied, or followed, their
innovations; being obviously intended to advocate the
doctrines they taught."* A still more erroneous
opinion was published by Professor Wilson, twelve
years before, in his "Sketch of the Religious Sects of
the Hindus," in which he has observed: "To the internal incongruities of the system, which did not affect
its integral existence, others were, in time, superadded,
that threatened to dissolve or destroy the whole. Of
this nature was the exclusive adoration of the old
deities, or of new forms of them; and even, it may be
presumed, the introduction of new divinities. In all
these respects, the Puráńas and Tantras were especially
instrumental; and they not only taught their followers
to assert the unapproachable superiority of the gods
they worshipped, but inspired them with feelings of
animosity towards those who presumed to dispute
that supremacy. In this conflict, the worship of
Brahmá has disappeared, as well as, indeed, that of
the whole pantheon, except Vishńu, Śiva, and Śakti,
or their modifications. With respect to the two former,
in fact, the representatives have borne away the palm
from the prototypes; and Kŕishńa, Ráma, or the Linga,
are almost the only forms under which Vishńu and
Śiva are now adored in most parts of† India.": In

---

* Vol. I., Preface, p. XVI.
† Colonel Kennedy here omitted the very important words "most parts of".
‡ Professor Wilson's collected Works, Vol. I., pp. 3—5.

this Sketch, however, Professor Wilson at the same time observes that "the worshippers of Vishńu, Śiva, and Śakti, who are the objects of the following description, are not to be confounded with the orthodox adorers of those divinities."* And yet he also states that *the present state of the Hindu faith is of, comparatively, very recent origin.*[1][†]

It would, hence, appear that Professor Wilson has formed his opinion of the Hindu religion from the *exception*, and not from the *rule*, and that he has given an importance to the sects that have originated amongst upwards of a hundred and thirty millions of people, to which they are not entitled. For it would, no doubt, be considered as a strange mode of judging of the established religion of England, were an opinion to be formed of it from the sects which prevail there: but such seems to have been the manner in which Professor Wilson has contemplated the Hindu religion; and it is too evident that it is in support of this erroneous view of the subject that he has ascribed to the Puráńas a modern origin, and contents which they do not contain. But I am certain that not a single Puráńa inculcates the *exclusive* worship of a particular deity, and that not a passage which is genuine can be found, in any Puráńa,‡ which would inspire the followers of

---

[1] This Sketch is contained in Vols. XVI. and XVII. of the *Asiatic Researches.* I refer, throughout this letter, to the part contained in Vol. XVI.

---

* Professor Wilson's collected Works, Vol. I., p. 30. † *Ibid.*, p. 12.
‡ In p. 347, *infra*, Colonel Kennedy asserts, however, that "there are no means of distinguishing those parts of them [the Puráńas,] which

one deity with feelings of animosity towards those
who presumed to dispute its supremacy.[1] So far, indeed, is this from being the case, that every sect—as Professor Wilson himself admits,—has found it necessary
to compose works for the purpose of teaching and supporting its peculiar tenets; which circumstance, alone,
is sufficient to prove that the Puráńas were not adapted for the promotion of such an object, and, consequently, that those works could not have been written
in subservience to sectarial imposture, as Professor
Wilson supposes.

It is also undeniable that the great mass of the
Hindus are Smártas, though all who are so do not
adopt this name;[2] that is, they consider both Vishńu

---

[1] In the Sketch referred to, Professor Wilson has quoted
several Sanskrit authorities, which, if genuine, would disprove
this statement: but he has specified neither the book nor the
chapter of the Puráńas from which they are said to be taken;
and it would appear that he had not, himself, verified them.
Not being able, therefore, to ascertain this point, I must consider* these quotations to be spurious; for they are at complete
variance with numerous passages that occur in the Puráńas,
which expressly inculcate that Vishńu and Śiva ought, both, to
be worshipped.

[2] The Brahmans of the Deccan, for instance, and of Gujerat,
call themselves Śaivas; but they are, in reality, Smártas, as they
do not reject the worship of Vishńu, though they consider it of
less importance than that of Śiva. The same is the case with
many of the Brahmans in other parts of India, who call themselves Vaishńavas, but consider Śiva as entitled to adoration.
This, however, is in strict conformity to the Puráńas, in which

are thought to be ancient and genuine from those which are thought
to be modern and spurious."

* Most venturesomely.

and Śiva to be entitled to adoration, but some of them
identify either Vishńu or Śiva with the Supreme
Being, — an opinion which is clearly inculcated in
several of the Puráńas. But, though, in some of those
works, Vishńu is represented to be, in some degree,
inferior to Śiva, still the latter is frequently introduced, in the Śaiva Puráńas, as enjoining the necessity of worshipping Vishńu, and explaining the mysterious nature of his incarnations; and, in the same
manner, though, in the Vaishńava Puráńas, the supremacy is ascribed to Vishńu, still the fullest justice
is done to the divinity of Śiva. The *exclusive* votary
of Vishńu, on the contrary, refuses all adoration to
Śiva; and, in the same manner, the *exclusive* votary of
Śiva denies Vishńu to be a proper object of worship;
and such votaries, therefore, of these deities are, with
reference to the population, by no means numerous
in India. It is equally unquestionable that the substitution of the Linga for the image of Śiva occasioned
no alteration in the worship of that god; for, in the
ritual prescribed for the worship of the Linga, as contained in the *Linga Puráńa*, it is said: "Having bathed
in the prescribed manner, enter the place of worship;
and, having performed three suppressions of the breath,
meditate on that god (Śiva,) who has three eyes, five
heads, ten arms, and is of the colour of pure crystal,
arrayed in costly garments, and adorned with all kinds
of ornaments. Thus, having fixed in thy mind the real
form of Maheśwara, proceed to worship him with the
proper hymns and prayers." The Linga, therefore, is

the terms Vaishńava and Śaiva denote the *preferential*, but not
the *exclusive*, worshipper of either Vishńu or Śiva.

worshipped by all Śaivas and Smártas; for it is, in fact,
the only type under which Śiva has been adored from
remote times. The worship, also, of Ráma is scarcely
known in India;* and Professor Wilson is, certainly, in-
correct in stating that the worship of Bála Gopála,
the infant Kŕishńa, is very widely diffused amongst
all ranks of Indian society; for the votaries of Kŕishńa
are by no means numerous, and are to be found only
in Bengal,[1] and in some parts of Hindostan proper.
Much of the reasoning, however, adduced in the
Preface to the Translation of the *Vishńu Puráńa*, to
prove the modern compilation of the Puráńas, is
founded on the supposition that the date of the Puráńas in which Kŕishńa is mentioned—particularly the
Brahma Vaivarta,—must be subsequent to the establishment of the sect of "the worshippers of the juvenile Kŕishńa and Rádhá, a form of belief of known
modern origin."† But, in that Preface, Professor Wilson gives it, as his opinion, that the Mahábhárata "is,
evidently, the great fountain from which most, if not
all, of the Puráńas have drawn;"‡ and, in the Sketch
above referred to,§ he remarks: "The worship of
Kŕishńa, as one with Vishńu and the universe, dates,

---

[1] Mr. Ward remarks: "Six parts out of ten of the whole
Hindu population of Bengal are supposed to be disciples of this
god. The far greater part of these, however, are of the lower
orders; and but few of them Brahmans." Vol. I., p. 200.

* If Colonel Kennedy's information had been coextensive with anything approaching the whole of India, he would never have hazarded this
remark.
† Vol. I., Preface, p. LXVI.   ‡ *Ibid.*, p. XCII.
§ Professor Wilson's collected Works, Vol. I., p. 121.

evidently, from the Mahábhárata." According to this statement, therefore, it is evident that, as the worship of Krishńa dates from that poem, and as its composition preceded that of the Puráńas, the date of none of those works can in the least depend on the time when the sects of Vallabha and Chaitanya originated,—unless, indeed, Professor Wilson supposes that the *Mahábhárata* was not written until after the year 1520, A. D. In that Sketch, also, Professor Wilson has observed: "The worship of Krishńa, as one with Vishńu and the universe, dates, evidently, from the Mahábhárata; and his more juvenile forms [actions?] are brought pre-eminently to notice in the account of his infancy contained in the Bhágavata: but neither of these works discriminates him from Vishńu; nor do they recommend his infantine and adolescent state to particular veneration." And, further: "In this description of creation, however, the deity [Krishńa,] is still spoken of as a young man; and the Puráńa [the *Brahma Vaivarta*], therefore, affords only indirect authority, in the marvels it narrates of his infancy, for the worship of the child."* These remarks are quite correct, as far as relates to the veneration of Krishńa; for I have shown, in my former letters, that in not one of the Puráńas is the worship of Krishńa, either as a child or a young man, inculcated, or even indicated. It is, hence, evident that, although the accounts of Krishńa's boyhood, which are contained in several of the Puráńas, may have suggested to Vallabha and Chaitanya the design of establishing the worship of Krishńa, still those Puráńas could not have been written

---

* Professor Wilson's collected Works, Vol. I., p. 121 and p. 124.

for the purpose of promoting a form of belief which is
not even mentioned in them.

Professor Wilson, at the same time, extends the prevalence of this worship, by identifying the infant
Kŕishńa with "the juvenile master of the universe, Jagannátha";* and yet he fixes the date when the temple
of Jagannátha was erected, in A. D. 1198,† and that
when Vallabha lived, in about A. D. 1520.‡ The worship, therefore, of Jagannátha cannot be the same as
that of Kŕishńa established by Vallabha; and, in fact,
there is not the slightest resemblance between them:
because Jagannátha is worshipped as an incarnate
form, or, rather, as a type, of Vishńu, by all Hindus;
and, on the contrary, the worship of Kŕishńa is not
generally practised, and prevails only in particular
parts of India. The legend, also, relating to Jagannátha
has no further reference to Kŕishńa than the name;
for it is said, in it, that the temple of Purushottama
was erected by a king named Indradyumna, a fervent
votary of Vishńu, who being much distressed for the
want of a proper image to place in it, Vishńu appeared
to him, in a dream, and informed him that, the next
morning, he would find, in the sea, a sacred tree from
which the image was to be made. In the *Brahma Puráńa*, it is, further, said that, when the king had, accordingly, found the tree, and brought it on shore,
Vishńu and Viśwakarman (the artificer of the gods) appeared to him, and that Vishńu directed the latter to
form from the tree the images of Kŕishńa, his brother
Balabhadra, and sister Subadhrá, which command

---

* Vol. I., Preface, p. XXII.   † *Vide supra*, p. 312.
‡ Professor Wilson's collected Works, Vol. IIL, p. 120.

Viswakarman immediately executed. Although, therefore, the images worshipped at Jagannátha bear these
names, the adoration is, in reality, addressed to Vishńu,
as the lord of the universe; and, consequently, in the
ritual prescribed for it, there is no mention whatever
of "the infant Kŕishńa, Govinda, Bála Gopála, the sojourner in Vŕindávana, the companion of the cowherds
and milkmaids, the lover of Rádhá."*
Professor Wilson also seems not to have taken into
consideration that the ten *avatáras* of Vishńu are an
essential part of the Hindu religion; as it appears to
be sufficiently ascertained that they are alluded to in
the Vedas,† and it is certain that the son of Devakí,
or Kŕishńa, is mentioned in at least two of the Upanishads—the *Chhándogya* and *Náráyańa*. The veneration, therefore, of Kŕishńa, as an incarnate form of
Vishńu, which is all that is prescribed in the Puráńas,
must be of as remote a date as the most ancient known
state of the Hindu religion;‡ and the mention, consequently, of Kŕishńa, in any of the Puráńas, as an *avatára* of Vishńu, but not as a peculiar object of worship,—in which character he is never described in those
works, §—can afford no grounds for supposing that
the present Puráńas are modern and sectarian compilations. Before, therefore, Professor Wilson identified
that veneration with the worship of Kŕishńa established
by Vallabha and Chaitanya, and hence inferred the

---

* Vol. I., Preface, p. XXII.
† The knowledge of this allusion seems to be the peculiar property
of Colonel Kennedy.
‡ That is to say, as old as the *mantras* of the *Rigveda*!
§ For disproof of this assertion, see Book V of this Work, *passim*.

comparatively recent date of the Puráńas, as now
extant, he should have produced, from those works,
some passages which either expressly or virtually inculcate that worship; but he himself acknowledges,
as I have before observed, that no such passages exist,
and thus admits that this objection to the genuineness
and antiquity of the Puráńas rests, solely and entirely,
on inferences drawn from suppositions imagined by
himself, but which are supported by neither probability
nor by any authority whatever.

It is, hence, evident that, in presenting the sects
which exist in India as a correct representation of the
actual condition of the Hindu religion, and in maintaining that the present state of the Hindu faith "is of,
comparatively, very recent origin,"* Professor Wilson
has taken a most erroneous view of the subject. For
the great mass of the Hindus adhere to that religious
system which has prevailed in India from the remotest
times, and which, alone, is inculcated in the eighteen
Puráńas. Even Professor Wilson himself has observed
that "the origin and development of their doctrines,
traditions, and institutions [of which that system is
composed,] were not the work of a day; and the
testimony that establishes their existence three centuries before Christianity carries it back to a much
more remote antiquity, to an antiquity that is, probably, not surpassed by any of the prevailing fictions, institutions, or beliefs of the ancient world."† As, however, it is only from the Puráńas that a complete
knowledge of those traditions and doctrines can be

* Professor Wilson's collected Works, Vol. I., p. 12.
† Vol. I., Preface, p. XCIX.

derived, it is obvious that there are either no grounds
for ascribing to them a remote antiquity, or that it
must be admitted that the Puránas are ancient compositions, and not modern compilations written by
eighteen obscure individuals between the eighth and
seventeenth centuries: because there are no other
works with which the legends, and descriptions of
scenery, men, and manners, and of rites, ceremonies,
and modes of worship, contained in the Puránas, might
be compared, in order to ascertain whether they are
of ancient or of modern date. And the supposing,
consequently, with Professor Wilson, that the Puránas
are an intermixture of ancient and modern ingredients,
can be of no avail; for there are no means of distinguishing those parts of them which are thought to
be ancient and genuine from those which are thought
to be modern and spurious. But the internal evidence
of the Puránas proves that those works did not accompany, or follow, the innovations introduced into
the Hindu religion by Śankara Áchárya, Rámánuja,
Madhwáchárya, and Vallabha; and that they are not
intended to advocate the doctrines taught by those
sectaries. For not one of their sects is mentioned, or
alluded to, in the Puránas, in which works the only
deities who are represented to be objects of worship
are Vishńu, Śiva, Deví, Gańeśa, and Súrya; and the
worshippers of these deities are, indisputably, held to
be the five orthodox divisions of the Hindus. Professor
Wilson's supposition, therefore, that the Puránas were
written in subservience to sectarial imposture, being,
thus, disproved, it follows that the whole of his reasoning, to prove their modern date, founded on their

"exhibiting a sectarial fervour and exclusiveness,"* is totally futile and fallacious.

The Puráńas, consequently, do not contain—as Professor Wilson states,—the doctrines of sects of known modern origin; as, besides the sects just referred to, he only particularizes, in the Preface to the Translation of the *Vishńu Puráńa*, the Sáktas and Jainas as being mentioned in the Puráńas. But, in my former letters, I have sufficiently shown that the tenets and practices of the Sáktas are so completely at variance with every principle of the Hindu religion, that it is impossible that they could be noticed in books which the Hindus hold to be sacred. I also pointed out, in my last letter, † that the term *Árhata* did not—as Professor Wilson assumed,—indicate either Jina or the Jainas; but I stated, erroneously, that it applied, in the passage which I quoted, to Buddha.¹‡ On subsequently comparing, however, the eighteenth chapter of Book III. of the Translation of the *Vishńu Puráńa* with the original, I found that the one did not agree with the other; for the terms "Bauddhas" and "Jainas", which are introduced into the Translation and the notes to it, *do not occur in the origi-*

---

¹ This mistake was occasioned by my trusting to the Translation, in which it is said: "These Daityas were induced, by the arch-deceiver, to deviate from their religious duties (and become Bauddhas)."

---

* Vol. I., Preface, p. V.
† *Vide supra*, pp. 322, 323.
‡ The whole truth is, that the Colonel not only criticized Professor Wilson's rendering without reference to the original, but that he interpolated it without acknowledgement, in foisting in the word "Buddha", so distinguished, typographically, that it seems to be quoted. The excuse offered in note 1, above, is very feeble.

nal. It is, therefore, singular that Professor Wilson should have made such a translation as this: "The delusions of the false teacher paused not with the conversion of the Daityas to the Jaina and Bauddha heresies;" * and that he should have remarked, in a note: "We have, therefore, the Bauddhas noticed as a distinct sect:" because the original is, simply: "O Maitreya, after Máyámoha, the great deceiver, had deluded the Daityas by various heretical doctrines, they relinquished the excellent faith inculcated by the Veda and Smṛiti."[1] It even appears, from the whole of this legend, that it does not apply to Vishṇu's appearance as Buddha, but to some other occurrence, which is not mentioned in any other Puráṇa than the *Vishṇu:*[†] for it thus commences, according to the translation: : "There was, formerly, a battle between the gods and demons, for the period of a divine year, in which the gods were defeated by the demons under the command of Hráda." But the only dissemination of heretical doctrines, through the instrumentality of Vishṇu, which is mentioned in any other Puráṇa, is that in the city of the Tripura Asuras and that in Kásí; to neither of which this legend applies; as it is said, in it, that Máyámoha, the name of the illusory being emitted from Vishṇu's body, "having proceeded (to earth), beheld the Daityas,

---

[1] मैत्रेय तब्बुधर्में वेदक्षृत्युदितं परम् ॥
अन्याव्यन्यपाख एड प्रकारैवङ्कभिर्द्विज ।
इतियाक्सोहयामास मायामोहोऽतिमोहकृत् ॥

---

* Vol. III., p. 211. Colonel Kennedy quotes only a portion of the sentence corresponding to his own translation given just below.
† For refutation of this, *vide infra,* p. 378, note †.
‡ Vol. III., p. 201.

engaged in ascetic penances, upon the banks of the
Narmadá river."* Professor Wilson, therefore, has
given to this chapter an interpretation not authorized
by the original, in which nothing occurs which indicates that the composer of this Puráńa intended to
describe either Buddha or Jina, under this illusory
form, or to adopt, or allude to, their doctrines, in the
words spoken by it.†

I have adverted to this remarkable deviation from
the faithful manner in which translations should always
be made,‡ because the purport of this legend clearly
shows that the terms "Jainas" and "Bauddhas" cannot
be contained in any manuscript of the *Vishńu Puráńa*.
But Professor Wilson may have supposed that the
term *Árhata* denoted the Jainas, and may have understood, from the words *budhyadhwam* and *budhyate*,§
that they applied to the Buddhists; and to this there
could be no objection, had he expressed his opinion
in a note, and not introduced into the text, the title
of the chapter, and the index, the term "Jainas" and
"Bauddhas". As, also, the illusory form addressed

---

* Vol. III., p. 207.

† On the contrary, it is beyond doubt that both Jina and Buddha, by
implication, are represented as forms of Máyámoha. First, in the *Vishńu-
puráńa*, we have mention of the establishment of the Árhatas by this
"Deluder by illusion", who then metamorphoses himself, and establishes
a sect by which the Bauddha is, unmistakeably, intended. The Árhatas
must be either Jainas or Bauddhas; and the Chapter referred to shows
that they were, unquestionably, the former. But I have anticipated Professor Wilson's Reply.

‡ The Colonel, practically, was scarcely so austerely punctilious as
his principles. *Vide supra*, p. 348, note ‡.

§ On the gross error here accepted, *vide infra*, p. 362, note †, and
p. 377, note ‡.

only the same Daityas,* it is evident that he could not have induced them to adopt the doctrines of both Jina and Buddha; and Professor Wilson, therefore, should have selected either the one or the other as being the false teacher here intended. But it is undeniable that Jina or the Jainas are not mentioned, in the Puráńas, under these names;† and there is no reason, as I have before shown, for supposing that they are denoted by the term *Árhata*;‡ as no conclusion can be justly drawn from an isolated word which occurs in the Puráńas, unaccompanied by any explanation of its intent and meaning. It will, hence, appear that this legend cannot apply to the Jainas: nor can it apply to Buddha; for he, according to the Vaishńava Puráńas, was not an illusory form emitted from the body of Vishńu, but an actual incarnation of Vishńu,§ born in Kíkaṭa.‖ When, therefore, Professor Wilson has so misunderstood and misinterpreted a passage in a Puráńa which he has himself translated, it must be evident that no reliance can be placed on the correctness of the opinions which he expresses with respect to the age, and the scope and tendency, of the eighteen Puráńas. He has, however, intimated that he intends laying before the Royal Asiatic Society analyses of all the Puráńas, similar to the one of the *Brahma Puráńa*, published in No. IX. of the *Journal* of that Society. But it is obvious that

---

* Not those already perverted, but "others of the same family". See Vol. III., p. 210.

† For Paurániḱ mention of the *Jina-dharma*, or "religion of Jina", see Vol. IV., p. 43, note 1.

‡ Who are the Árhatas, then?

§ But why assume that the Puráńas may not contradict each other?

‖ *Vide supra*, p. 178, notes 1 and ¶.

such mere details of the contents of each Puráńa can afford no information respecting the variety of subjects treated of in those works; and it is certain that, if these details are accompanied with such comments as have been already published by Professor Wilson, the analyses will convey the most erroneous notions of what is actually contained in the Puráńas. For Professor Wilson supposes that the Puráńas exhibit "a sectarial fervour and exclusiveness"; that they contain the doctrines, or allusions to the doctrines, of philosophical and religious sects of known modern origin; and that, in them, circumstances are mentioned, or alluded to, or legends are narrated, or places are particularized, of which the comparatively recent date is indisputable. But no one of these suppositions—as I have evinced, in the course of these letters,—rests on any grounds whatever; and nothing contained in the Puráńas in any manner justifies Professor Wilson's opinion, that those works are pious frauds, written for temporary purposes, and in subservience to sectarial imposture. As, however, he not only entertains such an opinion, but even supposes that the Puráńas were compiled by eighteen obscure individuals, between the eighth and seventeenth centuries, it will be evident that no analyses which Professor Wilson may give of those works will convey a correct, complete, and impartial account of the traditions, doctrines, and modes of worship which are described in the eighteen Puráńas.

In the remarks, therefore, contained in these letters, my object has been to evince that Professor Wilson has taken a most erroneous view of the remote and

actual state of the Hindu religion, and that his preconceived opinions on this subject have led him to assign
a modern origin to the Puránas, and to support this
statement by ascribing to them sectarian doctrines
which they, certainly, do not contain; and that all his
reasoning to prove the modern compilation of those
works is futile, contradictory, unfounded, or improbable. In this I have, perhaps, succeeded; for, as Professor Wilson has not quoted any passages from the
Puránas, in which sectarial fervour and exclusiveness
are exhibited,* and in which circumstances of comparatively recent date are mentioned,† it may be concluded
that he knew of no such passages; as their production
would, at once, have proved the point which he wished
to establish. This negative argument acquires the
greater force from Professor Wilson having stated that
he has collected a voluminous series of indices, abstracts, and translations of all the Puránas; and, consequently, if any passages occur, in them, which inculcate the *exclusive* worship of Vishńu or Śivu, or the
worship of Ráma, Kŕishńa, or Śakti, or which mention
the Jainas,‡ or any modern sect, or any comparatively
recent event, he could have had no difficulty in producing such passages, in support of his statements;
and their non-production, therefore, must be considered
as strong proof of their non-existence. The supposition,
however, that the Puránas were written in subservience
to sectarial imposture, was judiciously selected, by Professor Wilson, as his principal argument in proof of

---

* *Vide supra*, p. 340, notes 1 and *.
† Professor Wilson does refer to the prophetic parts of the Puránas.
See Vol. I., Preface, pp. XVI. and XVII. ‡ *Vide supra*, p. 323, note †.

their modern compilation; for the internal evidence of the genuineness and antiquity of those works depends entirely on their exhibiting a faithful representation of the Hindu religion as it existed in remote times. But Professor Wilson has not yet proved that the Puráńas contain sectarian doctrines; and I am convinced that, when the Puráńas are more fully examined, and the Vedas more completely known, it will be ascertained that the rites, ceremonies, and doctrines of the Hindu religion, described in the Puráńas, are, essentially, the same as those described in the Vedas, and that no essential difference exists between the ritual of the Vedas and the modes of worship prescribed in the Puráńas, except the adoration of images; and I can affirm, from actual perusal, that the theological parts of the Puráńas conform, in every respect, to the doctrines which are contained in the principal Upanishads; and these, it is admitted, are portions of the Vedas. *

With regard, however, to the legends which occur in the Puráńas, I may be allowed to avail myself of the following remarks which I have made in another work: "'I observe, however (Mr. Colebrooke remarks), in many places [of the Vedas], the groundwork of legends which are familiar in mythological poems: such, for example, as the demon Vŕitra, slain by Indra, who is, thence, named Vŕitrahan; but I do not remark anything that corresponds with the favourite legends of those sects which worship either the Linga or Śakti,

---

* The multiplied errors of this passage it must be unnecessary, at this day, to point out. The writers of the Puráńas paid little intelligent heed to the Vedas, of which, for the rest, the Upanishads cannot, with any propriety, be considered as portions.

*or else Ráma or Kŕishńa. I except some detached por-
tions the genuineness of which appears doubtful; as
will be shown towards the close of this Essay.'* But,*
instead of considering the allusions to popular mythology which occur in the Vedas as being the *groundwork* of subsequent legends, would it not be more con-
sonant with reason and probability to conclude that
these allusions actually referred to well-known legends?
For, otherwise, it will be evident that they must have
been altogether unintelligible,—expressed, as they were,
with so much brevity, and, in fact, merely mentioned
in that cursory manner which is usual in adverting to
circumstances perfectly notorious. In which case, it
would also appear most likely that the legends had
been previously collected, and rendered accessible to
every one by being recorded in those very works which
are still extant under the name of Puráńas; for it is
quite impossible to discover, in the Puráńas, a single
circumstance which has the remotest semblance to the
deification of heroes, a notion totally unknown to the
Hindus."[1]†

It, hence, appears that there is an intimate correspondence between the legends, rites, ceremonies, and
doctrines described in the Vedas and Puráńas; and
even Professor Wilson admits that there is "abundant
positive and circumstantial evidence of the prevalence

---

[1] Researches into the Nature and Affinity of Ancient and
Hindu Mythology, p. 188.

* Colebrooke's *Miscellaneous Essays*, Vol. I., p. 28, note •. Colebrooke
does not italicize this passage.

† Here, again, Colonel Kennedy has come to a conclusion widely
different from that ordinarily entertained.

of the doctrines which they [the Puráńas,] teach, the
currency of the legends which they narrate, and the
integrity of the institutions which they describe, at
least three centuries before the Christian era;"* and
that "the testimony that establishes their existence
three centuries before Christianity carries it back to
a much more remote antiquity."† But it is evident
that such a correspondence with the Vedas, and with
the ancient state of the Hindu religion, could not exist
in the Puráńas, unless they were written at a period
when the traditions, the ritual, and the doctrines of the
Vedas still constituted the prevailing form of the Hindu
religion; and it is, therefore, utterly improbable that
(as Professor Wilson supposes,) the Puráńas, as now
extant, could have been compiled between the eighth
and seventeenth centuries, when the Muhammadans
were extending their dominion over the greatest part of
India, and when the Hindu religion had lost much of
its original purity. His reasoning, consequently, is
altogether ineffectual to prove that the Puráńas are
modern compilations; for it is not supported by either
probability or proof, or by the internal evidence of
those works; and it, thus, entirely fails in demonstrat-
ing that the Puráńas were written or remodelled for
the purpose of promoting the innovations introduced
into the Hindu religion by Śankara Áchárya, Rámánuja, Madhwácharya, and Vallabha, and of advocating
the doctrines which they taught. All the remarks,
therefore, on this subject, which Professor Wilson has
yet published, are completely erroneous; and it may,

* Vol. I., Preface, p. XCIX.
† Ibid.

in consequence, be concluded that there are no valid grounds for disputing the genuineness and antiquity of the eighteen Puráńas.

Bombay, 29th December, 1840.

VANS KENNEDY.

PROFESSOR WILSON'S REPLY.

SIR: Col. Vans Kennedy has lately favoured you with a series of letters upon the subject of my views of the modern date and sectarian spirit of the works termed, by the Hindus, Puráńas. I entertain great respect for the Colonel's talents and industry, but none whatever for his love of disputation, or his pertinacity of opinion, and attach little weight to deductions that are founded upon imperfect investigation, and prejudices much more inveterate than any which he accuses me of cherishing. I have, therefore, no intention of entering upon any refutation of his notions, or vindication of my own. Having put forth conclusions drawn from a deliberate and careful scrutiny of the premisses which warrant them, I am contented to leave them to their fate: if they are sound, they need not be defended; if they are erroneous, they do not deserve to be defended. I have implicit faith in the ultimate prevalence of truth; and, as I am satisfied that my conclusions are, in the present instance, true, they have nothing to apprehend from Colonel Vans Kennedy.

Neither is it necessary, now, to expend time upon any discussion as to what the Puráńas are. The con-

futation of Colonel Vans Kennedy's doctrines of their
high antiquity and pure theological character is to be
found in the works themselves. Translations of two
of them have been published,—that of the *Vishńu Puráńa* by myself, and that of the *Srí Bhágavata* by M.
Burnouf; and an appeal to these, which are now accessible to all who may be interested in the inquiry,
will show how utterly untenable is Colonel Vans Kennedy's theory. If he objects to the particular examples
here named, let him choose his own. He will pardon
me for suggesting that he would be more usefully and
creditably employed in translating and publishing some
other Puráńa or Puráńas than in depreciating the
better directed labours of other Sanskrit scholars. The
result of such translations will, I have no doubt, con-
firm the conclusions which I have not found it possible to avoid, and with respect to which the opinions
of M. Burnouf coincide with mine. The Puráńas, in
their present form, are not of high antiquity, although
they are made up, in part, of ancient materials; and,
in the legends which they relate, and the practices
which they enjoin, they depart as widely from what
appears to be the more primitive form of Brahmanism
as they do from the subjects which authorities of unquestionable weight, as well as their own texts, declare
should form the essential constituents of a Puráńa.

Whilst, however, I think it a work of supererogation
to refute errors which the Puráńas themselves are at
hand to correct, I must beg leave to set Colonel Vans
Kennedy right on a matter not of opinion, but of fact.
Conscious, no doubt, that his arguments will not bear
the test of comparison with the original works, he has

attempted, at the close of his last letter, to insinuate
a suspicion that the translation is not to be trusted, and
charges me with having misunderstood and mistrans-
lated a passage that is of some importance as a criterion of the date of the Puráńa. He does not say that
I have done so purposely, in order to fabricate a false
foundation for my opinions; but the tendency of his
animadversions leads to such an inference. To this
inference I cannot stoop to reply; but I shall have no
difficulty in showing that the charge of misapprehension applies not to me, but to Colonel Vans Kennedy.

Now, I will not venture to affirm that, in a work of
some extent and, occasionally, of some difficulty, I
have never mistaken my original; that I have always
been sufficiently careful in expressing its purport; that
I may not have, sometimes, in the course of a translation not professing to be literal,* diverged more than
was prudent from the letter of my text. The latter
may have been the case, in the passage in question;
and Col. Vans Kennedy is literally correct in stating
that the very words "Jainas and Bauddhas" are not
in the Sanskrit, where they are found in the English.
At the same time, had he fully comprehended the
sense of the preceding passages, had he been aware
that all which had gone before related to Jainas and
Bauddhas, he must have admitted that their specification, which was recommended by the consideration
of perspicuity, and by the construction of the English

---

* Whatever Professor Wilson may have meant, his words are: "In
rendering the text into English, I have adhered to it as literally as was
compatible with some regard to the usages of English composition."
Vol. I., Preface, p. CXVI.

version, was warranted by the context, and was, therefore, unobjectionable.*

I will not think so meanly of Col. Vans Kennedy's
criticism, as to suppose it possible that it would cavil
at words, or that it would attach any importance to
the insertion of the terms "Jainas and Bauddhas" in
the place where they occur, if it could be substantiated
that, in all the preceding parts of the chapter, the text
has had them in contemplation. This he denies, and
I maintain. We shall see which is right.

The eighteenth Chapter of the third Book of the
Vishńu Puráńa describes, in the first part, the apos-
tacy of certain persons from the Brahmanical faith,—
from the Vedas and Smŕitis—in consequence of the
doctrines of a false teacher, who is Vishńu in disguise.
The heresies into which they fell were *two*. Col. Vans
Kennedy's interpretation is "*one*"; and here is the
source of his misapprehension. That he labours under
an erroneous view of the sense of the passage, a brief
examination of it will irrefutably demonstrate.

In the first place, then, speaking of those who first
became followers of the false prophet, the text says,
expressly: "They were called *Árhatas*, from the phrase
which the deceiver made use of, in addressing them,
'*arhatha*' (Ye are worthy) of this great doctrine."† So
far there can be no question that the Árhatas are named,
by the *Vishńu Puráńa*, as one set of schismatics.

---

* The words in question—Vol. III., p. 211,—are "Jaina and Bauddha";
and, since Professor Wilson tacitly professed to translate on a uniform
plan, he should have included them in parentheses, just as, in the preceding paragraph, he has parenthesized the words "and became Bauddhas".

† Compare the rendering in Vol. III., p. 209.

It is very true that we have not the name of the
other apostate sect enunciated; but it is indicated in a
manner not to be mistaken. "Know ye," says the
teacher,—*budhyaswa.* * "It is known," reply the disciples,—*budhyate.*† If these inflexions of the verb *budh*,
'to know,' do not clearly intimate the followers of a
faith who, from the same root, are named *Bauddhas*,
I should like to know to what other class of Indian
religionists it can apply.‡

It is not, however, from inferences, even thus palpable, that I am justified in limiting the designation of
Bauddhas to the sect here described. Col. Vans Kennedy is told, in my Preface, that I have, invariably,
consulted an able commentary on the text of the
Vishńu Puráńa; and to this commentary he either
has, or has not, referred: if he has not, he has come
to his task of criticism very ill-prepared; if he has, he
should, in candour, have admitted that what he is
pleased to term my misunderstanding or misrepresen-
tation of the text was shared by learned Hindus, who,
most assuredly, could not be suspected of any disposition to derogate from the sanctity and antiquity of
such sacred books as the Puráńas. If the word
Bauddha is inaccurately specified, the error is as
much the commentator's as mine. Col. Vans Kennedy
may, possibly, set a higher value upon his own erudition than that of any native Pandit: he must not expect others to agree with him in an estimate; and, at
any rate, he is bound, in fairness, to admit the existence
of such an authority, supposing him to be aware of it,

---

* Correct to *budhyadhwam*. Moreover, *budhyaswa* means "know thou".
† See note † in the next page. ‡ *Vide infra*, p. 368, note †.

when he condemns an interpretation which it fully
justifies. Ratnagarbha, the commentator on the *Vishńu
Puráńa*, explicitly states that, "in the repeated use
of the words *budhyaswa** and *budhyate*,† it is the intention of the text to explain the meaning of the denomination *Bauddha* (*Evaṁ budhyatety-atra puna-
ruktir Bauddha-pada-niruktyarthá*.)" I have been fully
authorized, therefore, in inserting the term *Bauddhas*.

Having, thus, vindicated, unanswerably, the propriety
of employing the word *Bauddha*, we come to that of
Jaina. It has been shown that the Árhatas are named;
and by these, I affirm, Jainas are intended. Col. Vans
Kennedy asserts that the term is applied, in this very
place, to Bauddhas, and adds: "It is singular . . that
Professor Wilson should assume, in direct opposition
to the authority of the Puráńa which he has, himself,
translated, that the term *Árhata*, when it occurs . . . .
in the Puráńas, should be considered to apply to Jina,
and not to Buddha.": I am not aware that I have
said any such thing:§ but that is of no matter. In the
passage in dispute, I do understand *Árhatas* to mean
Jainas; and I am not so singular, in this understanding, as Col. Vans Kennedy fancies. I again appeal to

---

* See note • in the preceding page.

† The commentator, having to do with a verb, would not have used
the term *punarukti*, 'iteration', unless he had been referring to a repetition of the same mood. The text—see Vol. III., p. 211, note §,—exhibits *budhyata, budhyadhwam*, and *budhyata* again. Professor Wilson
omitted to translate the first, hastily misrepresented the second, and
mistook the third. If *evam* in the text, and *iti* in the commentary, had
been preceded by *budhyate*, the result would have been *budhyata evam*
and *budhyata iti*. ‡ *Vide supra*, p. 323.

§ As much may, however, fairly be taken as implied in Vol. I., Preface,
pp. LXXIX., LXXX.

the commentator, in support of my translation. The Colonel, not perceiving that two different sects are described, asserts, as just seen, that *Arhatas*, in this place, means *Buddhists*. Had he taken pains to be better informed, he would have found that there was sufficient authority for distinguishing them in this passage, and he would not have made an assertion so utterly at variance with the general purport of the whole of the description. *Arhata* does not mean *Buddhist*; for the commentator expressly observes, of the object of the text, when describing the operations of the false teacher: "Having expounded the doctrine of the Árhatas, he proceeded to explain the doctrine of the Bauddhas (*Árhata-matam uktwá Bauddha-matam áha.*)" Ratnagarbha, therefore, unequivocally asserts that *two* sects (not *one*) are here described, and that Árhatas are a different class of sectarians from Buddhists or Bauddhas. Col. Vans Kennedy is, therefore, wholly mistaken in understanding the passage to relate to *one* sect of schismatics only, and is wholly wrong in confounding Árhatas and Buddhists.

That Árhatas are not, in this place, Buddhists, is undeniable, upon authority which few will fail to prefer to Colonel Vans Kennedy's; and it only remains to determine what they are. To any one at all acquainted with the practices and tenets of the Jainas, as they have been explained by Mr. Colebrooke, they are sufficiently well indicated by allusions in the text of the *Vishńu Puráńa*, in the passage in question, to leave no doubt that they are intended. If Jainas are not meant, what are the schismatics here described by their doctrines, and designated by the term *Árhatas?*

They are not Bauddhas; that is settled: and, when no perversity of ingenuity can identify Árhatas with Bauddhas, there is no alternative left but to identify them with Jainas. That the term does, very commonly, denote Jainas, is familiar to all who ever heard of either. Perhaps Colonel Vans Kennedy will admit this; perhaps he will, also, admit that the celebrated Jaina teacher and lexicographer Hemachandra is some authority for the accurate designation of the sect of which he was so distinguished an ornament, and that he gives the word *Arhat* as a synonym of *Jina*, *Tirthankara*, and the like.* This is a mere waste of words. When *Árhata* does not mean a *Bauddha*, it means a *Jaina*. It cannot mean a Bauddha, in the passages of the *Vishńu Puráńa* which are now under discussion; because the Bauddhas are also specified and distinguished by both text and commentary: it, therefore, does mean Jaina; and, consequently, I am fully authorized in inserting the words *Jainas* and *Bauddhas* in the Translation.† The misapprehension is not mine; it is my critic's: with which restitution of what appertains to him, and not to me, I take my leave of him, and of all further controversy with him.

H. H. WILSON.

COLONEL KENNEDY'S REJOINDER.

SIR: The letter of Professor Wilson, inserted in the number of your Journal for May last (received here

---

* *Haima-kośa*, I., 24.

† This conclusion is not easy to accept. *Vide supra*, p. 360, note *.

on the 7th instant), has much surprised me; as I do
not understand why he accuses me of "love of disputation" and "pertinacity of opinion": for the opinions
expressed in the letters which I, some time ago, transmitted to you are contained in my work on Ancient
and Hindu Mythology, published in 1831; and, to prepare materials for that work, I actually read, and carefully examined, all the eighteen Puráńas, except the
Bhavishya. When, therefore, Professor Wilson, in the
Preface to his Translation of the *Vishńu Puráńa,* took
so very different a view of the genuineness and antiquity of the Puráńas, as now extant, nothing could be
more unobjectionable than my examining critically
the remarks contained in that Preface, and making
public the result of that examination. Nor could it be
reasonably expected that I should admit the correctness of that view, when it appeared to me to have
been formed on insufficient and erroneous grounds.

In his letter, Professor Wilson very politely observes: "Conscious, no doubt, that his arguments will
not bear the test of comparison with the original
works,[1] he has attempted, at the close of his last letter,
to insinuate a suspicion that the translation is not to
be trusted." I have, however, neither insinuated nor
stated any objections to the accuracy of that Translation,
except in one instance, in p. 340,[*] in which Professor
Wilson has thus translated a passage of the *Vishńu
Puráńa:* "The delusions of the false teacher paused

---

[1] On the contrary, I have, in my former letters, transcribed
the original Sanskrit, in the few instances in which I have speci-
fically contradicted the statements of Professor Wilson.

[*] Vol. III., p. 211, in the present edition.

not with the conversion of the Daityas to the Jaina and Bauddha heresies." Of this passage I transcribed the original Sanskrit, in my last letter, in order to show that the terms *Jaina* and *Bauddha* were not contained in it. But I further observed: "Professor Wilson may have supposed that the term *Árhata* denoted the Jainas, and may have understood, from the words *budhyadhwam* and *budhyate*, that they applied to the Buddhists; and to this there could be no objection, had he expressed his opinion in a note, and not introduced into the text, the title of the chapter, and the index, the terms *Jainas* and *Bauddhas*." I, thus, anticipated all that Professor Wilson has said on this point, in his letter; and, as he admits, in it, that these terms are not to be found in the original, the question is, simply: Is a translator at liberty to insert, in the original text of the work which he translates, a name which is not contained in it, and then to argue that the work must be of modern date, because that particular name occurs in it? Such is the case, in the present instance; for Professor Wilson affirms that the Jainas are mentioned in the *Vishńu Puráńa*, and adopts this circumstance as a criterion for fixing the dates when the Puráńas were composed: but this name is not to be found in that Puráńa; and I, therefore, justly objected to its being introduced into the Translation.

Professor Wilson, however, in his letter, remarks: "I will not think so meanly of Colonel Vans Kennedy's criticism, as to suppose it possible that it would cavil at words, or that it would attach any importance to the insertion of the terms 'Jainas and Bauddhas' in the place where they occur, if it could be substantiated that, in all the preceding parts of the chapter, the text has had them in contemplation." But it is precisely to this that I object; for I contend that, in judging of the genuineness and antiquity of the Puráńas, their text should be allowed to speak for itself, and not as it may be interpreted by translators and commentators. For, with respect to the passage in dispute, I observed, in my last letter: "Professor Wilson, therefore, has given to this chapter an interpretation not authorized by the original, in which nothing occurs which indicates that the composer of this Puráńa intended to describe either Buddha or Jina, under this illusory form, or to adopt, or allude to, their doctrines, in the words spoken by it." To this he replies, in his letter: "In the first place, then, speaking of those who first became followers of the false prophet, the text says, expressly: 'They were called *Árhatas*, from the phrase which the deceiver made use of, in addressing them, '*arhatha*' (Ye are worthy) of this great doctrine.' So far there can be no question that the Árhatas are named, by the *Vishńu Puráńa*, as one sect of schismatics." Admitted. He proceeds: "It is very true that *we have not the name* of the other apostate sect enunciated; but *it is indicated*[1] in a manner not to be mistaken. 'Know ye,' says the teacher,—*budhyadhwam.** 'It is known,' reply the disciples,—*budhyate.* If these inflexions of the verb *budh*, 'to know', do not clearly

---

[1] The italics, in these two instances, are mine.

* Here Colonel Kennedy silently corrects an inadvertence of Professor Wilson. *Vide supra*, p. 361, note •.

intimate the followers of a faith who, from the same
root, are named *Bauddhas*, I should like to know to
what other class of Indian religionists it can apply."
But there is nothing whatever, in the original, which
shows that the second address of this false teacher
was intended to inculcate doctrines different from
those taught in his first address.* On the contrary,
the former appears to be, clearly, a continuation of
the latter; and, as it is not said, in the original, that a
sect was denominated from the word *budhyadhwam*,†
in the same manner that it is said that a sect was denominated from the word *arhatha*, it is most probable
that, in this passage, the *Árhata* sect is, alone, intended.
But Professor Wilson observes: "If Jainas are not
meant, what are the schismatics here described by
their doctrines, and designated by the term *Árhatas?*
They are not Bauddhas; that is settled: and, when no
perversity of ingenuity can identify Árhatas with
Bauddhas,[1] there is no alternative left but to identify
them with Jainas."

---

[1] Professor Wilson seems to forget, here, his note in p. 339:

* The Sanskrit text distinctly enough points to two forms of hetero-
doxy. The first is intimated as the Jaina, by mention not only of one
of the names of its professors, but, also, of one of the differentiae of
their doctrines; and the stanza to which reference is made, just above,
intends, undeniably, the Bauddha. The writer of the *Vishńu-puráńa*
seems to regard the Jainas and the Bauddhas as, in some sort, cognate.
That he represents the Jainas as preceding the Bauddhas manifests that
his information as to the history of these two classes of religionists was
far from exact,—a striking argument of his modernity.

† If Colonel Vans Kennedy had recognized that the original has *budhyata*, *budhyadhwam*, and *budhyata*,—and all in one line,—could he have
resisted the conclusion that these words indicate Buddha? See, further,
note ‡ in p. 377, *infra*.

‡ Vol. III., p. 209, note 2, in the present edition.

It is in this singular manner that Professor Wilson attempts to prove that the Puránas, as now extant, are modern compilations; for he entirely disregards the original text, and substitutes, for it, his own inferences and assumptions. In this instance, he admits, in his letter, that it is the term *Árhata*, and not *Jaina*, that is contained in the original; and he, further, admits that, in it, the name *Bauddha* is not enunciated, but merely indicated; and yet he maintains that he was "fully authorized in inserting the words *Jainas* and *Bauddhas* in the Translation." He remarks, also, that, though "Colonel Vans Kennedy may, possibly, set a higher value upon his own erudition than that of any native Pandit, he must not expect others to agree with him in an estimate." But I may be permitted to observe that long experience has convinced me that, although commentaries on Sanskrit works are, no doubt, of much use, yet they are by no means safe guides for ascertaining the plain and unsophisticated meaning of the text. In objecting, therefore, to the translation of the passage in dispute, I did not think it necessary to notice whether or not it agreed with the commentary; and Professor Wilson has, now, most unfortunately for his argument, referred to it: for the commentator never uses the word *Jaina*, but always *Árhata*;* as in the passage quoted from the commentary in p. 43 of the *Asiatic Journal* for May last.† Conse-

of the Translation of the *Vishńu Puráńa*: "Here is further confirmation of the *Jainas* being intended by our text; as the term *Árhata* is, more particularly, applied to them, although it is also used by the Buddhists."

* *Vide infra*, p. 376, note †.   † *Vide supra*, p. 363.

quently, Professor Wilson has no right to quote the
commentary of the *Vishńu Puráńa*, as an authority
in support of his assumption, that the *Árhata* of the
Puráńas means the Jaina sect.* It is, however, on this
assumption that Professor Wilson, when speaking of
the date of that Puráńa, hesitates not to state: "Both
Bauddhas and Jainas are adverted to [in it]. It was,
therefore, written before the former had disappeared.†
But they existed, in some parts of India, as late as the
twelfth century, at least; and it is probable that the
Puráńa was compiled before that period."¹ Thus, from
a few verses of the *Vishńu Puráńa*, in which no sect
is mentioned except the *Árhata*, Professor Wilson assumes that the *Bauddhas* and *Jainas* are adverted
to, in it, and, hence, fixes the compilation of the *Vishńu
Puráńa* at some time before the twelfth century. On
the total invalidity of such a mode of reasoning I need
not remark; but it seems extraordinary that he should
have called attention to it by his ill-judged letter; as
he has, by the arguments contained in it, fully confirmed all that I have said relative to his assertions
and statements being at complete variance with what
is actually contained in the Puráńas, and to his being,

---

¹ Preface to the Translation of the *Vishńu Puráńa*, p. LXXII.‡

* This is mere paltering. Árbata, when it does not mean Bauddha,
means Jaina; and Professor Wilson, in p 363, *supra*, quotes the commentator Ratnagarbhu as saying: "Having expounded the doctrine of
the Árhatas, be proceeded to explain the doctrine of the Bauddbas."
† Is this logic conclusive? Save in a spirit of prophecy, the Bauddhas
could not be spoken of before they appeared. But why might not a Hindu
writer make mention of them after their disappearance, just as well as
during their presence?
‡ See Vol. I., Preface, p. CXI.

in consequence, unqualified to express a correct opinion
respecting their age, and their scope and tendency.

I do not, therefore, understand what Professor Wilson means by observing, in his letter, that he has "implicit faith in the ultimate prevalence of truth." I objected to his introducing into his Translation of the
Vishńu Puráńa the names of two sects which are not
contained in the original, and to his adopting these
names as a criterion for fixing the dates of the Puráńas; and he admits these facts. The truth, consequently, in this instance, belongs to my objections.
Although, also, he considers it quite superfluous to
enter into any controversy with me, yet it has been
hitherto supposed that discussion was the best means
of ascertaining the truth: and it is, surely, not sufficient
that the Professor of Sanskrit in the University of Oxford should be satisfied that his conclusions are true;
for it might be expected that he would be prepared
to support those conclusions, whenever controverted,
by argument and authority. Professor Wilson may
think that my deductions are founded on imperfect investigation and inveterate prejudice, and that the refutation of my doctrines of the high antiquity and pure
theological[1] character of the Puráńas is to be found in
the works themselves.* But this is not enough; for,
if my theory on these points is utterly untenable, it

---

[1] I have never described the Puráńas as being *purely theological*; as I have merely stated that their principal object is moral
and religious instruction; and I have, invariably, used the words
"mythology" and "theology" in order to show that these subjects
are of a distinct nature, although both are treated of in the Puráńas.

* *Vide supra*, pp. 357, 358.

24*

would, most assuredly, be much more conducive to
the prevalence of truth to expose its erroneousness
than to refer, for its refutation, to such voluminous
works as the Puráńas, which scarcely any person will
take the trouble to examine. The weight, however,
which should be attached to my opinions respecting
the genuineness and antiquity of the Puráńas, as now
extant, is not the point in question; for I observed, in
my last letter, that Professor Wilson had taken a most
erroneous view of the remote and actual state of the
Hindu religion, which had, alone, led him to ascribe a
modern origin to the Puráńas; but, that, "as he has not
quoted any passages from the Puráńas, in which sectarial fervour and exclusiveness are exhibited, and in
which circumstances of comparatively recent date are
mentioned, it may be concluded that he knew of no
such passages; as their production would, at once, have
proved the point which he wished to establish.* This
negative argument acquires the greater force from
Professor Wilson having stated that he has collected
a voluminous series of indices, abstracts, and translations of particular parts of all the Puráńas; and, consequently, if any passages occur, in them, which inculcate the *exclusive* worship of Vishńu or Śiva, or the
worship of Ráma, Kŕishńa, or Śakti, or which mention
the Jainas, or any modern sect, or any comparatively
recent event,† he could have had no difficulty in producing such passages, in support of his statements;
and their non-production, therefore, must be considered

* *Vide supra*, p. 340, notes 1 and •; also, p. 353, note †.
† For Pauráńik mention of the introduction of the Parsees into India, *vide infra*, pp. 381—385.

as strong proof of their non-existence." It is not, consequently, the opinions which Professor Wilson or myself entertains on this subject that should be considered, but that which is actually contained in the Puránas. I affirm that the Puránas do not contain what Professor Wilson has stated is contained in them; and, as I cannot be required to prove a negative, it remains with him to produce such passages, from those works, as will demonstrate that my affirmation is unfounded. Until, however, such passages are produced, I may be allowed to repeat my former conclusions, that Professor Wilson's opinion, that the Puránas, as now extant, are compilations made between the eighth and seventeenth centuries, rests solely on gratuitous assumptions and unfounded assertions, and that his reasoning, in support of it, is either futile, fallacious, contradictory, or improbable.

It is not, I may trust, necessary that I should disclaim all intention of depreciating, by what I have written at any time, the labours of any Sanskrit scholar. In the present instance, in particular, as I had given some time and some attention to the examination of the Puránas, and to acquiring information concerning the remote and actual state of the Hindu religion, I saw no reason for refraining from making public my objections to the view which Professor Wilson had taken of the age, the scope, and the tendency of the Puránas, in the Preface to his Translation of the *Vishńu Puráńa*. It must, also, be evident that, if the opinions expressed respecting any part of Sanskrit literature were not controverted, when erroneous, it would be impossible that the real nature of that literature could ever be ascertained. Had, therefore, Professor Wilson been solicitous for the prevalence of truth, he should not have been indignant at the remarks on his theory, which you obliged me by publishing in the *Asiatic Journal*; but, on the contrary, he should have taken the trouble of examining my objections, and of exposing their erroneousness, if unfounded; but, if founded, candour and the love of truth should have induced him to acknowledge that he had called·in question, on insufficient grounds, the genuineness and antiquity of the eighteen Puráńas.[1]

Bombay, 17th July, 1841.

VANS KENNEDY.

NOTE.

Professor Wilson seems to have misunderstood the reason which led me to point out, in my last letter, that he had misunderstood and misinterpreted a passage in a Puráńa which he had, himself, translated: for, in his reply, he merely defends the introduction, into the translation, of the words "Jainas" and "Bauddhas";

---

[1] It is singular that Professor Wilson has, in one part of his letter, adopted my view of the subject; as he actually speaks, in it,* of "learned Hindus, who, most assuredly, could not be suspected of any disposition to derogate from the sanctity and antiquity of such sacred books as the Puráńas." It would seem, therefore, that, however satisfied Professor Wilson may be with the truth of the conclusions which he has published, he, nevertheless, fluctuates in his opinion respecting the sanctity and antiquity of the Puráńas, as now extant, or their being modern compilations, made for the purpose of sectarial imposture.

* *Vide supra,* p. 361.

but he says nothing with respect to his having adopted
the names of these sects as a criterion for fixing the
modern dates at which he thinks the Puráńas were
written. It was, however, to this that I particularly
objected, in my former letters; for, in p. L. of the Preface to the Translation of the *Vishńu Puráńa,** Professor Wilson states that "the date of the Kúrma Puráńa is, avowedly, posterior to the establishment of the
Jaina sect; and that there is no reason to believe that
the doctrines of Arhat or Jina were known in the
early centuries of our era."† And, in his notes to
the Translation, pp. 339, 340, 341,‡ he remarks:
"Here is further confirmation of the Jainas being
intended by our text."—"We, have, therefore, the
Bauddhas noticed as a distinct sect. If the author
wrote from a personal knowledge of Buddhists in India, he could not have written much later than the
tenth or eleventh century." [1]—"We may have, in this

ᵗ But why not much earlier? As it is sufficiently proved that
Buddha flourished in the sixth century *before* our era.

---

* See Vol. 1, Preface, p. LXXIX. If Colonel Vans Kennedy had
quoted more ingenuously, the reader would have seen that, in the passage which Professor Wilson translates from the *Kúrma-puráńa*, the
Bhairava, Váma, and Yámala scriptures are named with the Árhata; and,
the former being modern, there is a strong presumption that the term
Árhata is meant to denote a faith more recent than the Bauddha,—
namely, the Jaina. Still more cogent, as against the Colonel, is his own
fuller rendering—in pp. 286, 287, *supra*,—of the passage in question.
For, there, besides the scriptures just enumerated, those of the Kapálas
are specified; and the Kapálas are not known as a sect of much antiquity.

† Suspicion of mistake or forgery not being entertained, already in the
fifth century of our era the Jainas must have been a sect of some considerable age. For a Jaina inscription, said to be dated in the Śaka year
411, corresponding to A. D. 489, see the *Journal of the Royal Asiatic
Society*, Vol. V., pp. 34ᴇ, 341. ‡ See Vol. III., pp. 209, 211, 214.

conflict of the orthodox divinities and heretical Daityas,
some covert allusion to political troubles, growing out
of religious differences, and the final predominance of
Brahmanism. Such occurrences seem to have preceded
the invasion of India by the Mohammedans, and prepared the way for their victories."

But, after thus making use of the names "Jainas"
and "Bauddhas", to prove the modern compilation of
the Puráńas, Professor Wilson now admits that these
names are not to be found in the original; but he maintains that he was fully authorized in inserting them in
it, by the context and commentary. Yet, in his letter,
he quotes no part of the context,* in order to evince
that it relates to the Jainas and Buddhists, and rests
his argument, in support of its being these sects that
are intended in the passage in dispute, solely on the
words *Árhata*, and *budhyadhwam*, and *budhyate*.
But the commentator does not say that *Árhata* means
Jaina;† and Professor Wilson assigns no other reason

---

* The English translation, even apart from Professor Wilson's supple-
mentations, is quite sufficient to show that the Jainas and Bauddhas
are meant to be described.

† I think I am not wrong in saying that Hindu writers, as a rule,—
so far as I have examined them,—affect the terms Arhat and Árhata,
rather than Jina and Jaina. Possibly the former may have become,
comparatively, more dyslogistic, as they easily might, by suggestion;
for, though Jina was the name of a Buddha,—but one not much heard
of, apparently, in later times,—Arhat denoted another Buddha, whose
name was of more frequent mention, perhaps from its adoption by the
Jainas. These religionists, while professing no reverence for Buddha,
did profess reverence for Arhat, an equivocal designation, and which re-
minded of the Bauddhas; and this fact, it may be, influenced the Hindus,
with their hatred of Buddhism and everything therewith cognate, to call
the Jainas, by preference, Árhatas. It should seem that the Jainas,
among themselves, were more generally denominated Jainas.

for supposing that these two sects are one and the
same than that, as the *Árhatas* cannot be Bauddhas,
they must be Jainas. I am, however, obliged to observe that the original does not in any manner admit
of this translation in p. 339:* "In this manner, exclaiming to them, 'Know' (*budhyadhwam*), and they
replying, 'It is known' (*budhyate*), these Daityas were
induced, by the arch-deceiver, to deviate from their
religious duties (and become Bauddhas)." For, in the
original,—at least, according to my copy of it,—it is not
said that the words *budhyadhwam* and *budhyate* were
spoken by this emanation of Vishṇu and the Daityas;
but they are distinctly ascribed to Parásara, the narrator of the Puráṇa, who, after relating what was said
by this false teacher, proceeds to narrate that it was
thus by saying "know ye", and, they replying "it is
known", that Máyámoha caused the Daityas to forsake their religion.[1][†] The word *budhyadhwam*, how-

[1] पराशर उवाच ।
एवं बुध्यध्वं बुध्यतैवमितीरयन् ।
मायामोहः स दैतेयान्धर्ममत्याजयन्निजम् ॥ [‡]

Vishṇu Puráṇa, Part III., Chap. XVIII.

On the waning of the Bauddhas, while religious rivalry was still
active, and controversial debate still ran high, no doubt the Hindus
transferred to the Jainas a liberal share of the animosity of which their
heretical congeners had been the object.

See, further, *infra*, p. 379, note †.

* See Vol. III., p. 210.

† See my translation of the passage, in Vol. III., p. 210, note §.
Professor Wilson, in his rendering of the passage, omits, as he frequently
omits, the introductory words "Parásara said". But the omission, in
this instance, is of no help to Colonel Vans Kennedy's argumentation,—
if such it may be called.

‡ For the correct reading of the first verse, see Vol. III., p. 210,

ever, is used in this address of the false teacher, but
evidently in its usual sense; for Professor Wilson thus
translates the sentence in which it occurs: "Understand
my words; for they have been uttered by the wise."*
There are, consequently, no grounds whatever for
supposing that the words *budhyadhwam* and *budhyate* were, in this passage, intended to indicate the
"Bauddhas"; and, as this emanation of Vishńu was
not Buddha,† it must be evident that the doctrines
which he is here represented as teaching could not be
the same as those which were first taught by Buddha.
The original, therefore, did not justify this gloss of
Professor Wilson, "and become Bauddhas": for it is not
said, in it, that, after the false teacher had addressed

---

note §. Provided there is not a typographical oversight, was it because
he could make nothing of the word बुध्यत which he leaves out, that
the Colonel abridged the text?

In thinking, like Professor Wilson, that the word coalescing with एवं
is बुध्यते, he evinced forgetfulness of a most elementary rule of Sanskrit
grammar.

Though Professor Wilson misapprehended the sense of the stanza in
question, his very confident critic did not take a single step towards
setting him right.

* See Vol. III., p. 210. The original is:

बुध्यध्वं मे वचः सम्यग्बुधैरेवमुदीरितम् ।

† According to the *Padma-puráńa*, the god Śiva declares:

दैत्यानां नाग्रनाथीय विष्णुना बुद्धरूपिणा ।
बौद्धग्राख्रमसत्रोक्तं नग्रनीलपटादिकम् ॥

"In order to the destruction of the Daityas, the false Bauddha system—
with *its* naked *images*, blue vestments, and the rest,—*was* enunciated
by Vishńu in the form of Buddha."

Here there is a distinct reference, in direct contradiction of Colonel
Kennedy's positive assertion.

I have no copy of the *Padma-puráńa* at hand, by which to verify
this extract. It will be found quoted in p. 6 of my edition of the
Sánkhya-pravachana-bháshya, in the *Bibliotheca Indica*.

the Daityas* a second time, a second sect was originated; and it appears evident that, throughout this passage, the text relates to no other sect than the *Árhata*, which is, alone, mentioned in it.

It is, hence, undeniable that Professor Wilson has not "vindicated, unanswerably, the propriety of employing the word *Bauddha*"; and, consequently, the singular futility of his argument, with respect to the Jainas, becomes the more conspicuous. The Árhatas "are not Bauddhas (he says); that is settled: and, when no perversity of ingenuity can identify Arhatas with Bauddhas, there is no alternative left but to identify them with Jainas." But, as Professor Wilson has not produced, and I am certain that he cannot produce, any Sanskrit authority which proves that the *Árhata* of the Puránas is the same as the Jaina sect,† and, as

---

* But not those who had already been proselytized. *Vide supra*, p. 351, note *.

† There is no question that the Puránas were written after the rise of the Jainas, and that the authors of the Puránas, equally with their successors, designated them, preferably, as Árhatas. *Vide supra*, p. 376, note †.

I do not mean, however, that the Jainas were called Árhatas only. *Vide supra*, p. 351, note †.

In Nágeśa Bhaṭṭa's gloss on Govardhana's *Saptaśati*, entitled *Guru-vyákhyá*, the subjoined verses, which follow a denunciation of Sáṅḍilya as heretical, are quoted from the *Linga-puráṇa*:

पाञ्चरात्रं भागवतं वीजं दैगम्बरं तथा ।
लोकायतं च कापालं सौमं पाशुपतं तथा ॥
लाकुलं(?) भैरवं वामं ग्राह्मं ग्राह्मवयामले ।
एवंविधानि शास्त्राणि विरुद्धानि महामुने ॥
स्वतः प्रमाणभूतेन वेदेन मुनिसत्तम ।
वैदिकशास्त्राणि शास्त्राणि मनस्यापि न संस्मरेत् ॥

Doctrines here specified, and stigmatized as repugnant to the Veda, are the Páncharátra, the Bhágavata, the Bauddha, the Daigambara, the

he here admits that it is not the same as the Buddhist sect, it must, consequently, follow that the "Jainas" and "Bauddhas" are neither mentioned nor indicated* in the passage in dispute; and that he, therefore, attempts in vain to show that he was fully authorized in inserting the names of these sects in his translation.

V. K.

Lokáyata, the Kápála, the Sauma, the Páśupata, the Lákula(?), the Bhairava, the Váma, the Śákta, the Śámbhava, and the Yámala.

It would be very riskful to deny that the term Daigambara here points to one of the two grand divisions of the Jainas.

The preceding passage I have been obliged, from want of access to manuscripts, to take on trust.

* As to palpable indication of the Bauddhas there, *vide supra*, p. 368, note †.

CORRIGENDA, &c.

VOL. I.

PREFACE.

P. VII., note †. That Colonel Wilford was acquainted with the *Jyotirvidábharaña* appears from the *Asiatic Researches*, Vol. IX., pp. 82, 131.

P. XLV., note *. *Read* editor's note in p. LV. *infra.*

P. LVI., l. 11. The Translator had, erroneously, "Kroshfuki," where I have put Kraushfuki.

P. LXII., ll. 10 — 14. The work there described is properly entitled *Vahni-puráña*, and differs from the *Agni-puráña.*

P. LXIV., l. 15. The following observations touching the Magas were communicated by Professor Wilson to Père Reinaud, and will be found in his *Mémoire Géographique, Historique et Scientifique sur l'Inde, etc.*, pp. 391 — 397:

"In the brief notice of the Bhavishya Puráña which I have given in the Preface of the Vishñu Puráña, it is stated that the greatest part of the work relates to the worship of the Sun, and that, in the last chapters, there is some curious matter relating to the Magas, worshippers of the Sun; as if the compiler had adopted the Persian term Mugh, and connected the fire-worshippers of Iran with those of India. But the subject, it is added, requires further investigation.

"The last twelve or fourteen chapters of the Bhavishya Puráña are, in fact, dedicated to the tradition, of which a summary and not altogether accurate account has been given by Colonel Wilford, in the Eleventh Volume of the Asiatic Researches, and which records the introduction of the worship of the Sun into the north-west of Hindusthán, by Sámba, the son of Kríshña. This prince, having become a leper, through the imprecation of the irascible sage Durvásas, whom he had offended, and despairing of a cure from human skill, resolved to retire into the forest, and apply himself to the adoration of Súrya, of whose graciousness and power he had learned many marvellous instances from the sage Nárada. Having obtained the assent of Kríshña, Sámba departed from Dwáraká; and, proceeding from the northern bank of the Sindhu (Indus), he crossed the great river the Chandrabhágá (the Chinab), to the celebrated grove of Mitra (Mitravana), where, by fasting, penance, and prayer, he acquired the favour of Súrya, and was cleansed of his leprosy. By Súrya's injunctions, and as a mark of his gratitude, Sámba engaged to construct a temple of the Sun, and to found, in connexion with it, a city on the banks of the Chandrabhágá. As he was in some uncertainty what form of the Sun he should set up, a miraculous image of great splendour appeared to him, when bathing, which floated on the current and, being wafted to the shore, was accepted by Sámba, as sent to him by the original, and was, accordingly, placed, with due honour, in the temple dedicated to the Sun.

"After narrating these events, several chapters of the Puráña are occupied with the instructions communicated to Sámba by Nárada, regarding the ceremonies to be observed in the construction of the temple and the daily worship of the image. Sámba is desirous of retaining learned and pious Brahmans for the purpose of performing the appointed rites, and receiving the donations he may make to the Sun; but Nárada, in the spirit of the prohibition found in Manu, against the performance of idol-worship, as a source of emolument, by Brahmans, apprises Sámba that no Brahman can undertake the office of ministering priest without incurring degradation in this life, and punishment in the next. He, therefore, refers Sámba to Gauramukha (White-face), the Purohita (or family-priest) of Ugrasena, king of Mathurá, as the only person who could tell him whom he might most suitably employ as the officiating priests of the Sun; and Gauramukha directs him, in consequence, to invite the Magas to discharge the duty, as they are, in an especial degree, the worshippers of Súrya.

"The Magas, according to the legend narrated, not very distinctly, by the compiler of the Puráña, were at once the progeny of Agni and Áditya (Fire and the Sun,) by Nishkumbhá, the daughter of a holy sage named Ŕiju or Ŕijwáhwa (*ŕju*, upright, and *áhwá*, appellation), of the race named Mihira. She was dedicated to Agni by her father; but the Sun, fascinated by her beauty, assumed the form of Agni, and begot a son, named Jalagambu, from whom sprang the Magas. Ŕiju, displeased with his daughter, condemned her offspring to degradation; but the Sun, at Nishkumbhá's entreaty, although he could not raise the Magas to a level with the Brahmans, conferred upon them the almost equal distinction of being his chosen ministers.

"Although Gauramukha could inform Sámba what priests the prince ought to employ, he is represented as ignorant of the place where they dwelt, and, referring Sámba again to the Sun, Súrya desires him to repair to Sáka-dwipa, beyond the sea of salt water, in which region the Magas corresponded with the caste of Brahmans in Jambu-dwipa or India; the other three castes being the Magasas, Mánasas, and Mandagas, equivalent to Kshattriyas, Vaiśyas, and Súdras: there were no mixed castes in Sáka-dwipa. It may be here observed that a similar enumeration of the tribes of Sáka-dwipa occurs in other Puráñas, as in the Vishñu Puráña, where, instead of Magas, the Translation has Mŕigas: but this may be only a various and, perhaps, an inaccurate reading of the original manuscript.

"In obedience to the commands of Súrya, and with the help of Kŕishña, who lent him the use of Garuda for the journey, Sámba went to Sáka-dwipa, and induced eighteen families of Magas to return with him to India, to fulfil the function of ministering priests in the temple of the Sun, which he now completed, building, at the same time, around the temple, a spacious city, which was called, after him, Sámbapura. The legend also relates that the Yádava prince prevailed upon his kinsmen, the Bhojas of Dwáraká, a branch of the race of Yadu, to give their daughters, in marriage, to his Magas; and their descendants were, thence, called Bhojakas. But, in a subsequent passage, with an inconsistency not unfrequent in some of the Puráñas, it is said that ten only of the eighteen families received damsels of the tribe of Bhoja, whilst the other eight, who were of the rank only of Súdras, although equally worshippers of the Sun, were married to Sáka maidens: their descendants were named Mandagas.

So far there is little, in the legend, beyond the name Maga, and the worship of the Sun, to suggest any connexion between it and the history of the fire-worshippers of Persia. But there are other particulars mentioned, which are of a more explicit tenour. They cannot, however, always be satisfactorily made out, in consequence of the obvious inaccuracy of the texts, arising, in a great measure, from the usual carelessness of the copyists, but partly from the occurrence of terms, probably ill understood and imperfectly represented by the original writer. There are three copies of the Bhavishya Purána in the Library of the East India House, and two in the Bodleian. One of each collection omits the legend: of the remaining copies, the Oxford manuscript is the most correct; but it abounds in mistakes. Dr. Maximilian Müller has kindly furnished me with a transcript of the passages I required, and has enabled me to collate them with the East India House copies, from which, although some particulars remain doubtful, yet enough may be extracted to establish the identity of the Magas of the Puránas with the followers of Zoroaster.

"In answer to various questions relating to the practices of the Magas, put by Sámba, the Sage Vyása professes to give him some account of them, beginning with the explanation of their name, which is not very intelligible. Apparently, it may be rendered: 'The Magas are so called because they do not proceed by a contrary Veda' (*viparyastena vedena Magá náyantyato magáñ*; as if from *má*, 'not', and *gá*, 'who goes'); the writer considering the precepts of the Zend authorities as not opposed to those of the Vedas. The Sun, Vyása continues, in the form of fire, bears or wears (*dhárayate*) what he calls a *kúrcha*; and, therefore, the Magas are wearers of it (*kúrchadháriñañ*): the word ordinarily implies a bunch of peacock-feathers; but it may have, in this place, some other sense. The Magas eat in silence, whence they are called *Mauninañ* (silentiaries). They are also termed *Vachúrcha*, from *Vacha*, said to be a name of the Sun, and *archá*, 'worship'. They have four Vedas, termed *Vada, Viswavada, Vidut*(?), and *Angirasa*(?). Gepa or Gesha (perhaps for Sesha), the great serpent, having cast off his skin in the Sun's car, it became the origin of what is here called the *Amáhaka*, which is given by the Magas, on solemn occasions, and with appropriate *mantras* or prayers. This is somewhat differently told a few lines afterwards All creatures, it is there said,—Gods, Rishis, Rákshasas, Nágas,—assemble, at stated periods, in the chariot of the Sun; and, on one of these occasions, Vásuki, the king of the serpents, dropped his old skin: it was picked up by Aruña, and given, by him, to the Sun, who put it on round his waist, in honour of Vásuki, as if unseparated from the body of the Nága, whence it was called *Avyanga* (from *a*, 'not,' *vi* 'apart from,' and *anga*, 'the body'). From its being thus worn by the Sun, it became sacred, in the estimation of his worshippers; and they, therefore, constantly wear it. Whoever goes without it is impious and impure, and falls into hell Like the *Munja* of the Brahmans, it is said, it should be put on in the eighth year from conception. It is to be made of cotton, or wool, of one colour: the best kind is 132 inches (or fingers) long; the next, 120; and it should never be less than 108 inches in length. Other names appear to be applied to it, as *Amáhaka, Sára-pradhána, Bháva-sára*, and *Sára-mara*; but this is uncertain, as the passage is corrupt, and some other article may be intended, invested with which, and the *Avyanga*, the worshipper is said to be *Pa-*

Chitánga. Again, in place of the *Darbha*, or sacred grass of the Brahmans, the *Pavitra*, or purificatory instrument of sacrifice of the Magas, is said, by Vyása, to be called *Varsma*, or (in another place,) *Varsama.*

"A variety of other particulars are briefly mentioned, some of which are intelligible, others uncertain. A Maga must not touch a dead body, nor a woman at certain seasons; he should (not?) cast a dead dog on the earth, and should not die without worshipping the Sun. He should let his beard grow, travel on foot, cover his face in worshipping, and hold what is called the *Nirnaka* in the right hand, and the *Sankha* (conch-shell?) in the left; and he should worship the Sun at the three Sandhyás, and at the five festivals. Other details are too questionably particularized to be specified; but more than enough has been cited to establish the fact that the Bhavishya Purána intends, by Magas, the Mughs of the Persians, the Magi of the Greeks, and the Parsees of India. Thus, the rule of eating in silence, the covering of the mouth at worship, the prohibition of touching a corpse, or, at least, the impurity thereby contracted, are characteristic of the Parsee faith. A still more decisive indication is furnished by what is related of the *Avyanga*, which is, clearly, the sacred girdle of the Parsees, called, most commonly, *Kusti* or *Kosti*, but also *Aiwyonghám*, according to Anquetil du Perron, as quoted by Dr. John Wilson, in his notices of the Parsee religion. The latter also observes, almost in the words attributed to Vyása: 'The *Kusti* bears some analogy to the *Munja* of the Brahmans.' According to him, the *Kusti* should be put on when the child has attained the age of seven years, seven months, and ten days, (which agrees well enough with our text); and the wickedness of not wearing it, and the consequences of such impiety, are similarly described in Zend and Pehlevi works. Unluckily, I have not, at present, the means of consulting Anquetil du Perron; or some other analogies might be traced. But there can be no doubt that another term which occurs in the Sanskrit text is identifiable in the Zend, and that the *Varsma* or *Varsama* of the Bhavishya Purána is the *Barsam* or *Barsom* of the Vendidád,—a bundle of twigs of the pomegranate, in place of the bundle of sacred grass used by the Brahmans, and equally an essential part of the apparatus employed in the worship of Fire, or oblations offered to that element, in both religions.

"It is evident, therefore, that the Bhavishya Purána, in the legend of Sámba, has in view the introduction of the fire-worship of Iran; and it is curious to find so prompt an adoption by the Brahmans, and such a cordial tolerance of a foreign system of religious practices and belief. The only question that suggests itself concerns the period at which this took place, the time at which the Brahmans acknowledged the high-priests of the Sun as little inferior, in sanctity, to their own order;—whether it followed the flight of the Parsees to Gujerat, in the beginning of the eighth century, or whether it occurred some few centuries earlier, when, we have reason to infer from numismatic evidence, Persian princes or satraps exercised authority on the north-west frontier of India. Either period would not be incompatible with the probable date of the Bhavishya Purána, which, in its actual form, cannot pretend to very remote antiquity. That the legend is of the more recent era is most likely; and this is confirmed by the circumstance of Sámba's being fabled to have gone from Dwáraká, in Gujerat, to bring the Magas from their native country to India. That the Parsees ever made their way into the Punjab is very questionable; and no traces are recorded of their presence on the banks of the Chandrabhágá; nor have we any notice of the remains of a temple of the Sun in that quarter, although, according to Colonel Wilford, there was a city of Sámba in the same direction."

Instead of "Nishkumbhá", the preferable reading of MSS. seems to be Nikshubhá. Nor is Rijwáhwa called by a second name, "Riju".

For the castes in Sáka-dwípa, see Vol. II., pp. 199, 200. It will there be learned, from one of my annotations, that, in lieu of "Mríga",—the only reading known to Professor Wilson,—I found, in most of my copies, the undoubtedly correct 'Maga'.

P. LXV., l. 3. *Read* Yudhishfhira.

P. LXXXVI., l. 18. See, for Hayagriva, Vol. V., p. 2, notes 1 and र.

P. XC., l. 12. *For* Kámákshyá *read* Kámákhyá. And see Vol. V., p. 88, notes 2 and •••.

P. XCIX., l. 22. *Read* beliefs.

P. CXV, l. 1. I have corrected Professor Wilson's "Ratnagarbha Bhafta". *Bhattáchárya* is a title which has been used, I believe, only in Lower Bengal; whereas the title of *Bhatta*, there unknown, seems to have been current in almost every other part of India.

P. CXV., l. 3 *ab infra*. Instead of 'Chitsukha Yogin', Professor Wilson had, erroneously, "Chit-sukha-yoni."

For Chitsukha Muni, perhaps the same as Chitsukha Yogin, see my Sanskrit Catalogue, pp. 155 and 206.

P. 2, l. 2. One of my MSS. here interpolates the following stanzas:

विश्वेश्वरं विश्वसृजं वरेखं
विश्वं विश्रुहं वरदं वरिष्ठम् ।
अनादिमध्यान्तमलच्यरूपं
विष्णुं विभुं विप्रहितं गतोऽस्मि ॥
उत्पत्तिस्थितिसंहारमोषाणां चैककारणम् ।
नारायणमणीयांसं प्रयतोऽस्मि अगन्नृतम् ॥

P. 6, l. 7. Instead of the five stanzas which, according to the text followed by the Translator, begin the work, three of my best MSS. give only the last of them, preceded by the following:

श्रीश्रीनिधानं गुबरत्नराजितं
परायरं ब्रह्मसुधामुधिं भजे ।
हयो हरेविष्णुपुराणकौस्तुभो
यस्मादभूद्भासविभुश्च विश्वकृत् ॥

P 6, l. 16. "All the Hindu systems consider vegetable bodies as endowed with life." So, and correctly, remarks Professor Wilson, in his collected Works, Vol. III., p. 381. *Charáchara*, or the synonymous *sthávara* and *jangama*, is, therefore, inaccurately rendered, in pp. 6, 47, 64, 149, 183, and elsewhere, "animate and inanimate", "sentient beings" and "unconscious", "conscious and unconscious beings", &c. &c. 'Locomotive and fixed' would be better, since trees are considered to possess souls.

P. 8, note †. See Vol. III., p. 35, note ‡‡.

P. 32, notes, l. 14 *ab infra. Read* Swayambhú.

P. 46, ll. 1, 2. The original is :

तत्सम: मोक्षते विद्यमिल एयोपचारत: ।

The term उपचारत: here implies 'metaphorically'.

P. 55, notes, l. 5. *Read* Swayambhú.

P. 60, notes, l. 2 *ab infra.* Read *Sthúlamaya.*

P. 65, note *. Also see *Original Sanskrit Texts,* Part I., pp. 50, 51 (2nd ed.).

P. 66, notes, ll. 3—5 *ab infra.* Dr. Muir translates, more correctly: "Every substance (*vastu*) is brought into the state of substance (*vastutá*) by its own inherent power." *Original Sanskrit Texts,* Part. I., p. 51 (2nd ed.).

P. 70, notes, l. 7 *ab infra.* For the term *mukhya,* see *Original Sanskrit Texts,* Part I., p. 57, text and note 104 (2nd ed.).

P. 80, note, l. 7 *ab infra.* For the term *ambhámsi,* see *Original Sanskrit Texts,* Part I., p. 24, note 36 (2nd ed.).

P. 84, ll. 13 *et seq.* For a similar passage, translated from the *Taittiríya-samhitá,* see *Original Sanskrit Texts,* Part I., p. 16 (2nd ed.).

P. 85, notes, l. 11. Instead of 'Shodasin', the Translator had "Sorasi". Many errors of this stamp have been corrected silently.

P. 95, l. 7. Professor Wilson had "Gaveduká", instead of 'Gavedhuká'; for which see Vol. V., p. 175, notes 3 and ‖.

P. 95, notes, l. 10. The *udára* is a wild grain, according to the commentators.

P. 95, notes, l. 11. For the Professor's "Kodrava", I have put 'Kora-dúsha'. On this word the commentator Sridhara makes a remark which plainly evinces that he was not an inhabitant of Eastern India.

P. 96, l. 10. Where I have printed 'drop', the first edition had "dross". The error was typographical, the original word being *bindu.*

P. 98, notes, l. 4. "The city of the Gandharvas is, properly, Alaká,—on Mount Meru,—the capital of Kubera." Professor Wilson, in Professor Johnson's *Selections from the Mahábhárata,* p. 11.

P. 108, l. 1. For the origin of the name Uttánapáda, see *Original Sanskrit Texts,* Part I., p. 72 (2nd ed.).

P. 109, l. 4. Daksha's daughters by Prasúti furnish several of the Má-tris, according to divers enumerations of the members of this group.

P. 111, notes, l. 11. It is observable that we here have Dandanaya, but Danda and Naya in p. 110.

P. 112, text and note *. Raurava is one hell, and Naraka is another. See Vol. II., p. 214; p. 215, note ‖; and p. 216.

P. 114, l. 13. The words "whose essence is the elements" scarcely render aright the original expression, *bhúta-bhávana.*

P. 116, ll. 4, 5. In Áswaláyana's *Gṛihya-sútra,* IV., VIII., 19, we find the following names: Hara, Mṛida, Sarva, Śiva, Bhava, Mahádeva, Ugra, Bhíma, Paśupati, Rudra, Sankara, Íśána.

P. 117, L. 2. *For* Ushá *read* Ushas. The latter is classical; the former, Vaidik. Compare *apsará* and *apsaras*.

P. 117, L. 7 and note ‡. According to the *Mahábhárata, Ádi-parvan, śl.* 2589, Anila had two sons, Manojava and Avijnátagati. Which of the two is the same as Hanumat is undecided. Can Anila be synonymous with Íśána? If not, there are two Manojavas with mothers of the same name, Śivá.

P. 119, L. 10. Instead of Gauri, some MSS. yield Bhútigauri.

P. 119, ll. 23, 24. Dhaneśwara is the term there rendered "the god of riches"; and Kubera is not named in the original.

P. 129, L. 9. Instead of my 'Sumeru', the former edition had "Meru", which I find in no MS.

P. 139, L. 21. उपचारत:—a word often misapprehended by the Translator,—here means 'metaphorically', not "who is not in need of assistance". Further, परमेषु:, rendered "the supreme god", is explained as meaning 'lord of the great Má', *i. e.*, Lakshmi. The original of the sentence is as follows:

प्रोच्यते परमेष्ठो हि यः शुब्धोऽप्युपचारतः ।
प्रसीदतु स नो विष्णुरात्मा यः सर्वदेहिनाम् ॥

"May he who, though pure *of connexion with all things*, is, by a figure of speech, called lord of the great Má", &c.

P. 144, note *. My list of corrigenda, entirely overlooked by Professor Müller, points out several gross typographical errors; and these he has reproduced.

P. 147, note, last line. Ordinarily, at least, Ráhu is described as a Dánava, or son of Danu.

P. 148, notes, L. 7. Ráhu is generally considered to be the ascending node; Ketu, the descending.

P. 152, L. 4. Besides this Lakshmi, the text of the *Vishńu-puráńa* mentions another, of less note, daughter of Daksha, and wife of Dharma. See the Index..

P. 152, L. 7. The first edition had, for Niyati, Niryati,—an error of the press.

P. 154, notes, l. 14 *ab infra.* "Agastya is a celebrated person in Hindu legend. He is fabled to have prostrated the Vindhya mountain, as well as to have drunk the ocean dry. The traditions of the South of India ascribe to him a principal share in the formation of the Tamil language and literature; and the general tenour of the legends relating to him denotes his having been instrumental in the introduction of the Hindu religion and civilization into the Peninsula." Professor Wilson, in Professor Johnson's *Selections from the Mahábhárata*, p. 51, note 2.

P. 155, L. 7. *Read* Abhimánin.

P. 155, notes, L. 7. *Read* Śankhapád. See Vol. II., p. 262, note †, *ad finem.*

P. 156, notes, L. 5. Pávaka, I think, is called parent of Kavyaváhana.

P. 156, note 2. See Vol. III., p. 166, note *.

P. 159, note, L. 3. Instead of 'Áyushmat', the former edition had "Áyushmanta", which is impossible.

P. 165, l. 5. The word "Madhuvana" is not in the original.

P. 177, l. 2. Variants of Slishfi are Srishfi and Sishfi.

P. 177, l. 8. Araṅya seems to be as common a reading as Anaraṅya.

P. 177, l. 9. For the patriarch Vairája, see Vol. II, p. 86.

P. 178, l. 1. The original here not only names Pṛithu, but calls him by his patronym, Vainya.

P. 178, notes, l. 12. The unwarrantable "Suvithi" stood, in the former edition, for my 'Swarvithi'.

P. 182, notes, l. 10 Read Bhramaras.

Pp. 187—191. For a passage on the milking of the Earth, see the Atharva-veda, VIII., X., 22-29,—especially, 24. I have to thank Dr. Muir for this reference.

P. 194, l. 2. It would have been an improvement, for clearness, to put Samudra, instead of "ocean". Ságara, a well-known proper name, also means "ocean".

VOL. II.

P. 5, last line. The original word for "region" is áyatana.

P. 7, ll. 3 and 19. Read Keśava.

P. 9, notes, l. 8 ab infra. Read by.

P. 21, notes, l. 2. Professor Wilson had "Kakud" where I have substituted 'Kakubh'

P. 22, l. 3. For definitions of the Vasus and Rudras, see the Bṛihad-áraṅyaka Upanishad, III., IX., 3, 4.

P. 29, l. 3. On the number of the gods, see the Bṛihad-áraṅyaka Upanishad, III., IX., 1, 2

P. 29, notes, l. 5. Read Sastradevatás.

P. 71, l. 6. Simbiká was half-sister of Viprachitti.

P. 85, ll. 4, 5. Soma, here called monarch of Brábmans, was, himself, a Kshattra, according to the Bṛihad-áraṅyaka Upanishad, I., IV., 11.

P. 86, l. 5. For Vairája, see Vol. III., p. 168, note ‡.

P. 100, l. 3. The Translator had "Medha" where I have put 'Medhas'.

P. 105, notes, ll. 5, 6. Arhat is synonymous with Jina; Árhata, with Jaina. See Vol. V., p. 376, note †.

P 112, note, l. 14. Instead of Kubera, we have Soma, in p. 240.

P. 117, l. 8. The Gandhamádana mentioned in p. 122 is a different mountain.

P. 120, l. 3. Burnouf considers the Sítá to be the same as the Sihoun. Introduction à l'Histoire du Bouddhisme Indien, Vol. I., p. 540.

P. 120, note ‡. The Sanskrit name of the Oxus seems, through the Chinese, to be Vakshu. And this form I have found, more than once, in MSS.

P. 121, notes, l. 10 ab infra. Read Sarayu.

P. 128, notes, l. 7. Read Narmadá.

P. 137, notes, l. 10. Read मधुरा.

P. 143, notes, l. 12 ab infra. Professor Wilson had "Stháneśwara" where I have put 'Sthánwiśwara'. This, the correct form, I learned from the *Harsha-charita*. The first word in the compound is Sthánu, a name of Śiva.

P. 149, l. 1. According to Mr. Molesworth's Maráthi Dictionary, a river Pravará falls into the Godávari at Tonken.

P. 152, l. 1. Read *Púrnásá*.

P. 155, notes, l. 13 *ab infra*. *Read* 131.

P. 159, notes, l. 10. *Read* Kundiña.

P. 163, notes, last line. For Káśi *read* of the Káśis.

P. 166, note ∗. *For* third *read* fourth.

P. 166, note ††. The Máhishiki river is named in the Bengal recension of the *Rámáyaña, Kishkindhá-kánda*, XLI., 16.

P. 166. Erase note §§.

P. 172, notes, l. 6. *Read* occur.

P. 172, note ‡‡. For Kuśasthali and Kuśávati, see Vol. III., p. 320, note ‖.

P. 174, note 1. "The Sauvíras, although applied here to a particular family, denote, as is subsequently shown, a tribe or people either identical, or closely connected, with the Sindhus; for Jayadratha is indifferently termed Raja of the Sindhus or Saindhavas and Raja of the Sauvíras. They are sometimes named in concert, as Sindhu-sauvíras, and, whether the same as the dwellers on the Indus, or a kindred tribe, must have occupied much the same territory,—the western and southern portion of the Punjab." Professor Wilson, in Professor Johnson's *Selections from the Mahábhárata*, p. 65, note 3.

P. 177, note 1. For the supposed modern representatives of the Dahae, see Sir H. M. Elliot's *Supplemental Glossary*, pp. 414, 415.

P. 178, l. 2. *Read* Karnátakas.

P. 211, notes, l. 5. *Read* Puloman.

P. 221, text and note 1. According to Sir David Lyndesay's less pagan notions,—which he shared with S. Thomas Aquinas and Peter Lombard,—a humbler class than the gods, the elect, will be indulged with the felicity of contemplating the discomforts of the damned:

"Thay sall reioyis to se the gret dolour
Off dampnit folk in hell, and thare torment;
Because of God it is the inste ingement."

P. 236, ll. 10, 11. Compare the *Bhagavad-gítá*, IX., 16.

P. 255, notes, l. 7. For 1809 *read* 2010, in correction of Professor Wilson.

P. 287, note ∗. For Rambha, see Vol V., p. 12, text and note ‖.

P. 288, note †. For Ápúraña, see Vol. V., p. 251, note †.

P. 293, notes, l. 12 *ab infra*. *Read* Sakra.

P. 316, note 1. It does not appear that the *Bhágavata-puráña* mentions Jambúmárga. Probably it is named by the scholiast Śrídhara: for Professor Wilson not seldom confounds commentary and text.

P. 318, l. 4. A Sauvíra is an inhabitant of Suvíra. Read, therefore, 'king of the Sauvíras'.

P. 340, l. 32. *Read* l. 11 *ab infra*.

P. 341, l. 25. Mahárashtra, it seems, was a designation known to Hiouen Thsang.

P. 343, ll. 21—23. Erase the note.

390   CORRIGENDA, &c.

VOL. III.

P. 2, notes, l. 4. *Read* Yámas.

P. 6, notes, l. 18. *Read* Vaṃśavartins.

P. 7, notes, l. 2. The inverted commas should come at the end of the sentence in the line preceding.

P. 16, l. 1. *Read* Ákúti.

P. 18, notes, l. 3. *Read* Vaikuṇṭha.

P. 44, notes, l. 5. *Read* Śánti.

P. 55, note †. For the meaning of *prâṇâyáma*, see Vol. V., p. 231, note ';'.

P. 60, l. 6. Kṛita seems to be the right name. See Vol. IV., p. 143, text and note †.

P. 77, note 1. Compare Vol. V., pp. 229, 230, text and annotations.

P. 80, notes, l. 2 *ab infra.* For father *read* grandfather.

P. 87, note ‡. For p. 110, note §, *read* p. 113, note †, and p. 114, notes ‡ and §.

P. 131, notes, l. 8 *ab infra.* The real designation of the work there named is, I find, *Pránakṛishṇiyaśabdábdhi.*

P. 131, notes, l. 14. Taráchandra Chakravartin prepared the revised English translation; and the Bengalee translation was the work of Viśwanátha Tarkabhúshaṇa. See the London *Asiatic Journal*, 1832, Part I., p. 335.

P. 164, note †. See p. 221, note ||, in the same volume.

P. 167, notes, l. 13. *Read* Váruṇa.

P. 179, notes, l. 10 *ab infra.* Read I., LXXXIX., 3.

P. 183, note †. For Vol. II. read Vol. I.

P. 187, notes, l. 8 *ab infra.* Read *Brahmáṇḍa-puráṇa.*

P. 197, l. 4. The Manu intended is Vaivaswata; for whom see p. 13 of the same volume.

P. 198, notes, l. 9. *Read* vague sense.

P. 209, l. 1. *Read* Árhatas.

P. 209, note 2. Professor Wilson should have written 'Árhata'. See Vol. V., p. 376, note †.

P. 217, note •. Read *Ṛishi.*

P. 218, l. 9. Instead of "Raja of Káśi" the correct rendering is 'Raja of the Káśis'.

P. 220, l. 3 *ab infra.* The translation is not literal here, and yields neither "king of Káśi" nor 'king of the Káśis'.

P. 230, note ||. See p. 20, note 1, in the same volume.

P. 245, l. 5. *Read* Tṛiṇabindu.

P. 249, notes, l. 3. It is meant that Ánarta and the rest were brothers.

P. 249, note ¶. *Read* IX.

P. 266, notes, l. 4. *Read* Rantinára. Also see Vol. IV., p. 129.

P. 266, notes, l. 8. *Read* Matinára. Also see Vol. IV., p. 129, notes 2 and ||.

P. 267, l. 21. The learned reader may be amused by the whimsical etymologies, of a like character to this, given in the annexed stanza

CORRIGENDA, &c. 391

from Appayya Dikshita's *Śivatattwaviveka*:

द्विसिधातो: सिंहग्राव्दो वश आक्षी ग्रिव: भूत: ।
वर्षंबलयत: ग्राव्द: पम्र क: कम्रपो यथा ॥

P. 280, note •. Yauvanáśwa is, of course, the patronym of Ambarisha.

P. 283, notes, l. 2. 'Duḥsaha' is a more ordinary form than "Dussaha".

P. 321, notes, l. 5. *Read* Tárápíḍa.

P 325, notes, l. 2. For a Yájnavalkya, in connexion with the Yoga philosophy, see Vol. V., p. 230, note ‖.

P. 325, note 4. Viśwasáhwan is, probably, one with the Viśwasaha of p. 323.

P. 330, notes, l. 2. See Vol. IV., p. 344; supplementary annotation on p. 84.

P. 334, l. 1. *Read* Ritujit.

P. 336, note §. *For* 353 *read* pp. 244, 245.

VOL. IV.

P. 17, note 1. For Richika, see Vol. III., p. 80, note †.

P. 30, l. 6. Compare p. 136, note 1, in the same volume.

P. 40, note ‡. Compare what is said of Tálajangha in p. 57.

P. 57, l. 3. *Read* Tálajanghas.

P. 63, notes, l. 13. *Read* Ruchaka.

P. 67, notes, l. 6. *Read* Romapáda.

P. 95, l. 3. *Read* Ávaha.

P. 97, note ‡. *Read* Dhrishtá.

P. 100, notes, l. 18. *Read* Śúra.

P. 111, notes, l. 3 *ab infra. Read* Hamsa, Suvamśa.

P. 112, note ‖. For Cháruhásini, see Vol. V., p. 69, note §; p. 81, note §; and p. 83, note §.

P. 114, notes, l. 10 *ab infra. Read* p. 96.

P. 123, notes, l. 10. Insert a comma after "Brihaspati".

P. 129, note ‖. *Erase* another, Atitára.

P. 132, notes, l. 12 *ab infra.* It is observable that, in p. 102, we have had a Bhíma son of Anila.

P 141, notes, l. 4. *Read* Dridháśwa.

P. 142, note ††. *For* Dhritaráshtra *read* Dhritaráshtra's charioteer, according to the more usual legend.

P. 144, note 3. *Read* Riksha.

P. 148, notes, l. 6. *Read* Arimejaya.

P. 157. Erase note §.

P. 171, note 1. For Śreńika, father of Kúnika, see the *Journal of the Bombay Asiatic Society*, Vol IX., p. 154.

P. 178, l. 5 and note ‖. For "Chandapradyota" and his son Pálaka, see the *Journal of the Bombay Asiatic Society*, Vol. IX., p. 147.

P. 182, note ••. *Read* is Udáyin. For Udáyin, said to have been son of Kúnika, see the *Journal of the Bombay Asiatic Society*, Vol. IX., pp. 147, 154.

P. 184, note 2. A *mahápadma* is only a thousand millions, according to the *Liláwati*. Elsewhere a simple *padma* is said to be ten thousand millions. See Vol. V., p. 187, note †, and p. 188, note ‖.

P. 202, l. 1. For Gardabhila, said to have been king of Ujjayini, and father of Vikramáditya, see the *Journal of the Bombay Asiatic Society*, Vol. IX., pp. 139, 143, 148, 154.

P. 215, note *. For Pushpamitra, see the *Journal of the Bombay Asiatic Society*, Vol. IX., p. 148.

P. 216, l. 1, and p. 217, notes, l. 1. For Viśwasphatika, see the *Journal of the Bombay Asiatic Society*, Vol. IX., p. 146.

P. 217, note ‡. For Kantipuri *read* Kántipuri.

P. 223, notes, l. 11 *ab infra*. *Read* Chandrabhágá.

P. 248, ll. 7, 8. "The increaser of the Bhojas" would be the correct rendering. See p. 260, note ९, in the same volume.

P. 279. Erase note ‡.

P. 308, note 1. See Vol. V., p. 231, notes 1 and ¦.

VOL. V.

P. 2, note ९. For Hayagríva, as slain by Vishnu, see p. 90.

P. 2, notes, l. 7 *ab infra*. *Read* बभूवुरयतीः.

P. 26, notes, l. 12 *ab infra*. *Read* निष्कास्य.

P. 53, notes, l. 9. *Read* *Harivamśa*.

P. 74, notes, l. 5. *Read* *Gaja-gámini*.

P. 140, notes, l. 6. *Read* *Viráta-parvan*.

P. 169, notes, l. 3 *ab infra*. *Read* *Vamśánucharita*.

P. 176, l. 6. *For* sage *read* age.

P. 190, notes. l. 4. By the original expression, here rendered "four fingers", 'four finger-breadths' is intended.

P. 209, notes, l. 3. *Read* Tat-práptaye.

P. 250, l. 4. *Read* Ríshi.

P. 250, l. 5. *Read* Ribhu.

P. 290, notes, l. 5. *Read* Vámáchárins.

P. 319, l. 5. *Read* Brahmáńda.

P. 326, l. 1. "Váma Yamáchárin", it may be surmised, is a typographical error for 'Vámáchárin'.

P. 356, l. 4 *ab infra*. *Read* Madhwáchárya.

P. 358, l. 5. *Read* Śri Bhágavata.

POSTSCRIPT.

The MSS. of the *Vishṅu-puráṅa* and of its commentaries used by the Editor belong, chiefly, to himself, and are the best, or copies of the best, which he was able to discover during a long and extensive search in India. He has also carefully examined all the oldest and most valuable MSS. which he knows to exist in England, and an especially excellent one obligingly lent to him by the accomplished Principal of the Benares College, Mr. Griffith. The Madras, Bombay, and Calcutta impressions he has, further, constantly had by his side; and he has frequently consulted them, but to little useful purpose. With few exceptions, the Sanskrit works brought out under the supervision of Hindus are inferior even to indifferent manuscripts; and this must continue to be their character, so long as they betray a systematic disregard of the most elementary principles of editorial probity.

As regards the original and the translation of a book, until the text of the first is duly ascertained, the other can be worth very little; and the MSS. of the *Vishṅu-puráṅa*—which is still inedited,—present a choice of lections in almost every line. Professor Wilson sometimes employed one MS., sometimes another; and there are but rare indications that he compared together even two, out of all that were accessible to him. The consequence of impatience of collation is inevitable; and it not seldom happens that he unfortunately had before him, and followed, the very worst reading from among a variety of good and bad.

Had the Editor clearly foreseen, in time, what awaited him, rather than do that which he has done, he would have bazarded a critical edition of the *Vishṅu-puráṅa* in the original, and an entirely new translation. The one has long been all but ready for the press; but its appearance has been defeated by one manœuvre after another, and now can never be realized. An independent version of his own would, certainly, have cost him much less trouble than the invidious labour which he has expended on these volumes. Of notes he would have been sparing; inasmuch as, in the whole compass of Sanskrit literature, he could not consider the text of even a dozen works to be sufficiently settled to warrant an appeal to them, except in a most general way, for purposes of comparison or illustration.

Though many of Professor Wilson's notes have no very intimate connexion with his translation, others have such a connexion; and some of them are necessary to its very intelligibility. To make a selection, from among these categories, as subject-matter for remark, would have been difficult, and, the question of difficulty apart, would have been liable to objection. Emendations, to be rendered at all convincing, every here and there demanded the production of new matter; and, sometimes, when such matter has lain at the Editor's elbow, it has been offered to the reader, notwithstanding its being only indirectly germane to the occasion. As for his annotations, however, he does not lay the least claim to their being exhaustive. He has given mere specimens, — at best, suggestive of the peril which, in the dawn of the exploration of Sanskrit literature, attends on peremptory statement or positiveness of conclusion, — and equally so where he has amended the Professor's renderings, and, in short, in the discharge of his revisory functions generally. Still, in one important respect he has been solicitous of thoroughness. By citations from, and references to, the other publications of Professor Wilson, he has studied — not unsuccessfully, he trusts, — to make him, as far as possible, his own commentator, corrector, and supplementer.

A copious disquisition on the Puránas as a class, and on the *Vishńu-puráńa* in particular, is reserved against the emergence of some other opportunity for publishing it.

The sixth volume will be occupied with a full index to the entire work.

LONDON,
July, 1869.

Printed by Unger Brothers (Th. Grimm), Berlin, Friedrichsstrasse 24.

www.ingramcontent.com/pod-product-compliance
Lightning Source LLC
Chambersburg PA
CBHW032341280326
41935CB00008B/405